The Biblical Seminar

75

Biblical Semantic Logic

Biblical Semantic Logic

A Preliminary Analysis

Arthur Gibson

SHEFFIELD ACADEMIC PRESS
A Continuum imprint
LONDON • NEW YORK

Copyright © 2001 Sheffield Academic Press
A Continuum imprint

Published by Sheffield Academic Press Ltd
The Tower Building, 11 York Road, London SE1 7NX
370 Lexington Avenue, New York NY 10017-6550

www.SheffieldAcademicPress.com
www.continuumbooks.com

British Library Cataloguing-in-Publication Data

A catalogue record for this book is available from the British Library

Typeset by Sheffield Academic Press
Printed on acid-free paper in Great Britain by Bookcraft Ltd, Midsomer Norton,
Bath

ISBN   1-84127-338-4 (hardback)
          1-84127-173-X (paperback)

For Stanley and Wendy Porter

CONTENTS

PREFACE

This book is about applied language studies of the Bible's Old and New Testaments. In the book's title the expression 'Semantic Logic' marks the introduction of insights in mathematical logic and logic theory of meaning to biblical studies. The book does not presuppose knowledge of formal logic; and the reader should be disabused of the assumption that these insights are of only obscure theoretical linguistic interest. Current research in logic advertises its crucial connection with general questions of meaning and theology. However, as a systematically pursued subject (as opposed to merely peripheral treatment), logic has not previously been applied to study of the original Bible languages. Partly for this reason the book is modest in scope—not least because it is concerned with applied linguistics—and it is a preliminary investigation to prepare the way for more extensive and detailed projected books. Accordingly, certain more advanced issues of importance (such as intuitionism, model logic, theory of truth and identity)[1] I defer for attention elsewhere, even where certain solutions to those issues are implicitly deployed below. Nevertheless, I have attempted to steer around various disputed positions in logic; and where that has not been expedient, a given view is adopted (usually a standard interpretation held in respect), so as to articulate an introduction of logic to applied linguistic items without the distraction of lengthy technical discussion of multiple alternatives. The book is a considerable simplification of the original research.

There might be theologians who suppose that each discipline has its own differing logic which is 'true for it', and they will demur from my imposition of standard logic. It is not enough to demur; the

---

[1] See, for example, M. Dummett and R. Minio, *Elements of Intuitionism* (Oxford, 1977); R. Rorty, *Philosophy and the Mirror of Nature* (Oxford, 1980); and D. Wiggins, *Sameness and Substance* (Oxford, 1980).

following study shows that standard logic fits the subject—a proof is
in the fit. It is true that each subject will display differing choice of
logical procedures and patterns of logical organization in analysis; but
the foregoing dispute is only confusedly pitched at that level. Such
variety is achieved by deployment of standard logic. It is only at a
more fundamental level that claims for a differing logic from standard
can be advanced. For example, it is either true or false that 'there was
a Rephaim cult at Ebla as expounded by Matthiae's explanation of
rp'um'. This book's logic rests on the semantic principle in this type
of reasoning (including the consequent senses of *true, assertion, negation* and *conjunction*), that a point in a finite domain is either true or
false; and this accommodates a number of alternative interpretations
of logic. For a person to retreat to his 'own logic' requires that he
violates this principle and its consequences; so if someone opposes
the logic of the following pages, except if I have made a mistake he
will need to lay out his 'logic' and yet withdraw the claim that it
primarily deals with truth—in which case, either way, he concedes
defeat. I leave the formal proof of this to be read elsewhere.[2] Howbeit,
such a critic is often confused on another account which obscures his
appreciation of the foregoing. He mistakes theological principles for
principles in logic—acting as though laws of logic can be revised in
conformity with individual subjects. Even logicians who favour (a
suitably refined) reconstruction in this direction have not shown what
such a logic could be, nor proved the need for fundamental revision of
standard logic, in the appropriate sense used above. So it is incorrect
to respond to logical criticisms of scholars' statements by appeal to
the non-standard (alleged) logic of their subject-matter, as a means of
avoiding the censure and new positive proposals advanced in this
book. This would unwittingly comply with a *reductio ad absurdum*

---

[2] See S. Haack, *Deviant Logic* (Cambridge, 1974) and *Philosophy of Logics*
(Cambridge, 1978), pp. 228ff. The above principle applies to the macro-
scopic world. It is often held that it does not apply to the quantum mechanical field. But recent work in cosmology might indicate that it does apply
(for example see B.S. Dewitt and N. Graham (eds.), *The Many Worlds of
Interpretation of Quantum Mechanics* (Princeton, 1973), and W. Israel and
S.W. Hawking, *General Relativity* (Cambridge, 1979, Chs. 12 and 14). This is
primarily owing to H. Everett III's original work which interprets quantum
mechanics as part of a universal wave function, an element of Hilbert space,
with causal and deductive properties. Current cosmology (e.g. Hawking's
1977 theorem) appears to support the application of Everett's thesis to the
large scale structure of space-time and creation (singularities).

sequence whereby a person used the logically faulty element of his presentation as 'proof' that he is right by reference to its uniquely deviant logic; but deviance in logic is precisely the question which has not been proved. Of course, this is not to dispute that this book deals with only one feature among many areas in biblical studies and biblical linguistics. And many topics which are introduced could do with a separate book on their texture and problems; but one has to start somewhere.

The numerical decimal classification of this book (e.g. I.I, sub-sections I, 2, etc.) indicates the breakdown of the subject being analysed, while the alphabetical notation (a, b, c, etc.) is to note the introduction of cases (for example, scholars' statements and ancient texts) which are to be examined. Both the decimal and alphabetical classifications conform to the structural sequence consequent on the priorities specified in I.0–I.I below.

Since (with one exception) the citation of Near Easten texts is in transliteration, quotation marks have not been placed round the quotations; but they should be assumed. For reasons of economy and the following the absence of Dāgēš Forte and Massoretic vocalization in the relevant ancient texts, these formations are not incorporated into transliterated expressions.[3]

Where a translation of a scholar's work is especially influential, or more widely used than the original, and I want to discuss an aspect of the translation's influence and/or the author's treatment, I cite the translation as though it were the author's work. I ask to be excused this slight infelicity, since I am concerned with influence and not primarily provenance; and the particular author has some-times adopted the translation in question elsewhere; the custom is followed, also, in the interest of brevity. A standard biblical (King James Version) translation or translation of other texts is added to aid those who are not familiar with the other languages.

Cambridge, October 1980

---

[3] The editions of the Bible to be employed in the present book are: K. Elliger and W. Rudolph *et al.* (eds.), *Biblia Hebraica Stuttgartensia* (Stuttgart, 1977); *Vetus Testamentum Graecum Auctoritate Gottingensis editum* (Göttingen, 1954–); and K. Aland, M. Black, C.M. Martini, B.M. Metzger and A. Wikgren (eds.), *The Greek New Testament*, 3rd edn. (London, 1975). (But other versions are reproduced where authors quoted employ them.) Abbreviations for the above texts are BHS or MT, LXX, and NT respectively.

PROLOGUE

Biblical Semantic Logic (hereafter *BSL*) was published in 1981. Since it is now out of print I appreciate Sheffield Academic Press's offer to republish the book and invitation to provide some account of developments in the field, my own work and that of others, subesequent to the original publication. I appreciate the assistance of Philip Davies in expediting the republication of *BSL*.

One way of attempting to open up past literature such as the Bible to wider analysis is to apply the most general representational means for examining it and its interpretation. Logic is such a means. *BSL* furnishes a means to assess how some logic applies to biblical semantics and interpretation. Conversely, it also queries the identity of logic and the development of its identities by highlighting usage in natural languages as a criterion for testing our grasp of logic. Finally, since *BSL* operates linguistically within the context of Near Eastern narratives and their intertextual relations to the Bible, it also tests for the applicability of its analyses to this context, and so opens up the quest for a logic of comparative literature.

1   *Developing the Agenda of* Biblical Semantic Logic

My own work in carrying forward the agenda of *BSL* can be briefly indicated. *Text and Tablet* (2000a) applies logic to relations between, on the one hand, a range of Old Testament and Near Eastern narratives, inscriptions and tablets, and on the other hand, archaeology and historical analysis, showing the positive consequences of *BSL* for exegesis, the external worlds associated with the Bible, and relevant ancient Near East narrative and archaeology.

In 'God's Semantic Logic' (1997a), and *Text and Tablet* (2000a: Part 1), I provide a logical theory for ancient representation of God in the Bible, and in the Dead Sea Scrolls' use of the Bible. This theory enhances the delineation and interpretation of the elements that are tested in *BSL*. In 'Modern Philosophy and Ancient Consciousness'

(1998) I examine the prospect for relating analytical and other philosophies of mind to map Mesopotamian mentality. This study and others (such as 'God's Semantic Logic' and my forthcoming *Counter-Intuition, Beyond Human Meaning?* and 'Relations between Rhetoric and Philosophical Logic') argue that logics devised for interpretation of ancient texts and sites can provide insights into how language and image relate to what the mind is and how we can characterize the identities of the unconscious.

BSL showed that one major cause of mistakes is that the impact of false simplification had distorting effects on our study of ancient narratives and inscriptions. 'Ockham's World and Future' (1998a) shows how such effects are consequences of some Ockhamist influences. This study criticizes Ockham's claims for simplicity, supporting and extending the generalization in *BSL*'s criticism of reductionism and hypostatization.

BSL also argued that formal analysis applies to creative literatures, though obviously many versions of formalism are incapable of depicting literary usage. *Infinite Literary Logic: A Treatise on Logic, Literary Creativity and Philosophy of Mathematics* (forthcoming e) provides a basis for showing how logic relates to creative literature.

BSL leaves space for the issue of creativity, while its use of logic facilitates the claim that creativity and logic belong together. I have developed this in the context of an overall philosophy (see Gibson 1987, 1997, 2000, 2000a, forthcoming d).

There is a separate project exploring relations between literary creativity and philosophical analysis. The practice of philosophers composing creative literature has a firm place in French literature, as with Sartre's novels and plays, but hardly in English, though Wallace Stevens's poetry approaches this boundary. This situation was impressed on me by Frank Kermode, who offered to guide me in literary research while I taught him Hebrew. Kermode subsequently suggested that I compose some poetry to explore connections between sense and creativity. The first result is *Boundless Function* (Gibson 1987), which ventilates some difficult relations between literature, philosophy, and the external world, especially involving the Bible and Mesopotamia. The complex and intentionally problematic ironies in this philosophical poetry (see Gibson 1987: 11-14, 21-45, 51-57, 63-69, 75-84) develop a creative theory of meaning and deploy some logical criteria proposed in *BSL*. Such a poetic fission of linguistic, philosophical and creative elements is new. The poetry queries our separation of subjects into institutionally rationalized pigeonholes while it presupposes the need for clarified distinctions and for one to reflect on the identities of meaning. I have extended this work in *God and the Universe* (2000), in contexts of formal philosophy, and in *Text and Tablet: Near Eastern Archaeology, the Old Testament and New Possibilities* (2000a), in relation to ancient irony and nuance.

Such lines of enquiry involve some puzzling relations of logical order to chaos and semantic indeterminacy. In 'Philosophy of Psychotic Modernism: Wagner and Hitler' (2000b) I examine how logic is operable in one of history's abnormal spacetimes, that of Hitler. I explain how this type of theory applies to ancient social power structures and demonology, while suggesting that some ancient pre-Greek Sumerian mentalities embody archetypes mirrored in some modernist and contemporary functions of the mind, as deployed in political and religious influence. This queries the use of Greece as a fount for types of the unconscious. *What is Literature?* (forthcoming d) examines how this situation relates to contemporary and ancient literature, arguing that the emergence of the unconscious originates in a literate society in trauma. 'Modern Philosophy and Ancient Consciousness' (1998) and *Text and Tablet* (2000a) deploy a range of modernist and post-structuralist phenomena in an examination of ancient Near Eastern worlds. This aims to lay a foundation for a philosophy of history that implicitly questions the nature of 'modern philosophy', as does the application of logic in *BSL* to pre-Greek culture.

BSL also applied, interpreted, and disputed, some of Frege's logic, at a time when reassessment of it had just got underway. *BSL* presumed that Frege was wrong to exclude literary and native speaker use of tone from logic.[1] This attack was intended to open the way to a theory that certain types of live metaphor are properties of logic and of higher mathematics, that there is a continuum between literary functions and higher logics, in appropriate and exotic ways. One implication of this is that inferential instability is internal to logic, and starting in 1987, I introduced the term 'counter-intuition' for this phenomenon. *Counter-Intuition* (forthcoming a) is devoted to this topic.

BSL suggested a link between semantics of ancient literature and cosmology as well as pure mathematics. *God and the Universe* (2000) is the first large-scale analysis to present and explore these scenarios.

---

[1] My *Epigraph* and argument in Gibson 1987 took this dispute further.

This book and *Beyond Human Meaning* (forthcoming b) propose a qualitative conception of mathematical infinity, as a series of live metaphors by which to depict qualitative elements in creative literary usage.

Internal to creativity in logic and literature is the topic of transcendence. Biblical literature abounds with exotic uses of transcendence. Accordingly, a philosophy and logic of the Bible should address conceptions of this type of feature. In 'Logic of the Resurrection' (1999), *God and the Universe* (2000), and *Infinite Literary Logic* (forthcoming e), the logic voiced in *BSL* is extended to the formulation of conceptions of transcendence.

2   *A Review of Recent Literature Relevant to* Biblical Semantic Logic

(a) *Analytical Philosophy of Language and Logic*

BSL's use of Wittgenstein's *Philosophical Investigations* has been taken further in Boghossian's (1989) review of rule following, while Cartwright's (1999) idea that groups of theory models, rather than one true theory, apply to study of language offers something quite similar or complementary to *BSL*. I have in fact (Gibson 2000a) applied Cartwright's suggestions to the Old Testament, and I am sympathetic to Popper's (1994) concern to acknowledge that there is myth *in* theoretical frameworks. The researches by McGinn (1984), Cavell (1995), Stern (1995), and in the volume edited by Sluga and Stern (1996) on Wittgenstein (1999; see also Wittgenstein 1996) impinge on *BSL*'s concern to formulate a logic of representation, while my recent book (Gibson 2000) offers an explicit theory of how expression of God in the Bible can be represented by such means. Arthur Danto's studies on visualization in art and its relations to literature (see Danto 1994) comprise a basis for launching investigations of ancient narrative, as I have suggested (Gibson 2000a).

Dummett (1993, 1993b) continued the quest (see Dummett 1981) in ways that have important consequences for *BSL*'s use of Frege. Hale (1994, 1996) has also constructed significant foundations for refining and querying Dummett's theories of names and singular terms. In contrast *BSL* (and Gibson 2000, 2000a) also considers a logic of vague predicates; such an approach can be extended by Williamson (1996), and differently by Sangali (1998).

BSL used the early work of Hintikka; his later work is also of special interest for those who want to give more attention to reinterpreting analytical philosophy and logic from within its axioms (see

Hintikka 1998, 1998a) to sustain aspects of *BSL*'s formal priority. Integrated with this perspective is *BSL*'s account of fallacies, which can be supplemented by Hansen's and Pinto's (1995) edited collection of studies on the topic. As an alternative to the possible world semantics mentioned in *BSL*, it now seems to me that Lewis's (1986) indexical plurality of worlds is an appropriate map for structuring some ancient Near Eastern religious worldview logic. The technical logic foundations of Cignoli *et al.* (2000), which were developed after the publication of *BSL*, are of significance for those who wish to pursue a many-valued logics approach. Tenant's (1997) thesis on anti-realist logics may also be fertile for some areas of biblical semantic logic.

Biblical scholars are divided over the applicability of Chomsky's earlier work to biblical texts. Areas that require more attention than they have received, however, are his recent theories (see Chomsky 1995, 1995a, and especially 2000) on the problems of text, language and mind, which hold enormous promise for research into ancient language.

(b) Semantics and Grammatical Research
Although there is much yet to achieve in logic research in conjunction with comparative and related linguistics, the type of linguistic research that *BSL* hoped and allowed for, which is an ideal tool for exposing logical structures, now occupies an influential position. Important new linguistically based insights into relations between Sumerian and themes related to the Old Testament include Klein's (1997) examination of the Sumerian versus biblical views on the origin and development of languages on Earth, which backs Noah Kramer's view (see Kramer's 1987 revised edition of *Sumerian Mythology*). Although a brief study, W.G. Lambert's (1995) assessment of some new Babylonian *WL* significantly adds to the rationality exposed in his earlier work (1960).

The use of deviant logics is considered in *BSL*. Although Livingstone's (1986) investigation of Assyrian and Babylonian scholars' rationalities and Leick's (1994) study of sex and eroticism in Mesopotamian literature only implicitly address issues of reasoning, yet their insights are extremely important for fresh judgment in this sphere, as I have recently argued (2000a).

There is also the splendid study on structural Babylonian grammar by Buccellati (1996), which has many logical insights, often implicitly formulated. Textual and lexical resources have improved in areas covered by *BSL* with additions such as Conti's (1992) index of Eblaic

texts and Black, George and Postgate's (1999) Akkadian dictionary
(both of which have import for concepts of reason mirrored in some
Old Testament themes). George's (1999) edition of the *Epic of Gilgamesh*, as well as Hadley's (2000) analysis of the language of the cult of
Asherah, though they do not address logic, stand as models of the sort
of study *BSL* advocated, and the latter approach to titles and names
exemplifies the criteria that *BSL* proposed. Also important is Huehnergard's (1989) research on Akkadian at Ugarit.

The revised English edition (1992) of Moran's *Les Lettres d'El-
Amarna* (1987) is complemented by Izre'el's (1997) analysis of how
the ancient scholars approached issues in the Amarna scholarly tablets, while Cochavi-Rainey's (1998) assessment of Egyptian influence
in the Amarna sphere, with Parkinson's (1997) and Nili's (1993)
examination and presentation of a range of Egyptian tales, are valuable resources for constructing some logics of Old Testament comparative intertextual semantics of the Old Testament world. Further
afield, yet similarly illuminating, is the collection of research studies
edited by MorPurgo Davies and Duhoux (1985) on Linear B. Martin
Bernal's forthcoming *Moses and Muses* promises to be a research of
challenging importance for the interpretation of many of these
arenas.

(c) Ancient Logic and the Bible
Although some research has been done on rational relations between
the biblical worlds and Classical Greek ones, yet there remains extensive work of high quality in Classical research that could generate
fresh programmes for biblical research on rationality. The collection
of studies edited by Gentzler (1998), and Williams's (1993, 1998)
work are fine starting points. In a different vein, work by philosophers of science such as Hesse (1995) highlight the value of qualified
alignments between modern and ancient rationalities as devices to
recover ancient meaning. Some progress has been made on the relations of stylistics to rational representation, as with Miller (1996);
and the use of comedy as a reasoned genre has attracted some attention in Whedbee (1998). Fresh possibilities can emerge from unexpected directions; for example, Molyneaux's (1997) research on the
representational depiction in the private tombs of the Late Eighteenth Dynasty Egypt reveals concepts of meaning related to shape,
which readily complements some of *BSL*'s treatment of semantic
expression as a species of visualizing representation (cf. also Gibson
2000a).

(d) Theology and Philosophy of the Bible

Milbank (1991, 1997) has raised fundamental questions about the identity of theology that has been influential in the last century. It is time for a reassessment of the impact of such theology on the Bible. Addinall (1991) has furnished us with a valuable discussion of the comparative philosophical currents that are often presupposed in, and predispose, discussion of biblical rationality, while Barr (1993) has mapped some contrasts, both misleading and correct, between thematic reasoning within the Bible and Barthian theology concerning faith and nature. Neil MacDonald (2000) has provided very significant research on how some of Barth's interpretation related to Kant, Hume and Wittgenstein facilitates construction of worldviews in the Bible. Neusner's (1988) and Neusner's and Chilton's (1997) researches on the connection between Jewish and Christian rationalities connect with *BSL*'s interest in the use of logical semantics representation.

(e) Mesopotamian Rationality and the Bible

BSL was written within Near East and Mesopotamian perspectives, rather than those of a biblical theology, though there are important researches within the latter priority, for example Ingraffia (1995). Alter's and Kermode's (1997) collection also offers much of interest that relates to reason in the Bible.

There are too many developments in Near East and Mesopotamia contexts for one here to represent even the categories of research relevant to biblical semantic logic. Fundamental to the perspective of *BSL* is the presupposition that biblical and Mesopotamian semantics and logic have extensive interconnections. Algaze (1993) made an indirect important contribution to this position when he framed seminal generalizations that were functions of the Uruk world system and its similarity to adjacent cultures. Robson's (1999) account of the pervasive awareness of mathematical understanding throughout a variety of Mesopotamian pragmatic and conceptual cultures assists us in allowing for considering that bivalent logical comprehension was a typical property within levels of such societies.

(f) Bible, Mentality and Archaeology

BSL was written before the wave of current interest in the ancient mind, though it addresses many central areas of this agenda. Rogerson's (1985) study of the application of sociology to the Old Testament helped to provide a more refined interpretation of the ancient world than some previous, theologizing approaches. Hodder (1999) has prepared the way for a fresh approach to the use of rationality in relation to mentality and archaeology, while I (Gibson 2000a) have tackled such matters in relation to biblical narrative. Shapiro (1997) has formulated some concepts for interpreting the contingent relations between such inner and outer worlds, while Schacter (1997) provides a powerful hypothesis on the memory as a means to access elements of the past, and Hacking (1994, 1998) employs analytical philosophy to inform us about the retrieval of memories when blocked by the 'semantic contagions' of false consciousness and memory, a notion that I apply (Gibson 1998, 2000a) to ancient semantics and semiotics. Such progress blends with other conceptions arising from archaeological research pertinent to the logic or semantic schemes of, for example, Gardin (1980) and the edited collection by Forte and Siliotti (1997).

These advances are complemented by the work of Robson (1999), which has illustrated the quite advanced theoretical competence of many ancient writers and thinkers, in contrast with some previous primitivizing assumptions. Important for this is correct theorization about the Greek–Hebrew axis in Old Testament influence, of which Dalley and Reyes (1998), and Pearson (1999, 2001), are important instances.

(g) Mediaeval Logic and the Bible

The work of Peter Geach is cited in *BSL*, one of whose strands is the excavation of neglected areas of logic in the mediaeval worlds. Since the publication of *BSL* this research has developed apace. It has special applications that can be modified for biblical semantics and logic, though there is much more preparatory work to be done in implementing such projects. G.R. Evans (1984) made a start; Marenbon (1987) and his edited volume (1998) have pioneering interpretations in some other areas, as has Pasnau (1997). In Priest (1995) we have a revival of a mediaeval view that a given proposition is both true and false. I have argued (Gibson 2000c) that this type of formal view does apply to some ancient rationality, though it is not—as Priest seems to hold—true for the foundation of logic.

Logic should not only encourage readers to articulate relevance (see Anderson and Belnap 1992), but also stimulate us to expect and search for surprise, as the study of paradox in *BSL* illustrates. Progress in the history of ideas since publication of *BSL* typifies this situation. The ways that later scholars draw on the past can be an inadvertent rewriting of it, which nevertheless may offer neglected or eclipsed insights into biblical semantics. For example *BSL* offered logic for the view that *'lhym* is not a proper name, but like a logical function—a role-term. This conclusion is supported by the Dead Sea Scrolls, where the Melchizedek Scroll (11QMelch) uses Ps. 82:1's *'lhym* as a role-term for a divine agent rather than God (see Gibson 1997a). Although sixteenth and seventeenth century Soncinians were ignorant of such matters, they had a similar view. Since the 1991 release of more of Isaac Newton's unpublished manuscript on biblical exegesis, we discover that his contact with such underground currents of thought led him also to the same conclusion. Snobelen (2001: 97-98) lays out aspects of the history of such ideas, and notes Keynes's view that Isaac Newton was a Judaic monotheist of the school of Maimonides. If there is some truth to this, it illuminates a way in which the mediation of semantic options and their logics might have been relayed through underground routes to contexts remote from their possible biblical origins.

(h) French Philosophical Research

BSL did not venture into French philosophy, but in later publications I have rectified that absence. Somewhat neglected or unknown outside France is French specialist research on logic, philosophy of mathematics and philosophy that is relevant for semantics, though there has been little explicit integration between such research and the Bible. There is space only for a selection of typical instances, though the time is ripe for large-scale investigation of these possibilities. Claude Imbert (1992) offers a profound exploration of how visualization can be associated with logic, but does not apply this to the Bible; yet it is a ready-made framework that, if connected to *BSL*, can yield important insights for the assessment of biblical reasoning. Other relevant pioneering work in France includes Bouveresse (1987, 1995, 1997), as well as Bourdieu (2000).

Many relations between philosophy and literary analysis are of value for further research into the Bible and semantic logic, originated and were refined by French philosophers, though these have yet to be systematically applied in this way. Notoriously, Derrida's research (1967, 1982, 1983, 1990) produces fragmentation of logical application to narrative. It is worth pursuing analysis of his studies outside of confrontational perspectives, however; I have done this (2000) and conclude that there is much of value, while partially disagreeing with him. Derrida's research (1987) on truth and painting in relation to literature has important lessons for scrutiny of biblical semantics, and can produce instructive tensions with Danto

(1994). Sartre's formulation of role functions is significant for future interpretation of the biblical logics of characterization. (Although Cumming (1992) does not introduce this theme to the Bible, his theory is a profitable basis for new work on the topic.) Deleuze and Guattari (1994) are significant for interrogating analytical philosophy's assumption that there is an exclusive contrast between a priori and empirical domains in relation to narrative representation. Gatens and Lloyd (1999) open up ways in which these matters derive from Spinoza and his concern with religious narrative.

For those who tend to dismiss French philosophy and literary culture as a series of transient fashions irrelevant to biblical rationalities (though no doubt universalized versions of them are susceptible to this criticism), it would be as well to reconsider how they may be treated as variable functions. Perhaps the deepest study of this is Marian Hobson's assessment (1998) of Derrida. One might even consider how a familiar, now anachronistic, notion such as structuralism could be refocused as superstructuralism (Harland 1987). Within the history of ideas, Foucault's research continues to be among the most important for stimulating us to rethink ideas of rationality and irrationality within both the ancient world and scholastic institutionalism (see, e.g., Foucault 1965).

(i) Rhetoric in the Bible

BSL did not address rhetoric in the Bible. The volume edited by Porter (1997) is a comprehensive survey of recent Classical and New Testament rhetoric researches.

Gibson (forthcoming c) addresses some ways in which we can recognize and map pathways between deductive logic and natural language usage. The fragmentary use of deductive rather than inductive logic, described by Aristotle—the *enthymeme*—is here investigated and related to biblical usage. Burnyeat (1994) has proved—as Ross (in his Introduction to Aristotle 1965) had supposed—that Aristotle's *enthymeme* is not an incomplete syllogism, as many New Testament scholars have assumed. Hence the futility of looking for quasi-syllogistic forms in the Bible, and worse still, altering biblical prose so that these forms accord with a syllogistic form. Aristotle's syllogism is far more finely tuned than to allow such paraphrasing of its identity. As Sorensen (1998) has shown, we need to be very careful how we interpret Aristotle here. The upshot of the progress in retrieving Aristotle's concept of *enthymeme* is, first, that probability and induction are not *internal* to its identity; and secondly, that through it deduction, of the sort that is not syllogistic, can be found within New Testament natural language usage. The first point is important, partly because enthymemic inference is frequently more complex or subtle than syllogism, and on occasions it is too complex to be expressed in syllogism. Thus, the deductive *enthymeme* in the Bible is a reflection of the refinement and originality of its writers, which is obscured when the *enthymeme* is treated as an incomplete syllogism.

(j) Greek Language
Stanley Porter (1992, 1994, 1999a, b) has pioneered a fresh approach to Greek grammar and idiom, which holds great promise for contributing to the exposure of the internal logics of texts in areas that did not maximally profit from earlier grammars. Progress in analysis of cultural insights for features of linguistic analysis is illustrated by the work of Derderian (2001) concerning mourning related to the emergence of literacy, with Dobrov (2001) in the realm of metafictional poetics, and Newiger (2000) on allegory and metaphor. The emerging research by Matthew Brook O'Donnell (1999, 1999a) uses refined computer analysis, which avoids the mechanizing shortcomings often associated with such analysis, and is an example of a new generation of work of special relevance for facilitating logical and mathematical analysis of biblical and other semantics.

BIBLIOGRAPHY OF RECENT WORK

Addinall, P.
  1991 *Philosophy and Biblical Interpretation* (Cambridge: Cambridge University Press)
Algaze, G.
  1993 *The Uruk World System* (Chicago: University of Chicago Press)
Alter, R.
  1981 *The Art of Biblical Narrative* (New York: Basic Books)
Alter, R., and F. Kermode (eds.)
  1997 *The Literary Guide to the Bible* (London: Collins)
Anderson, A.R., and Belnap N.F.
  1992 *The Logic of Relevance and Necessity* (2 vols.; Princeton, NJ: Princeton University Press)
Aristotle
  1965 *Aristotle's Prior and Posterior Analytics* (ed. W. D. Ross; Oxford: Clarendon Press)

Bahrani, Z.
    1998   'Conjuring Mesopotamia: Imaginative Geography and a World Past', in
            L. Meskell (ed.), *Archaeology under Fire* (London: Routledge): 159-74
Bakhtin, M.
    1984   *Problems of Dostoyevsky's Poetics* (ed. and trans. C. Emerson; intro. W.C.
            Booth; Theory and History of Literature, 8; Manchester: Manchester Uni-
            versity Press)
Banfield, A.
    1982   *Unspeakable Sentences* (London: Routledge & Kegan Paul)
Barr, J.
    1993   *Biblical Faith and Natural Theology* (Oxford: Clarendon Press)
Baudrillard, J.
    1996   *The Perfect Crime* (trans. C. Turner; London and New York: Verso)
Bernal, M.
            Moses and Muses (forthcoming)
Black, J., George, A., and Postgate, J.N.,
    1999   *A Concise Dictionary of Akkadian* (Wiesbaden: Otto Harrassowitz)
Blackburn, S.
    1998   *Ruling Passions* (Oxford: Clarendon Press)
Blazer, V.
    1999   'Elam: A Bridge between the Ancient Near East and India', in R. Blench
            and M. Spriggs (eds.), *Archaeology and Language. IV. Language-Change and
            Cultural Transformation* (London and New York: Routledge): 48-78
Boghossian, P.
    1989   'The Rule-following Considerations', *Mind* 98: 507-49
Bourdieu, P.
    2000   *Pascalian Meditations* (Cambridge: Polity Press)
Bouveresse, J.
    1987   *La force de la regle* (Paris: Editions de Minuit)
    1995   *Wittgenstein Reads Freud* (trans. C. Cosman; Princeton, NJ: Princeton Uni-
            versity Press)
    1997   *La demande philosophique* (Paris: Editions de l'eclat, 2nd edn)
Bowie, A.
    1996   *Philosophy of German Literary Theory: From Romanticism to Critical Theory*
            (London: Routledge)
Bradford, R.
    1997   *Stylistics* (London: Routledge)
Buccellati, G.
    1996   *A Structural Grammar of Babylonian* (Wiesbaden: Otto Harrassowitz)
Burnyeat, M.F.
    1994   'Enthymeme: Aristotle on the logic of persuasion', in D.J. Furley and
            A. Nehamas (eds.), *Aristotle's Rhetoric* (Princeton, NJ: Princeton University
            Press): 3-55
Cartwright, N.
    1999   *The Dappled World: A Study of the Boundaries of Science* (Cambridge:
            Cambridge University Press)

Catagnoti, A.
1998 'The 3rd Millennium Personal Name from the Habur Triangle in the Ebla, Brak, and Mozan Texts', European Centre for Upper Mesopotamian Studies. *Subartu*. IV. (Bruxelles: Brepots)
Cavell, S.
1995 *Philosophical Passages* (Oxford: Basil Blackwell)
Chomsky, N.
1995 *Language and Mind* (New York: Harcourt Brace Jovanovich)
1995a 'Language and Nature', *Mind* 104: 1-62
2000 *New Horizons in the Study of Language and Mind* (Cambridge: Cambridge University Press)
Cignoli, R.L.O., Itala, R., D'Ottaviano, M.L., and Mundici, D.
2000 *Algebraic Foundations of Many-Valued Reasoning* (Trends in Logic, 7; Dordrecht and London: Kluwer Academic Publisher)
Cochavi-Rainey, Z.
1998 'Egyptian Influence in the Amarna Texts', *UF* 29: 95-114
Conti, G.
1992 *Index of Eblaic Texts (published or cited)*, with A. Catagnonti and M. Bonechi (Quaderni di Semistica Materiali, 1; Florence: Dipartmento di Linguistica, Universita di Firenze)
Cumming, R.D.
1992 'Role-playing', in C. Howells (ed), *The Cambridge Companion to Sartre* (Cambridge: Cambridge University Press): 39-66
Dalley, S., and Reyes A.T.
1998 'Mesopotamian contact and influence in the Greek world', in S. Dalley (ed.), *The Legacy of Mesopotamia* (Oxford: Oxford University Press): 107-24
Danto, A.
1994 *Embodied Meanings* (New York: Noonday Press)
Davidson, D.
1980 *Essays on Actions and Events* (Oxford: Oxford University Press)
Day, J.
1997 'Resurrection imagery from Baal to the book of Daniel', in Emerton (1997): 125-33.
Deleuze, G., and Guattari, F.
1994 *What is Philosophy?* (trans. G. Burchell and H. Tomlinson; London: Verso)
Derderian, K.
2001 *Leaving Words to Remember: Greek Mourning and the Advent of Literacy* (Mnemosyne, bibliotheca classica Batava, Supplementum, 209; Leiden: E.J. Brill)
Derrida, J.
1967 *L'écriture et la différance* (Paris: Editions du Seuil)
1982 *Margins of Philosophy* (Chicago: University of Chicago Press)
1983 'The Time of a Thesis: Punctuations', in A. Montifiore (ed.), *Philosophy in France Today* (Cambridge: Cambridge University Press): 34-50
1987 *The Truth in Painting* (Chicago: University of Chicago Press)
1990 *Writing and Difference* (London: Routledge)

1998   *Monolingualism of the Other, or The Prosthesis of Origins* (trans. P. Mensah; Stanford: Stanford University Press)

Dobrov, G.
2001   *Figures of Play: Greek Drama and Metafictional Poetics* (New York: Oxford University Press)

Dummett, M.
1975   'What Is a Theory of Meaning?: I', in S.D. Guttenplan (ed.), *Mind and Language* (Oxford: Oxford University Press): 97-138 (= M. Dummett, *The Seas of Language* (2 vols.; Oxford: Clarendon Press, 1993, 1996): I, 1-33)
1978   *Truth and Other Enigmas* (London: Gerald Duckworth)
1981   *Frege: Philosophy of Language* (London: Gerald Duckworth, 2nd edn)
1993   *Frege and Other Philosophers* (Oxford: Oxford University Press)
1993a *Origins of Analytic Philosophy* (London: Gerald Duckworth)

Eco, U.
1984   *Semiotics and the Philosophy of Language* (London: Macmillan)

Evans, G.R.
1984   *The Language and Logic of the Bible: The Earlier Middle Ages* (Cambridge: Cambridge University Press)

Fine, K.
1985   *Reasoning with Arbitrary Objects* (Aristotelian Society Series, 3; Oxford: Basil Blackwell)

Foley, H.P.
1988   *Ritual Irony* (Ithaca, NY: Cornell University Press)

Forrester, J.
1980   *Language and the Origins of Psychoanalysis* (London: Macmillan)
1997   *Dispatches from the Freud Wars* (Cambridge, MA: Harvard University Press)

Forte, M., and A. Siliotti (eds.)
1997   *Virtual Archaeology* (London: Thames & Hudson)

Foucault, M.
1961   *Folie et deraison* (Paris: Plon)
1963   *Naissance de la clinique* (Paris: Presses universitaires de France)
1965   *Madness and Civilization* (trans. R. Howard; London: Routledge)
1966   *Les mots et les choses* (Paris: Gallimard)
1969   *L'archéologie du savoir* (Paris: Gallimard)
1972   *The Archaeology of Knowledge and The Discourse on Language* (trans. S. Smith and A. Mark; London: Tavistock)
1979   *The Will to Knowledge* (London: Allen Lane)
1989   *The Birth of the Clinic* (trans. A. Sheridan; London: Routledge)
1989b *The Order of Things* (London: Routledge)

Gardin, J.-C.
1980   *Archaeological Constructs: An Aspect of Theoretical Archaeology* (Cambridge: Cambridge University Press)

Garver, N.
1996   'Philosophy as grammar', in H. Sluga and D.G. Stern (eds.), *The Cambridge Companion to Wittgenstein* (Cambridge: Cambridge University Press): 134-70

Gatens, M., and Lloyd G.
1999   *Collective Imaginings* (London: Routledge)

Gentzler, J. (ed.)
1998   *Method in Ancient Philosophy* (Oxford: Clarendon Press)

George, A.
1999   *The Epic of Gilgamesh: The Babylonian Epic Poem and other Texts in Akadian and Sumerian* (London: Allen Lane, Penguin Books)

Gibson, A.
1987   *Boundless Function* (Newcastle: Bloodaxe)
1997   'Archetypal Site Poetry', in J. Milbank, *The Mercurial Wood: Sites, Tales, Qualities* (Salzburg Studies in English Literature, Poetic Drama and Poetic Theory; Salzburg, Austria: University of Salzburg Press): vii-xi
1997a   'God's Semantic Logic: Some Functions in the Dead Sea Scrolls and the Bible', in S.E. Porter and C.A. Evans (eds.), *The Scrolls and the Scriptures: Qumran Fifty Years After* (RILP, 3/JSPSup, 26; Sheffield: Sheffield Academic Press): 68-106
1998   'Modern Philosophy and Ancient Consciousness', in M.A. Hayes, W.J. Porter and D. Tombs (eds.), *Religion and Sexuality* (Sheffield: Sheffield Academic Press): 22-48
1998a   'Ockham's World and Future', in J. Marenbon (ed.), *Routledge History of Philosophy*. III. *Medieval Philosophy* (London: Routledge): 329-67
1999   'Logic of the Resurrection', in S.E. Porter, M.A. Hayes and D. Tombs (eds.), *Resurrection* (JSNTSup, 186; Sheffield: Sheffield Academic Press): 166-94
2000   *God and the Universe* (London and New York: Routledge)
2000a   *Text and Tablet: Near Eastern Archaeology, the Old Testament and New Possibilities* (Aldershot: Ashgate)
2000b   'Philosophy of Psychotic Modernism: Wagner and Hitler', in S.E. Porter and B.W.R. Pearson (eds.), *Christian–Jewish Relations through the Centuries* (R\LP, 6/JSNTSup, 192; Sheffield: Sheffield Academic Press): 351-86
Forthcoming a
        Counter-Intuition
Forthcoming b
        Beyond Human Meaning?
Forthcoming c
        'Relations between Rhetoric and Philosophical Logic', in S.E. Porter and D.L. Stamps (eds.), *Rhetorical Criticism and the Bible: Essays from the Florence Conference* (JSNTSup, 195; Sheffield: Sheffield Academic Press)
Forthcoming d
        What is Literature?
Forthcoming e
        Infinite Literary Logic: A Treatise on Logic, Literary Creativity and Philosophy of Mathematics

Gibson, A., and O'Mahony, N.A.
1995   'Lamentation sumerienne (vers - 2004)', *Dedale: Le pardoxe des representations du divin—L'image et l'invisible*, 1-2 Paris: 13-14

Goldhill, S.
1984   *Language, Sexuality, Narrative: The Oresteia* (Cambridge: Cambridge University Press)

1986   *Reading Greek Tragedy* (Cambridge: Cambridge University Press)

1990   *The Poet's Voice* (Cambridge: Cambridge University Press)

Hacking, I.

1994   *Rewriting the Soul* (Princeton, NJ: Princeton University Press)

1998   *Mad Travellers: Reflections of the Reality of Transient Mental Illnesses* (Charlotteville: University Press of Virginia)

Hadley, J.M.

2000   *The Cult of Asherah in Ancient Israel and Judah: Evidence for a Hebrew Goddess* (Cambridge: Cambridge University Press)

Hale, R.

1994   'Singular Terms', in B.F. McGuinness and J.L. Oliveri (eds.), *The Philosophy of Michael Dummett* (Dordrecht: Kluwer Academic Publishers): 17-44

1996   'Singularity Terms (1)', in M. Schirn (ed), *Frege: Importance and Legacy* (Berlin: W. de Gruyter): 438-57

Hammond, G.

1983   'The Bible and Literary Criticism: I and II', *Critical Quarterly* 25.2: 5-20 and 25.3: 3-15

Hansen, H.V., and Pinto R.C. (eds.)

1995   *Fallacies* (University Park, PA: Pennsylvania State University Press)

Harland, R.

1987   *Superstructuralism* (London: Methuen)

Harris, A.C., and L. Campbell

1995   *Historical Syntax in Cross-Linguistic Perspective* (Cambridge: Cambridge University)

Hesse, M.

1995   'Past Realities', in I. Hodder *et al.* (eds.), *Interpreting Archaeology* (London: Routledge): 45-57

Hintikka, J.J.

1998   'Who is about to Kill Analytic Philosophy?', in A. Biletzky and A. Matar (eds.), *The Story of Analytic Philosophy* (London: Routledge): 253-69

1998a *The Principles of Mathematics Revisited* (Cambridge: Cambridge University Press)

Hobson, M.

1982   *The Object of Art* (Cambridge: Cambridge University Press)

1990   'On the Subject of the Subject: Derrida on Sollers in *La dissemination*', in D. Wood (ed.), *Philosophers' Poets* (London: Routledge): 111-39

1995   'What Is Wrong with Saint Peter's, or Diderot, Analogy and Illusion in Architecture', in W. Pape and F. Burwick (eds.), *Reflecting Senses* (Berlin: W. de Gruyter): 53-74, 315-41

1998   *Jacques Derrida: Opening Lines* (London: Routledge)

Hodder, I.

1999   *The Archaeological Process* (Cambridge: Cambridge University Press)

Horn, L.R.

1996   'Presupposition and Implicature', in Lappin (1996): ch. 11

Huehnergard, J.

1989   *The Akkadian of Ugarit* (Atlanta: Scholars Press)

Imbert, C.
   1992   *Phenomenologie et langues formulaires* (Paris: Presses Universitaires de France)
Ingraffia, B.D.
   1995   *Postmodern Theory and Biblical Theology* (Cambridge: Cambridge University Press)
Izre'el, S.
   1997   *The Amarna Scholarly Tablets* (Groningen: STYX Publications)
Jacobi, F.H.
   1787   *David Hume über den Glauben oder Idealismus und Realismus ein Gespräch* (Breslau: G. Loewe)
James, S.D.T.
   1984   *The Context of Social Explanation* (Cambridge: Cambridge University Press)
Kabbani, R.
   1986   *Europe's Myths of Orient* (London: Pandora)
Kermode, J.F.
   1964   *The Sense of an Ending* (New York: Oxford University Press)
   1979   *The Genesis of Secrecy* (Cambridge, MA: Harvard University Press)
   1983   *Essays on Fiction* (London: Routledge & Kegan Paul) = *The Art of Telling* (Cambridge, MA: Harvard University Press)
   1985   *Forms of Attention* (Chicago: University of Chicago Press)
   1990   *Poetry, Narrative, History* (Oxford: Basil Blackwell)
   2000   *Shakespeare's Language* (London: Allen Lane, Penguin Books)
Khalfa, J.
   2000   'Deleuze et Sartre: idée d'une conscience impersonnelle', *Les Temps Modernes* 55.608: 190-222
Klein, J.
   1997   'The Origin and Development of Languages on Earth: The Sumerian versus the Biblical view', in M. Coggin, B.L. Eichler and J.H. Tigay (eds.), *Tehillah le-Moshe* (Winona Lake, IN: Eisenbrauns): 77-92
Kramer, S.N.
   1987   *Sumerian Mythology: A Study of Spiritual and Literary Achievement in the Third Millennium B.C.* (Westport, CT: Greenwood Press, rev. edn)
Kristeva, J.
   1982   *Powers of Horror* (New York: Columbia University Press)
Kristiansen, K.
   1998   *Europe before History* (Cambridge: Cambridge University Press)
Kugel, J.L.
   1982   *The Idea of Biblical Poetry* (Yale: Yale University Press)
Lambert, W.G.
   1960   *Babylonian Wisdom Literature* (Oxford: Oxford University Press)
   1995   'Some New Babylonian Wisdom Literature', in J. Day, R.P. Gordon and H.G.M. Williamson (eds.), *Wisdom in Ancient Israel* (Cambridge: Cambridge University Press): ch. 2
Langton, R., and Lewis, D.
   1998   'Defining Intrinsic', *Australian Philosophical and Phenomenological Research* 58.2: XX

Lappin, S. (ed.)
  1996   *The Handbook of Contemporary Semantic Theory* (Oxford: Basil Blackwell)
Leick, G.
  1994   *Sex and Eroticism in Mesopotamian Literature* (London: Routledge)
Lewis, D.
  1980   *Collected Works*, I. (Oxford: Oxford University Press)
  1986   *Worlds in Plurality* (Oxford: Oxford University Press)
Livingstone, A.
  1986   *Mystical and Mythological Explanatory Works of Assyrian and Babylonian Scholars* (Oxford: Clarendon Press)
MacDonald, N.
  2000   *Karl Barth and the Strange New World within the Bible* (Carlisle: Paternoster Press)
Marenbon, J.
  1987   *Later Medieval Philosophy* (London: Routledge)
  1998   *Medieval Philosophy* (vol. 3, History of Philosophy; London: Routledge)
McGinn, C.
  1984   *Wittgenstein on Meaning* (Oxford: Oxford University Press)
Meiroop, M. van de
  1999   *Cuneiform Texts and the Writing of History* (Approaching the Ancient World; London and New York: Routledge)
Melzer, T.
  1995   'Stylistics for the Study of Ancient Texts', in W. Bodine (ed.), *Discourse Analysis of Biblical Literature* (Atlanta: Scholars Press)
Milbank, J.
  1991   *Theology and Social Theory* (Oxford: Basil Blackwell)
  1997   *The Word Made Strange* (Oxford: Basil Blackwell)
Miller, C.L.
  1996   *The Representation of Speech in Biblical Hebrew Narrative* (HSM, 55; Atlanta: Scholars Press)
Molyneaux, B.L.
  1997   'Representation and Reality in the Private Tombs of the Late Eighteenth Dynasty, Egypt: An Approach to the Study of the Shape of Meaning', in B.L. Molyneaux (ed.), *The Cultural Life of Images* (London: Routledge): 108-29
Moran W.L.
  1987   *Les Lettres d'El-Amarna* (Paris: Editions de Serf)
  1992   *The Amarna Letters* (Baltimore: The Johns Hopkins University Press)
MorPurgo Davies, A., and Duhoux Y. (eds.)
  1985   *Linear B: A 1984 Survey* (BCILL, 26; Louvain-la-Neuve: Cabay)
Neusner, J.
  1988   *The Incarnation of God* (Philadelphia: Fortress Press)
Neusner, J., and Chilton, B.
  1997   *The Intellectual Foundations of Christian and Jewish Discourse* (London: Routledge)
Newiger, H.-J.
  2000   *Metapher und Allegorie: Studien zu Aristophanes* (Hans-Joachim Newiger Series: Drama; Beiheft 10; Stuttgart: J.B. Metzler)

Nicholson, E.

1998   *The Pentateuch in the Twentieth Century* (Oxford: Clarendon Press)

Nili, Sh.

1993   *Where Can Wisdom Be Found? The Sage's Language in the Bible and in Ancient Egyptian Literature* (OBO, 130; Fribourg: University Press; Göttingen: Vandenhoeck & Ruprecht)

Nussbaum, M.C.

2000   *Women and Human Development: The Capabilities Approach* (Cambridge: Cambridge University Press)

O'Donnell, M. Brook

1999   'The Use of Annotated Corpora for New Testament Discourse Analysis: A Survey of Current Practice and Future Prospects', in S.E. Porter and J.T. Reed (eds.), *Discourse Analysis and the New Testament: Approaches and Results* (JSNTSup, 170/SNTG, 4; Sheffield: Sheffield Academic Press): 71-117

1999a   'Linguistic Fingerprints or Style by Numbers: The Use of Statistics in the Discussion of Authorship of New Testament Documents', in S.E. Porter and D.A. Carson (eds.), *Linguistics and the New Testament: Critical Junctures* (JSNTSup, 168; Sheffield: Sheffield Academic Press): 206-54

Owen, D.I.

1992   'Syrians in Sumer', *Bibliotheca Mesopotamia* 1992: 107-75

Parkinson, R.B.

1997   *The Tale of Sinuhe and Other Ancient Egyptian Poems* (Oxford: Clarendon Press)

Parpola, A.

1994   *Deciphering the Indus Script* (Cambridge: Cambridge University Press)

Pasnau, R.

1997   *Theories of Cognition in the Later Middle Ages* (Cambridge: Cambridge University Press)

Pearson, B.W.R.

1999   'Resurrection and the Judgment of the Titans: ἡ γῆ τῶν ἀσεβῶν in LXX Isaiah 26.19', in S.E. Porter, M.A. Hayes and D. Tombs (eds.), *Resurrection* (RILP 5/JSNTSup, 186; Sheffield: Sheffield Academic Press): 33-51

2001   *Corresponding Sense* (Leiden: E.J. Brill)

Pierce, C.S.

1931–58 *Collected Papers* (Cambridge, MA: Harvard University Press)

Popper, K.R.

1994   *The Myth of the Framework* (ed. M.A. Nottarno; London: Routledge)

Porter, S.E. (ed.)

1992   *Verbal Aspect in the Greek of the New Testament, with Reference to Tense and Mood* (SBG, 1; New York and Bern: Peter Lang, 2nd edn (1989))

1994   *Idioms of the Greek New Testament* (BLG, 2; Sheffield: Sheffield Academic Press, 2nd edn, 1994 (1992))

1994   *Katallassw in Ancient Greek Literature, with Reference to the Pauline Writings* (Estudios de Filología Neotestamentaria, 5; Córdoba, Spain: Ediciones El Almendro)

1996   *Studies in the Greek New Testament: Theory and Practice* (SBG, 6; New York and Bern: Peter Lang)

1997   *Handbook of Classical Rhetoric in the Hellenistic Period 330 BC–AD 400* (Leiden: E.J. Brill)

1999   *Early Christianity and its Sacred Literature* (with Lee M. McDonald; Peabody, MA: Hendrickson)

1999a   'Linguistics and Rhetorical Criticism', in Porter and Carson (eds.), *Linguistics and the New Testament*: 63-95

1999b   'Paul as Rhetorician and Epistolographer', in S.E. Porter and D.L. Stamps (eds.), *The Rhetorical Interpretation of Scripture: Essays from the 1996 Malibu Conference* (JSNTSup, 180; Sheffield: Sheffield Academic Press): 222-49

1999c   *The Paul of Acts: Essays in Literary Criticism, Rhetoric, and Theology* (WUNT, 115; Tübingen: J.C.B. Mohr (Paul Siebeck))

Postgate, J.N.
1992   *Early Mesopotamia* (London: Routledge)

Priest, G.
1995   *Beyond the Limits of Thought* (Cambridge: Cambridge University Press)

Rescher, N., and Brandom R.
1980   *The Logic of Inconsistency* (Oxford: Oxford University Press)

Reynolds, D.
1995   *Symbolist Aesthetics and Early Abstract Art* (Cambridge: Cambridge University Press)

Riffaterre, M.
1991   'Undecidability as Hermeneutic Constraint', in P. Collier and H. Geyer Ryan (eds.), *Literary Theory Today* (Cambridge: Cambridge University Press): 109-24

Robson, E.
1999   *Mesopotamian Mathematics, 2100–1600 B.C.* (Oxford: Clarendon Press)

Rogerson, J.W.
1985   'The Use of Sociology in Old Testament Studies', in J.A. Emerton (ed.), *Congress Volume: Salamanca, 1983* (VTSup, 36; Leiden: E.J. Brill): 245-56

Rooth, M.
1996   'Focus', in Lappin (1996): ch. 10

Rorty, R.
1984   'The Historiography of Philosophy: Four Genres', in R. Rorty, J.B. Schneewind and Q. Skinner (eds.), *Philosophy in History* (Cambridge: Cambridge University Press): 49-76

Ross, J.
1997   *The Semantics of Media* (Dordrecht: Kluwer Academic Publishers)

Salvesen, A.
1998   *Origin's Hexapla and Fragments* (TSAJ, 58; Tübingen: J.C.B. Mohr (Paul Siebeck))

Sangali, A.
1998   *The Importance of Being Fuzzy* (Princeton, NJ: Princeton University Press)

Schacter, D.L.
1997   *Searching for Memory: The Brain, the Mind, and the Past* (New York: Basic Books)

Schenkeveld, D.M.
1997   'Philosophical Prose', in Porter (1997): 195-264

Shapiro, E.R.
  1997   *The Inner World in the Outer World* (New Haven: Yale University Press)
Shennan, S.
  1997   *Quantifying Archaeology* (Edinburgh: Edinburgh University Press, 2nd edn)
Shoesmith, D.J., and Smiley T.J.
  1980   *Multiple-Conclusion Logic* (Cambridge: Cambridge University Press, corrected edn)
Smiley, T.J.
  1982   'The Theory of Descriptions', *Proceedings of the British Academy (1982)* 67: 321-27
Snobelen, S.
  2001   ' "The mystery of this restitution of all things": Isaac Newton on the return of the Jews', in J.E. Force and R.H. Popkin (eds.), *Millenarianism and Messianism in Early Modern European Culture* (Dordrecht: Kluwer Academic Publishers): 95-118
Sorensen, R.A.
  1998   'Logical Luck', *Philosophical Quarterly* 48.192: 319-34
Sperber, D.
  1985   *On Anthropological Knowledge* (Cambridge: Cambridge University Press)
Spitz, E.H.
  1985   *Art and Psyche: A Study in Psychoanalysis and Aesthetics* (New Haven: Yale University Press)
Sluga, H., and Stern, D.G. (eds.)
  1996   *The Cambridge Companion to Wittgenstein* (Cambridge: Cambridge University Press)
Stern, D.G.
  1995   *Wittgenstein on Mind and Language* (Oxford: Oxford University Press)
Striker, G.
  1998   'Aristotle and the uses of logic', in Gentzler (1998): 209-226
Tenant, N.
  1997   *The Taming of the True* (Oxford: Oxford University Press)
Thomsen, M.-L.
  1984   *The Sumerian Language* (Mesopotamia, 10; Copenhagen: Akademisk Forlag)
Tigay, J.H.
  1985   *Empirical Models for Biblical Criticism* (Philadelphia: University of Pennsylvania Press)
Tilley, C.
  1999   *Metaphor and Material Culture* (Oxford: Basil Blackwell)
Ucko, P.J.
  1968   *Anthropomorphic Figurines of Predynastic Egypt and Neolithic Crete* (London: A. Szmidla)
Watanabe, C.E.
  1998   'Aspects of Animal Symbolism in Mesopotamia' (unpublished PhD dissertation; Cambridge University Faculty of Oriental Studies)

Watterson, B.

   1997   *Amarna: Ancient Egypt's Age of Revolution* (Stroud, UK: Tempus)

Whedbee, J.W.

   1998   *The Bible and the Comic Vision* (Cambridge: Cambridge University Press)

Williams, B.

   1993   *Shame and Necessity* (Berkeley: University of California Press)

   1998   *Plato: The Invention of Philosophy* (London: Phoenix)

Williamson, T.

   1996   *Vagueness* (London and New York: Routledge)

Wittgenstein, L.

   1996   *Notes on Logic* in M.A.R. Biggs (ed.), *Editing Wittgenstein's 'Notes on Logic'* (2 vols.; Working Papers from the Wittgenstein Archives at the University of Bergen, 11)

   1999   *The Collected Manuscripts of Ludwig Wittgenstein on Facsimile CD-ROM* (ed. Wittgenstein Archives, University of Bergen; Oxford: Oxford University Press)

Young, J.E.

   2000   *At Memory's Edge* (New Haven: Yale University Press)

I

INTRODUCTION

1.0 BIBLICAL SEMANTIC LOGIC

1 Logic and Biblical Linguistics

The following work commences construction on a topic new to
biblical linguistics. This topic is the application of logic to do
semantics at the applied level. It would be premature to develop
an exhaustive mapping of logic on to biblical texts; I am concerned
with the prior task of introducing logical topics to biblical linguistics and giving a critique of some scholastic treatments.[1]
J. Macquarrie, commenting on J. Barr's work,[2] observed:

> In stressing the sentence as the minimal unit of discourse,
> Barr is saying precisely what Wittgenstein said. Barr explicitly
> says that his own inquiry is linguistic rather than logical,
> but he also remarks that in such an inquiry 'important
> questions of logic and of general philosophy are involved'.
> If Biblical theologians follow up some of the directions which
> Barr has indicated . . . they are bound to come to the question
> of the logical patterns in Biblical language . . . Such investi-
> gations could obviously profit from the techniques of logical
> analysis.[3]

To commence this task on a proper footing, we need to know first

---

[1] In an hermeneutical context, A. C. Thiselton's *The Two Horizons* (Exeter,
1980) underlines the importance of this type of concern. Additionally, see A. C.
Thiselton's judgement that philosophical semantics can supplement linguistic
semantics (cf. his study in I. Howard Marshall (ed.), *New Testament Interpretation* (London, 1977). But see J. Barr's review of this work in *Theology*, 81 (May
1978), 681, pp. 233–4).

[2] J. Barr, *The Semantics of Biblical Language* (Oxford, 1961).

[3] J. Macquarrie, 'Second Thoughts', *Expository Times*, 75 (Nov. 1963), 2, p. 47.
His Barr quotation comes from *The Semantics of Biblical Language*, p. 1. Actually,
Wittgenstein developed the point from Frege (cf. 2.1, 3 below).

the nature and level of consistency in biblical studies, since they are the medium for depicting biblical texts. At the level of biblical languages, Macquarrie's suggestions have not been implemented.[4] Their significance is deepened by research such as that by M. Dummett,[5] which exposes the importance of the application of logic to natural languages for a theory of meaning.

---

[4] i.e. with respect to the original (and not translated) languages; of course, in analysis of scholars' reasoning D. H. Kelsey, *The Uses of Scripture in Recent Theology* (Philadelphia, 1975), for example, has made a start.

[5] e.g. M. Dummett and R. Minio, *Elements of Intuitionism*, pp. 376–81, and especially P. T. Geach, *Reference and Generality* (amended edn., Cornell, 1968). See M. Dummett, *Truth and Other Enigmas* (London, 1978), chs. 9, 22, 23; and his *The Interpretation of Frege's Philosophy* (London, 1981).

1 Priorities

Any elements of logic in the present investigation are employed to grapple with current, applied semantic issues within biblical studies. Hence logic is subsidiary to biblical semantics – and to the latter's present states and modes, which will, because of formally primitive situations within biblical studies, prevent my introducing theoretical matters which would otherwise hold my attention.

2 Orientalist Perspective

The orientalist context of biblical semantics, rather than a theologically associated approach, is the arena within which data are to be examined. Barr's own linguistic focus reflects this same perspective, for example in *Semantics* and to some extent in his work on comparative philology.[1] Barr showed that substantial misunderstanding was encased in mainstream interpretations of biblical linguistic phenomena, and he initiated a reconstruction of descriptive biblical linguistics. C. Rabin,[2] together with a few more recent linguists,[3] also developed other approaches.

Unfortunately, it is clear that such writers as D. Hill[4] and (I shall show) F. M. Cross[5] can respond to the situation produced by Barr's criticisms as though he had offered a recommendation about the *presentation* of, for example, the Kittel[6] dictionary or hypostatization of linguistic items, and that slight adjustment of description would remove the offending features while these traditional fragments of a theologico-linguistic scheme could be salvaged as they basically stand. Barr's own assessment[7] of Hill's views demonstrates that Hill has misunderstood Barr's analysis

[1] J. Barr, *Comparative Philology and the Text of the Old Testament* (Oxford, 1968).

[2] C. Rabin works in a rather different mould from J. Barr (cf. C. Rabin 'hattitaken semantiqa miqra'it', *Bet-Miqra'* (1962), pp. 17–27).

[3] e.g. J. F. A. Sawyer, *Semantics in Biblical Research* (London, 1972).

[4] D. Hill, *Greek Words and Hebrew Meanings* (Cambridge, 1967).

[5] F. M. Cross, *Canaanite Myth and Hebrew Epic* (Harvard, 1973).

[6] G. Kittel and G. Friedrich (eds.), *Theologisches Wörterbuch zum Neuen Testament* (Stuttgart, 1933, etc.).

[7] J. Barr's review of D. Hill's *Greek Words and Hebrew Meanings*, *New Black-friars*, 49 (April 1968), 575, pp. 376ff.

at important junctures, and (as I would state it) has confusedly
transposed indictments about the deep structure in such theologico-linguistic hypotheses to merely surface grammar criticisms.[8] I shall argue that this mistake, typically, is to some extent
due to the fact that further errors need to be exposed. These
errors were beyond the prescribed scope of Barr's pioneering
book,[9] even though he hinted at the possible and probable existence
of these types of mistakes and lifted a few out for comment. The
types of mistakes Barr did castigate (since they are still sometimes
to be found in the research literature) can benefit from further
characterization, from a logico-linguistic standpoint. It should
not be assumed that if an item falls into this category of characterization it is of solely logical interest. Logical analysis can point
out the behaviour of phenomena in language where inconsistency
is a matter of linguistic confusion. This confusion is often a matter
of elementary linguistic error but disguised from view by complex
confused presuppositions masked by an erudite hypothesis.

Outside the parameters of this negative task (which is nevertheless positive because it exposes what is the case in a state of affairs –
the negative part is in what is discovered, not the technique's use),
I wish to suggest and show by practice that such a logico-linguistic
analysis and its attendant devices are of descriptive and interpretative value in the identification and assessment of the nature and
contents of biblical and Near Eastern texts.

---

[8] I use 'surface grammar' quite generally here, as in J. Lyons' *Introduction to
Theoretical Linguistics* (Cambridge, 1968), p. 247.
[9] J. Barr, *The Semantics of Biblical Language*, pp. 1–2.

1 Analysis

One can summarize a recurrent weakness of some biblical scholarship exemplified in many of the following cases, and introduce a description of a corrective task of analysis, by quoting Barr's judgement:

> ... one of my chief doubts about the main current of biblical scholarship ... is that it is too simply empirical, too dominated by the *fact* of evidence in the form of quotable words, of entries in dictionaries, of discovered artefacts, and too little experienced in the analysis of the connexions between these facts and the variety of their possible interpretations. It has been too much controlled by a logic of discovery (whereby a new text from Qumran, a new word found in Ugaritic, are taken to prove something) and too little by a logic of analysis. The purely empirical aspect of scholarship needs to be supplemented by an analytic approach; or, we might say, a factual empiricism needs to be replaced by an analytic empiricism.[1]

Barr is rightly criticizing a simplistic empiricism which does not actually succeed in accurately describing the 'fact'. The logic of discovery has not been a logic of scientific discovery, but a naive realism in which first impressions are assumed to be what it is to be the particular fact. Barr's assessment has a corollary in K. R. Popper's viewpoint, which Popper has widely developed, embodied as follows:

> ... there is no such thing as ... the passive reception of a flow of information which impresses itself on our sense organs. All observations are theory impregnated ...
>
> Francis Bacon was rightly worried about the fact that our theories may prejudice our observations. This led him to advise

[1] J. Barr, *Biblical Words for Time* (rev. edn., London, 1969), pp. 198–9. An example of the type of study which does implement caution and avoid Barr's criticism is A. R. Millard's 'A Text in a Shorter Cuneiform Alphabet from Tell Nebi Mend (TNM 022)', *Ugarit-Forschungen*, 8 (1976), pp. 459–60; although it is short and does not employ formal analysis, it does not commit the aforementioned errors. Hence a formal analysis is not necessary to avoid Barr's criticism.

scientists that they should avoid prejudice by purifying their
minds of all theories . . . But to attain objectivity we cannot
rely on the empty mind: objectivity rests on criticism, on critical discussion . . .[2]

Merely because a scholar appears to be preoccupied with the
archaeological artefact or with a lexical item in a text this does not
entail that he is descriptively or analytically closer in accuracy to
it, although the negation of this point is often presupposed by
such scholars.[3] The proximity itself might be an ingredient in
generating subjective presentation of it (a naive realism).[4] Often,
of course, these scholars are influenced by intricate hypotheses
and networks; and if little attention is given to analytic empirical
exposure of the item analysed, then naive realism can provoke
the scholar to discard nonconforming features of data – scanned as
they are by interpretations of previously theory-impregnated
observation of data. In this situation there is an inconsistency
between various elements of a scholar's use of material and hypotheses and also often inconsistency within his usage of data and
drawing out consequences from his own – for a person is not always
cognizant of that to which he has committed himself. The theory
of *consistency is* logic; in view of this, it is relevant to the foregoing
issues to apply some distinctions drawn from logic to biblical
studies. Within language usage in dead texts, there are also patterns of usage which can easily be confused and mismatched to
accord with an hypothesis. The employment of some principles
from logic which are found in some form in natural languages[5]
or where substantial formal work gives an hypothesis that certain
structural properties recur in natural languages, renders it
possible to explore practical difficulties about exposing procedures
to do with preserving or removing consistency.

[2] K. R. Popper, 'The Rationality of Scientific Revolutions', p. 79: an unpublished MS when kindly sent to me by Professor Popper in proof form. It is
interesting to notice how Barr's and Popper's general positions coincide concerning criticism and interpretation.
[3] cf. M. Dahood, 'Comparative Philology Yesterday and Today' (a review of
J. Barr's *Comparative Philology and the Text of the Old Testament*), *Biblica*, 50
(1969), p. 75.
[4] cf. A. J. Ayer, *The Problem of Knowledge* (Harmondsworth, 1956), pp. 79,
81–3 for examination of this designation.
[5] This is based on the premise that the constant reuse of language involves
resort to a minimal set of recurrent properties, not on the presumption held by,
for example, an extreme supporter of N. Chomsky, *Syntactic Structures* (The
Hague, Paris, 1957).

Of course it would be foolish to impose some system as the criterion for what it is to be *all* acceptable properties in texts and hypotheses, given the ignorance at a formal level which exists in the literature. It is at once a strength and a possible weakness of the expedient to generalize,[6] when describing and interpreting linguistic phenomena, that investment is required in some structural features that are purported to exist; but this ought not to be gross uncritical investment, but rather a self-critical procedure which renders presuppositions and unsupported moves of interpretation explicit. Logic can fulfil this requirement and detect junctures where it has been neglected.

2   Logico-Linguistics

'Logico-linguistics' was coined by P. F. Strawson[7] to designate a collection of his studies of reference, meaning, intention, predication and generality, etc. The term reflects the type of content of the present book, although Strawson's position on logic is not adopted here; an approach closer to that of Frege and Wittgenstein is followed.[8] (Unfortunately, restrictions imposed by problems in biblical studies and its Near Eastern languages' commitments at an applied level will prevent inclusion of analysis of quantification and other important issues in the philosophy of logic.) In addition, to facilitate the development of an analysis combining logic and biblical languages, some theoretical linguistics by J. Lyons[9] will be utilized to clarify certain items. In the incomplete states of insight in formal areas of logic and in theoretical linguistics, together with the rudimentary stages in the application of both to biblical studies which currently obtain, it is no disrespect but pragmatic necessity to assume that an eclectic approach is proper. (Moreover, it could be the suitable route to a generalized theory of dead languages in the Near East, if, as I believe, an adequate linguistics of dead languages will

[6] See J. F. A. Sawyer, *Semantics in Biblical Research* (London, 1972), p. 115.

[7] In P. F. Strawson, *Logico-Linguistic Papers* (London, 1971); Strawson informs me (letter 28 Nov. 1975), as I supposed, that his own title was intended to echo L. Wittgenstein, *Tractatus Logico-Philosophicus* (London, 1922).

[8] As presented by M. Dummett, *Frege: Philosophy of Language* (London, 1973), etc.

[9] Principally in J. Lyons, *Semantics 1* and *2* (Cambridge, 1977); but cf. his *Introduction to Theoretical Linguistics* (Cambridge, 1968) and *Structural Semantics: an Analysis of Part of the Vocabulary of Plato*, Publications of the Philological Society, 20 (Oxford, 1963).

contain many fragments from presently distinct hypotheses, synthesized into a consistent form.)[10]

The foregoing general stance should sharply be differentiated from some superficially similar attempts to systematize[11] natural languages by groups such as the Prague functionalists,[12] the Münster group,[13] East Berlin generativists,[14] French structuralists,[15] the Münster-Bochum group,[16] or the e.g. Dutch text grammarians.[17]

An attempted formalization of biblical languages is outside the scope of this present research. The project is possible; but it presents a great and deep task in view of problems in analysing dead texts and in formal limitations of understanding in logicism.[18]

This is not to conclude that the scholars mentioned above have nothing of value to offer, but that their systematic position is unnecessarily speculative. Episodically, these scholars offer insights of relevance for biblical linguistics. For example, R. Harweg offers a substitution theory in which he draws[19] generalized conclusions from the antecedent/consequent ordering of sentences' contents, together with unitary substitutions and reorderings of items within sentences, to give insight into the structure of emphasis, priorities and sometimes theme of an author. Nor does it always require a 'logic of' natural language to produce such discoveries; T. Muraoka[20] has achieved substantially the same type of results for MT Hebrew without employing any formalism.

The logic to be presupposed as relevant here is that discovered by G. Frege.[21] In this perspective logic is the specification of a formally consistent ideal language. Consideration of logical form is a concern with generalization and universalization. Assessment

---

[10] Of course an eclectic approach needs to be governed by a notion of consistency from use.

[11] I would not employ 'systematize' for my own attempts.

[12] e.g. F. Daneš (ed.), *Studies in Functional Sentence Perspectives* (Prague, 1974).

[13] e.g. R. Harweg, *Pronomina und Textkonstitution* (Munich, 1968).

[14] e.g. H. Isenberg, 'Das direkte Objekt im Spanischen', *Studia Grammatica*, 9 (1968).

[15] J. Kristeva, 'Narration et Transformation', *Semiotica*, 4 (1969), pp. 422–48.

[16] e.g. W. A. Koch, *Vom Morphem zum Textem* (Hildesheim, 1970).

[17] e.g. T. A. van Dijk, *Some Aspects of Text Grammars* (The Hague, Paris, 1972).

[18] Logicism is a study of the foundations of logic, and is quite different from J. Barr's use of the term in *The Semantics of Biblical Language*, p. 93, etc.

[19] R. Harweg, *Pronomina und Textkonstitution* (Munich, 1968).

[20] T. Muraoka, *Emphasis in Biblical Hebrew* (Jerusalem, 1969).

[21] G. Frege, *Philosophical Writings of Gottlob Frege* (Oxford, 1960); cf. T. W. Bynum (ed.), *Conceptual Notation* (Oxford, 1972).

of interconnections in and between the rules of inference is a concern with logical systems.[22] I do not suppose that Frege's logic is indeed the perfected ideal language, and I shall not be concerned to relate its logicism to the Bible – except in so far as it is an indirect suppressed premiss behind my episodic use of philosophical logic which historically has its provenance in his work.[23] Wittgenstein's viewpoints and interests much more reflect my own in the present piece of work; nevertheless, of course, Frege's virtue of placing *use* at the roots of meaning and logic has grown into the central feature of an aspect of Wittgenstein's analysis of language.[24] I also share Wittgenstein's[25] and W. Haas's[26] dismay at the use of rules to militate for rules, rather than use in language to produce accounts of modifiable tendencies. Nevertheless (I do not say contrariwise), I recognize the use of principles and distinctions from philosophical logic in the later Wittgenstein when employed to explain natural language.[27]

Bertrand Russell[28] once held the view that classical logic could not contain vague predicates. This opinion is now known to be wrong. S. Haack[29] has now shown that vague predicates can so be expressed, and Wittgenstein[30] paved the way for this advance.

---

[22] For a discussion of some problems here see W. V. O. Quine, *Philosophy of Logic* (Englewood Cliffs, 1970).

[23] On this history see W. and M. Kneale, *The Development of Logic* (Oxford, 1962); and cf. P. T. Geach's account in G. E. M. Anscombe and P. T. Geach, *Three Philosophers* (Oxford, 1961), pp. 132–62; also, M. Dummett, *Frege: Philosophy of Language*, pp. 665–84.

[24] See M. Dummett, *Frege: Philosophy of Language*, pp. 192ff; it might be more explicitly acknowledged (in perhaps over-polarizing the early and later Wittgenstein, as some have done) that use (albeit formalized use) is a concept which was first introduced by him in the *Tractatus* (6.211, 3.326, 4.1272, 4.241, 3.325, 4.013, etc.) and not the *Philosophical Investigations*, although it is distinctively developed in the latter.

[25] L. Wittgenstein, *Philosophical Investigations*, secs. 1–244, and his *Philosophical Remarks* (Oxford, 1975), pp. 51–7, 58–9, 84–8.

[26] W. Haas, 'Syntax and the Semantics of Ordinary Language', *Aristotelian Society, Supplements*, 49 (1975), pp. 147–69. However, Haas appears out of touch with recent logicism.

[27] e.g. L. Wittgenstein, *Philosophical Investigations*, p. 11, and sec. 345. The recent work closest to developing both Wittgenstein's type of combination of philosophical logic and later treatments in the *Investigations*, is, I think, P. T. Geach, *Reference and Generality*.

[28] B. Russell, 'Vagueness', *Australasian Journal of Philosophy and Psychology*, 1 (1923), pp. 88–9.

[29] S. Haack, *Deviant Logic* (Cambridge, 1974), pp. 196–25.

[30] L. Wittgenstein, *Philosophical Investigations*, secs. 71, 77, 98, 100–1, and p. 200; I agree with Wittgenstein and M. Dummett (cf. *Frege: Philosophy of*

The task of logic is not mainly connected with ambiguity. However it would be rash to assume that this truth somehow excludes logic completely from the province of ambiguity, for it can be used to expose ambiguity. (J. E. J. Altham,[31] questioning the work of F. Sommers,[32] has queried the logical grounds for enforcing a judgement of ambiguity in relation to statements of truth-value.) Also, logic can be used to trap fallacious or quantificatious thinking.[33] Therefore, while restrictions exist on the capacity of logic as currently formulated, this is not tantamount to discounting the application of logical canon at relevant[34] junctures.

Central issues dealt with in philosophy and obliquely linked with matters to do with language have some relevance for biblical language studies, not least because of the conceptual load which biblical expressions often carry. The presuppositions of some scholars who analyse biblical texts have sometimes been converted into a characterization of these texts under the guise of descriptive activity which was actually sharply prescriptive.[35] Such conflations require exposure; and logical analysis is ideally suited for this task, not least by its capacity to generate conceptual insights. If attention is taken up with mistakes in biblical studies in the following passages, this is because clarification of the arena in which they have been made is a prerequisite for progress in descriptive semantics and conceptual analysis, for the mistakes are components in mainstream methods of some scholarship which have been, as it were, interwoven with biblical texts. Nevertheless, this negative task is positive in its effect and, because it can serve to introduce logical conceptions which exact particular respect from logicians and which many judge to have special value for the study of natural languages, it facilitates an investigation of the 'logical patterns' in biblical usage.

In fact, Barr has already informally advertised the value of analytical criticism: as N. W. Porteous[36] stated, Barr 'has an

Language, pp. 646ff.), that Frege was entirely wrong to say that vagueness is always a defect in natural languages, for which see S. Haack, *Deviant Logic*.

[31] J. E. J. Altham, 'Ambiguity and Predication', *Mind*, 80 (April 1971), 318, pp. 253–7.

[32] F. Sommers, 'Predicability', *in* M. Black (ed.), *Philosophy in America* (London, 1965), pp. 262–82.

[33] 'Quantificatious thinking' is Geach's (*Logic Matters*, pp. 56–7) translation of Frege's [*mechanische oder*] *quantifizierende Auffassung*, which displays the segmentation fallacy (studied in 1.3) and other confusions.

[34] i.e. relevant to analysing use in texts and scholarly use of texts.

[35] On presupposition see 5.2, 3 (d) below.

[36] See N. W. Porteous, 'Second Thoughts', review of aspects of J. Barr's *The Semantics of Biblical Language*, *Expository Times*, 75 (1963/4), p. 70.

uncanny gift for detecting fallacies' which has proved profitable for descriptive semantics. The present work takes Barr's stance as a demarcating point.

3 Linguistics

I will not attempt to review the comparatively small group of biblical linguists who are starting to introduce procedures from general linguistics, since the following study is to develop a line of its own and some of the work of these linguists (as I shall attempt to show) is not always of high quality compared with linguistic work in other languages. However, this assertion has a number of important exceptions (not all of whom are here mentioned), and I hope sometimes to draw on their work. One case is the fine research by T. Muraoka.[37] The former category is typified by some of the work of J. F. A. Sawyer[38] which, I show below, has considerable defects, despite its use of fragments of general linguistic theory.

J. Lyons[39] is well known to have attempted to introduce a (very roughly) Fregean type of reference into his semantics. At various stages I shall refer to his work for applied linguistic documentation, since I find his work of value, but it will become obvious that I have a conception quite distinct from his. The main reason for this is that I believe that actual use in a text ought to control the production of theory more closely than it does in Lyons's work, and that logic should be more directly linked with use when it is explained than is the case in Lyons's latest opus.[40] In certain other respects he is most helpful.

The analytical sharpness customary in logic and analytical philosophy or some theoretical linguistics is mostly quite foreign to the informal complexity in theological and biblical studies. In fact the orientation of biblical scholars even at the linguistic level is so different from a situation where logic is important at analytical *and* conceptual terminals, that one senses some scholars do not readily register the types of issues, distinctions and pursuits which are important for a philosopher and logician. The following argument restricts attention to logical topics which occupy positions of respect and importance in philosophical and logical

[37] T. Muraoka, *Emphasis in Biblical Hebrew.*

[38] J. F. A. Sawyer, *Semantics in Biblical Research* (London, 1972), etc.; his use of reference is loose (cf. p. 46), among other things.

[39] J. Lyons, *Structural Semantics; Introduction to Theoretical Linguistics; Semantics 1.*

[40] See J. Lyons, *Semantics 1* and *2*, pp. 138–229.

perspectives as developed in recent years. A narrow group of issues within this brief will be traced in the following pages. Where possible related biblical items and features will be used in different logic contexts to provide some continuity of examples, although the primary consideration is to present analytical aspects, especially concerning reference.

1   Hebrew Intuition

(*a*)   Questions whose answers, even if not definitively formulated, have clear if not easy treatments in logic and linguistics of live languages can remain as cloudy caprices in Near Eastern studies. In a dead language the identification of semantic values is a problematic task, even with coherent techniques. Componential treatment does not provide automatic routes to the specification of values because all componential approaches are intentionalistic in principle, and the linguistic actors no longer exist to furnish evidence of the relation of native intention to textual values. Even in a live language such a procedure is often precarious on account of the complex relation meaning has to collocational terms. Furthermore, where the basis of semantic identification in a live language regresses to intuitions about normal usage and a criterion founded upon this truth,[1] in the case of dead languages there is strictly no such possibility of sensing this particular type of intuition. This is because intuitions about dead languages regress to assumptions produced by and based upon theorizing about artificially[2] learned usage which arises from a scholastic context, rather than a field which is synchronic with the field of the ancient text, and in many cases lacks a reliable ancestral connection with it. This is an important consideration because it is easy to fail to distinguish the intuition contingent on live language usage from the artificially learned intuition which is based on inspection and theoretically charged interpretation of the frequency of distribution of expressions in a dead language text. It is from this state that one measures normality in a dead text; but this normality cannot guarantee knowledge of the intuition which produced the expression's position and use, because normalcy and frequency are not linked symmetrically in such a way as to reach a state of being guaranteed the same intuition – as in the case of native intuition. In short, a criterion of meaning of an expression's use in a dead language text resides partly in specifica-

---

[1] I am not here adopting N. Chomsky's view in *Current Issues in Linguistic Theory* (The Hague, Paris, 1964), pp. 79–81, and would wish to admit W. V. O. Quine's criticism of mentalism (in *From a Logical Point of View*, pp. 47–64).

[2] By 'artificially', of course, I intend no carping observation; it is a matter of fact that scholarly usage is produced from textual analysis and not native use.

tion of frequency at the intersection where intuition occupies that coordinate in a live language analysis. So intuition in relation to a dead language text is asymmetrical to intuition in a live language, even where the two forms of language are 'one' given language (e.g. Hebrew or Greek) if the patterns of normality and choice differ in the form of the language when it is dead and when it is revived or artificially mastered in scholastic situations. This distinction is easily confused or conflated or not given adequate attention. In an otherwise often helpful work, J. F. A. Sawyer[3] observes:

> . . . in linguistic research intuition can be said to play a less subjective role than it does in other disciplines . . . Intuition in other words plays a vital role in mutual intelligibility. People make and understand utterances they have never heard before and in the same way the present writer's knowledge of Hebrew is an important factor in the situation (however hard to prove or define), so that a classification of Hebrew vocabulary based on it is a possible starting-point, and, what is more, one on which there would be a very large measure of agreement . . . among similarly informed writers and scholars.
>
> A knowledge of Hebrew implies that I can intuitively recognise words of related meanings.

The psychological referent of an intuition is not an experience of understanding,[4] but merely a conforming response which operates as an assumption with the premiss that the response matches the requirement.[5] So there is nothing inherent in an intuition which functions to discover truth and exclude delusion. In some discipline such as a type of mathematics (*pace* Sawyer) where intuition is less subjective, it is superfluous since the calculative configurations furnish criteria of matching.[6] However, where Sawyer posits intuition, the 'need' for intuition in his

---

[3] J. F. A. Sawyer, *Semantics in Biblical Research*, p. 34.

[4] I here adapt and develop a feature of L. Wittgenstein. See *The Blue and Brown Books* (2nd edn., Oxford, 1969), pp. 140–57.

[5] See L. Wittgenstein, *The Blue and Brown Books*, pp. 140–3 on the arbitrary nature of the principle which produces the criterion of recognition in intuition in relation to language.

[6] i.e. superfluous in the sense that the mathematical move is a function of an explicit rule (cf. L. Wittgenstein, *Tractatus*, 6.2323–6.24; and the commentary of M. Black in *A Companion to Wittgenstein's 'Tractatus'* (Cambridge, 1964), pp. 342–3).

position arises because there is a probability of substantial difference between known values in their language game[7] and expressions
in a text at which intuition is directed. Lyons[8] appropriately
cautions about this type of untenable equation: 'intuitions have
no doubt been very much affected by our formal schooling . . . and
must never be taken on trust as a reliable guide to our actual usage
in spontaneous speech'. Yet it is precisely this which Sawyer
advocates, and, moreover, as a procedure for initiating semantic
analysis of a dead language. This commits him to the conflation
of the actor's response being categorial for the semantic requirement in live and dead languages, as well as initially identical for
each, although no two distinct diachronic phases of a language's
literature are ever semantically symmetrical or identically stable
in shifts of meaning.

All Sawyer's 'knowledge of Hebrew' actually 'implies' is that
one possesses a conforming response, a predisposition, to construe
observations on semantic values as a function of a presupposition.
The observation and presupposition[9] factors mingle, collide and
demarcate in arbitrary fashion when deployed to assess a dead
language by use of a live one. 'Implies', strictly, imports deduction;
but a conclusion drawn from empirical data involves inductive
inference[10] (and not deductive reasoning which can carry a consequence by mere form). But one cannot intuite semantic identification of a dead language item, since intuition is not an experience
of understanding; empirical observation prior to analysis also
fails us because this does not yield a paradigm of normalcy identical
to the live language. Hence Sawyer cannot, through intuition,
intuitively recognize words of 'related meaning'. Yet this intuition
is accordingly inductive. And if it is inductive, then it requires
observations to support it; but if it needs observational support
then it is not a mental propensity which can act as a truth-discover-
ing procedure. Also it is related to frequency and not intuition
(and so one is having intuitions about frequencies, not intuitions
about original native intuitions as in live language analysis),
thus raising the question of the need for proof at the intersection

---

[7] 'Language game' in Wittgenstein's analogy of two different types of games
using chess men where there is a likeness between them which does not furnish a
discovery procedure for the meanings in each (see *The Blue and Brown Books*,
pp. 183–4).

[8] J. Lyons, *Semantics I*, p. 27.

[9] Nor can one introduce T. S. Kuhn's tacit knowledge and intuition, since
these are tested; (see *The Structure of Scientific Revolutions* (2nd edn., Chicago,
1970), p. 191).

[10] cf. K. R. Popper, *Objective Knowledge* (Oxford, 1972), pp. 1–31.

where in live intuition all one requires is just that intuition as evidence. If the intuition is wrongly defined (by being conflated with another disparate live language intuition), then this could infect prescription of a discovery-procedure for identifying well-formed descriptions of proper intuitions. It is at this stage that a scholar's subjectivity could confuse proper intuition with misleading intuitions. For many groups of regular widely distributed terms, this difficulty might not arise; but for other terms and expressions these will be substantive problems which would benefit from differentiation of the two sorts of intuition.[11] And all confusion eventually distorts.

(b)   Sawyer's competence with Hebrew might sometimes save him from this type of mistake; but as an account of how intuition works, others' research demonstrates how easily intuition leads to semantic disasters. It is convenient to select an extreme example of such a mistaken set of confusions highlighting a very deviant illustration. By reason of his extremity this particular scholar is untypical (at least in the example below) of other scholars who commit the mistake, but the difference is one of extreme degree and not type, so the comparison holds good, with the foregoing qualifications. (I do not assume that this instance is typical of all Yonick's work;[12] and I appreciate that he is different from Sawyer in many respects.) Yonick claims:[13]

> In 1 Sam. 13:14, the expressions *nāgid* and *melek* are synonymous, but we also find another specification, namely, that the *nāgid* must be a man who acts according to the heart and will of Yahweh . . .
>
> The expressions *nāgid* and *melek* have the meaning 'shepherd', namely *noqēd*. Hence the king-leader is known also as the shepherd . . .
>
> Etymologically, *nāgid* and *noqēd* are related. In the Semitic languages of Mesopotamia, the forms *nagida, naqada, nagid, nagidu*, etc., are documented. Also in Old Akkadian, the word exists, and is a 'loan-word' in the Sumerian NA.GAD, but not *vice versa*. In the contexts, it is a royal title as in Ugaritic.

[11] cf. also J. Lyons's worry of a distinct sort over intuition (*Introduction to Theoretical Linguistics* (Cambridge, 1968), p. 154); on frequency, see his *Semantics 1*, pp. 42ff.

[12] I do not dispute that Yonick is not an influential figure; it is his type of error which is the main reason for citing his claims.

[13] S. Yonick, *Rejection of Saul as King of Israel* (Jerusalem, 1970), pp. 20-3.

In Sacred Scripture as in the other Semitic languages, *ngd*
and *nqd* are variations of the same concept.

(Actually the term alleged to be *melek* ('king') in 1 Sam. 13:14
is not this but *mmlktk* ('thy kingdom').) Yonick asserts synonymy,
but then unconsciously retreats to something like referential
identity[14] by making the contrary acknowledgement that a basic
specification of *nāgīd* is not shared by *melek*. The way Yonick
describes it (as 'must be a man who . . .') gives one warrant for
supposing that Yonick construed the import of this as a feature
possessed by the referent, not of the sense of the linguistic item.
(If one takes seriously the claim of synonymy, then this empirical
difference is all it could be.) On the one hand, if Yonick admits a
difference of meaning in a synonym then he is confused – in para-
doxical synonymy.[15] On the other hand, if he is attempting to
specify or actually is committed to describing a non-linguistic
property of the referent then he has committed a referential
fallacy.[16]

noqēd occurs twice in MT with *melek*. In neither of these occurrences does evidence exist to show that they both 'have the meaning
shepherd'.[17] More strangely still, Yonick affirms that the terms
nāgīd and *melek* have the meaning *noqēd*. Yet the semantic fields
of the first two terms differ from the latter since *melek* is regularly
employed of non-Israelites, but only rarely[18] (and probably in a

---

[14] See J. F. A. Sawyer, *Semantics in Biblical Research*, pp. 75–6 for explanation
of this terminology. In this reference expressions have the same referent but
not description.

[15] For definition of this term see P. T. Geach, *Logic Matters* (Oxford, 1972),
p. 84.

[16] J. Barr has given examples of this type of error (*Comparative Philology and
the Text of the Old Testament*, pp. 291–2) albeit without employing this terminology. It is possible that since Yonick comes from a Roman influenced tradition
he *might* have a confused notion of *suppositio* which neglects the distinction of
sense and reference (cf. C. L. Hamblin, *Fallacies* (London, 1970), pp. 123–4). For
a proper account of *suppositio* see P. T. Geach, *God and the Soul* (London, 1969),
pp. 43ff. on Aquinas.

[17] In Amos 1:1 the two terms have distinct subjects and differ in meaning. In
the other use in 2 Kgs. 3:4 the terms are employed with distinct values (cf.
Moabite Stone l. 1, and possibly l. 31, although J. C. L. Gibson reads *wq*––).
(*Melek* occurs in Amos 7:13, which becomes relevant if in 7:14 *bwqr* is replaced
by *noqēd*, as some authorities suggest without textual evidence, following
aipolos of LXX. I think this replacement is wrong; but if it is correct, it is another
case of semantic difference which opposes Yonick's view.)

[18] See Ezek. 28:2.

context of grim irony) is *nāgīd* used of a non-Israelite ruler.[19]
nāgīd and *melek* are at most hyponyms;[20] but sometimes they
cannot even be hyponymic (2 Chr. 31 : 13 employs *nāgīd* to specify
the head priest over the temple; of course Yonick has not given
attention to homonymy which might block semantic equations).

Yonick evidently reaches his conclusions partly by etymology
in relating *nāgīd* to *noqēd*; but this is an incoherent backwards
causality which purports to measure the later values of terms by
their (hypothetical) former history (which often turns out to be
an attempt to force semantic interrelations from homonymic
relations). The foregoing notice of how the relevant MT words are
employed is a barrier to Yonick's semantic derivations from etymology which ignore linguistic levels, since the etymological relations
are hypothetical ossifications of prehistory's connection with MT
usage. Here is a case of what Barr[21] has termed the root fallacy.

> It seems to be commonly believed that in Hebrew there is a
> 'root meaning' which is effective throughout all the variations
> given to the root by affixes and formative elements, and that
> therefore the 'root meaning' can confidently be taken to be
> part of the actual semantic value of any word or form which
> can be assigned to an identifiable root: and likewise that
> any word may be taken to give some kind of suggestion of
> other words formed from the same root.

Barr has some formal support for this distinction in the history
of philosophy where A. Fraunce[22] characterized the fallacy of
false etymology which has some strong resemblance to the root
fallacy.

The occurrence of this fallacy in Yonick's treatment is in conjunction with presumptions about universals in Semitic languages,
although perhaps Yonick was unaware of this requirement.

---

[19] *noqēd* is never used of a king 'who acts according to the heart and will of
Yahweh' (Yonick's claim), thus excluding this specification from the semantic
domain.

[20] I follow D. A. Cruse's approach to this term 'hyponym' and agree that
'traditional logical' notions (including Lyons's) are inadequate to deal with the
relation here indicated by that term (see D. A. Cruse, 'Hyponymic and Lexical
Hierarchies', *Archivum Linguisticum* (1975), pp. 26–31).

[21] J. Barr, *The Semantics of Biblical Language*, p. 100. See also 5.0 and 5.1
below for detailed analysis which is there linked to an example by Sawyer.

[22] A. Fraunce, *The Lawiers Logike* (London, 1588), f. 56. (I am not agreeing,
of course, with Ramus, but Fraunce's use of the 'Secondary arguments'; cf.
C. L. Hamblin, *Fallacies*, pp. 140–2). Barr does not make this connection.

Yonick has not only employed morphology as a mirror for semantics, but he also adopts certain feeding-points for semantic transfers between words by assuming such relations in, for example, *nagida/naqada* and even NA.GAD where he supposes that these are 'variations of the same concept' on the basis of postulated equivalences between characters of different value in distinct languages; a consonant cluster may seem to override the difference to produce apparent semantic equivalence, although there is no comparative linguistic warrant for this. If Yonick's credentials are laid out concerning this feature, he is involved in what Geach[23] terms a segmentation fallacy: where two propositions or expressions are deemed equivalent on some count, then it is false to slice them into segments and assert equivalence on all counts between each component.

The method articulated by Yonick reflects an hypostatization[24] of language where disparate forms and uses are drawn as 'variations of the same concept', a procedure which Barr has proved to be illicit for biblical analysis.[25] A suppressed premiss in Yonick's position, which is a concomitant of hypostatization, is to treat words as concepts, a feature which Barr has also criticized in detail[26] and which Geach has proved incoherent in the context of logic and language,[27] in the relevant sense.

Quite evidently, there is something wrong with Yonick's intuition and this error is exacerbated by his not inspecting its credibility. This is an extreme case, and in that respect untypical, but, in principle his mistakes will be shown to exist in a lesser degree in much stronger scholars who postdate Barr's and others' related researches. This indicates the need for further and possibly distinct analysis of areas in biblical and Near Eastern studies where these problems exist.

Beyond this fact, the foregoing example sketchily outlines the –

---

[23] See P. T. Geach, *Logic Matters*, pp. 55ff. and p. 99. Since Yonick's errors are represented by formal designations here, I am not to be seen to be committing an *argumentum ad hominem* (for which see E. M. Barth and J. L. Martens, 'Argumentum ad hominem', in *Logique et Analyse*, 20 (1977), pp. 76–96).

[24] For this term cf. G. B. Milner, 'Hypostatization', in C. E. Bazell, J. C. Catford, M. A. K. Halliday, R. H. Robins (eds.), *In Memory of J. R. Firth* (London, 1966), pp. 321–34, and the following reference.

[25] J. Barr, *The Semantics of Biblical Language*, pp. 38, 171, and 'Hypostatization of Linguistic Phenomena in Modern Theological Interpretation', *Journal of Semitic Studies*, 7 (1962), pp. 85–94.

[26] J. Barr, *The Semantics of Biblical Language*, pp. 38ff., etc.

[27] P. T. Geach, *Logic Matters*, pp. 289–301, etc.

usually suppressed – contiguity of some logical,[28] metaphysical,
philosophical and scientific[29] issues to the Bible.

2   Semitic Comparative Philology

(*a*)   Many interpretations of MT Hebrew texts utilize items in
other Semitic languages to induce actual or seeming identification
of semantic values in MT.[30] Cognizance or ignorance of the existence or fictional status of semantic universals can be dismantled
into two related topics:

(i) The attempt to produce a generalized scheme of rules for
describing the semantic domains of individual terms which are
assumed to occur in the set of (or a set of) Semitic languages.

(ii) Explanation of the transfer from language L_1 to language L_2
of an expression[31] or sequence of expressions, together with an
assessment of semantic values before and after transfer.[32]

(i) and (ii) relate to procedures which have influenced scholars
to approach the classification of semantic domains before diachronic criteria for identifying a linguistic item have been determined. Yet scholars have sometimes tended to assume that they
know a synchronic value (at time t_2) because a rough classification
of texts on a diachronic axis of time t_1 and t_3, and perhaps an
occasional text from t_2, is available. However, this can involve an
hypostatization of the diachronic axis as though it were a particular
synchronic axis – sometimes by appeal to roots.[33] This can be

[28] Yet I agree with Barr's criticism of 'logicism' (*The Semantics of Biblical
Language*, pp. 100–6).

[29] i.e. theory of empirical relations of texts to history.

[30] Often these identifications are not argued but assumed as evident, when
actually a substantial analysis is required to adduce connection (cf. M. Dahood's
claim that in Job 39:27 *wky* is 'apparent' as a name of a bird (i.e. 'falcon') from
Ugaritic *ky* (UT, 146:6; 1101:4), in 'Four Ugaritic Names and Job 39:5,
26–7', *Zeitschrift für die Alttestamentliche Wissenschaft*, 87 (1975), p. 220).

[31] J. Lyons (*Semantics 1*, pp. 18–24) uses 'expression' in a narrow way; I use
it to pick out a linguistic item without imputing any value judgement to that
item *by* so terming it.

[32] Where there are apparent similarities one often has an unstable situation
because if the large lexical overlap between L_1 and L_2 is early in the history of
separation from, for example, proto-Semitic, then the probability of confusing
only indirectly related homonyms is high, and extant items may only reflect
an untypical section of early usage (cf. J. Barr, *Comparative Philology and the
Text of the Old Testament*, pp. 156–66).

[33] J. Lyons (*Semantics 1*, p. 244) has said that the failure to preserve the distinction between synchronic and diachronic, coupled with lack of differentiation
between descriptive and prescriptive points of view, is to commit the etymological
fallacy; this has obvious relations to the previously mentioned root fallacy and

termed the Babel fallacy, and is a variation on the segmentation fallacy mentioned earlier, only that here the fallacy is committed in respect of sets of description of historical series of expressions.[34]

Sometimes a mistake involving the Babel fallacy is owing to lack of precision which permits temporal misplacement of data.[35] Issues are complicated both by the absence of an exact specified diachronic axis for all sections of MT texts and allegedly related comparative material, and by often dogmatic competing theses. Some of the errors produced could arise because of presuppositions which a scholar may hold in assumptions adopted (unconsciously or not) in interpretation of linguistic items. A case which illustrates one facet of such confusions is produced by S. A. Ryder's[36] analysis of the Western Semitic D-stem.[37] A three-fold thesis has often been upheld about the origin of D-stems: (i) D-stems are derived from B-stems;[38] (ii) a D-stem must therefore have a meaning distinct from the B-stem; and (iii) a D-stem's meaning is an intensification or pluralization of the root concept (*sic*) in the B-stem. These as presuppositions, which might function as premises in a scholar's exposition of a D-stem item, are not obviously false; they are credible possibilities, although one might be justifiably suspicious of the uniformity presupposed in the relation between (i) and (ii) and concerned about the possible artificial collapse of terms into a root concept which neglects possible asymmetry in diachronic history.[39] Ryder has offered

---

Lyons has not noticed that his fallacy is very close to Fraunce's fallacy of false etymology (see 1.3, *1* (*b*) and note 22 above), but it is worth keeping these two separate because of Lyons's specification.

[34] For the type of difficulties this produces see J. Barr's helpful analysis in 'The Ancient Semitic Languages – the Conflict between Philology and Linguistics', *Transactions of the Philological Society* (London, 1968), pp. 37–55.

[35] J. A. T. Robinson claims that massive error in dating NT MSS has produced similar mistakes (cf. *Redating the New Testament* (London, 1976), pp. 20ff.); conversely, if he is wrong, then he is a case of what he alleges.

[36] S. A. Ryder II, *The D-Stem in Western Semitic* (Paris, The Hague, 1974), e.g. pp. 164ff.

[37] A D-Stem as defined by A. Goetze's conversion of A. Ungnad's terminology is a stem with doubling (of middle radical). See A. Goetze, 'The So-called Intensive of the Semitic Languages', *Journal of the American Oriental Society*, 62 (1942), pp. 1–8, p. 3, note 39 (Ryder's references to pagination in this article (see *The D-Stem in Western Semitic*, p. 15, note 9, etc.) are entirely wrong). Also, A. Ungnad, *Babylonisch-assyrische Grammatik* (2nd edn., Munich, 1926), pp. 39ff.

[38] 'B-Stem' from Goetze's 'basic stem' (based on Ungnad's Grundstamm; cf. A. Goetze, *op. cit.*, p. 3, note 38).

[39] e.g. when there is no symmetrical semantic transitivity between values, in B-stem and D-stem forms, as a law-like fact: F. M. Cross *Canaanite Myth and*

arguments to suggest that customary views of the nature of D-stems are inaccurate; he proposes that D-stems had a separate, single point of origin and a basic function. He also posits a premiss involving causality, in considering that the D-stem is an extension of the triliteral root in order to conform to a quadriliteral pattern originally connected with denominative (or nominal) verbs.[40] Ryder discards (i)–(iii) above, arguing that D-stems place a greater emphasis on the object of action, while B-stems indicate emphasis on the doer of the act. In addition he proposes a number of unevenly shared semantic properties displayed by distinct uses of D-stems which he suggests previous accounts have obscured.[41]

In the cases where D-stems (or aspects of relations assumed to hold between them and other phenomena) have been held, or unwittingly presumed, to be universalized entities, substantial distortions will have been produced if Ryder is correct and former hypotheses were articulated. Such postures fail to weigh data sensitively; nor do they describe data adequately; they impose prescription as description. Even where universals are intuitively sensed within a group of linguistic phenomena, there is not infrequently a partial hypostatization. Sometimes the classification of, for example, a D-stem is not itself analysed but appealed to in a theologico-linguistic synthesis of texts and history (as in the foregoing example from Cross) as though it were a designation of a formulated universal warranting transitivity for some implication, which would not be supported by the objective description of actual uses which are presumed to be the D-stem's domain. This situation should give rise to concern, not least because the epistemological shape of the D-stem conception (with the probable exception of specifications by scholars such as Goetze and Ryder) has rather unclear, or subjectively assumed, partial provenance in Arabic grammars.[42] Ryder observes that even this Arabic depend-

---

Hebrew Epic (Harvard, 1973), pp. 128–9 maintains B-form *qp'* cannot have a sense 'to congeal' because D-stem form in Mishnaic Hebrew and Aramaic of Talmud is different (the B-stem is from Exod. 15:8).

[40] S. A. Ryder, *The D-Stem in Western Semitic*, pp. 21–53, 164ff.

[41] Ryder states (*op. cit.*, p. 166) concerning the alleged derivation of D-stems from B-stems that: 'We regard this designation as a linguistic rationalization, based upon a pseudopsychological or romantic confusion of a strengthened form with a strengthened meaning.'

[42] cf. A. Goetze's survey in 'The So-called Intensive of the Semitic Languages', pp. 1–2; also, S. A. Ryder, *The D-Stem in Western Semitic*, pp. 11–20; and cf. E. Speiser, 'The Durative Hithpa'el', *Journal of the American Oriental Society*, 75 (1955), pp. 120f.

ence is improper on occasions and Hebraists have sometimes misconstrued the significance of references which Arab grammarians have made to the D-stem.[43]

Outside these investigative confusions, the possible ontological identity[44] of what is a universal requires more refined treatment – including options not often mentioned – if error is to be avoided. Even where evidence for some universal is constructed, it is not self-evident by merely listing uniform occurrences of expressions what it is to be *that* universal. Apart from quantificational use of universal[45] I think that universals as propensities, dispositions,[46] or tendencies[47] require much more investigation. It is also of importance to examine how these possibilities relate to literatures which contain outstanding qualities of creative value and aesthetic or pragmatic (linguistic) innovative power, as compared with conformist (e.g. ritualist or colloquial) usage. It is possible that the two categories operate quite distinctly,[48] with the former maybe possessing unique properties which have wrongly been merged with disparate types.[49] It is not being assumed here that creativity, as opposed to productivity,[50] is rule-governed, but rather that the implementation of highly creative language in ordinary usage (by actors who are not the creators and postdate them) may have an innovatory power untypical of other items.[51]

One problem is that the causality of a term may not be available in extant texts; indeed it might not ever have been exposed to literary textual use. At this juncture if the canon of probability employed is logically arbitrary or incoherent, then, if fictional

---

[43] See S. A. Ryder, *The D-Stem in Western Semitic*, pp. 14 and 166, where he argues that Arabic *takṭīr* is misused by many Semitists to be a subjective heightening of experience, whereas he claims it is used in the sense of an expansion of the scope of the action of the root.

[44] i.e. the empirical status and identity of a universal.

[45] i.e. a rigid formal class quantifier (cf. J. Lyons, *Semantics I*, pp. 156ff.).

[46] For these two terms see J. L. Mackie's review of D. H. Mellor's *The Matter of Chance* (Cambridge, 1971), *Philosophical Quarterly*, 23 (1973), pp. 85ff.

[47] Of course, one would still be able to formulate rules of this tendency (cf. W. Haas, 'Meanings and Rules', *Proceedings of the Aristotelian Society* (1972/3), pp. 152f.).

[48] i.e. with respect to exhibiting universals.

[49] Of course formal work such as J. Kurylowicz's *Studies in Semitic Grammar and Metrics* (Warsaw, 1972), pp. 1–63, does not fall foul of such confusions, but more theologico-linguistically oriented works which do not take proper account of this type of research do.

[50] cf. J. Lyons, *Semantics I*, p. 76. Revelation is a neglected topic here.

[51] cf. also J. Barr, *The Semantics of Biblical Language*, p. 295.

causality is presumed, recovery of a term's actual semantic value is rendered impossible by theoretical confusion.[52]

(*b*)   Universals are often presupposed when associating linguistic entities by claiming that '*x* and *y* are the same'. Geach[53] proves that such an equation is incoherent; he concludes:

> . . . it makes no sense to judge whether *x* and *y* are 'the same', or whether *x* remains 'the same', unless we add or understand some general term – 'the same *F*'.

Frequently scholars treat sameness without at all distinguishing or attempting to establish what semantic *F* (i.e. a predicate or component of a predicate functioning as a criterion of identity[54]) obtains in statements concerning what element is the same in respect of an *x* and *y*. H. Ringgren[55] is characteristic of this lack of discrimination, and his description of the following Ba'al I*[56] reflects it:

ktmḫṣ . ltn . bṯn . brḥ
tkly . bṯn . 'qltn.[–]

F. M. Cross's translation of the above is 'When you (Ba'al) smote Lotan the ancient dragon/Destroyed the crooked serpent'. Ringgren, following standard exegesis, maintains that this Ba'al text is to be linked with Isa. 27:1:

'l lwytn nḥš brḥ
w'l lwytn nḥš 'qltwn
leviathan the piercing serpent,
even leviathan that crooked serpent

Ringgren states 'lotan is clearly identical with the leviathan of the Bible, the monster which was defeated by Yahweh at creation,

---

[52] Here 'causality' is linguistic conditions which produce a semantic value which is their effect.

[53] P. T. Geach, *Reference and Generality* (amended edn., Cornell, 1968), pp. 39–46, 148–53, and p. 39 for the following quotation.

[54] For definition of this terminology see 3.1 following.

[55] H. Ringgren (trans. J. Sturdy), *Religions of the Ancient Near East* (London, 1973), pp. 148–9.

[56] Here produced from J. C. L. Gibson, *Canaanite Myths and Legends* (Edinburgh, 1978), pp. 68–9. The following translation of Cross's appears in his *Canaanite Myth and Hebrew Epic* (Harvard, 1973), p. 119.

and which in Isaiah 27:1 is described in exactly the same words as here [in the Ba'al I* text].'[57] But Ringgren does not offer any account of in what respect the characterization 'in exactly the same words' holds; clearly, within such an opacity many different and differing candidates could obtain. Ringgren supposes certain relations are synonymous in some way; but what he does specify is of little assistance: the Bible does not mention and describe a monster lotan which was defeated by Yahweh at creation, and the MT quotation above is in the future tense while the Ugaritic is past. So the suggested description for sharing sameness only occurs outside MT, while yet Ringgren offers it as evidence that an entity is identical in MT and the Ugaritic text. Of course, I am not assuming that no relation exists between the two texts; but, rather, that to assert that one does with incoherent specification is of little value and misleading. Further since Ugaritic and Hebrew are two distinct, albeit related, languages,[58] it seems a mistake to propose that the relation inheres in 'described in exactly the same words as'. What is it to be linguistic objects capable of receiving this designation?[59] What is it to be 'words' here? Graphemes, lexemes, functions of a sentence? If Ringgren has ascribed conceptual value of sameness to the relation, as he appears to have done, then the latter is required; but why tie the description to words, since the words are words in different languages? The words are not 'exactly the same' in an unqualified sense because, for instance, one could not insert the Ugaritic quotation above into the MT without a semantic change,[60] or at least syntactic problems. All these problems arise because Ringgren has failed even informally to specify what F it is that produces sameness and has linked his assertion irrelevantly to 'words'.

To be sure, there appears to be some reproduction or, more cautiously, similarity, at some level between items in the MT and Ugaritic texts. Yet Ringgren offers no synchronic connection between the two; nor does he indicate a diachronic sequence of

---

[57] H. Ringgren, *Religions of the Ancient Near East*, p. 149.

[58] cf. M. Sekine, 'The Subdivisions of the North-West Semitic Languages', *Journal of Semitic Studies*, 18 (1973), 2, pp. 208–9, 211, 213, 215, 220. This relates to the fact that discontinuity may be obliterated by Ringgren's assertion.

[59] For proof of the acuteness of this problem see C. Lewy, *Meaning and Modality* (Cambridge, 1976), pp. 1–47.

[60] Consider J. Barr's analysis of value judgements assumed in reading a text (in 'Reading a Script without Vowels', in W. Haas (ed.), *Writing without Letters* (Manchester, 1976), pp. 71–100) which require or presuppose decisions taken or neglected in ascribing values to expressions which can produce differing identifications of items.

derivation which would preserve a connection of the same F (if F is filled by culling from hints in Ringgren's narrative).

It is not sufficient to meet these problems by maintaining that Ringgren is merely speaking of a coincidence in the terms *lotan* and *lwytn*. One requires a criterion of identity[61] and not solely the occurrence of 'the same' type of subject term to reach a valid conclusion about coincidence of reference. Of course one cannot speak of identity of referents since these terms dismantle into mythological references whereby a set of predicates in the genre from which they come constitutes the supposed referent; that is, mythological referents have no empirical referents, and so intended[62] references reduce to the linguistic predicates associated with them in use, as J. Woods has shown.[63]

These objections do not comprise an argument in principle against the connection of *lotan* with *lwytn*. But since empirical evidence indicates[64] that Ugaritic society terminated by the first millennium, contact between its language and text and those of the Isaiah period is not immediate. This diachronic rather than synchronic relation of texts originally containing the Ugaritic and also the Hebrew MT forms[65] needs sensitive exposure and not polemical conflation.

Barr[66] has pointed out that there is an important second level within religious language: it is a reflection upon (criticism of, a correction of, or a more general formulation of) expressions which previously occur in an earlier first-level discourse. The Ugaritic Ba'al I* text is a first-level discourse while Isaiah 27 is a second-level text, if there is employment of an identical item

[61] See the explanation of this expression in 3.1.

[62] For this sense of intended and its relation to identity, cf. P. T. Geach, *Logic Matters*, pp. 153–65.

[63] J. Woods, *The Logic of Fiction* (The Hague, Paris, 1974). I carefully employ 'reduce' here so as not to impose a particular thesis about the specific nature of the reduction at this stage in analysis.

[64] e.g. W. F. Albright, *Yahweh and the Gods of Canaan* (London, 1968), pp. 139ff.

[65] Other MT occurrences of *lwytn* (Job 40:25; Pss. 74:14, and 104:26) do not significantly alter the strength of this point and display distinct contexts from the Ba'al I* text. Ebla material may yield dissimilarities. M. J. Dahood) after discussion with G. Pettinato) informs me that *be-ri-um*, which he identifies as the equivalent of Ugaritic *brḥ* and translates as 'wicked' or 'evil', occurs in the Tell Mardikh texts where it requires these translations; either way, this yields discontinuity with MT or lengthy diachronic history unaccounted for by Ringgren.

[66] J. Barr, 'The Language of Religion', in *Proceedings of the Study Conference in the Methodology of the Science of Religion* (Turku, 1973), L. Honko (ed.), *Science of Religion* (The Hague, 1979), pp. 429–41.

in both.[67] To regard the semantic values of linguistic phenomena as strictly reciprocal and hence intersubstitutional in the two levels (of Ugaritic and Hebrew) is a misunderstanding of the distinction of level and commits one to confusing an axis as synchronic instead of diachronic. Linking these two foregoing points of mediation between Ugaritic and Hebrew MT texts and second-level discourse produces a possibility of tendency towards semantic separation of items, which requires investigation whenever an equation is proposed; Ringgren neglects this task and merely asserts the equation in a particularly strong form with misleading examples.

A stage in the semantic history between first- and second-level text can (but does not have to) be metaphor. Metaphor is (roughly) the transference of an expression from one semantic domain to another, which involves the preservation of words but a change in their value(s). In a rather different context Barr[68] has examined instances of the mistaken identification of two expressions which revealed that a shift to metaphorization had lain undetected in a diachronic phase between the two uses. T. A. van Dijk[69] has demonstrated that metaphorization processes and products of them in the Indo-European group of languages[70] entail a 'blocking' of the regular derivations by which one can normally reach a description of a semantic value. The heavy employment of metaphor in Semitic and biblical texts, encouraged perhaps by theological usage,[71] advertises the need for caution in a context where Ringgren, for instance, moved into an equation of synonymy without such scrutiny.[72]

---

[67] Of course, the items do not have to be semantically different in the first and second levels; but there is a probability that values will change from t_1 to t_2, especially when the relevant period is over hundreds of years.

[68] J. Barr, *Comparative Philology and the Text of the Old Testament*, pp. 241ff. cf. J. Lyons, *Semantics 1*, pp. 263–4 for examples and classification of metaphor.

[69] T. A. van Dijk, *Some Aspects of Text Grammars: A Study in Theoretical Linguistics* (Paris, 1972), p. 255.

[70] I am not here assuming that there is some universality in the notion of metaphorization in all languages, but that the cited examples in Indo-European languages are in the same category as those to which metaphor can be applied in many MT cases.

[71] To be sure, inclination in theological language to produce changed expressions has also to be measured in conjunction with the tendency in certain uses to provoke institutionalization which generates some ossification.

[72] Whether or not there is change, it is clear that some scholars never address themselves to the two levels of discourse and terminology which would expose this (e.g. J. Gray, 'A Cantata of the Autumn Festival: Psalm 68', *Journal of Semitic Studies*, 22 (1975), 1, pp. 2–26).

In addition, if the Baʿal I* *lotan* and Isaiah 27 *lwytn* are possibly further fossilized into some type of idiom, or if there has been idiomatization in non-MT usage and the occurrence in MT is a pun by reversal of this semantic history, then the foregoing problems emerge in a stronger (albeit slightly modified) form. A deceptive feature of idiomatic usage is that it can be homophonous,[73] homomorphous or sometimes homonymic[74] with complex or simple expressions in normal (i.e. non-idiomatic) usage, while its semantic values differ. If this type of asymmetry is not noticed, and idiomatic usage is employed as evidence for values exhibited by its lexemes[75] in previous non-idiomatic semantic history, by perhaps a sort of premiss presuming semantic universals which are 'self-evident', then evidence will actually be counter-examples to the proposal.

The occurrences of *brḥ* with *lotan* in the Baʿal text and *lwytn* in the biblical passage fit in well with the foregoing situation. W. Haas[76] has noticed that pun and irony expressions often have uses where the pun is constructed by resisting the fossilized use of the idiom; this effectively converts the idiom to a previous stage in its history (metaphor, etc.), and hence pun is produced by contrast. Since the Ugaritic field in which *brḥ* occurs is different from that of MT, and the semantic values of both have some separate ingredients,[77] then there are grounds for postulating a pun (as a possibility) by the latter against the former.[78] If this is so, then clearly MT and Baʿal I* are not 'exactly the same words' in an unqualified sense, reference or tone;[79] and it is precisely at the interface of these changes that opinions can wrongly be transferred if distinction of levels is not appreciated. Also, the terms were used in a civilization later destroyed (before MT Isaiah usage), and it was only centuries afterwards that they entered into pun-

---

[73] cf. J. Lyons, *Semantics 1*, p. 22.

[74] J. Lyons claims that homophony is a form of partial homonymy (*Semantics 1*, pp. 21–2).

[75] For lexeme, cf. J. Lyons, *Semantics 1*, pp. 19ff.

[76] Mentioned by Professor Haas in a lecture and cited with his permission, which I here acknowledge, although my formulation of the point is slightly different from his own.

[77] That is to say, if we follow F. M. Cross, *Canaanite Myth and Hebrew Epic*, pp. 118–20 or RSV Isaiah 27:1 (cf. J. Barr, *Comparative Philology and the Text of the Old Testament*, p. 323, number 67).

[78] In a valuable (albeit often theoretically confused) paper A. L. Oppenheim ('Idiomatic Akkadian', *Journal of the American Oriental Society*, 61 (1941), pp. 251–71) showed that many Akkadian complex homonyms had more than one idiomatic semantic value (sometimes as many as four).

[79] For a discussion of 'tone' see 2.0, 1 (*b*) following.

contracts within a polemical context in another (albeit related) language employed in a distinct socio-linguistic group. In such a situation similarities disguise differences and fine distinctions can conceal fundamental shifts of nuance and meaning, while yet there is undeniably some sort of relation between the two.

A problem hinted at above is also contingent on the nature of changes and shifts in usage: in mythological, idiomatic and some metaphorical expressions there is a failure of normal (i.e. previously employed) reference. This is akin to reference failure in logic,[80] and for analogous reasons. Semantic 'impurities' (which are quite normal linguistic features in natural languages) infect the linguistic items in use. Especially where pun or irony is present through, for example, metaphor and idiomatic puns, there might be only seeming references related to cancelled ontologies.[81] Obviously, it is a complex problem to unpack the components and interrelations in such phenomena; this itself indicates a need for care rather than a blanket description of the type Ringgren offered. Where idiomatized usage of a piece of theological language from another (dead) culture, without irony or pun, is evident in a text (such as Isaiah), then, if an exeget is neglectful of the semantic asymmetry between uses (here, Ugaritic and MT), he may miss the fact that idiomatization has 'killed off' the purported reference in the first-level discourse, because complex homonymy has been wrongly taken as evidence of unqualified synonymy. This ossification of reference is particularly important in theological polemics and is easily missed owing to the subtle interplay of often specialized[82] terminology in a context in which it is being controverted.

(c) Morphological similarities, which have no other connection at all, and certainly no semantic one, also become the objects for

---

[80] cf. S. Haack, *Deviant Logic*, pp. 126–9.

[81] i.e. play on what in another theological (Ugaritic) use was a term to which an alleged reference was attached, but now by idiomatization or theological opposition (by Isaiah 27 type of use) which cancels the referential use, there is play on the previous contracts of the item, as a sort of polemical demythologization pun which resorts to reversal (de-ossification) of a value for irony. For a consideration of this seeming reference see P. T. Geach, *God and the Soul* (London, 1969), pp. 110ff.

[82] Specialized terminology, in virtue of that fact, might become idiom for many uninitiated users. See J. Barr (*The Bible in the Modern World* (London, 1973), pp. 171–2) for the application of reference to the use of 'literal' as employed by some fundamentalists in certain theological contexts, and some of their critics' objections, together with the type of reference in allegorical genre. Barr's discussion is helpful as a point of comparison regarding the switch of reference in two distinct uses and how misunderstanding can be generated.

confused synthesis in comparative philology. G. R. Driver's treatment of *ṣnḥ* is an example of this type of confusion, although an extreme one.[83] I will not dwell in detail on this case since I have examined it elsewhere,[84] except to highlight relevant features for present purposes. Driver was a scholar of major influence; and yet his study of *ṣnḥ* is, I consider, more deviant than Yonick's[85] claims for *nāgīd*. Barr[86] rightly stressed that the NEB translation (which Driver informed me[87] was directly based, at his own insistence, on his own proposal) is not worthy of serious consideration as a contender for the original meaning of Judg. 1:14 (NEB 'broke wind'). Yet Driver insisted that it appear as the NEB rendering of Judg. 1:14, without an alternative footnote translation, even though it had never before been proposed and though no other scholar had offered (or has offered) any linguistic support for it. Thus it seems that Driver himself did not consider his proposal to be an inordinate one,[88] and, although it is an extreme example of his procedure in linguistic analysis, in this respect it might properly reflect – because it makes explicit tendencies in his work – a characteristic facet of his linguistic procedures.[89]

Driver argued that *ṣnḥ* means 'broke wind', while most translations have a rendering similar to 'alighted'. *ṣnḥ* only occurs in MT three times, and two of these are parallel texts (Josh. 15:18; Judg. 1:14), the other being Judg. 4:21 which Driver rendered[90] 'ran out' in his article – but 'oozed out' in Judg. 4:21 (NEB).

LXX Judg. 1:14 has two words (*egogguze kai ekrazen*) for *ṣnḥ*; but the parallel LXX text in Josh. 15:18 has yet another single

[83] G. R. Driver, 'Problems of Interpretation in the Heptateuch', in *Mélanges bibliques ... André Robert, Travaux de l'Institut Catholique de Paris*, 4 (Paris, 1957), pp. 73–5.

[84] A. Gibson, 'ṢNḤ in Judges 1:14: NEB and AV Translations', *Vetus Testamentum*, XXVI (1976) 3, pp. 275–83.

[85] S. Yonick, *Rejection of Saul as King of Israel*, pp. 20–3.

[86] J. Barr, 'After Five Years: A Retrospect on Two Major Translations of the Bible', *The Heythrop Journal*, 15 (1974), p. 387.

[87] In the period September 1973 to October 1974 Professor Driver corresponded with me on this topic and related matters, which I here acknowledge.

[88] However, R. Murray and E. W. Nicholson informed me that the revisers of the projected revision of the NEB have decided to withdraw the Driver translation of Judg. 1:14 and restore the type of translation for which I argued and which Nicholson had independently supported.

[89] It is pertinent to note that, although the *ṣnḥ* case is idiosyncratic, there is a large group of other Driver examples which are extreme; e.g. cf. J. Barr, *Comparative Philology and the Text of the Old Testament*, pp. 290f., etc., where a treatment of some of them can be found.

[90] G. R. Driver, 'Problems of Interpretation in the Heptateuch'.

term *boaō*, and not the Judges' LXX terms. (In Judg. 4:21 LXX has *kai diexēlthen en tē gē* for MT *wtṣnḥ b'rṣ*.)

Driver maintained that the LXX translations of *ṣnḥ* accurately reflect its original semantic value. However, purely dismissively and without proof, he rejected the LXX translation of Judg. 4:21. Driver asserted that the referent of the LXX terms 'must be' a sound or (anal) noise, although no LXX usage entails this conclusion (nor did Driver offer any, but a classical Greek citation which even then did not contain the same Greek term[91]). Nor does any LXX use of the three relevant terms occur in an anal context, but always oral. This referential switch is a referential fallacy, which can be termed the oral/anal fallacy.[92] Also, since Driver stated, of a possibility,[93] that the LXX terms 'must express'[94] sounds (as opposed to indicating a phonetic value which stands for a semantic value), he committed a modal fallacy,[95] that of promoting possibility to necessity without empirical or logical warrant.

These connections offered by Driver were taken by him to 'imply'[96] that the Akkadian *ṣanāḫu* is the cognate synonym for *ṣnḥ*. Driver asserted that *ṣanāḫu* 'easily lends itself to such a translation'[97] as 'broke wind'. But in all extant texts where *ṣanāḫu* occurs there is no trace of anything like this meaning, and it possesses the sense of excretion of faecal blood (appearing as a rare term in medical texts).[98] It is odd that *ṣanāḫu* and *ṣnḥ* should be judged to be linked at all semantically because they appear in two different languages in two quite odd and widely separated semantic fields (i.e. medical and domestic/theological fields). Barr has exposed a tendency on Driver's part to reduce a semantic problem[99] (or even invent a difficulty where there is none) to its

[91] From Aristophanes: see G. R. Driver, 'Problems of Interpretation in the Heptateuch', p. 5.

[92] This bold designation was proposed by G. E. M. Anscombe when we discussed the phenomenon and its relation to fallacy.

[93] Without proof that it could have been an *empirical* possibility (cf. A. R. White, *Modal Thinking* (Oxford, 1975), pp. 5–18).

[94] G. R. Driver, 'Problems of Interpretation in the Heptateuch', pp. 73–5.

[95] See P. T. Geach, *Logic Matters*, p. 155.

[96] See G. R. Driver, 'Problems of Interpretation in the Heptateuch', p. 74.

[97] The vagueness of this expression tends to betray weakness.

[98] It can also be associated with diarrhoea (F. Kuchler, *Beiträge zur Kenntnis der assyrischen-babylonischen Medizin*, pl. 11, iii 44); it *may* have phlegmatic blood as its object (cf. *The Assyrian Dictionary* (Chicago, 1962), pp. 96, 100) but these possible, untypical readings (which are in any case problematic) were not available when Driver wrote his study (and I am examining Driver's actual argument, as it stands).

[99] J. Barr, *Comparative Philology and the Text of the Old Testament*, pp. 290–1.

alleged empirical referential associations. That is to say, to attempt a resolution of a semantic value by importing a description into it of some linguistically non-specified property of the referent which is postulated to be in relation to the term under analysis. This is explicitly present in Driver's[100] onomatopoeic treatments of a number of words, where some extra-linguistic feature is deemed an analogue of a semantic value and the latter conjectured by description of the former (although it usually presented as vice versa).

The notion of choice is important as a factor in assessing the possibility of a semantic value being ascribed to a term where an alternative exists.[101] Nowhere does Driver mention that there is a standard term for 'break wind' in Akkadian (ṣarātu)[102] which is obviously not matched with ṣnḥ. However, Driver does cite an Arabic term 'aḍraṭa which is similar in some respects in form and in semantic value to ṣarātu.[103] Nevertheless, he does not observe that this item is nearer the normal Akkadian word which is not selected by him for equation with ṣnḥ; clearly, such opposition tends further to weaken ṣanāḫu as a candidate for matching with ṣnḥ because not only is there no text with ṣanāḫu meaning 'broke wind', but there is another term which has that value and holds the position when such a semantic choice is made.

Of course even on grounds of morphological universals (which it is appropriate to mention since Driver seems to be arguing from form to meaning)[104] the type of argument Driver offered cannot be reconstructed into a viable presentation because the main morpheme ṣnḥ differs from ṣrt, and ṣanāḫu is different in meaning. Even if proto-Semitic[105] were articulated as an assumption here, since there is no evidence that ṣanāḫu or ṣnḥ meant 'broke wind', it still requires an analytical movement through to the alleged hypothetical referent associated with these verbs, and a supposed transfer of an extra-linguistic non-specified feature ('broke wind', in seeming association linguistically with excrement (linked with

---

[100] e.g G. R. Driver's ' "Another Little Drink" – Isaiah 28:1–22', P. R. Ackroyd and B. Lindars (eds.), *Words and Meanings* (Cambridge, 1968), pp. 47–67; cf. p. 48, etc.

[101] cf. J. Lyons, *Introduction to Theoretical Linguistics*, pp. 413–14.

[102] BM 98743 exhibits the untypical spelling zarātu. Driver does not refer to the Akkadian ṣarātu at all.

[103] G. R. Driver translates this term as 'farted'.

[104] A procedure which is illicit, as proved by J. Barr, *The Semantics of Biblical Language*, pp. 89ff.

[105] cf. J. Barr, *Comparative Philology and the Text of the Old Testament*, pp. 75–81.

ṣanāḫu)). This has no linguistic support and involves the root fallacy and hypostatization, yet presumably is the sort of approach Driver adopted as a framework.[106] Owing to Driver's expressed seriousness about his proposal for the value of ṣnḥ, and also the chronic linguistic confusions adduced above, even though Driver's scholasticism is here exhibited at its most far-fetched, he cannot be interpreted as impishly offering a conjecture on Judg. 1:14.

Wittgenstein spoke of our 'craving for generality'[107] and of our employing confused analysis of language seemingly to achieve that generality. He also argued that we utilize our apprehensions about 'family resemblances',[108] which we purport to discover in language games, and often mistakenly connect unrelated properties of actual and possible items (while also confusing one category with the other).[109] I think that this is at least analogous to what Driver has done in respect of ṣnḥ, and to what has happened in some senses in the other cases in current research cited here. One modification of this sketch is worthwhile: fallacies have family resemblances which generate products that display family relations. In the foregoing example each fallacy (or rather the unanalysed error it characterizes) generates a relation which supports its antecedent error, and produces a self-confirming, self-supporting series of analytical moves constituting a matrix of fallacious interrelations which comprise the scholar's informal 'philosophy of language'. Where the premisses of this philosophy are inconsistent, as they are, the projection of the qualities, which the premisses house, into the attached analysis will tend to obscure and disguise the confusions and fallacies, because they are thus programmed presuppositions acting roughly uniformly on all the abstracted phenomena. (At different junctures, and in regard to particular topics analysed, this philosophy might be at one time dominant,

[106] This usage of form as though it were a marker in itself for meaning of a particular value could be construed as falling under the fallacy of illicit process (C. L. Hamblin, *Fallacies*, pp. 196–7) whereby a term distributed in the conclusion (here, in a semantic analysis), which is the semantic value postulated, 'can' be absent from all the premisses; Driver disguised this absence by importing form as necessarily carrying the meaning in the premiss(es).

[107] L. Wittgenstein, *The Blue and Brown Books* (2nd edn., Oxford, 1969), p. 17.

[108] L. Wittgenstein, *Philosophical Investigations* (3rd edn., Oxford, 1967), secs. 66–7, 77, etc. Although I judge Bambrough to be wrong in his interpretation, it is instructive to examine the following two studies on this topic: R. Bambrough, 'Universals and Family Resemblances', and H. Khatchadourian, 'Common Names and "Family Resemblances" ', in G. Pitcher (ed.), *Wittgenstein* (London, 1968), respectively pp. 186–204 and pp. 205–30.

[109] cf. R. Bambrough, 'Universals and Family Resemblances', p. 204.

at another time only implicit, and in other situations merely episodically implemented.) There will also be an acceptance among
other scholars of the view in direct proportion to their sharing
these presuppositions as part of their theologico-linguistic or
orientalist *Weltanschauung*. This confused procedure among some
scholars, and set of sequences involving fallacies, contingent on
misuse of functional properties in linguistic data being examined,
can be termed the generative syndrome.[110]

Frequently underlying this generative syndrome complex, are
metaphysical norms which are sometimes causally unconnected
or often directly linked with a linguistic *Weltanschauung*. Nor are
metaphysical premises solely the domain of conservative theologico-linguists; for the position of claiming that there is no
metaphysically true viewpoint is itself a metaphysical judgement
which can influence semantics.

[110] I have culled 'generative' from 'generative grammars' in respect of their
speculative over-use as prescriptions when few constraints govern their production. (It would not be surprising to see T. Boman's *Das hebräische Denken* revived
by innate grammars; cf. 2.1, 2 (b) below.)

1   Septuagintal Relations

(a)   It is not infrequent for a text's meaning to be defined by its future history.[1] Often MT Hebrew is measured by its later LXX translations. The later history of LXX MSS and their recensions are only now becoming clear in some respects. There is already a long tradition of inbuilt interconnections between the specifications of semantic values in MT and LXX[2] which is sometimes confused and always complex. Further, pointed and consonantal texts have been misdescribed, merged with LXX MSS in analysis and fed in unevenly to support opposed assessments. It is evident that the LXX MSS are weak and strong at different points as probable readings of MT semantic values, and it is also evident that many scholars differ over precisely where and how these ascriptions apply. Certain problems relating to the present inquiry are portrayed in this state of affairs.

D. W. Gooding's impressive work on the 3 Reigns Miscellanies[3] demonstrates that the Miscellanies are not designed to follow the MT, nor to be brought into conformity with MT at a later date, nor to follow any other Hebrew text tradition exclusively.[4] However, Barthélemy had already offered a differing viewpoint on the text history of the Miscellanies.[5] This was partly taken up by F. M. Cross[6] and also J. D. Shenkel.[7] Barthélemy affirmed that the (kaige) first Palestinian recension did treat of the Miscellanies and influenced their contents, although he did not cite examples of this relation. Gooding maintains that the textual variations already existed, and suggests that the translators accepted them without attempting to bring them into conformity with MT. Their pur-

---

[1] By meaning I here indicate the original meaning; and cf. J. F. A. Sawyer's important observation (*Semantics in Biblical Research*, p. 113) about the significance of later contextualizations.

[2] cf. the survey by P. Walters (ed. D. W. Gooding), *The Text of the Septuagint* (Cambridge, 1973).

[3] D. W. Gooding, *Relics of Ancient Exegesis* (Cambridge, 1976).

[4] *ibid.*, p. 110, etc.

[5] D. Barthélemy, *Les Devanciers d'Aquila* (Leiden, 1963), pp. 142ff.

[6] F. M. Cross, 'The Contribution of the Qumran Discoveries to the Study of the Biblical Text', *Israel Exploration Journal*, 16 (1966), pp. 81–95.

[7] J. D. Shenkel, *Chronology and Recensional Development in the Greek Text of Kings* (Harvard, 1968).

pose, Gooding supposes, was specifically midrashic, 'to make midrashic capital out of them'.[8]

The position that one adopts concerning the semantic values to be ascribed to the MT text will, if LXX data are considered and used in a certain construction, be influenced in a particular direction contingent on whether one's view of the Miscellanies is that they are a recension which returns to the MT, or midrashic elements formed as a variation without there having been a different Hebrew *Vorlage* (Gooding opposes the claim that there is a different Hebrew *Vorlage* to be instantiated behind the Miscellanies).[9]

(*b*)   In the Miscellanies 3 Reigns 9:24 is missing, and is transposed to 9:9. J. A. Montgomery[10] noted that Stade[11] set out 3 and 4 Reigns to indicate items from an alleged royal annal.[12] Montgomery sought to establish that certain Hebrew formations (for example, where '*z* ('then') is prefixed) are, in Stade's words, 'used for additions which give the impression of having been inserted from other works'.[13] These words of Stade's which Montgomery quotes, Montgomery judges to embody 'an extraordinary amount of caution', and he holds to the view that pertinent archival elements in Reigns do indeed come from official records. However, I think that neither Stade nor Montgomery is cautious enough in his presentation. Even Stade's qualified language presents data as though they were actually his interpretation. His style of discourse masks the place where proof is absent, for instance by employing such expressions as 'additions which give the impression': impressions are not received; sense data are interpreted responses by an observer or analyst.[14] Montgomery mentioned Akkadian instances of alleged equivalent uses of lexical items, and

---

[8] D. W. Gooding, *Relics of Ancient Exegesis*, p. 110.

[9] *ibid.*, p. 62, etc. (Incidentally, 'instantiated' is employed formally (roughly) in the sense of a specific designation's replacing a variable (where, in this context, a variable *x* stands in place of (an hypothetical unknown) *Vorlage*, the instantiation of which yields its name, allegedly).)

[10] J. A. Montgomery, 'Archival Data in the Book of Kings', *Journal of Biblical Literature*, 53 (1934), pp. 46–52.

[11] In the Polychrome Bible.

[12] This was of course a device in presentation in the Polychrome Bible which presupposed Stade's opinion on provenance which was asserted in the editorial introduction.

[13] J. A. Montgomery, 'Archival Data in the Book of Kings', p. 47.

[14] See for theory K. R. Popper, *Objective Knowledge* (Oxford, 1972), pp. 62ff.; cf. A. J. Ayer, *The Problem of Knowledge*, pp. 84–133, and P. T. Geach, *Mental Acts* (2nd edn., London, 1971), pp. 45–7.

the suggested parallel cases on the Moabite Stone. Montgomery's is also an hypothesis-laden interpretation of data which is employed in an attempt to prove (in one short article) that such expressions came from royal archives[15] because they are introduced by the same type of item (which nevertheless is not proved to be semantically identical). I am not objecting to such a conclusion in principle; but only in practice can its viability be assessed. Montgomery imposes a causal connection between items such as 'z and its purported Akkadian and Moabite counterparts as proof that Reigns have been drawn from royal annals (I term this argument p). Such an argument is fallacious: an Ignoratio Elenchi fallacy,[16] of alleging to prove p, while unwittingly demonstrating q. Here q might represent a description of a common stylistic feature in Reigns, Akkadian and Moabite, and infer a common technique of recording history. However this does not imply even a synchronic causal connection of deriving that custom; nor even upon such a causal connection could one load a thesis that this implies that if the style is associated with data in Akkadian royal annals, then Reigns derived its contents (at relevant points) from royal annals: that is a fallacy of inferring.[17]

(c)   All this is relevant for an assessment of Gray's[18] views because he adopted Montgomery's thesis without any further analysis of it, and implemented it through 1 and 2 Kings. When Gray deals with 1 Kgs. 9:24, which commences with 'k ('But'), he asserts, without evidence of variant readings and in an absence of any analysis, that here the MT is corrupt and should read 'z. Not surprisingly this aligns the verse with Montgomery's and Gray's hypothesis on the royal annals.

After this move Gray claims that 9:24 is 'An excerpt from an archival source, here doubtless displaced from its context and included at this point as referring to public works to which the corvee was applied'.[19] Hence within a semantic field, Gray has

---

[15] J. A. Montgomery, 'Archival Data in the Book of Kings', p. 49.

[16] I refer to the modern definition of the fallacy, rather than the medieval treatments (cf. C. L. Hamblin, *Fallacies*, p. 273).

[17] See C. L. Hamblin, *Fallacies*, p. 222f.

[18] J. Gray, *1 and 2 Kings* (2nd, fully revised edn., London, 1970). The type of care which is absent in Montgomery and Gray is present as a standard caution in other scholars such as S. P. Brock (e.g. 'The treatment of the Greek Particles in the Old Syriac Gospels', in, J. K. Elliott (ed.), *Studies in New Testament Language and Text* (Leiden, 1976), p. 81) where he admits *gyr* as a Syriac loan-word from Greek *gar*, but resists semantic implication between them in usage.

[19] J. Gray, *1 and 2 Kings*, p. 252.

injected an hypothesis, presented it as a universal of that field without warrant (and with premisses asserted, and upholding it concerning proof from other alleged relations between it and two other languages), introduced a speculation about a variant reading as fact, and applied the 'universal' 'z to induce a conclusion about the displacement of MT 9:24. To say the least, this is a modal fallacy.[20]

Of course there is no text of MT without 9:24 in its place. The Miscellanies contain 9:24 at 3 Reigns 9:9; and in a footnote Gray[21] cited the LXX reading as evidence of interference with the (*sic*) text to support his use of Montgomery's replacement of 'k with 'z. Clearly, a dislocated LXX does not imply a corruption in MT, especially where MT texts do not contain the seeming corruption. (And as a weak probability, albeit with a qualification of nil observational support, its inductive character would act as an implication block on Gray's conversion of possibility to actuality.)[22] Gray presumes that LXX is following a different Hebrew *Vorlage*,[23] and along with Montgomery[24] supposes that the LXX *tote*, which translates 'k as though it is to be read 'z, shows 'k to be an error.

Yet Barthélemy's work and Gooding's research particularly confirm earlier scholars' caution over the translation claims of the Miscellanies. Since Gray notices some of these midrashic elements in the Miscellanies,[25] it is inconsistent of him – in the absence of an offer of further proof – to adopt the semantic values in the Miscellanies occurring in a dislocated text to assert that they are the measure of a postulated Hebrew reading which disagrees with MT. Strangely, Gray blanks off the distinction between the Miscellanies' midrashic, distorting recensions and the projected original LXX text in his only mention of evidence in a footnote,[26] because he refers to 'the Septuagint' and not the various recensions upon which, elsewhere, he has commented.

[20] cf. P. T. Geach, *Logic Matters*, p. 155; S. Haack, *Deviant Logic*, pp. 78–80. This type of reference I make to fallacies mainly to render the type of error explicit, rather than strap formal logic on to these scholars; surely it is clear that these errors are provable from applied linguistic studies in any case.

[21] See J. Gray, *1 and 2 Kings*, p. 252 footnote.

[22] J. Barr has documented this inconsistent shift in other contexts, in *Comparative Philology and the Text of the Old Testament*, pp. 285–7.

[23] J. Gray, *1 and 2 Kings*, Introduction and 1 Kgs. 9:9.

[24] J. A. Montgomery, 'Archival Data in the Book of Kings', p. 49.

[25] See J. Gray, *1 and 2 Kings* Introduction.

[26] *ibid.*, p. 252, footnote. Of course, the LXX readings are not a criterion for the MT text since the latter is not always exactly mirrored by the former, and the former's translators' understanding, not MT, is echoed in LXX.

2 New Testament Semantics

Many relations between the Old and the New Testaments enable one to consider issues in each in adjacent contexts, as some of Barr's work shows.[27] Some of the reasons for this are internal to NT and OT, and others external. On the one side, NT makes massive use of OT material, and its language historically and semantically ebbs and flows from OT *milieux*. On the other side, scholars' exegesis of NT language often reflects preoccupation with constructing relations of interdependence or polarity between OT and NT. What scholars have deemed equivalent to internal functions have sometimes turned out to be external, and vice versa.[28]

(*a*) Barr demonstrated[29] that some theologico-linguists dealing with NT language wrote in total neglect of linguistic semantics. One of these was J. A. T. Robinson.[30] Robinson has since become much more influential, as well as being one of the NEB translators. Barr observed that[31] Robinson's derivation of ideas from the alleged consequence of 'one' Hebrew and two Greek words for 'flesh' (*bśr*, *sarx* and *sōma*) revealed Robinson's confusion about the functional relation of necessary and possible options in semantic history.[32]

Features of the generative syndrome can be traced in Robinson's later writings which have a family resemblance to his somatic semantics in the earlier study criticized by Barr. A facet of this resemblance is a programmed norm in Robinson's analysis of Christology of John; he states in connection with John 1:

> . . . becoming man means living as a man, experiencing a human existence: for . . . to be the subject of such experiences *is* to be human. But to *be* a man is more than to experience life as a man. The fact that I, a human being, might decide to experience life *as* a dog . . . does not make me a dog. (Robinson's own italics.)[33]

---

[27] J. Barr, *The Semantics of Biblical Language*, e.g. pp. 161–205; *Old and New Interpretation* (London, 1966).

[28] cf. J. Barr, *Old and New Interpretation*, pp. 176ff.

[29] J. Barr, *The Semantics of Biblical Language*, p. 35.

[30] J. A. T. Robinson, *The Body* (London, 1952), pp. 12f.

[31] See J. Barr, *The Semantics of Biblical Language*, pp. 35–7.

[32] This is, of course, another example of the modal fallacy; cf. D. Hill's remarks on *sōma* and his reference to Robinson (D. Hill, *Greek Words and Hebrew Meanings*, p. 282).

[33] J. A. T. Robinson, *The Human Face of God* (London, 1972), pp. 108–9.

The opening expression 'becoming a man means living as a man' is, to say the least, a trivial quasi-tautology,[34] even with an awareness of Robinson's hostility towards certain trinitarian views. Despite the fact that Robinson is analysing a topic to clarify matters, he obscures the status of his usage. If he intends the first occurrence of 'man', in this quotation, to be a subject term with a reference, he has offered us an incredibly obvious equation. If he supposes that the first use of 'man' here is a mass term for humanity (note, a partial hypostatization if so), then this is hardly less trivial, since the second 'man' is merely a member of this class. Indeed, since it is necessarily the case (on either of these two readings) that both of the expressions 'becoming a man' and 'living as a man' must be true if one of them is, it is superfluous for Robinson to argue that one means the other even as causal and existential[35] truths. If it be responded that here (and one of my reasons for the foregoing sequence was to exact this point and force its exposure) these readings of Robinson are wrong because 'man' (in the first use) is a name for a concept such as (roughly) the state of fully experiencing what it is to be in the human condition of life's apprehensions, then Robinson is committed to the mistake Barr adduced[36] where words are assumed to be concepts. Of course there is no reason why Robinson should not erect an object language in which this occurs and that 'man' be a designation for it; but this is precisely what he does not do, and cannot do by using 'man' as though it unaided carried that conceptual meaning. In any case one ought to have an explicit unambiguous analytical language when describing issues, whereas here Robinson fills his metalanguage[37] with mystical unanalysed prose.

Robinson's next statement 'But to *be* a man is more than to experience life as a man' is even worse than his opening judgement. The significance Robinson attaches to this expression is advertised by his following comparison. Robinson contrasts a human being's experiencing life '*as* a dog' (Robinson's *italics*)

---

[34] 'Quasi-' is here employed along the lines of P. T. Geach's use of the term (*Logic Matters*, pp. 161–5, 206f.).

[35] 'Existential' is employed above in its logical sense (associated with existence objectively) and not with the sense used by Sartre, and this is the case throughout the present work.

[36] J. Barr, *The Semantics of Biblical Language*, pp. 226ff.

[37] For explanations of object and metalanguages see 2.0, 3, and cf. J. Lyons, *Semantics 1*, pp. 10–13. It is illicit to suppose that Robinson is right to use such language because he is describing mystical prose, since asymmetry of analytical and creative language is necessary for classification and separation (cf. P. T. Geach, *Logic Matters*, pp. 85–7: vague terms can have precise definition).

with, the consequence he draws from this, 'does not make me a dog'. So much is obvious. Yet his comparison of this with '*be* a man' and 'as a man' is impossible in a consistent analysis. Robinson is attempting to strike a distinction of identity between 'to *be* a man' and 'as a man', in the sense that the former is displaying something more than the latter. '*Be*' is here[38] merely a necessary condition for using the term 'man' with referential force; the italics may give it emphatic stress, but that cannot evoke an escape to transcendental realms where inconsistency has the virtue of consistency. If one construes 'as a man' with predicative force, then, if it is a predicate and not merely an unused predicable,[39] it must be attached to a subject term by which it and its (perhaps implicit) quantifier carry the value of 'be' in the deep grammar; in short, if this predicate really is usable or used, that entails its being employed in conjunction with an equivalent value to 'to be'. Conversely, if one wants to unpack 'as a man' into a subject term 'man' with its own reference, then as it stands it is being employed with a value which is equivalent to 'to be', for that to be the case. Either way, where '*be* a man' and 'as a man' are used of a person it is a necessary condition that he is a man in the second as well as the first expression.[40] As Geach states in a related context:[41] ' "man" in predicate position relates rather to the nature by which Christ is a man' (and Geach is dealing with the term's connection with 'as'). This opposes a serious non-trivial comparison in Robinson's examples.

I appreciate that Robinson is attacking what he believes to be a view of Christ as a trinitarian hollow man without the properties of being a man. However, incoherent language and conflated levels of language are to be eschewed, especially where one is analysing similar confusions. If a protagonist of Robinson's view wanted to respond that he is speaking on the ontological level and not second intention level of abstract logic,[42] nevertheless the

---

[38] cf. A. N. Prior, *The Doctrine of Propositions and Terms* (London, 1976), pp. 107–34.

[39] 'Predicable' is Geach's term for a predicate when it is not in use, but, for example, in a list for possible use (cf. P. T. Geach, *Reference and Generality* (emended edn., Cornell, 1968), pp. 24ff., etc.). cf. J. Barr's *The Semantics of Biblical Language*, pp. 58ff., which makes helpful comments on the surface and deep grammar of Semitic copulas, etc.

[40] On person, cf. P. F. Strawson, *Individuals* (London, 1959), pp. 42ff.

[41] P. T. Geach, *Logic Matters*, p. 300.

[42] For explanation of this terminology see P. T. Geach, *Logic Matters*, p. 297f., i.e. ontological level – discourse about objects; second intention level – discourse about concepts and terms.

foregoing catches Robinson out at both levels. Indeed, later in his book he renounces the ontological level by introducing a mythological mode of discourse;[43] but this is a stylistic switch for he still purports to apply his account there to characterize referential functions and ontological referents. Nor is this weakness acceptable by reason of Robinson's notice that allegedly equivalent hypostatization occurred in late Judaism of the OT period,[44] for reasons offered above.[45] In the foregoing case theological motifs, themes and presuppositions heavily influence Robinson's language. This is precisely the type of feature which Barr found massively distorts biblical linguistic analysis, and the impact of this feature on Robinson's earlier and later analyses is comparably destructive of his position.

(b) In contrast to Robinson's approach there is need to avoid an opposite extreme where a speculative text-grammar logic (e.g. French structuralist or Dutch text-grammar logics) is utilized as a criterion at a systematic level. This is especially dangerous when it tends to be married to a traditional syllogistic logic with its misleading weaknesses. B. Olsson[46] in his analysis of John's Gospel is one scholar who adopts such an approach. Conversely, to attempt an investigation of, say, 'reason' in parts of the NT without any considerations of substantive logical distinctions renders the project of little value; D. W. Kemmler[47] studies NT 'reason' without any attention whatever to sense and reference or other analytical distinctions.[48]

(c) Another approach, by G. B. Caird,[49] does make some use of distinctions related to sense and reference; but he appears confused

[43] J. A. T. Robinson, *The Human Face of God*, pp. 116–20.
[44] See J. A. T. Robinson, *The Human Face of God*, p. 149.
[45] i.e. there is a precise description for vague predicates.
[46] B. Olsson, *Structure and Meaning in the Fourth Gospel* (Lund, 1974).
[47] D. W. Kemmler, *Faith and Human Reason* (Leiden, 1975).
[48] It is interesting to note that while scholars such as J. Barr and J. F. A. Sawyer have implemented a fragment of descriptive application of reference in MT analysis, with Barr also mentioning sense, little corresponding work has been done in NT semantics, although it is urgently needed (a need which the following partly supplies). In a context of the philosophy of religious language some analysis of non-biblical terms has been commenced (cf. P. T. Geach, *Providence and Evil* (Cambridge, 1977) and generally the discussion by J. Barr (*Biblical Words for Time*, pp. 198–207) on some relations between philosophy and biblical language studies which have relevance for investigations in the latter.)
[49] G. B. Caird, *The Language and Imagery of the Bible* (London, 1980).

over the various interpretations and the distinctions associated with them. For example, he observes:

> Yet even this simplest of acts [of naming] is compounded of two elements: a name both identifies and describes. In the terminology made popular by J. S. Mill, a name denotes a person or thing having certain qualities and connotes the qualities which all such persons or things have in common (*A System of Logic*, p. 20). Modern linguists draw the same distinction by means of the terms sense and referent: the sense is what we are saying, the referent what we are saying it about.[50]

It is entirely wrong to suggest that the explanations of 'denotes' and 'connotes' in Mill correspond to theses about 'sense' and 'referent'. The sense/referent (and reference) relation was devised by Frege to oppose and demolish the type of position advanced by Mill. This is obvious in Dummett's analysis of the distinction, where he observes that 'Examples of this kind are meant by Frege to controvert only the position taken up by Mill.'[51] A reason for Frege's attack was, as Geach explains it, 'Mill's term "denoting" simply embodies the fundamental confusion of the two-name theory between the relations *being a name of* and *being predicable of*.'[52] In the following chapters I deal with these distinctions in detail. After the above quotation, Caird makes an exception of proper names, proposing that 'they only identify: they have denotation, but no connotation.'[53] Someone may think that Caird might be excused this incorrect view (where he related sense and referent to these terms as explanation in the above quotation), since he uses it immediately to warn against fanciful etymology in proper name exegesis. However, later Caird asserts that 'Strictly speaking, a proper name is a word with denotation but no connotation, reference but no sense; and etymology is an attempt to provide it with connotation also.'[54] Now strictly, a proper name does have sense in the various standard expositions of sense and

[50] *ibid.* p. 9. I do not deal with Caird's book in detail because it is, as he states, 'written for amateurs' and 'for those who read the Bible in English' (pp. vii and 2), being a non-technical work. But the above example is of interest since it is the statement, of an eminent scholar, which is implemented throughout his book, and is related to similar confusions documented in the following pages.

[51] M. Dummett, *Frege: Philosophy of Language* (London, 1973), p. 97.

[52] P. T. Geach, *Logic Matters*, p. 51.

[53] G. B. Caird, *The Language and Imagery of the Bible*, p. 9.

[54] *ibid.* p. 45.

reference. At least, the sense is the reference. Further, different proper names of the same referent have some difference of sense on Frege's interpretation (so the explanation of sense being solely reference in a proper name cannot exhaust its sense). For example, the cases of the Evening Star and the Morning Star (neither of which are descriptions since they refer to a planet, but one user might not know that both proper names refer to the same planet).[55] These proper names have different senses, different modes of presenting the same reference. This reflects, as Dummett mentions, 'Frege's doctrine that proper names have a sense and are not, as Mill thought, mere labels attached to objects.'[56] Caird's non-standard habit of using the term 'referent', and not employing 'referring' (and he rarely utilizes 'reference'), imitates J. S. Mill's treatment of 'denoting terms' as primitive references which the mind apprehends as directly mediating the subject. Mill's exposition abstracts from the muddled *suppositio* doctrines of, for example, William of Ockham, which obscure and collapse the correct distinction between referring and referent (this history is analysed in detail by Geach[57]). Chapter 4 and section 5.2 below develop these features in connection with their appearance in other scholastic writings, since Caird's approach is not unique, although it absorbs some modern terminology into earlier viewpoints.

(*d*)   It is consistent to suppose that a presupposition[58] about comparative normality of distribution and value is an actual and required (suppressed) premiss behind the adoption of a use of 'synonymously'. Scholars are not infrequently neglectful of this constraint, and contrarily introduce identity signs[59] and a term such as 'synonymously' in a way which cannot correlate with a conjunction of these factors. R. Bultmann[60] is such a case; J. T. Sanders[61] (who sometimes implements an element of Bultmann's

---

[55] See Frege's influential study 'On Sense and Meaning', in P. Geach and M. Black (eds.), *Translations from the Writings of Gottlob Frege* (3rd edn., Oxford, 1980), pp. 56–78.

[56] M. Dummett, *Frege: Philosophy of Language*, p. 545. This is not to agree to fanciful etymologizing, although ch. 3 below will show how proper name paronomasia can be harnessed properly to sense and reference.

[57] P. T. Geach, *Reference and Generality*, pp. 3–106, 144–66.

[58] Presupposition and related items are examined in 5.2, *3* (*d*); cf. also 3.1.

[59] i.e. '=', 'is', etc.; cf. identity in 3.1.

[60] See examination of Bultmann in 2.0, *3* (*d*) and 5.2, *2* (*b*), 5.2, *3* (*c*).

[61] J. T. Sanders, *The New Testament Christological Hymns*, Society for New Testament Studies: Monograph Series, 15 (Cambridge, 1971), e.g. pp. 10, 63, 93.

theologico-linguistic mysticism[62] also reflects the same confusion where his equations assert synonymy, yet dissolve into other phenomena when investigated. Sanders opens a study of Phil. 2:6–11 by an English translation of the text which he for the most part adopts as the criterion for the semantic values of the Greek (without any proof for the relevant values). From this translation he abstracts items, stating[63] 'The second line in either case then explicates what was said in the first line; this is done synonymously in the second stanza ("likeness" = "fashion", "of men" = "like a man") . . . "Humbled himself" is the equivalent . . . to "emptied himself"'.[64] First, 'explicates' is not compatible with 'synonymously' and possibly 'equivalent', since if the items were strictly synonymously related, one synonym could not explicate the other, but would (semantically) be the other's value. Second, 'of men' and 'like a man' are semantically asymmetrical regarding 'of' and 'like' and quantificationally distinct in *men/man*; so it is, at the most, only at some levels that the equated components share semantic values, with differences at others, while Sanders distinguishes neither group. Third, of course, Sanders's equation can be reconstructed, for example, as an hyponymic[65] relation, but he does not offer it at this level or use it in this way. Fourth, where these three points apply, theologico-linguistic procedure employed to produce a theological conclusion can easily obscure levels not consequently differentiated, and so assume separate semantic levels to be members of one level. In this situation, clearly, theological assumptions can dictate the permissibility of semantic equations which violate levels without the mistake's being noticed by the scholar.

[62] This employment of the term 'mysticism' to designate a linguistic feature is akin to the use of it to indicate some Arabic phenomena by P. Morewedge in 'Critical Observations on Some Philosophies of Mysticism', *International Journal for Philosophy of Religion* (1977), pp. 409–24.

[63] Sanders takes Phil 2:6–11 to be an exhibition of *parallelismus membrorum*, following J. Jeremias (cf. *The New Testament Christological Hymns*, p. 9, note 1) and apparently assumes that the (alleged) reception by the text of this description permits the adoption of synonymy between paralleled components. Of course, the absence of synonymy would block the alleged connection for any use, not merely for logico-linguistic usage; hence Sanders cannot be allowed to discard the problem as being of solely logical interest.

[64] J. T. Sanders, *The New Testament Christological Hymns*, p. 10.

[65] For this usage of 'hyponymic' see J. Lyons, *Semantics 1*, pp. 291ff. It is worth observing that not only do semantic values indicating sense (information) become misused, but the referential function can be distorted and confused with a warrant for sense synonymy where merely identity of reference is present.

Here Sanders has indiscriminately generalized over a domain of semantic levels when actually a level-specific description is required both to render explicit the appropriate semantic features, and to prevent over-statement of the position, relation and significance of the phenomenon which is being interpreted. What D. Crystal[66] has said of translation theory can helpfully be used to hint at Sanders's use of English in semantic problems, and also summarize a more general set of difficulties in procedures and problems in biblical linguistics:

> Readiness to look critically at the metalanguage of translation, I would argue, is a prerequisite for progress in this field.

What Crystal notices about translation is relevant for semantics, when he speaks of the

> . . . complexity underlying some of the common-place evaluative phrases used about the acceptability of a translation[67]

the neglect of which can obscure description and generate prescription. No formal metalanguage adequate to handle natural languages yet exists; but it is a concern with semantic hygiene and description which warrants a logico-linguistic exploration in that direction.

---

[66] D. Crystal, 'Current Trends in Translation Theory', *Bible Translator*, 27 (July 1976) 3, pp. 322–9.

[67] *ibid.*, p. 328. In this perspective it is interesting to consider scholastic explanation of texts as a sort of paraphrase (in intent), which further aligns Crystal's observation with my comments.

2

MEANING

2.0 SENSE AND REFERENCE

1 Sinn and Bedeutung

(a) Gottlob Frege[1] formulated the distinction between the sense (*Sinn*) and the reference (*Bedeutung*)[2] of an expression. J. Barr,[3] alluding to W. V. O. Quine's[4] interpretation, has employed the notion of reference to discriminate between confused and consistent treatments of MT items. Frege took the distinction to clarify the nature of different sorts of expressions, from individual words to sentences, though not all expressions are uniformly susceptible of analysis by the distinction.[5] In the expression *yhwh mlknw* ('Yahweh is our king'), in Isa. 33:22, each semantic element displays sense, among other things. The sense of a proper name, Frege claimed, is its reference, while the sense of the remainder of the expression is the information it exhibits. It should not be supposed that reference is restricted to the grammatical subject of an expression. In the expression in Job 40:3, *wy'n 'ywb 't-yhwh*

---

[1] G. Frege, 'Sinn und Bedeutung', *Zeitschrift für Philosophie und philosophische Kritik*, 100 (1892); trans. as 'On Sense and Meaning' in P. T. Geach and M. Black (eds.), *Philosophical Writings of Gottlob Frege*, pp. 56–78.

[2] As W. and M. Kneale point out (in *The Development of Logic* (Oxford, 1962), pp. 495–6), although *Bedeutung* matches 'meaning' almost exactly in normal uses, Frege's specialized, innovatory use is based on the simple verb *deuten* from which *Bedeutung* is derived – in which term the metaphorical sense of 'point' (hence, refer) is evident in Frege's exposition.

[3] *Comparative Philology*, pp. 118, 291 (n. 3), and 292.

[4] W. V. O. Quine, *From a Logical Point of View* (Harvard, 1966), pp. 9–47, etc. Barr's use of reference is brief and rare.

[5] cf. P. T. Geach, 'Names and Identity' in S. Guttenplan (ed.), *Mind and Language* (Oxford, 1975), pp. 139–58; M. Dummett, *Frege: Philosophy of Language* (London, 1973), pp. 81–294. See P. T. Geach (*Reference and Generality*, pp. 47–80) for discussion of confusions which result(ed) if reference is not clearly understood; and W. V. O. Quine (*Word and Object*, pp. 113–86) for the clarification of reference in relation to other linguistic phenomena.

wy'mr ('Then Job answered Yahweh and said'), the two proper
names have references (although it may require a logical reification
of the statement, on one interpretation, consistently to determine
the second reference).[6]

(b)   Preliminary notice of another related aspect of Frege's
treatment of language is appropriate here in order to isolate and
temporarily ignore it, so that it is not confused with sense and
reference. This feature is tone. Sense and reference, for Frege,
are phenomena which are relevant for determining an expression's
truth or falsehood. Tone is whatever is outside that scope; I
follow Dummett[7] by using this term (which renders Frege's two
words *Beleuchtung* and *Färbung* for these phenomena). Frege was
not interested in tone; it needs much more research to develop it
and will certainly be a general term covering disparate entities. The
following variations in choice of items in 2 Sam. 22 and Ps. 18[8]
illustrate tone differences: *'qr'/'šw'* ('cried'); *w'hyh/w'hy* ('I was');
yšʿw/yšwʿw (*NEB* 'cry'/'cried'); (here, the application of tone to
discriminate between subsidiary and substantial (sense) elements
in uses of items could be a device for assessing an aspect of the
relation holding between first- and second-level texts (distinguished above in 1.3, 2 (b)), illustrated in 2 Sam. 22 and Ps. 18).
Tone, in Frege, is not an element of a logical expression's truth or
falsehood; of course this does not imply that tone is non-semantic,
nor outside the scope of truth.

2   Reference

(a)   Frege's reference distinction has often been lifted out of its
formal *Sitz im Leben*, and profitably employed in other linguistic
hypotheses where it holds the status of an almost system-free
general principle. J. Lyons[9] in a theoretical context and J. F. A.
Sawyer[10] in applied biblical linguistics have made general, albeit

---

[6] On connecting sense and information see J. D. B. Walker, *A Study of Frege*
(Oxford, 1965), pp. 92–105; and M. Dummett, *Frege : Philosophy of Language*.
cf. J. Barr, *Comparative Philology and the Text of the Old Testament*, p. 291, n. 3,
and J. Lyons, *Semantics 1*, pp. 41–50.

[7] See M. Dummett, *Frege: Philosophy of Language*, pp. 2f., 83–8 (including
'force').

[8] Verses 7/7, 24/24, and 42/42; cf. LXX readings also. As Dummett has remarked to me, tone is a ragbag designation for items of disparate linguistic
significance, as these texts illustrate.

[9] J. Lyons, *Structural Semantics*, pp. 50–1; *Introduction to Theoretical Linguistics*, pp. 404–5, 424–8.

[10] J. F. A. Sawyer, *Semantics in Biblical Research*, pp. 77–82.

distinct, use of reference. Scholars like R. M. Kempson[11] have attempted to preserve some features of Frege's philosophical logic, while incorporating reference into their own theoretical systems. Wittgenstein[12] agreed with Frege's sense and reference distinction and utilized it and Frege's overall formal framework. He did, however, advance different theses about the significance of sense and reference.[13] Such applications of reference can be taken as evidence that an analysis about reference in biblical languages and scholarship need not be an implementation of Frege's programme for language, and even if it were it might produce insight for other conceptions of language. However, biblical scholars have largely ignored it.

(b)   There is lack of clarity in some scholars'[14] consideration of the relation of reference *to* a referring term, and it is not uncommon to discover the absence of such a treatment where it is required. In the ordinary use of 'reference' there is a conceptual ambiguity which coheres in the term's being a mirror for that for which it stands. Frege himself used the word *Bedeutung* in three characteristic ways in his later work.[15] First, reference is the *referring* of a term. Second, the thing to which it refers is a *referent*. Third, the relation between a referring term and its referent is that of *reference*. (Dummett[16] claims that this variety of uses is a harmless deviation in Frege, since he does not confuse distinct roles; even so, Russell's Paradox was not discovered[17] by Frege in his own work, and since we do not have a consistent theory of the nature of meaning, it is as well to expose ambiguity to surveillance.)

(c)   Barr,[18] Lyons,[19] and Sawyer[20] rightly assume that the terms

[11] R. M. Kempson, *Presupposition and the Delimitation of Semantics, Cambridge Studies in Linguistics*, 15 (Cambridge, 1975), pp. 31–7, 85–112.

[12] See Tractatus, *4* to *6*; and, outside the formal position of the *Tractatus*, in *Philosophical Investigations*, e.g., pp. 46–139 secs. 108–502.

[13] cf. G. E. M. Anscombe, *An Introduction to Wittgenstein's Tractatus* (4th edn., London, 1971), p. 17.

[14] e.g. J. Lyons, 'Firth's Theory of "Meaning"' in C. E. Bazell, J. C. Catford, M. A. K. Halliday and R. H. Robins (eds.), *In Memory of J. R. Firth* (London, 1966), p. 293, etc.

[15] cf. M. Dummett, *Frege: Philosophy of Language*, pp. 93–4.

[16] *ibid.*, p. 94.

[17] G. Frege, *Grundgesetze der Arithmetik, begriffsschriftlich abgeleitet* (Jena, 1903) Vol. II, Appendix.

[18] *Comparative Philology*, p. 292.

[19] *Introduction to Theoretical Linguistics*, p. 404.

[20] *Semantics in Biblical Research*, p. 77.

furnishing arguments for references do in fact refer. Barr is the
most explicit: he states,[21] of the term *mqwm* appearing on some
Canaanite and Aramaic inscriptions, that 'the writers, *referring to*
a tomb or area around it, called it a "place"' (Barr's italics).
This type of interpretation of a referring term accords well with
Frege's link of a referring term with its referent in striking a
reference (for example as expounded and illustrated by Anscombe).[22] Hence, referring is the root of reference. The function
of a referring term is to designate the referent by standing for it[23]
(to the explanation of function I return in 2.3).

That referring is a linguistic function is important for investi-
gating reference in ancient texts and scholars' translations and
description of their semantic contents. If a scholar has misunderstood or misused a referential function, then this will proportionately distort his account of semantic data. This is especially
important, as well, for biblical theology.

3 Linguistic Referents

(*a*)   In the foregoing, *mqwm* is said to be the referring term for the
referent which is a tomb. Likewise, a linguistic item itself can be a
referent where a scholar has a translation or a quotation from a
text. For example, in J. A. Fitzmyer's study of MT quotations in
Qumran and related texts[24] there is a citation from the Cairo
Genizah text of the Damascus Document. Namely: *k'šr 'mr byn
'yš l'štw wbyn 'b lbnw* (CD 7:8–9). This transcribed form is a
referring expression, the referent of which is the relevant portion
of the Damascus Document, *when* in a context of analysis where
the text is set up as the object language. In such an investigative
situation, then, the texts analysed constitute the object language,
and the language in which the analysis is done is the metalanguage.
One might interpret this as a difference of linguistic levels, or as

---

[21] J. Barr, *Comparative Philology*, p. 292.

[22] G. E. M. Anscombe, *An Introduction to Wittgenstein's Tractatus*, pp. 17,
98–112.

[23] To bring this out, E. E. Dawson has suggested that the referring term is
represented by 'A', the relation of reference by 'R' and the referent by 'A₁',
so ARA₁. He is, of course, characterizing the type of picture theory of meaning
proposed in the *Tractatus* (e.g. 4.0311); cf., the similar illustration in G. E. M.
Anscombe, *Introduction to Wittgenstein's Tractatus*, pp. 100ff. Also, for the argument that here Wittgenstein is developing Frege's legacy, see P. M. S. Hacker,
Insight and Illusion (Oxford, 1972), pp. 14ff.

[24] J. A. Fitzmyer, *Essays on the Semitic Background of the New Testament*
(London, 1971), p. 18.

a matter of logic, or both. Geach,[25] among others, has shown that a quotation (e.g. the above transcription) can be a sort of logical proper name in the metalanguage, which refers to its referent – the equivalent expression in the object language which is contained in the text.[26] Often, in English the marking of such an expression, which represents and refers to a referent which it reproduces, is achieved by employing quotation marks. So, when Fitzmyer cites the translation in English of CD 7:8–9, one reads a statement in quotation – which itself becomes a referring expression in English designating the referent CD 7:8–9.

The foregoing illustration from Fitzmyer and the connected description of the referential relation support the suggestion that where a scholar is examining an ancient text's semantic values in an object language/metalanguage investigative situation, reference (referring and referent) is an intrinsic feature of his activity; this is emphasized by the fact of 'referring' being a linguistic function of terms which he employs. In contexts of quotation, it might be considered that there is no room for misuse of reference; one does not discover error in Fitzmyer in the above context and I cite him because he is clear, accurate and thus exhibits consistent articulation of referential aspects in which I am interested. Nevertheless, even in Fitzmyer's example (a relatively straight-forward case of quotation) there are multiple instances of reference which could be confused. CD 7:8–9 is itself quoting Num. 30:17 (Heb.); hence there is in CD a usage of an MT text, so CD is, in its *Sitz im Leben*, a metalanguage text. Num. 30:17 is in CD the object language which CD quotes. Given this, Fitzmyer has choices from which to select: of regarding Num. 30:17 as CD's or his object language, while taking care to preserve CD as his object language.[27] There are other issues concerning CD which compli-

[25] P. T. Geach, *Logic Matters*, pp. 190–3, 201–9.

[26] There are certain formal devices and drill to be applied for handling the conversion of such quotations-as-names into a form where their content can be investigated in the metalanguage; cf. W. V. O. Quine, *Mathematical Logic* (2nd edn., Cambridge, Mass., 1951), sec. 4 following. Some of this drill has weaknesses, and various approaches have drawbacks and strengths; but I assume that the general fact of their being some form of reference to a text is evident.

[27] There is also a troublesome issue where there is no correspondence at one stage of the CD quotation of MT: the MT text of Num. 30:17 has *byn-'b lbtw* ('between the father and his daughter') whereas CD's citation reads *wbyn 'b lbnw*; here reference fails, though it is implied by CD, because there is no matching term for the relevant expression in MT. One might couch the failure of reference here employing T. J. Smiley's proposal for formalizing and developing Frege's presupposition concerning reference (see T. J. Smiley, 'Sense without Denotation', *Analysis*, 20 (1959–60), pp. 125–35) and S. Haack's (*Deviant Logic* (Cam-

cate the task of keeping track of references. C. Rabin claimed that the two recensions of the text at 7:9–8:2 are faulty copies of one archetype.[28] J. Murphy-O'Connor[29] alleged that there is some omission due to haplography, but that the omission was noticed at a later stage in writing and the Amos-Numbers' midrash was reintroduced at 19:7–13a. In the complex of competing explanation, and in other possible coherent contentions, references are switched, inverted in direction and perhaps conflated. The archetype of CD is an object language; but it is, in the context of analysis, an hypothetical, referentially opaque entity'[30] since it is constructed through a matrix of textual and literary assessments of metalanguage texts which are later recensions (allegedly) of the archetype. Obviously, if the temporal axes and causal relations are unclear, or confusedly interpreted even if intuitively clear, then it is possible and probable that some scholar will treat what is actually a metalanguage text containing a referring expression (e.g. the CD archetype) as an object language containing linguistic referents. With recensions this is more probable, especially where temporal relations are proximate yet it is important to keep them separated. A particular scholar's thesis will pick out a recension as prior to another because it is a construct in his thesis; he ought, however, to have built a diachronic axis from a set of synchronic descriptions, which it is not always possible to produce. Further, if confusion arises about the identity of the archetype text and recensions, then the referential relation of CD to MT texts, and possible NT allusions to or use of either of them, will be proportionately distorted. Hence, the matrix of assessment from which conclusions are to be drawn may well comprise a vicious circle of promoting possibilities to (seeming) actualities. Reference permits one to expose and fix this vagary.

(b) If J. T. Milik's opinion, that the Similitudes' passage in Enoch[31] is to be dated post-NT, is right (and classified as a later

---

bridge, 1974), pp. 137–47) appraisal and defence of it. In this context, the failure of reference function at a metalogical level would be identifiable as either false, or a lack of truth-value, yet not an intermediate *ad hoc* speculative value based on some modal models.

[28] C. Rabin, *The Zadokite Documents* (Oxford, 1958), p. viii.

[29] J. Murphy-O'Connor, 'The Original Text of CD 7:9–8:2 = 19:5–14', *Harvard Theological Review*, 64 (1971), pp. 379–86.

[30] This type of employment of 'opaque' to do with reference has its provenance in W. V. O. Quine, *From a Logical Point of View* (2nd rev. edn., Harvard, 1961), p. 142.

[31] J. T. Milik, 'Problèmes de la littérature Hénochique à la lumière des frag-

insertion in Enoch), then an example of the foregoing confusions would be found in Charles's interpretation of this text, where object language was deemed metalanguage.[32]

(c) While a referring term, by so functioning, specifies its referent, the converse is not true; as Frege said,[33] 'there is no route back from a referent to the referring term.' At a linguistic level Barr[34] has exposed a recurrent tendency for scholars to perform analyses as though it is in fact possible to achieve a route back from the referent.

(d) In addition to misuse of reference, it is not uncommon for related phenomena to be put in place of reference. Concerning John's Gospel, Bultmann alleged[35] '*swmly*' is to be understood throughout . . . as *plērōma* ['fullness']'. To produce such a meaning relation, a contrastive paradigmatic equivalence is required between John and, for example, Od. Sal.; but each example, cryptic in its brevity, cited in Bultmann,[36] does not yield one equivalent contract in the semantic fields of both texts. (And no synchronic link with the Mandean texts is demonstrated, although it is assumed; yet by now it is fairly clear, for instance, through the research of E. M. Yamauchi,[37] that the possibly relevant Mandean texts post-date John by centuries.) Hence Bultmann does not have the criteria of identity and application[38] to produce a refer-

---

ments araméens de Qumrân', *Harvard Theological Review*, 64 (1971), pp. 33–78, and *Ten Years of Discovery in the Wilderness of Judea* (London, 1959), p. 33; cf. his *The Book of Enoch* (Oxford, 1976).

[32] cf. R. H. Charles, *Apocrypha and Pseudepigrapha of the Old Testament* (Oxford, 1913), vol. 2, pp. 180ff.

[33] M. Dummett, *Frege: Philosophy of Language*, p. 227; I am indicating a strictly linguistic situation here, not where archaeological data and text interrelate.

[34] J. Barr, *The Semantics of Biblical Language*, pp. 22ff., etc. (Barr's treatment is not within the perspective of this Fregean distinction of sense and reference, of which Barr was, then, unaware, although it nicely confirms it.)

[35] R. Bultmann, *The Gospel of John* (Oxford, 1971), p. 77 n. 1. (This is one of a large group; cf. pp. 33, (133), 157, 468, 603, 630, often involving hypostatization and word concepts.)

[36] In Od. Sal. 7:11 'father' is not equivalent because of its contract with 'aeons and *their*'; 'his' in 17:7 is in opposition to 'of grace . . .' in John 1:14; the claim of the synonymity for 'eternal life' in Od. Sal. 9:4 with fullness is foreign to John; I grant that 14:14 is analogous, but the semantic field and identity of 'father' do not carry the equation.

[37] E. M. Yamauchi, *Gnostic Ethics and Mandean Origins* (Harvard, 1970), pp. 70ff.

[38] For presentation of these criteria see 3.1 below. The conclusion by M. L.

ence, in his analysis, as a function of his comparison of John with Gnostic texts, to a word (e.g. *swmly'*) which could be a source influence, although he brandished (irrelevant) information of a recondite sort which obscures this move. He takes the mistaken assumption of synonymy between the words to infer their synonymy; since an assumption is not an operation of proof he is wrong.

Further, Bultmann acted quite as though discovery of a Greek semantic value were to be achieved by scooping out the 'content' of an item in language A and transporting it to language B text. Haas[39] has shown that translation and related activity is, rather, a process of *matching* expressions in A with B – displaying the same field position.

Also, Bultmann's procedure is multilingual in its approach to identifying a term's semantic value. Yet semantic analysis for fixing the value of a well-known, widely distributed, term should be monolingual, built on its uses in its own semantic field.[40]

If a theologico-linguist has excluded such points of analytical method, he might suppose that '*swmly*' is to be understood throughout . . . as *plērōma*'[41] is an identification (where $a = b$), whereas, in actuality, it is the terminus of a thesis which commences by supposing that a possibly can refer (or be made to refer) to b, and/or that a and b can be referred to as members of one semantic class (or field). This exposes the need for criteria of distribution, normality and value by which a and b are placed in such synonymy. Such criteria are absent in Bultmann, and the absence is hidden by mere assertion of semantic identity between a and b. (Whether or not in some general form Bultmann's view might be developed into a coherent account is irrelevant to detection of this group of weaknesses occupying a central position in his explanation.)

Appold (*The Oneness Motif in the Fourth Gospel* (Tubingen, 1976), p. 169) is pertinent: 'Research has demonstrated the untenability of postulating an extrapolated model gained by distilling motifs from a wide range of divergent texts and then by placing them together into a constructed myth which is to serve as the measure of the essence of Gnostic religion.'

[39] W. Haas, 'The Theory of Translation' in G. H. R. Parkinson (ed.), *The Theory of Meaning* (Oxford, 1968). (cf. S. Isard, 'Changing the Context' in E. L. Keenan (ed.), *Formal Semantics of Natural Language* (Cambridge, 1975), where from a distinct standpoint and using oral situations, Isard makes a related point.)

[40] J. F. A. Sawyer, *Semantics in Biblical Research*, p. 116.

[41] Surely, even from Bultmann's position, *swmly'* and *plēroma* should here be in reverse order? Identity in synonymy is to be recognized as an incomplete expression for a is identical with (the same as) b with respect to a property A (and not absolutely all properties); cf. P. T. Geach, *Logic Matters*, p. 239f.

(e) Prior to Bultmann's stating the above point, there is a characteristic Bultmannian use of (seeming) referring expressions (where
he ascribes a referring function to a non-referring term). In the
statement *plērēs charitos kai alētheias* ('full of grace and truth'),
John 1 : 14,[42] Bultmann claims that *charis* and *alētheia* both 'refer',
and he also assumes that the latter 'denotes'. Some writers use
these terms properly, that is, applying them to an item which does
refer in its functional context; others apply them incorrectly from
a formal standpoint, albeit relatively harmlessly (where one would
construe the stylism charitably, but perhaps not imitate it) as
(roughly) equivalent to 'carrying the sense of'. In the above quotation Bultmann invents a (seeming) linguistic referent which is a
concept[43] by hypostatizing not only the non-referring terms but
also the postulated functions of referring, reference and referent.
This nest of hypostatization serves Bultmann as a (*suppressio
veri*) take-off device for projecting an ontological programme onto
NT Greek. It should be noticed that in linguistic analysis it is
not necessarily wrong to give a non-referring term a type of analytical referent, where this is a technique for expressing, say, the
normal usage of a word in a society;[44] some socio-linguistic analyses
have made use of analogous techniques.[45] However, the 'referent'
of the Bultmannian hypostatized reference *is* a concept, or thesis,
or state of reality – not a linguistic referent which names a group
of uses in literature or society (although some might wish to
reconstruct it as such). And Bultmann's procedure does not admit
of being treated as introducing hypostatization solely at the metalanguage level, but does instantiate it in biblical language as a
recurrent, typical feature.[46]

[42] R. Bultmann, *The Gospel of John*, pp. 73–4.

[43] Concerning another term on the same page (see *The Gospel of John*, p. 73,
note 1) Bultmann speaks of 'the concept *eikōn*'. J. Barr has exposed this type of
inconsistent treatment of language (cf. *Semantics of Biblical Language*, e.g.
pp. 18ff.; and 'Hypostatization of linguistic phenomena in modern theological
interpretation', *Journal of Semitic Studies*, 7 (1962) pp. 85–94) for which the above
is the logical underpinning in his examples, I suggest, and in Bultmann's case.
Of course, outside Bultmann's norms in a theological vein, other scholars commit
the same mistakes (e.g. G. Ebeling, in *Introduction to a Theological Theory of
Language* (London, 1973); see my analysis in the *Heythrop Journal*, 15 (October
1974) 4, pp. 423–40.

[44] cf. C. K. Barrett, *The Gospel of John and Judaism* (London, 1975) pp. 30ff.

[45] For example, P. Henry, 'On processing of message referents in contexts'
in E. A. Carswell and R. Rommetveit (eds.), *Social Contexts of Messages* (European Monographs in Social Psychology, 1, London, 1971), pp. 77–95.

[46] I come back to the question of intentional hypostatization of terms in
biblical languages in 2.2, 3.

(*f*) Such attribution of reference to non-referring terms at a
theological level of analysis is a terminus of a tendency to misplace
referential functions at a grammatical level, which is already in
evidence in the last century. Some of the grammars exhibiting
this have had substantial influence on some scholars' classification
of functions in biblical language.[47] *GK*[48] regularly exhibits an
incorrect analysis of referring:

> Peculiar to Hebrew is the employment of the article to
> denote a single person or thing (primarily one which is as
> yet unknown, and therefore not capable of being defined)
> as being present to the mind under given circumstances.
> In such cases in English the indefinite article is mostly used.
>
>   Thus Am. 5:19 *as if a man did flee from a lion* (*h'ry*, i.e., the
> particular lion pursuing him at the time), *and a bear* (*hdb*)
> *met him*, etc., cf. 3:12, 1 Kg 20:36 (Jn 10:12).

If Geach[49] is right in his interpretation of the definite article (and
in avoiding certain implausibilities in Frege's and Russell's
theses)[50] in relation to its connection with subject terms (although

[47] e.g. A. Müller, *Hebräische Schulgrammatik* (Halle, 1878): cf. English trans.
and ed. by J. Robertson, *Outlines of Hebrew Syntax* (Glasgow, 1888) e.g., sec. 149.
Frequently, initial confusion is produced through, for example, collapsing a
construct expression into one inseparable semantic component, by which a
scholar then wrongly concludes that any reference associated with the subject-
term is also – generalizing to other contexts – shared by the items in conjunction
with the subject-term. Hence, hypostatization of the relation of terms at a
grammatical level induces a scholar to ascribe reference to non-referring terms.
cf. Barr's related examination of the construct state in which he detects substantial
mistakes pertinent to the construct in, e.g. A. B. Davidson, *Hebrew Grammar*
(see revision 'throughout' by J. Mauchline (26th edn., Edinburgh, 1966),
which still leaves in Davidson's mistake, and which illustrates my own remarks),
pp. 64ff. cf. J. Barr, *Semantics of Biblical Language*, pp. 92ff. (Importantly, it is
not sufficient to conclude that reference is made because, for example, a Gnostic
author intended it; Bultmann's 'refers' requires, and Bultmann is committed
(cf. P. T. Geach, *Logic Matters*, pp. 163, 146–65 for proof) to referring to the
author's intention to refer; but he does not recognize nor show how he could
know this.)

[48] W. Gesenius, *Hebrew Grammar* (ed. and enlarged by E. Kautzsch) trans.
by A. E. Cowley from the 28th German edn. (2nd English edn., Oxford, 1910),
p. 407, sec. 4.q.

[49] P. T. Geach, *Reference and Generality* (emended edn.), pp. 55–175. Geach's
view is that this article is a quantifier.

[50] cf. M. Dummett, *Frege: Philosophy of Language*, pp. 168ff. Also, R. M.
Kempson, *Presupposition and the Delimitation of Semantics*, ch. 5, for another
approach, or for a distinct programme with grounds for reaching the same
conclusions: N. Chomsky, *Reflections on Language* (London, 1976), pp. 78–134.

there are problems with which one has yet to deal), or if T. J. Smiley's[51] approach is followed, then the definite article in the above specified type of context (howbeit not the *GK* formulation of it) does not have a referential function; the subject term does. It is a conflation of functions so to designate the article, since the article specifies the scope of the item which refers.[52] (*GK* could not be employing 'denote' as a harmless stylism because it states that the article 'is to denote a single person or thing'; but *that* meaning function precisely is referring, and that is what nouns of person and thing do.)[53] It may be objected that, e.g., in Amos 5 : 19 cited by *GK*, *h'ry* is a figuratively employed item, so does not refer. Of course, I do not need to argue that reference is there solely because 'denotes' is; but metaphor can carry reference. Since, in the foregoing, referring has been linked with functions some terms have in their contexts, if (the morphologically) identical terms appear without the same functions, I am not committed to imposing referring on them. However, *GK* might have too little noted the comparative function of *k'šr*, and therefore have unnecessarily required of the Grammar to indicate of *h'ry*: 'i.e., the particular lion pursuing him at the time'. Yet there was no particular, nor indeed any, lion pursuing him because

[51] cf. unpublished notes by T. J. Smiley of his 1973 Cambridge lectures on 'Definite Descriptions', the use of which I here acknowledge. Smiley takes implicit features of Russell's treatment in *Principia Mathematica* and develops the view that the definite article is a quantifier and formalizable as such in accordance with *P.M.* Of course, some article usage in MT pertains more to emphasis than quantification, but this feature is not relevant to the above.

[52] cf. P. T. Geach, *Logic Matters*, pp. 129–65. Nor does the Hebrew article ever take the referential function of an independent substantive (i.e. where it is not relying on some antecedent and conjoined pronoun, etc.), neither is it predicated of, nor is it pluralized – all evident indications (if taken with relevant considerations) that it does not refer.

[53] See W. P. Alston, *Philosophy of Language* (Englewood Cliffs, 1964), pp. 14–19, and 17 n. 8; I am not in citing this subscribing to the referential theory of meaning mentioned by the author. I. White shows that exactly the same type of uses of the article to those of Hebrew mentioned by *GK* above occur in English ('Singular Objects': a paper (unpub.) delivered at the Cambridge Faculty of Philosophy General Seminar 18 October 1972); so the use is not 'peculiar to Hebrew'. For example, 'as if the detective is running from the criminal' (unknown criminal); this example (which is my own, based on White's analysis) illustrates the case that non-intentional verb contexts, which are indeterminate (in addition to those mentioned by White) about the identity of a referent but refer, can use the definite article and do present the same problems of intentionality in some respects. But the following suggests this issue is not pertinent to Amos 5 : 19, etc., because *GK* has applied the wrong description. (But also see 'denoting' in 1.4 *2* (*c*) above.)

the 'lion' functions figuratively in a comparative expression. If it
has a reference, then it refers to the causal agency by which the
man (or referent of the figuratively used 'yš) is fleeing (and fleeing
– ynws – can be construed as figurative for some other experience).
Even if the article did denote, it would be attached to that agency,
not to some lion; of course, in that GK connects the article with
'a lion', it is tantamount to resting on a premiss which presumes
that the object of the article is lion; this is the case, but as a linguistic, not empirical, item. Whether or not one treats the article
as a specifier of the scope of the noun, rather than as a stylistic
feature of a figurative expression which severs its normal role, in
view of the foregoing, is a separate question contingent on its
function in figurative contexts. Whatever the answer to this
question is, it is nevertheless quite clear that GK has given the
article a false function of denoting, and this has induced (with
other contributory factors) a wrong ascription of bestial referent
to the noun, which might itself rest on a presupposition about a
dualist approach to meaning.[54]

(g)   Nida and Tabor display[55] a confusion over the source of
reference in the expression tō haimati autou ('his blood'), Rom. 5:9.
They state that 'In the expression "justified by his blood" (Rom.
5:9), blood, which normally designates a mass object, actually
refers to an event, namely, the atonement.' Nida and Tabor are
not employing the term 'refers' generally, but are using it in a
chapter on 'Referential Meaning', in a quite explicit manner to
represent the referential function. Strictly, the pronoun is the
source of indicating reference, since its antecedent is Christos in
5:8, where the pronoun is a substitution instance of that subject.
In cases when there is this type of substitution (and not mere
replacement of a function with a value asymmetrical to the subject),[56] the pronoun functions to relay the referring role of the

[54] P. T. Geach (Reference and Generality, pp. 6f., 32f., 55ff.) points out that in
scholastic philosophy (e.g. with Ockham) there was an early confusion of associating different theses and indiscriminated uses of suppositio and stat pro, and
relatedly of 'denoting' and 'denotes' in the last century (and others) which may
have fed through to other scholarly spheres and contributed to muddled analysis.
Geach suggests, with others, that, owing to this confusion, forms of 'denotes'
should cease to be used in referential contexts.
[55] E. A. Nida and C. R. Tabor, The Theory and Practice of Translation, Helps
for Translators Vol. 8 (Leiden, 1969), pp. 88–9.
[56] I do not wish unguardedly to generalize this judgement for other similar
uses without allowing for problems of quantification and reference through
subordinate clauses (cf. W. V. O. Quine, Methods of Logic (rev. edn. London,

subject term which, interpreted narrowly, is a reference within the linguistic level from pronoun to subject. The metaphoric *haimati* is what I wish to term a transform metaphor[57] (i.e. where a context advertises, by style and/or argument and semantic choices, that the semantic value of the metaphor is to strike associations which are derivable from the overall context of the text).[58] In Rom. 5:9 the possessive pronoun informs one that something (*haimati*) is ascribed to the subject; Nida and Tabor misunderstand this relation and invert it to: the subject is ascribed to something (*haimati*). Once this confusion is articulated and disguised it is easy to assume, as they do, that 'blood' refers, but wrongly so. Nor is it clear, even given Nida's and Tabor's view, that 'blood' merely directly refers to an event which is the atonement. 'Blood' is rather an ingredient of an exposition of redemptive teleology which is exhibited by the event in Romans,[59] of which 'atonement' is an element so termed by theological convention. Hence it is slightly misleading and circular to claim that 'blood' refers to an event, which event is named by a theological motif; this itself tends to reveal that what is actually being handled is not referring and referent but relations of words to words.

(*h*)   In between the positions of employing a referring term like 'denotes' as a harmless stylism and its misuse in a damaging thesis, is an intermediate use. In some scholars[60] there is no particularly entrenched distortion but a tendency to hypostatize a term to a small degree and an informality of analysis which together tend to generate weak or stretched conclusions in which data and imaginative activity combine uneasily.

1958), pp. 83ff.; J. E. J. Altham and N. W. Tennant, 'Sortal Quantification' in E. L. Keenan (ed.), *Formal Semantics of Natural Languages*, pp. 46–58; and especially 'Quantification theory' (unpub.) paper of T. R. Baldwin delivered at the Cambridge Faculty of Philosophy General Seminar, 24 February 1971).

[57] I was stimulated to the above formulation by W. Haas's remarks on poetic metaphor (which he applies to poetry) in his 1975 Research Lectures on Semantics, from which I drew the feature of transformation, which I here acknowledge, although my explanation is different from his own.

[58] I am not of course smuggling a word concept back in here; but claiming that a transform metaphor value is a summary aspect of the *Sinn* and perhaps tone.

[59] Rom. 3:21–31, especially v. 25.

[60] e.g. A. A. MacIntosh, 'A consideration of the problems presented by Psalm II:11–12', *Journal of Theological Studies*, new series, 27 (April 1976) pt. 1 pp. 2 and 11. Conversely, however (although this is no aid to MacIntosh), M. Foucault (*The Archaeology of Knowledge* (London, 1972), pp. 89ff.) has rightly stressed the complex tonal relations between referring term, context and referent which logicians may badly neglect.

2.1   Logico-Linguistic Context of Reference

1   *Hypostatized Structures*

It is extremely interesting to note that Frege, Wittgenstein[1] and Barr all inveighed against the practice of hypostatizing meanings,[2] and have criticized lack of attention to the use and context of a word in analysis of language.[3]

In earlier sections I have considered some misuse of reference and related confusions regarding individual words or expressions, not least of which was the hypostatization of a term. Some scholars attempt to generalize from employment of these individual treatments to systematize a conception of structures inherent to biblical languages; or – to emphasize the probable provenance of such attempts – a scholar may allow his (often unconsciously held) presuppositions in respect of individual expressions to specify his conception of language in general. I term the product an hypostatized structure and the process by which it is produced collective hypostatization.

In collective hypostatization, already hypostatized items are held up as markers of a typical set of functions in ancient language seemingly to characterize standard usage and often (alleged) ways of thinking in ancient times. If the components of such a linguistic calculation are hypostatized, then so must its conclusion be an hypostatization. Particularly is this the case where this type of analysis is employed to attempt an exposure of the rules of meaning (*sic*) supposedly embodied in ancient language: the rules themselves are hypostatizations.[4]

[1] cf. G. Frege, *Die Grundlagen der Arithmetik: eine logisch-mathematische Untersuchung über den Begriff der Zahl* (Breslau, 1884); in later works the feature of attention to context played a less explicit part in Frege's writing, yet is still there. L. Wittgenstein, *Tractatus, Philosophical Remarks, Philosophical Investigations*.

[2] See M. Dummett's account (in *Frege: Philosophy of Language*, pp. 92ff., 155–7) of Frege and Wittgenstein.

[3] See M. Dummett, *Frege: Philosophy of Language*, pp. 192–6. Wittgenstein also related these points generally to religious language (albeit with unexpected consequences); see his *Lectures and Conversations on Aesthetics, Psychology and Religious Belief*, ed. by C. Barrett (Oxford, 1966). For J. Barr's treatment of hypostatization and meaning, see references in the foregoing Section 2.0, *3*. cf. D. M. MacKinnon's (unpub.) essay, 'Some Recent Discussions of Religious Faith'.

[4] See L. Wittgenstein, *The Blue and Brown Books* (2nd ed., Oxford, 1969), pp. 19ff.

2 Morphology and Logic

(a) W. Haas[5] has explained that relations of graphemes to phonemes (and adjacent topics of semantic values) can be mistakenly identified. He cites the example of a confusion between a relation of correspondence and a relation of reference. I demonstrated above that such confusions around reference assume many forms; in the sphere of morphology and its relation to semantics, muddled description of relations can likewise be produced in, and as a result of, collective hypostatization. Where, for example, a relation of postulated correspondence is actually also mingled with descriptive elements which assume reference is in the relation, then the nature of the correspondence (which might only be a morphological, yet deemed semantical, relation) between P and Q expressions may wrongly be described as a referential relation. When this happens, then the task of proving that there is a semantic mirroring of contents of P in Q might be excluded as redundant because, it may be thought, reference between P and Q itself exemplifies grounds for there being reference to the same meaning in each expression. In fact, often such claims are only supported by a morphological similarity (between homonyms), where form is taken as a criterion of meaning. Such a muddle over individual pairs of expressions can exist in a synthesis about groups of expressions and structures which are being 'matched'.

(b) Before Barr's cautionary investigations in *The Semantics of Biblical Language* it was, for some, customary to examine biblical languages in styles displaying the above characteristic confusions. The work of T. Boman[6] is an example, albeit a rather idiosyncratic one. The situation is complicated when scholars, often episodically and even within the scope of one article, intentionally or unwittingly slide from some sort of linguistic procedure into an adoption of and/or merger with some form of 'logical' structure. In Boman's case the lapse is probably unintentional. Since logic itself, superficially, has a strong family relation to morphology, it is easy for scholars to produce apparently cogent arguments which can mask initial confusions and conflations.

---

[5] W. Haas, *Phono-Graphic Translation*, Mont Follick Series Vol. 2 (Manchester, 1970), pp. 20–9. See also J. Barr, 'Reading a Script without Vowels', in W. Haas (ed.), *Writing without Letters* (Manchester, 1976), pp. 81ff.

[6] T. Boman, *Das hebräische Denken im Vergleich mit dem Griechischen* (2nd edn., Göttingen, 1954); English trans. (with revision of German text) *Hebrew Thought Compared with Greek* (London, 1960). German pagination given hereafter.

Barr's portrayal of Boman's misunderstanding depicts Boman's contrary position in such a confusion. Barr described Boman's conception of an aspect of verbs. One should categorize this conception as an instance of an hypostatized structure which draws systematically misleading conclusions. I reproduce Barr's characterization of Boman's views:

(1)   Verbs are dynamic
       Stative verbs are verbs
       Therefore stative verbs are somehow dynamic and indicate an action or activity of the subject.[7]

Boman intends the evidence for (1) to be linguistic;[8] Barr observes that, rather, Boman's argument is a 'general logical one'[9] although superficially it appears to be a linguistic argument. While Barr is right to criticize Boman, further dismantling of (1) is required to determine the 'logical' status of Boman's view as displayed here.[10] The conclusion of (1) relies on a suppressed premiss, that

(2)   Morphology of stative verbs
       implies
       [Knowledge of the] ontology of their referents.

(c)   The distinction between token and type is helpful for categorizing different classes of things in analysis and expression. A token is a particular instance of a thing; a type is the set of things which are defined by it. For example, consider the difference between *zaqen* and זָקֵן ('be old'). At a level of token letters, they are different words. In a context of type letters, they are the same word. As a token, *zaqen* is a particular group of

---

[7] J. Barr, *The Semantics of Biblical Language*, pp. 55f.

[8] T. Boman, *Das hebräische Denken im Vergleich mit dem Griechischen*, pp. 21ff.

[9] See J. Barr, *The Semantics of Biblical Language*, p. 55.

[10] These criticisms do not entail that any (more rigorous) treatment of related issues of morphology and meaning relations about verbs, producing points of asymmetry between Hebrew and other languages, is wrong. (e.g. E. Jenni (*Das hebräische Pi'el* (Zürich, 1968)) avoids the obvious mistakes of Boman's procedure, and offers semantic generalizations connected with morphological evidence, although I do not think he is entirely free of Boman's type of shift from form to meaning.) In logic some uses of 'morphology' are more inclusive than linguistic uses, albeit more precise and specific; as an example of this, and linked with ontology see A. Tarski, *Logic, Semantics, Meta-mathematics* (Oxford, 1956), pp. 403–4.

marks; not marks *for* זָקֵן, but mere marks. When one introduces *zaqen* as a particular group of marks for זָקֵן, then one
assumes a premiss of type. That is to say, it requires a conception
of each word's standing to display one entity, and that this entity
can be represented by different modes of expression. Such an
entity, thus far, is not yet a semantic value, but only that entity
which can be written in different ways. Once this token/type
distinction is struck, it can be applied at any level in the universe
of discourse: to include or exclude items in respect of a class.
Scholars might incorrectly group as one entity two tokens which
differ, or employ a false type-marker at a semantic level to classify
two tokens; one might contaminate semantic types with an ontological type; another could wrongly infect the definition of a
semantic type with a mistaken ideology.[11] Boman exemplifies
some of these errors, and so it can be shown that (1) is bad logic.

Boman took it that he could collapse all verb uses in MT
(pertinent to his thesis) to one (hypostatized) label 'Verbs are
dynamic'. Since 'verb' is a syntactic category, one would expect
'dynamic' to mark some feature of that category; but Boman
shifts levels and applies 'dynamic' to a semantic level. Here
Boman is assuming that, accordingly, there can be a complete
matching of the type verb with the semantic type value; Barr has
demonstrated[12] that the semantic values in usages of these verbs
do not support Boman's jumping of levels, yet alone reduction of
syntactic to semantic type hypostatization. It is clear that Boman
has presumed that verbs, which are actually tokens of different
semantic types, can be pitched into one type, and been misled by
morphological parallels.

Precisely this absence of channel for transmitting the hypostatization of differing semantic values as one 'dynamic' value between morphological and semantic levels is expressed in Barr's
reproduction in (1)'s consequent 'Therefore stative verbs are
somehow dynamic . . .': the 'somehow' is an empty term which can

---

[11] I follow a general explanation of token/type distinction: e.g. C. S. Peirce,
Collected Papers, ed. by C. Hartshorne, P. Weiss and A. W. Burks (Cambridge,
Mass., 1931–58), vol. 4, sec. 537; and for detailed introduction of relations of
semantic, ontological, etc., levels in this context, see P. T. Geach, *Logic Matters*,
pp. 238–47; and the connection of these matters with reference are expounded
briefly in C. Thiel, *Sense and Reference in Frege's Logic* (Dordrecht, 1968),
pp. 142–57.

[12] J. Barr, *Semantics of Biblical Language*, pp. 46–84. For the same confusions
in ancient and modern philosophical writers see W. and M. Kneale, *The Development of Logic*, pp. 49f., L. Wittgenstein, *Tractatus*, secs. 3, esp. 3.331, and 5,
particularly 5.252.

only be filled with a specification at the non-semantic level. Boman's ambiguity in hypostatization converts the empty term into a receptacle for semantics.

The conclusion of Boman's argument can be described as 'Therefore stative verbs . . . indicate an action or activity of the subject'. But semantics is not symmetrical with ontology. Boman's conflation of morphology with semantics is here presumed to imply that semantics can dictate an ontological state, since the form 'is' a map of whatever a thing does. Cassiodorus[13] in the sixth century proved this sequence of sophism to be a paralogism; since Barr has in any case exposed its linguistics, I merely note that his criticisms are reflected at a logical level. Boman has lifted ontology as a type (not many types, as there are) and postulated a conceptual synonymy of it (at the appropriate juncture) with the semantics of verbs. Wittgenstein's work outlines, notoriously, that surface structure (e.g. verb morphology) has repeatedly bewitched the perception of those who expound language and its relation to the world.[14] Boman is an obvious case of this, and illustrates the destruction of consistent distinctions by which such illusions are generated.

Boman's logic is faulty; and I use the term 'pseudological' to describe this type of analysis.[15] Frequently in such a context, because of the misuse of logic by someone, logic has been dealt a disservice by its being supposed that logic is pseudologic. Scholarly works which Barr justifiably criticizes for linguistic deviance, which mischievously, loosely or incorrectly deploy the terms, technique (or vague, implicit uses) of logic, should not be included as factors in an analysis of the possibility of applying some logic to the investigation of biblical languages. Contrariwise, this truth does not oppose logic's being employed to describe and catch the operations of pseudologic.

(d)   Where a seeming connection has been adduced in language which appears to possess logical features, yet when further scrutiny produces evidence that the linguistic data counter such a connection, closer examination of the 'logical' features will

---

[13] J.-P. Migne (ed.), *Patrologia Cursus Completus Series Latina*, vol. 70, cols. 1194–6.

[14] L. Wittgenstein, *Philosophical Investigations*, e.g. sec. 109ff.

[15] W. Haas has coined this term in a paper examining some philosophical views which have some general similarity to the topics mentioned above (see W. Haas, 'On Speaking a Language', *Proceedings of the Aristotelian Society*, new series, 51 (1950–51), pp. 129–66, cf. p. 130, where pseudo-logical occurs).

betray a misuse of logic (when the connection is pseudological). Of course, this is not to impose some artificial language's norms as canonical for linguistic norms in the Bible, but rather to distinguish between consistent and inconsistent uses of data. Nevertheless, since most linguists assume or formulate a generalized system or interpretation of linguistic phenomena, there is an overlap, at times, between functions in the texts which are analysed and the explanatory functions of the terms which are members of the hypothesis which is purported to explain functions in linguistic phenomena.

For example, F. I. Andersen[16] explicitly adopts a notion of sentence type from the Summer Institute group.[17] Although based on a largely empirical investigation of languages by the Summer group, and of Hebrew Pentateuchal sentences[18] by Andersen, the notion is part of a particular theoretical structure conjecturing the nature of certain parts of languages.[19] To the extent that such a feature of a theoretical structure in function matches the function of the allegedly corresponding usage of items in biblical language, Andersen's contention will be vindicated. Yet if 'type' only fits certain token sentences in MT Hebrew, while having been generalized to cover all typical sorts, Andersen will have generated hypostatization in elements of the explanatory structure. In this case the concept of a function (assumed or specified) will be an hypostatized structure, not least because Andersen injects details of generative models into his account.

T. Collins[20] has pointed out that Andersen's definition of apposition and its relation to the parameters of being a sentence are not very satisfactory, having left the specification of it so that it could include two simple sentences, when he is supposedly stating the conditions for apposition in a compound sentence type. In addition to these unclear specifications, it is worth noting that

[16] F. I. Andersen, *The Sentence in Biblical Hebrew* (The Hague, Paris, 1974), pp. 24ff.

[17] K. L. Pike, 'A Guide to Publications Related to Tagmemic Theory' in T. A. Sebeok (ed.), *Current Trends in Linguistics*, 3 (The Hague, Paris, 1966), pp. 365–94; and R. E. Longacre, *Grammar Discovery Procedures* (The Hague, Paris, 1964), pp. 7–34, and *Hierarchy and Universality of Discourse Constituents in New Guinea Languages*, vol. 1 (Washington, 1972).

[18] cf. T. Collins's criticism about the untypical selection of MT sentences, which F. I. Andersen employed; in Collins's review, *Journal of Semitic Studies*, 20 (1975), 2, pp. 252–4.

[19] For documentation of this, cf. R. E. Longacre's *Grammar Discovery Procedures*, pp. 7–34, by W. L. Chafe's review, *Language*, 41 (1965), pp. 640–7.

[20] See Collins's review, *Journal of Semitic Studies*, 20 (1975), 2, p. 253; and F. I. Andersen, *The Sentence in Biblical Hebrew*, pp. 36–60, and p. 55.

Andersen's prior use of reference and hypostatization of terms
has contributed to his confusion and to the production of the error
noted by Collins.

In the section containing the confused specification of apposition,[21] Andersen does not cite any MT Hebrew examples, but
uses English illustrations:

> Sentence-level apposition resembles phrase-level apposi-
> tion. A typical phrase-level apposition places in juxta-
> position two words or phrases with a common referent, or at
> least some overlap in their fields of reference. Examples:
> *Dr. Livingstone, the explorer*; *red apple*. *Dr. Livingstone* and
> *the explorer* are identical. The phrase in apposition identifies
> the Head. In *Dr. Livingstone, an explorer* the apposition
> phrase classifies the Head. *Red* and *apple* are both class
> names; the apposition phrase refers to the overlap class
> of objects which are both *red* and *apple*.[22]

I leave aside the uneasy equation of phrase and sentence levels.
Andersen stated that 'Dr. Livingstone' and 'the explorer' are
identical; but in what respect identical? Andersen's mode of
expression hardly allows restriction of identification to one feature.
Since 'the explorer' contains semantic information which is
absent from 'Dr. Livingstone', it is evident they are not identical
in regard to semantic information. Clearly, it is reference which
is Andersen's concern.[23] When Andersen comments 'A typical
phrase-level apposition *places* [my italics] in juxtaposition two
words or phrases with a common referent' he is not informing
one of anything which apposition uniquely does, but merely
observing a necessary condition of an expression which mentions
a subject (which has a reference) twice. So it is misleading to lift
out such a referential feature only as a criterion which occurs in
phrase-level apposition and designate its being there intrinsically
because of apposition. Indeed, sometimes in phrase-level apposition there is no reference: phantom limb, the pain. So Andersen's
specification does not fit this sort of type, nor any intentionalistic
uses.

Moving to Andersen's 'red apple' now obliquely advertises

---

[21] F. I. Andersen, *The Sentence in Biblical Hebrew*, p. 36, sec. 3.0.

[22] *ibid.*; cf. R. E. Longacre, *Grammar Discovery Procedures*, pp. 74–100.

[23] For other important judgements see J. Barr's review of Andersen, *Journal
of Theological Studies*, 27 (1976), 1, pp. 151–3. cf. also a proper handling of
descriptions in P. T. Geach, *Reference and Generality*, pp. 48ff., 123ff.

what is behind his formal structure. It is strange that Andersen should have presumed that 'red' and 'apple' are class names in a section on grammar. Red is a predicative adjective, and as such does not refer but is applied to the referent of its subject term, and hence is true of it, if the expression itself is true. (I return to sentential structure later.) Given this, its function just is its semantic value, which does not involve reference except by application to an object through the means of its subject term's reference. Therefore there is no referring function 'to' a class of 'red'. If it were such a name of a class of 'red', it would be referring to that class not to the red property of a particular apple. Hence if Andersen's naming of 'red' is true, then his application is false; and if his naming is false, then his application is false. If the apposition phrase did refer to the overlap class of objects which are both 'red' and 'apple', then 'red apple' would refer to a class and not to any particular 'red apple'; but Andersen's phrase in apposition is to a particular apple. Hence, given either Andersen's contention of there being an overlap class, as a premiss – or its negation – Andersen's view of the apposition phrase 'red apple' is false. Not less is the probability that 'red apple' is not even an apposition phrase. It is evident that Andersen has wittingly or unwittingly prefixed a Platonic thesis of objective (hypostatized) meaning entities[24] at a general level, or, rather, a nominalist[25] two-name theory. Of the former, Barr has traced this in Boman,[26] and it also relates to my own tracking of Boman's misuse of reference above.

Although Andersen offers insights of value at some points, the above shows that in his work there is a formalized revival of those referential confusions criticized by Barr in *The Semantics of Biblical Language*. Andersen disguised the confusions by a formal

[24] While this is in Plato in the Forms (e.g. the *Republic* sec. 596, *A*) it is there guardedly developed, often while avoiding the confusion Andersen falls into – of nominalizing the predicate (e.g. in the *Sophist*); I have in mind the 'Platonic' traits in some nineteenth-century scholars which generally influenced, and still do indirectly affect, some scholars (cf. B. Bosanquet, *Logic* (Oxford, 1888), vol. I, pp. 9–100).

[25] By 'nominalist' I do not indicate the use of the term by some theologians (e.g. T. F. Torrance, *God and Rationality* (Oxford, 1971), pp. 36 and 128; cf. resulting distortion, p. 46), nor to the correct use of 'nominalization' in some applied linguistics (e.g. J. F. A. Sawyer, *Semantics in Biblical Research*, p. 63), but rather the strictly philosophical usage which antedates both of these uses. It is where a predicate is regarded as a name by which it is deemed logically, functionally symmetrical with substantive names; and had its strongest exposition by William of Ockham, being mediated to the modern era via J. S. Mill's *Logic*.

[26] J. Barr, *Semantic of Biblical Language*, pp. 105ff.

treatment which obscures the metaphysics assumed in the grammar and one would require an exhaustive analysis to generalize
this over all Andersen's study. Though I restrict my remarks to
the above citation, one should remember that Andersen is implementing a systematic thesis which is obviously firmly embedded
in his remarks on sentence types. Further, Andersen's book
continually emphasizes the empirical nature of his interest – to
produce hypothesis from data.[27] Yet it is apparent from the foregoing that at least part of his descriptive procedure is directed by
an unacknowledged dualist theory of meaning with a highly
speculative metaphysics, where meanings are, on occasions,
entities to which use refers[28] when the use to which Andersen's
view is applied is without a referential value.

(e)   Such an amalgam is at the same time too narrow and too
wide as a description of functions: too narrow because it excludes
certain non-referential features; too wide because it invents
reference where there is none. Conversely, Andersen comments on
'meaning' when, in one respect, he should be specifying reference,
which he does not mention. In a section (related to the above
quotation) defining 'Synonymous Apposition' Andersen states:[29]

> When two clauses in apposition are identical in both meaning
> and grammatical structure, the result is the *parallelismus
> membrorum* so highly favoured in Hebrew, especially in
> poetry.
> Example: '*dh wṣlh šm'n qwly*
>   *nšy lmk h'znh 'mrty*
>   Ada and Zilla, heed my-voice!
>   Wives of Lemek, hear my-speech
>   (Gn. 4:23)

I agree with Sawyer[30] that, in assessing alleged synonymy in
parallelismus membrorum and related structures, one should take
account of semantic interference in the associative field whereby
hyponymy might be enriched to a type of synonymous relation
between terms in apposition clauses. I also concur with Sawyer's
evident observation that referential identity[31] does not imply
synonymy. To these points can be added the comment that in

---

[27] F. I. Andersen, *The Sentence in Biblical Hebrew*, e.g. p. 19.
[28] I return to the relation of 'use' to 'mention' later.
[29] F. I. Andersen, *The Sentence in Biblical Hebrew*, p. 38, sec. 3.3.
[30] J. F. A. Sawyer, *Semantics in Biblical Research*, pp. 74ff.
[31] J. F. A. Sawyer, *Semantics in Biblical Research*, p. 76.

such circumstances predicates will often share a closer semantic relation in apposition than their substantives. Andersen does not discriminate between the two groups in this context and never offers an explanation of pertinent distinctions about reference and synonymy.

In the foregoing quotation Andersen supposes that the cited clauses are 'identical in both meaning and structure'. If one accepts that *qwly* ('my voice') is a type of metonymy metaphor, then one could regard it as synonymous with *'mrty* ('my speech'); but even this is loose and inexplicit, since as such *qwly* might be interpreted as identical because it referred to that 'speech', rather than its being the same semantic value as *'mrty*. However, I leave this aside, for it is with the substantive terms that 'identical in both meaning and grammatical structure' is inaccurate. *'dh* and *ṣlh* are proper names; *nšy* ('wives of') is not and is a role term in construct plural, linked with the proper name *lmk* – which has no corresponding reference in respect of the opening clause. Therefore, in opposition to Andersen's claim, the substantive terms in each clause exhibit substantial semantic differences both of sense and reference. Of course, there is some close relation which is heightened by interface mixing in the associative field, but that should not be deemed to produce identical meaning when the clause displays the above evidence of asymmetry concerning the clause in apposition. There is some referential identity shared by these clauses, yet there is also the additional reference for *lmk*; and the sense of the two substantive units in the clauses are semantically distinct in some respects. So in a section on synonymy, especially, it is misleading to claim of partial referential-identity groups of substantives that they are 'identical in both meaning and structure'.

3   Reference and Predication

In the foregoing I have not criticized the right of scholars mentioned to hold theses about language, but objected to unwitting articulation of premises and contrary use of data or dogmatic (unspecified) implementation of a non-linguistic hypothesis. However, for treatments of phenomena to acquire explanatory power and generalizability, it is expedient to make certain assumptions, although one should make them explicit, rather than smuggle them in, or deny them. The previous section contains some of my own assumptions which are standard aspects of logic, which I here state, and I also propose other notions in summary form.

Proper names refer; but predicates are ascribed to the referent of the proper name, that is, are true of, rather than refer to, the referent.[32] Predicates apply to referents only if they are attached to referring terms which have referents. A predicate, unexceptionably, is a linguistic unit in use, in accordance with the previous condition. Once it is excised for listing or analysis, or when this happens to a member of a predicate, then the reference linked to the predicable alters. To ignore this is to hypostatize expressions. That is to say, if an item is removed from the object language being analysed (in a text), then it becomes, in the metalanguage, a logical indicator for its use in that (or any) text; and the discovery procedure for its semantic value must take account of this for recovery of its value.[33] In the metalanguage the 'predicate' or subset of the predicate is in the relation of being a type (when deployed, for example, in a lexical context of analysis, that is, when it might be said 'the Hebrew word W means F in the MT'). Sometimes in this context, its referent may be the totality of uses of that particular word type in MT. Behind such a truth, of course, is Frege's point that only in the context of a sentence does a word stand for anything.[34] Wittgenstein leaned heavily on this point, not only in his later[35] but also in his earlier work,[36] as Dummett has pointed out.[37] In live speech, such an assertion of meaning-condition raises some issues;[38] but in a 'dead' language, set in a literary text, a sentential context is typical and necessary for intelligibility.

Geach[39] has composed the term 'predicable' to represent a predi-

[32] See A. Prior, *Objects of Thought* (Oxford, 1971), pp. 144ff.

[33] An abstracted term is not a consistent entity, except as a sign for its use in a source text. Neglect of this can lead to deeming words as entities, in themselves, as substances to which an interpretation might be applied, then imposed again on any of its uses, whereas information from its uses should produce the interpretation. J. Barr's *The Semantics of Biblical Language* (ch. 7) contains analysis of this form of clipping-off of the referential connections of an item with its *Sitz im Leben*, though without the above characterization.

[34] G. Frege, *Die Grundlagen der Arithmetik*, and see 'Sinn und Bedeutung'. To Frege's use of context, one would also wish to give due attention to other levels of an item's contextualization adjacent to semantic considerations expressed here (cf. J. F. A. Sawyer, *Semantics in Biblical Research*, pp. 6ff.).

[35] L. Wittgenstein, *Philosophical Investigations*, secs. 30ff.

[36] L. Wittgenstein, *Tractatus*, 3.326ff.; see also Frege quoted by Wittgenstein in his *Philosophical Remarks*, sec. 12.

[37] M. Dummett, *Frege: Philosophy of Language*, pp. 192ff.

[38] See W. Haas, 'On Speaking a Language', and in relation to ancient languages, cf. A. H. Gardiner, *The Theory of Speech and Language* (Oxford, 1932), pp. 110ff.

[39] P. T. Geach, *Reference and Generality*, pp. 23ff.; this device should not be

cate when it has been abstracted from its sentential context. Such a terminological distinction is a helpful marker in indicating the status of an expression in the interchanges between object-language and metalanguage levels, which lack of clarity can obscure. The predicable is, hence, a predicate which is divorced from its actual uses; it, then, has a relation of extension (if assessed and described properly) to its actual uses. Yet if a predicable (or subset of it) is hypostatized, and the recognition of its extensional relation to its textual source and meaning is accordingly masked, then sometimes a scholar might wrongly presume to furnish another differing route to a 'referent' by virtue of associating an exegesis with the hypostatized predicable. If a scholar succeeds in directing attention to the actual extension which the text has as its subject, this by no means guarantees that his attachment of a description will be right.[40] And not infrequently, the attempt to reach an (alleged) extension without constructing the semantic value from the totality of uses is precisely because there are problems of identification which resist easy solution. Here the value which a scholar chooses in bypassing textual analysis by his process of hypostatization will necessarily be conjectural.

4   Reference through Hebrew to Semitic Languages

(a)   Sometimes scholars extend some of the confusions documented above when handling comparative material. In a morphological analysis of the 'verbal element' yhwh ('Yahweh'), F. M. Cross[41] traces it to Semitic liturgical epithets through Amorite personal names such as ya-wi-DINGER.IM through to Ugaritic dū yakāninu; he then postulates the existence of a sentence name supposed to have been in a cultic formula (neither name nor formula are extant, but hypothetical). He concludes that the MT use of yhwh arises from the term's being dislodged and introduced into the MT type of usage.

The morphological parallels are not perfect; morphology cannot imply semantics, yet Cross presumes it does. The diachronic and synchronic axes are unspecified. Name, formula, and point of dislocation (from formula into MT) are theoretical,

---

confused with the systematic nominalization of predicates in a logic programme (cf. S. E. Böer, 'Proper Names as Predicates', Philosophical Studies, 27 (1975)).

[40] J. Barr's criticisms of some such transfers show this (cf. his Comparative Philology and the Text of the Old Testament, pp. 164ff., and 164 n. 1).

[41] F. M. Cross, Canaanite Myth and Hebrew Epic (Harvard, 1973), pp. 44–75; cf. pp. 62f., 71, and 66.

although they are key stages in the proposed route. Also, with the arbitrariness of diachronic and sociolinguistic hypotheses in the arena being analysed, it is perilous to venture, let alone assume, valid authoritative assertions, not least because of the Tell Mardikh tablets,[42] though the situation was still substantially unclear prior to their discovery.

There is apparent explanatory power,[43] and there is actual explanatory power. The former does not possess criteria of falsifiability, refutability and testability; the latter is that possible property of a proposal which exists because the proposal is an empirical statement. By 'empirical statement' I intend, with Popper,[44] a statement which is accessible to being shown true or false by a finite series of observation statements. An 'observation statement' is simply a true description of an observable or veridically observed entity.[45] Since Cross's cultic formula is not known to exist, there is no finite series of (actual) observation statements to support it. Hence, a proposal, that the cultic formula did exist, is not an empirical statement because there are no criteria for its being tested for truth or falsehood. That is to say (in one respect), scrutiny of Cross's proposal cannot test for falsehood because the entity which is alleged to exist is not available for one to match with regard to descriptive information. And any inductive argument in such a circumstance must regress to a premiss with this fatal weakness as its content. So even a weaker presentation of Cross's proposal as a conjecture[46] would fall under this criticism. In sum:

---

[42] See G. Pettinato, 'Testi cuneiform del 3. millennio in paleo-cananeo rinvenuti nella campagna 1974 a Tell Mardikh – Ebla', *Orientalia*, 44 nova ser. (1975), 3, pp. 361–74; and cf. P. Matthiae, 'Ebla nel periodo delle dinastie amorree della dinastia di Akkad Scoperte archeologiche recenti a Tell Mardikh', *Orientalia* 44 nova ser. (1975), 3, pp. 337–60. (The grading of speculations as authoritative criteria is illustrated in respect of the Tell Mardikh = Ebla debate, when, prior to the foregoing discoveries, M. C. Astour violently opposed the identification (see his 'Tell Mardikh and Ebla', *Ugarit-Forschungen*, 3 (1971), pp. 9–19).)

[43] I here use K. R. Popper's expression and implement his thesis since I agree with his general position on induction. (See *Conjectures and Refutations* (London, 1963), pp. 34ff.)

[44] K. R. Popper, *Objective Knowledge* (Oxford, 1972), p. 12, n. 19.

[45] *ibid.*, pp. 7ff.

[46] I employ 'conjecture' in the special sense of Popper's use of the term in the context of Hume's problem of induction as criticized by Popper *Objective Knowledge*, ch. 1), although Popper uses it also in a larger context of consistent conjectures (cf. *Conjectures and Refutations*, pp. 33ff.). On my use of Popper, in a context of Frege-Wittgenstein referential theory, see Popper's own agreement with Wittgenstein's implicit use of the same type of criteria mentioned above as being Popper's, in *Conjectures and Refutations*, pp. 39f. However (as Geach

where there is no empirical test for truth or falsehood, there is no support for a claim that a thing exists.[47] But Cross asserts it does.

An important consequence of this is that where a proposal is made which falls under this criticism, there is no (extension) reference between the statement containing the proposal and the alleged referent (i.e. Cross's alleged cultic formula). This is fatal for Cross's proposal, because he requires reference since it is the link between MT *yhwh* and its origin. Namely, Cross requires the cultic formula, as an empirical entity, as the genetic source of MT *yhwh*, yet the formula is an hypothetical construct without any extant attachable observation statements. Hence, he does not succeed in referring to that which he postulates as the source of *yhwh*. The 'referent' is a pseudological fiction.[48] (These remarks, suitably stated, also apply to the derivations Cross associates with the Amorite, Ugaritic and MT links.) Cross might argue that at some future time *t*, he expects it to be found, and so projectively observation statements will exist, which is often an Albrightian type of response to a more traditional presentation of objections like some of the above criticisms. However, he is no nearer to his assertion's truth on this response. For that concedes there is no present actual ground to support the proposal, except by the future which does not exist for one to refer to it;[49] and the possible future discovery equally furnishes the possibility of truth *or* falsehood as a property[50] of Cross's proposal. And since there is no present empirical observation statement to describe the 'referent' there is logically a nil probability to be affixed[51] to quantify Cross's proposal. Therefore an assurance of expected substantiation is literally worth nothing. This is not to say, that – as a piece of imagination, in a re-presented form – such a suggestion might not have some interesting features; however, too often they are

---

mentioned to me), Popper has confusedly said that (cf. *Conjectures and Refutations*, p. 40) Wittgenstein proposed verification in the *Tractatus*; in fact, he never uses the term or the thesis there.

[47] Imagination and intuition are not being objected to here; but, rather, that the grounds for testing them should be empirical description and not their 'fact' of existence.

[48] Such a referent is an hypostatization of a mentalistic item.

[49] For proof of this see S. Haack's *Deviant Logic* in its study of future contingents (pp. 73–90).

[50] For this technical sense of 'property' see K. R. Popper, *Conjectures and Refutations*, pp. 391ff.

[51] cf. K. R. Popper, *Objective Knowledge*, p. 59; and for some formal background, his *Conjectures and Refutations*, pp. 58–65, and pp. 59–60 note 25.

offered as evident truths with a (seeming) derivation from evidence. Also, as with Cross,[52] such procedures are frequently supposed to guarantee the veracity of a 'fact', which is then subsequently articulated as an antecedent, together with similar sets of conjecture, to infer (falsely) further conclusions of a generalized type.

(b)   After I had applied the notion of hypostatization to substantive expressions and predicates in some scholars' treatments, Barr observed[53] that hypostatization might be involved with a whole sentence. If Cross's cultic formula is admitted to be a sentence (of an unusual form), it would constitute a (somewhat untypical) example of sentence hypostatization, drawn into focus by a misuse of MT *yhwh*.

Even when there are textual referents to which an hypothesis refers, inexact specification of the data's relations, and scant attention to the limitations concerning what information reference can consistently be used to impart about a referent, can generate weak or faulty analysis. A case of weak analysis is furnished by a piece of J. J. M. Roberts's work.[54] After this, I come to an example of faulty analysis produced by G. R. Driver and mentioned by Barr.[55]

(c)   A. R. Millard[56] has argued that Roberts's study of the 'earliest Semitic pantheon' has (even allowing for the incomplete spread of pertinent texts available and the obscurity of some contexts for extant texts) certain investigative limitations, though it contains valuable information. In an example with which Millard does not deal, Roberts has an entry for the Sargonic *Iši-Rašap* (which Roberts translates '*Rašap*-Went-Forth'). His entry reads:[57]

Rašap is a *pars* or *paras* formation from a root unattested in

[52] F. M. Cross, *Canaanite Myth and Hebrew Epic*, pp. 44ff.

[53] Barr offered the instructive illustration, that someone might argue: a. He fell on the ground; b. He fell on the dust; c. His action is the same in a. and b.; Ergo: ground = dust; which is clearly fallacious at a semantic level. This example is related to the Boman type of argument concerning verb categories, but Barr's point holds generally (see, for example, my analysis of G. R. Driver's use of sentences in disparate texts in his argument for *ṣnḥ*, in sec. 1.3, 2 above).

[54] J. J. M. Roberts, *The Earliest Semitic Pantheon: A Study of the Semitic Deities Attested in Mesopotamia before Ur III* (Baltimore, 1972).

[55] J. Barr, *Comparative Philology*, p. 290.

[56] A. R. Millard's review, *Journal of Semitic Studies*, 19 (1974), 1, pp. 87–90.

[57] J. J. M. Roberts, *The Earliest Semitic Pantheon*, p. 48, entry 61; see also p. 111 n. 397.

Akkadian, but well known in West Semitic, which together with the West Semitic element *iṣi* suggests one is dealing with a West Semitic deity. The name is to be connected etymologically with Middle Hebrew *ršp* and Jewish Aramaic *ršp'*, 'flame'. The plural of the word is used in the Old Testament for flames, but the singular occurs in contexts where it must mean something like pestilence. 'Flame', however, appears to be the original meaning of the root. The meaning pestilence only occurs in passages where at least a trace of mythological flavour is left, which suggests that this meaning is secondarily derived from the character of the West Semitic god Rašap, 'Flame', who was regarded as a god of pestilence. In a list of gods from Ugarit he is identified with the similar Mesopotamian deity Nergal, and the later Greeks identified him with Apollo. The link between Rašap's name 'Flame' and his character as a god of pestilence may very possibly be the high fever which accompanies many epidemic diseases.

I quote the entry in full out of fairness to Roberts, and because one can observe the cumulative use of semantic-empirical associations of a conjectural nature promoted to a factual status. The MT items to which Roberts alludes post-date the Sargonic term, although he assumes a form of causal connection between the two sets: 'etymologically' disguises a diachronic group of data. If Roberts is appealing to a Middle Hebrew term as it is found in MT in the role of an attested instance of a word hyponymic with the Sargonic term, or at least where semantic derivation is producible from some type of overlap between the two, then one requires evidence of in which temporal direction Roberts assumes the reference to go: that is, is Roberts's metalanguage citation of the Sargonic item from its object language assuming that the Sargonic item is prior to the MT uses? Presumably so; yet it is, then, strange of Roberts to adopt this stance, unless 'etymologically' is an incoherent attempt at hypostatizing the total diachronic paradigm of related Semitic morphemes to give a (seeming) account of the meaning of the Sargonic term in the perspective of its alleged (perhaps merely morphological) future history in other Semitic languages.

Of course, Roberts's entry hints at 'a trace of mythological flavour' in the passages in MT[58] from which he culled the meaning

---

[58] MT passages which Roberts cites (*The Earliest Semitic Pantheon*, p. 111,

'pestilence'. Howbeit, this cannot be taken as an obvious embodiment of any Sargonic usage, since the referent is that of *yhwh*. It would present immense difficulties to establish that group of uses as coming from the same source as the Sargonic term, and with the particular semantic locus Roberts alleged, not least because a 'flavour' is hardly a central ingredient of a semantic value. Nor is 'flavour' exactly a precise indicator of some feature; neither is the 'mythological' mien of a term's alleged usage, if present as a strand in a context, an evident guarantee of the presence of other semantic entities, which on occasions might display it. This is especially so when the referents of the deities are distinct and have different and differing descriptions predicated of them when the relevant term is employed – indeed the MT item is not included in a naming epithet of *yhwh*, nor linked with the name, while the Sargonic use only occurs in such a naming position. I am not claiming that there is no indirect diachronic relation between Sargonic and MT items; it is my contention that, rather, given the variables contingent on such a relation, if these variables are not carefully made explicit, so that material and functions can be related, and separated, there is no useful semantic conclusion to be extracted from analysis. The relative paucity of relevant material from the pre-Ur III period has little to do with Roberts's weakness, which is produced from neglect of the direction of reference and its implications, together with the restricting functions of reference to distinct levels of linguistic activity. Hypostatization of diachronic sequences[59] has resulted in a confused merger of separate linguistic levels through measurement of the semantic value of the Sargonic item by assessment of its (supposed) future history, which is a backward causality unwarranted by the history of language.

The qualifications Roberts subsumes in the conclusions constitute at least one example of the *secundum quid*[60] fallacy.

---

n. 398) are Hab. 3:5 and Deut. 32:24. The Ugaritic data in Roberts's thesis can be criticized in a similar way to his MT remarks.

[59] Implication and consequence are operations which are specially prone to misuse in diachronic semantics: see J. Lyons, *Structural Semantics*, pp. 117ff., etc., and H. M. Hoenigswald's review of this work, *Journal of Linguistics*, 1 (1965), pp. 191–6; also, J. Lyons, *Introduction to Theoretical Linguistics*, pp. 90–1. For theory which might be applied to Roberts's subject see H. M. Hoenigswald's significant treatise *Studies in Formal Historical Linguistics*, Formal Linguistic Series 3 (Dordrecht, 1973).

[60] Not to be confused with the accident fallacy; for an account of *secundum quid*, see C. J. Hamblin, *Fallacies*, pp. 28ff., 208–13, and L. M. de Rijk, *Logica Modernorum* (Assen, 1962–7), vol. 2, pt. 2, p. 580.

That is to say, he excluded appropriate qualifications from
regulating his conclusions (though, in some form, they are present
in data or interpretation), when due account of them would
restrict his power to generalize conclusions from predicable items
associated with subject terms; an example is his statement 'The
meaning pestilence only occurs in passages where at least a trace
of mythological flavour is left, *which suggests that this meaning is*
secondarily *derived from the character* of the West Semitic god
Rašap, 'Flame' who was regarded as a god of pestilence.' (my
italics).[61] If the passages to which Roberts referred are the MT
texts (which are documented prior to his remark), then his point
as it stands is false: the use of a noun in a type of context[62] associated with a referring term m does not at all 'suggest' (imply or
require) that the meaning of the noun is in any way at all 'derived'
from the alleged character associated with the referent of another
referring term n, the contradictory of which involves committing
the referential and etymological fallacies, displaying a category
error.[63]

Roberts could be assuming that MT *rašap* is a late phase in a
semantic ancestral chain of *ršp* whose component links are semantically symmetrical respecting this value; but this would be mere
metaphysics, not diachronic semantics. Also, the one Ugaritic
text to which Roberts refers (in a footnote)[64] has been carefully
differentiated from the required 'mythological' sense,[65] and
Driver[66] renders *rašap* there as a common noun, not PN (I will
often employ 'PN' abbreviating 'proper name'). Further, the Ebla
texts,[67] as characterized by G. Pettinato, have *Rasap* in paleo-
Canaanite and in Sumerian contexts as a PN, which shows that

[61] J. J. M. Roberts, *The Earliest Semitic Pantheon*, p. 48 entry 61. I am not of
course assuming that Roberts's manipulation is intentional, but generated from
patterns and habits of thinking about data.

[62] Even 'mythological' is prescriptive, not descriptive, cf. J. C. L. Gibson,
'Myth, Legend and Folklore in the Ugarit Keret Aqhat Texts', *Vetus Testamentum*, supps., Congress Vol., 1974 (1975), pp. 60–8.

[63] This is an analogue of the root fallacy in PN dress.

[64] J. J. M. Roberts, *The Earliest Semitic Pantheon*, p. 111, n. 399; i.e. Keret, I, *i*,
lines 15–19: *rsp*[.]*mtdt.ǧlm*.

[65] See J. C. L. Gibson, 'Myth, Legend and Folklore'.

[66] G. R. Driver, *Canaanite Myths and Legends*, p. 29.

[67] i.e. TM.75.G.2000 and TM.75.G.2238 respectively. The former in a bilingual list links the PN with Nergal, so perhaps mitigating the occurrence of *s*,
but not *š* of MT texts in Pettinato's transliteration (cf. G. Pettinato, 'The Royal
Archives of Tell-Mardikh-Ebla', *Biblical Archaeologist*, 39 (1976), 2, pp. 49–50).
Of course, in any case the Ugaritic term, if taken as a PN, is still ossified and much
earlier than Middle Hebrew, so semantic symmetry cannot be assumed.

this PN, long prior to Middle Hebrew, had been, as a PN, ossified. So it is unsound and tenuous to presume uniform semantic history for an item which is ossified and has homonyms or polysemes.

Moreover, Roberts's own indication of data reflects a diachronic gap somewhere in our knowledge of possible relations between '*Iṣi-Rašap*' and an (hypothetical) proper name '*Rašap*' in Keret I because he mentioned (in the foregoing quotation) that '*iṣi*' is a West Semitic element which is a component of the proper name. So '*Iṣi-Rašap*' not the allegedly attested '*Rašap*', is (in Robert's repressed premiss) the first point of referential contact and source in West Semitic for which one should look. It requires additional reconstruction to induce a link between this West Semitic name '*Iṣi-Rašap*' and a proposed '*Rašap*' in Keret I, a point of which Roberts makes no mention. Accordingly, this diachronic gap, which would actually be a stage in the transmission of (the meta-linguistic) reference from the Sargonic item, to West Semitic provenance of it, to Ugaritic Keret I, is obliterated by Roberts making a direct connection with the Ugaritic Keret I text. So to the error of a reference which adverts to the future (supposed) history of an item instead of its past (inversion of reference), one should add Roberts's omission of the diachronic gap,[68] which, if excluded, enables a case to appear stronger than it is. Such a diachronic gap suppressed in a purported[69] reference, I term a referential gap. Of course, where in fact there is such a gap, there is reference failure, which is fatal for Roberts's presentation of his case.

(*d*) Many of the above cases of confusion postdate Barr's *Semantics* by a decade or more; it is possible that the reforms in procedure and analysis which Barr's criticisms demand have not been fully appreciated or implemented. This may also be due in some degree to the need for further exposure of the depth and nature of the confusions, as portrayed in a logico-linguistic context. It is evident from the foregoing that logic supports Barr's scrutiny of errors. Nevertheless, such a truth can be used to infer that the

[68] One might not be able to fill a diachronic gap with evidence; my point is that the fact of this analytical gap should be acknowledged; where it is smudged, impossible conclusions 'can' be drawn, and so its acknowledgement is of central importance. I do not suggest that this is conscious rigging by Roberts; but the fact of its being unconscious results in its being all the more pervasive, rather like a metaphor running out of control taking its 'user' with it when he thinks he is using it.

[69] 'Purported' is here employed strictly, as in D. Bostock, *Logic and Arithmetic* (Oxford, 1974), p. 54.

study of meaning, if strictly linguistic, is strictly logical, which point Barr[70] may have appeared to have countered: 'The approach to the study of meaning must be strictly linguistic, rather than logical, in character.' Clearly, Barr has used the term 'logical' rather generally as is indicated by the use of 'character', although on the same page he wrote of 'conceptions of a logical rather than a linguistic nature'. Fortunately Barr illustrates his intended use by an instance (which he regards as an extreme case) from Driver's[71] philological analysis of *ntr*. Driver supposed that *ntr* means 'tear' (rend), but that the *piel* is used of insects meaning 'hopping', and relates this to Arabic *tarra* meaning 'be severed' and *tarr* 'prancing, trotting'. Driver stated:

> There can be no objection to connecting *n-t-r* as applied to locusts with *tarr* as applied to light horses; and the underlying idea by which verbs of rending or tearing asunder are linked to verbs denoting trotting quickly or prancing or hopping seems to be that of separation from the ground, whereby the beast appears to be now touching the earth and now suspended in mid-air.[72]

Barr remarks on the morphological presuppositions on which Driver's type of treatment rests, and consequently observes that 'the procedure is logical rather than linguistic in type because it works by consideration of common features in the referents rather than by working out a process of meaning transfer within stages of linguistic usage'.[73] Barr has agreed that his use of the term 'logical' is too general and was written in ignorance of post-Frege developments in logic. For 'logical' the term 'pseudological' might more aptly be employed, being restricted to some of traditional logic's distinctions. This is not to consign traditional logic to be pseudologic, but so to label the misguided application of it

[70] J. Barr, *Comparative Philology*, p. 290, and see p. 126, n. 1.

[71] G. R. Driver, 'Difficult Words in the Hebrew Prophets', in H. H. Rowley (ed.), *Studies in Old Testament Prophecy*, T. H. Robinson Festschrift (Edinburgh, 1950), pp. 52–72. It is possible that in the foregoing quotation from J. J. M. Roberts from *The Earliest Semitic Pantheon* (p. 48) in the last sentence, 'The link between Rašap's name and "Flame" and his character as a god of pestilence may possibly be the high fever which accompanies many epidemic diseases', there could be exactly the same type of mistake Barr is criticizing in Driver, where Roberts is shifting an argument over the referent of the name and drafting in a semantic value which depicts an alleged situation adjacent to the referent not prescribed in the predicative function of textual predicates.

[72] G. R. Driver, 'Difficult Words in the Hebrew Prophets', pp. 70ff.

[73] J. Barr, *Comparative Philology*, p. 290.

(or unwitting adoption of its tenets)[74] to dictate (not describe) linguistic structures and procedures.

The crucial distinction between sense and reference was not clearly formulated until 1892.[75] It is clear from the preceding examinations that some scholars in nonphilosophical spheres still do not appreciate its significance and how it obtains upon and restricts connection in certain circumstances. A traditional confusion of sense and reference occurs, as I have indicated, in the employment of 'denote' (and Geach has shown that this is a common situation in a number of subjects)[76] which tends to echo the pre-Frege confusion. Driver used 'denoting' in the foregoing quotation to structure a link with verbs and actions (not descriptions of actions – which are the verbs themselves). Here Driver falls into the same type of error as Boman did (see 2.1, 2 above), but also the error, like Roberts,[77] of taking empirical states associated with a referent which is attached to the referring term as evidence of what a predicate means. Of course, where the semantic value of the predicate is a description of that empirical state, this is legitimate. Yet where the value of a predicate-function is unknown (or seemingly known, yet disputed by a controversial proposal) the sum of possible predicables is larger than the actual predicate; so there is room for massive error. Particularly is this the case when terms are ascribed (referring) roles (e.g. verbs) – which they do not and cannot have; this will tend to mask misdescription.

However, Driver's sharpness implemented a shade of metaphysical grammar[78] to combat the lack of actual connection

---

[74] For aspects of this adoption discussed see G. E. M. Anscombe and P. T. Geach, *Three Philosophers* (Oxford, 1961), pp. 5–63 and 131–62; P. T. Geach, *God and the Soul* (London, 1969), pp. 42–64. cf. also the interesting question of the possible Oriental influences on traditional logic via translation and its modification on some doctrinal points subsequently, in summary form: A. H. Basson and D. J. O'Connor, 'Language and Philosophy: Some Suggestions for an Empirical Approach', *Philosophy*, 22 (1947), pp. 52ff.; N. Rescher, *Studies in Arabic Philosophy* (Pittsburgh, 1966).

[75] By G. Frege, 'Sinn und Bedeutung', in Geach and Black, *Translations*.

[76] P. T. Geach, *Reference and Generality*, pp. 1–107; cf. the Egyptologist A. H. Gardiner (*The Theory of Speech and Language* (Oxford, 1932), pp. 57–60, etc.) who showed considerable vexation when attempting to tackle the sense and reference distinction without the device and explanation produced by Frege. Gardiner offered a rather painful half-formed explanation using denotation (although he mentioned (p. vii) that Bertrand Russell had read the book manuscript, Gardiner appears to have had no knowledge of Russell's or Frege's views about reference). I conjecture this distorts his treatment of Egyptian grammar.

[77] J. J. M. Roberts, *The Earliest Semitic Pantheon*, p. 48.

[78] For exposition of this expression see L. Wittgenstein, *Zettel*, sec. 55, etc.;

between 'rending', 'tearing' and 'trotting', 'prancing', 'hopping'
which his distortion produced. He did this when he specified 'the
underlying idea by which verbs' in these categories are 'linked'.[79]
Here although Driver expressed the notion as an 'idea', yet he
employs the term to indicate an empirical series of positions.
Therefore Driver constricts the notion of a term's function by
ascribing 'denoting' to it, which is supported by an appeal to a
non-functional[80] phenomenon – metaphysical ideas (dual meanings?) whose role is to structure and warrant extra-linguistic
entities as though they are mirrored at a semantic level. Such
entities consequently relate to an empirical action or position
(which Driver does not make the semantic value, e.g. of 'rending'
or 'trotting'), from which the semantic value (e.g. trotting) is
supposed to be derived. These features (of denoting, metaphysical
postulate, empirical analogue) produce a meaning, as Barr showed,[81]
quite irrelevant to the value in textual usage of the terms. Driver's
technique ignores: (1) the range of consistent possible content
derivable from a predicable (or subset of it) is strictly equivalent to
its actual semantic range in use as a textual predicate in the set of
literatures which is the object language of investigation; (2) texts
in languages other than the object language can be deemed as
constituents of the object language if and only if there is quotation
in the latter from those texts (and here quotation involving predicate items), and articulating criteria which restrict generalization
in an appropriate way and preserve distinct levels.

It is clearly arguable that some scholars' analyses of biblical and
Semitic languages embody some confusions which are reflected
in traditional logic and its application to language, although explicit use of that logic (e.g. proof syllogism) is very rare. Indeed
in contexts where some logic might have been explicit, certain
biblical scholars have exhibited an abysmal lack of interest in or
use of it,[82] or in making explicit the presuppositions they have.
Logicians[83] have shown that traditional logic has done damage to
philosophy and theology in some areas; indirectly, confusions
from the legacy of traditional logic may have influenced the study

---

Remarks on the Foundations of Mathematics, p. 23; *Philosophical Grammar*,
sec. 112; *Philosophical Investigations*, sec. 97f., 371–3, 572; cf. P. M. S. Hacker's
account which lifts out relevant principles, *Insight and Illusion*, chapter VI.

[79] G. R. Driver, 'Difficult Words in the Hebrew Prophets', p. 70.

[80] By 'non-functional', I intend absence of linguistic function.

[81] J. Barr, *Comparative Philology*, p. 290, and references on p. 331.

[82] See D. W. Kemmler, *Faith and Human Reason*.

[83] e.g. Y. Bar-Hillel, *Aspects of Language* (Jerusalem, 1970), pp. 98–9, etc.;
P. T. Geach, *Logic Matters*, pp. 289–301, 318–27.

of ancient Near Eastern languages.[84] Nor has such influence certainly ceased, not least owing to the above examples which postdate Barr's *Semantics*. Geach has noticed[85] and argued against Chomsky[86] that some of the confused parts of traditional logic have been unwittingly smuggled into recent linguistic theory (e.g. Chomsky's analysis of referring phrases (i.e. noun phrases), substitution and quantification). It is not surprising, then, to discover that J. W. M. Verhaar[87] has unearthed systematic mistakes and ill-formed[88] hybrids in respect of some contemporary theologians' usage of linguistics, philosophy and logic. Apart from this, as Geach[89] has pointed out, traditional logic of the sixteenth to twentieth centuries contained some deep, subtle distortions which have been passed over at a general level to the learned public of those centuries – and still is, in some Colleges of Unreason.[90] These institutions substantially influenced the teaching and research of languages, and would and still could regulate some scholars (especially in subjects and/or norms entrenched in a classical tradition) in their assumption of what it is to be logical and how (psuedo)logic pertains to language. This appears to be true of biblical studies.

(*e*)   The absence of an explicit use of logic does not entail inability to apply logic to assess presence or absence of consistency. A recurrent phenomenon in M. Dahood's discourses is the presence

[84] cf. A. H. Gardiner, *The Theory of Speech and Language*, pp. 273ff.; N. Rescher, *Studies in Arabic Philosophy* (Pittsburgh, 1966); W. F. Albright, 'Neglected Factors in the Greek Intellectual Revolution', *Proceedings of the American Philosophical Society*, vol. 116 (1972), pp. 225–42; J. Barr, *The Semantics of Biblical Language*, pp. 64ff.

[85] P. T. Geach, *Logic Matters*, pp. 6, 44f., 54, 66, 116 esp.

[86] N. Chomsky and P. T. Geach in debate in *Educational Review*, 22 (1969), 1, pp. 5–25: 'The state of language': 'Should traditional grammar be ended or mended?' (ed. A. Wilkinson).

[87] J. W. M. Verhaar, 'Some Notes on Language and Theology', *Bijdragen: Tijdschrift voor Filosofie en Theologie*, 30 (1969) 1, pp. 39–65.

[88] I employ 'ill-formed' in the sense used in logic, meaning 'not consistently expressed'.

[89] In discussion, which I here gratefully acknowledge, and for helpful correspondence.

[90] 'Colleges of Unreason' is a Geachian term: see P. T. Geach, *Logic Matters*, pp. 6, 54 and 70, which precisely relates to his programmatic distinction between some traditional and mathematical logics. Chomsky has not seen fit to take up most of Geach's criticisms on this line of demarcation and its critical import for some of Chomsky's attitude towards the synthesis of traditional logic and his work; but see generally his responses to Quine, in N. Chomsky, *Reflections on Language*, pp. 179–250.

of illogical treatment of proposals, particularly when reference to texts is involved. Many of his notices of innovatory suggestions are short, but his choice of this presentation is not a brief for neglect of reason. In a short study on causal *b* in Nahum 3:4 Dahood[91] commits a modal fallacy (i.e. where a possible conclusion is stated as an actual conclusion).[92] Dahood's article commences:

> Though causal *min* (*AV* 'of'; *NEB* 'for') has long been identified in *mrb* ('multitude') of Nah. 3:4a, the causal force of the two *beths* in the second half of the verse remains to be pointed out. This recognition leads to a new etymology for unexplained *hmkrt* ('selleth') . . .[93]
> The causal meaning of the preposition in *mrb* suggests that *b* in *bznwnyh* ('through her whoredoms') and *bkšpyh* ('through her witchcrafts') carries a similar significance, much like the parallelism of these causal prepositions in Isa. 28:7a and Ps. 6:8.[94]

The article[95] (which *concludes* twenty lines or so after the end of this quotation) furnishes three other MT parallels, which illustrate Dahood's point *if* the point is true (while the remainder of the article turns to explain the proposed root *nkr*). The conditional 'if' it is excluded by a modal shift.[96]

First Dahood introduces an admission that the causal force of the two *beths* has yet to be 'pointed out'. (Perhaps this is an authoritarian euphemism for 'needs to be proved', or ought so to be designated?) Second, Dahood presumes an inference by the mere fact of recognizing the existence of his opinion as fact (i.e. the 'fact' of causal force in the two *beths*). That is to say, Dahood presents possibility as actuality: his supposition is expressible in the form 'If there are two *beths* in φ-type expressions,

---

[91] M. Dahood, 'Causal *Beth* and the Root NKR in Nahum 3:4', *Biblica*, 52 (1971), pp. 395–6.

[92] For exposition of this see P. T. Geach, *Logic Matters*, pp. 155–6; S. Haack, *Deviant Logic*, pp. 78–80. Dahood's mistake may also be interpreted so as to fall under the classification of the Boethian fallacy of different modality, whereby the distinction between potentiality and actuality is confused: see C. L. Hamblin's discussion in *Fallacies*, pp. 211ff., etc.

[93] Here Dahood quotes the relevant verses.

[94] cf. M. Dahood, *Psalms I* (New York, 1966), p. 38. This citation Dahood provides in the above quotation.

[95] M. Dahood, 'Causal *Beth* and the Root NKR in Nahum 3:4', p. 395.

[96] On how the shift might be consistently achieved, see J. Hintikka, *Knowledge and Belief* (Ithaca, 1962), pp. 16ff.

and Dahood believes *beths* in φ to be causal, then *beths* in φ are causal'. Since such a characterization renders the disguised – apparently secure – credentials in Dahood's treatment explicit, it may come as a shock to advocates of Dahood who may find it difficult to credit Dahood with this extremely naive mistake. However, Wittgenstein[97] has shown to what extent the bewitched language bewitches thought and analysis. The foregoing characterization unpacks the components in Dahood's rhetoric[98] which are held out of sight by Dahood's literary style. Dahood quite evidently processes data by the canon of polemical and mentalistic semantics of his own literary style which is attended by a tendency to subjectivism.[99] No doubt much of this is habitual, and the modal upgrading is probably an unconscious marking up of hypotheses to theories.[100]

It might be noticed also that Dahood employs an Ugaritic illustration to support his contention, which is *bm nsq whr bḥbq ḥmḥmt* – 'From kissing there is conception, from embracing, pregnancy'.[101] Dahood obtained this example from Gordon,[102] and referred to Gordon's description of Ugaritic *b* as evidence, where the above expression is cited. In Gordon's section on *b* (§10.5) he is concerned to show that 'from' is central and normal for this class of *b* usages; only in the last sentence does Gordon offer the observation (with the above illustration) that *b* has a causal sense. However, first, it is clear that even in this illustration

[97] I employ 'bewitched' here as a term of art, from L. Wittgenstein, *Philosophical Investigations*, sec. 109ff.

[98] 'Rhetoric' is employed in the classical sense (cf. E. M. Cope, *An Introduction to Aristotle's Rhetoric* (London, 1867), pp. 4f.). Perhaps Dahood is to be compared with Isocrates, not Aristotle in use of rhetoric.

[99] For 'mentalistic semantics' see W. V. O. Quine's 'Mind and Verbal Dispositions', in S. Guttenplan (ed.), *Mind and Language* (Oxford, 1975), pp. 83–95. I do not agree with the theory of mentalistic semantics (neither does Quine), but use it here to indicate the type of approach which might portray Dahood's use of language from an internal standpoint. One aspect of his style is a tendency to psychologize objective states (e.g. his employment of 'This recognition . . .' above), and its being substituted for the task of proving the causal *beths* as premisses for recognition of that 'fact'. Here the psychologization produces distortion which invokes a subjectivist assessment (perception is deemed the ingredient which is the discovery procedure for truth, not analysis).

[100] For the hypothesis/theory distinction, cf. S. Amsterdamski, *Between Experience and Metaphysics* (Dordrecht, 1975).

[101] C. H. Gordon, *Ugaritic Textbook* (Rome, 1967), p. 96; cf. M. Dahood, 'Causal *Beth* and the Root NKR in Nahum 3:4', p. 396.

[102] See the fairly unchanged original form of Gordon's formulation in *Ugaritic Grammar* (Rome, 1940), pp. 68ff.

bm and *bḫbq* could (I do not say should) take the value 'from' rather than an explicit causal 'for' or 'because', as indeed Gordon's translation exhibits. Given this, the metaphoric expression can be construed as a 'source' (less probably, instrumental) use within the range of the value 'from'. Barr[103] has observed that previously there has been misuse of Ugaritic data in applying its *b* to Hebrew, since Ugaritic has no *mn*. Such a fact indicates that the antonymic structure, tensions and possible choices in Ugaritic were different from those of Hebrew. So to offer an illustration[104] as proof, in view of features in semantic fields which are asymmetrical, is working from a contrary premiss. Further, even accepting that the Ugaritic *b* does possess the causal value, Gordon's positioning of it in his treatment and its distribution in texts implies that the 'causal *b*' is not a central, normal value of the function *b*. To this is to be conjoined the point that biblical Hebrew, hitherto, has known of no relevant category of causal sense of *b*, but rather source and instrumental,[105] etc.

These phenomena advertise the danger of assertively (from either Ugaritic or Hebrew standpoints) ascribing an Ugaritic causal sense residing in an illustration as proof of a Hebrew use in a distinct semantic field, because for both fields such a value is fairly rare and untypical of central normalcy paradigms. Someone might claim Dahood's conclusion is reconstructible in terms of another analysis. I do not dispute this; I argue against what he has offered, not what might be produced, and readily admit that certain diachronic phases[106] and semantic fields in Ugaritic and Hebrew can be related in an appropriate way.

Dahood's use of 'recognition' obscures weaknesses in his illustrations. He purported to treat of actual relations between languages, whereas actually they are possible yet improbable ones.[107] Within biblical Hebrew, his evidence is actually a set of

---

[103] J. Barr, *Comparative Philology*, pp. 175–7; here Barr is dealing with an error of Dahood's, which falls into a similar category to the one with which I deal, although his example is to do with texts and items distinct from my own.

[104] An illustration which, if used for semantic purposes and yet has no relevant semantic supporting evidence, is an instance of the morphological/semantic confusion mentioned earlier.

[105] It is a recurrent confusion in language studies to conflate instrumental and causal at a conceptual level by not noting the asymmetry of cause and effect in respect of the two (cf. G. H. von Wright, *Explanation and Understanding* (London, 1971)).

[106] See J. F. A. Sawyer, *Semantics in Biblical Research*, p. 92.

[107] J. Barr demonstrates Dahood's confusion about probability and actuality over another case of *b* (see *Comparative Philology*, pp. 176–7).

alleged illustrations which he injects with the conclusion which requires proof, seeming by such appeal to prove his conclusion, although some of Dahood's opinions have great merit.

1 Mental Elements in Reference?

It is not uncommon to discover linguistic phenomena unguardedly psychologized: Ullendorff[1] wrote 'it is my intention to shew that the modes of thought in the Hebrew Bible are often very different from what they are commonly assumed to be . . .' Ullendorff cited Lev. 19:18 *w'hbt lr'k kmwk* ('thou shalt love thy neighbour as thyself' AV), and asked if this translation does 'translate the language and the thought of this verse accurately'. The use of 'of this' in the latter quotation appears to impute a psychological property to the sentence, although Ullendorff is obviously aware of differences in thought and language.[2] Ullendorff argued that AV and other translations follow the wrong LXX *seauton* rendering for *kmwk*, since the Hebrew text has neither reflexive pronoun nor accusative, and because, he assumed, translators have failed to appreciate a Semitic brachylogy which omits *ky*: 'thou shalt love thy neighbour, for he is as thou'.[3] I do not see that there is anything in Ullendorff's treatment which latches on to the thought categories which are his subject. His remarks about mental and linguistic entities are placed in apposition,[4] so one cannot rightly consider his use of 'thought' as a metaphor for linguistic phenomena in isolation from mental elements. Further, he employed (implicitly) the notion of linguistic choice[5] as a criterion of identification for the categories, including the absence of reflexive and accusative. Ullendorff additionally observed that in the use of the

---

[1] E. Ullendorff, 'Thought Categories in the Hebrew Bible', in R. Loewe (ed.), *Studies in Rationalism, Judaism and Universalism: in Memory of Leon Roth* (London, 1966), p. 276.

[2] *ibid.*, pp. 274, 278: 'And this latter interpretation is not only demanded by the language of the Old Testament, but also by the thought of the Hebrew Bible.' Unfortunately, although Ullendorff's subject is this set of categories he nowhere offers even a hint of how his use of 'thought' is related to language.

[3] *ibid.*, p. 276, and p. 277 for the phrase in Lev. 19:34.

[4] *ibid.*, p. 278.

[5] cf. J. Lyons's account of choice (*Introduction to Theoretical Linguistics*, pp. 213–37). I find the exposition of the thesis intuitively attached to *choice* obscure in many such accounts, though of value; nor, although helpful, is M. A. K. Halliday's more systematic, albeit individualist, framework entirely convincing (see, e.g., his *Explorations in the Functions of Language* (London, 1974); *Categories of the Theory of Grammar* (Indianapolis, 1972) (reprinted from *Word*, 17 (Dec. 1961), No. 3)).

verb *'hb* in Lev. 19:18 and 34, where the accusative *'t* is absent, *l* occurs to introduce the indirect, rather than direct, object. These are grammatical, not psychological, features. Of course, Ullendorff is not naively striking an identity equation between thought and language; yet he has taken indicators of linguistic features as transparent indicators of thought, to the extent of describing them as illustrative of 'modes of thought in the Hebrew Bible'.[6] If one were to attempt a reconstruction of his thesis, or acceptance of it as it stands, then there are substantial problems opposing the formulation of how a link is to be made with linguistic and psychological items, given Ullendorff's abstraction of grammatical items. While Ullendorff looks with favour on the change generated by Barr's *The Semantics of Biblical Language* and later work, in the foregoing illustration Ullendorff appears to fall foul of those very psychologizing tendencies which Barr exposed. This may not be an uncommon situation.[7]

It is of help to notice Ullendorff's introduction of a brachylogy; he does not offer a proof for its application to indicate an absent *ky*, but merely remarks on a failure of perception on the part of other scholars to appreciate its role. P. T. Geach[8] has shown that the employment of an argument with a brachylogy as one of its items involves some vexing difficulties, which Ullendorff ignored. First, to set up a link of intention with language entails an epistemic move: a belief about the relation of a mental state or event to the semantic values of a text is injected (i.e. Ullendorff's contention that a particular mode of thought is reflected in Lev. 19:18). All Ullendorff offers in support of his view is a series of linguistic possibilities which themselves rest on epistemic conjectures, which in turn are not self-evidently true and require proof – although they are offered as proof. Second, to promote a possibility to an actual feature of a text involves a modal fallacy.

[6] E. Ullendorff, 'Thought Categories in the Hebrew Bible', p. 276. Perhaps Ullendorff's examples, being like the above case, illustrate the type of mistaken conflation Barr was examining in *The Semantics of Biblical Language* (e.g. p. 265), although his criticisms were in a context of contrast.

[7] Of course, as Barr's citation of Ullendorff's earlier studies portrays (cf. *The Semantics of Biblical Language*, e.g. p. 101, note 5), the above error is not typical of all his work. Ullendorff is here mentioned in the context of a scholar who, although he writes on Hebrew, has wider linguistics interests, so I acknowledge that he is not quite a typical Hebraist; but his influence and his publications on Hebrew render him an appropriate case.

[8] P. T. Geach, 'The Perils of Pauline', *Review of Metaphysics*, 23 (1969), 2, p. 296 and in *Logic Matters*, pp. 153–65; cf. also from a different standpoint J. Hintikka *The Intentions of Intentionality and Other New Models for Modalities* (Dordrecht, 1975), pp. 43–75, etc.

Third, G. E. M. Anscombe has demonstrated that there is no obvious symmetry between the usage of direct/indirect objects as grammatical categories in a context of language, mind and psychological phenomena; but, rather, an intricate asymmetry, especially in contexts where brachylogy is ignored or alleged, because of the complexity in the relation of intention to language.[9] It is important in enforcing this third point to emphasize that Ullendorff has presented his assertion in the perspective of a description of psychological propensities ('thought categories') as though grammar were a mirror of mental reality, and style a marker of psychological emphasis.[10] In such a position grammar and style become criteria of an author's (semantic) intentions, which is roughly parallel to the error of dictating morphology and syntax as criteria of meaning.[11]

Except for subject terms which refer to the writer of a text, strictly, language does not refer to the mind.[12] The mind has an affinity with language which is proportionate to the efficiency of a writer and his linguistic medium. False description of the phenomena of mind and language produces interface noise at a descriptive level; where this interface noise obscures levels and relations the description ceases to characterize the phenomena. Particularly is this the case when the interface noise is a systematic (perhaps unconscious) injection of distorted assumptions and/or unwarranted universalization over disparate domains. The incoherent dualist hypothesis of meaning, which is often held in such a confused programme, can disguise the interface noise by deeming what is actually a non-semantic feature as a psycho-semantic item (although many linguistic functions do not house psycholinguistic information); 2.0 and 2.1 exhibit criticism of family-related theses where levels are mixed and interface noise has disguised confusion

[9] G. E. M. Anscombe, 'The Intentionality of Sensation: A Grammatical Feature', in R. J. Butler (ed.), *Analytical Philosophy* (2nd ser., Oxford, 1965), pp. 158–80.

[10] Nevertheless, I fully agree with T. Muraoka when he stated 'I am equally convinced that any attempt that does not positively evaluate and take into account the inner psychological aspects of emphasis is inevitably doomed to failure . . .', in *Emphasis in Biblical Hebrew*, p. iii.

[11] Of course, the theoretical basis for such confusions has a lengthy history, and has often resulted from overstatement of legitimate insights; for example, William of Ockham's universalization of Latin grammar as a model for mental language. P. T. Geach (*Mental Acts*, pp. 101–6), among others, has outlined the characteristic mistakes involved in the overdevelopment of the analogical relations between language and mind.

[12] The exception covers those expressions whose referents are themselves psychological.

as consistency. All these propensities obtain in a strand of form criticism where a text is employed to postulate the mental process which produced it,[13] in that linguistic scholarly customs are absorbed at a literary level and collectively generalized.

2   Semantic Intentions

(a)   G. M. Tucker[14] stated that form criticism is 'a means of identifying the genres of that literature, their structures, intentions'. Sometimes 'intentions' is employed loosely in such contexts; more often, there is a continual shift backwards and forwards to its literal and metaphoric usage – which generates equivocation. Tucker adds 'The term *intention* has been chosen here in preference to 'function' because it is both easier and more relevant to determine the effect which was intended than that actually accomplished.'[15] Surely this is entirely false. We can read a text to determine its function, yet also labour under the disability of dealing with a dead language whose psychological antecedents and world views no longer exist. It is a subtle task to make true statements about people's intentions[16] because mental states and causality are more remote from public view than the functions of a text's values; thus it is easier to determine the function and effect of a text than to measure intention and intended effects. In fact to argue as Tucker does is not only a misunderstanding about the nature of intention but opposes the conclusions of the pioneering work on intention by G. E. M. Anscombe.[17]

Tucker generates confusion at points by his conflating intentional expressions with 'the intention' he ascribes to a text. He abstracts[18] an intentional expression and promotes it to being the intention for the sentence in which it occurs. For example he

[13] cf. J. Barr, *The Bible in the Modern World*, p. 64 note 7. I do not here necessarily include the recent more critical form criticism developed by e.g. W. Richter in *Exegese als Literaturwissenschaft* (Göttingen, 1971).

[14] G. M. Tucker, *Form Criticism of the Old Testament* (Philadelphia, 1971), p. 1; and see G. M. Tucker and R. Knierim, *The Interpreter's Handbook of Old Testament Form Criticism* (Philadelphia, 1975); K. Koch, *The Growth of the Biblical Tradition* (London, 1969), pp. 5, 130; and G. von Rad, *Old Testament Theology* (Edinburgh, 1962), pp. 4f.

[15] G. M. Tucker, *Form Criticism of the Old Testament*, p. 17.

[16] cf. G. E. M. Anscombe, *Intention*, pp. 7ff.

[17] *ibid.*

[18] Tucker's abstraction has its corollary in the tendency to hypostatization exemplified in 2.1, *1* above. Form criticism in many respects is the generalization of such functions at a literary level of linguistic operation.

proposes that the opening of Amos 1:1–2 is not merely an intentional historical introduction; he claims that 'the intention is much deeper': 'to establish the concrete historical setting for the historically oriented prophetic words.'[19] Here language is merely psychologized.

No linguist or philosopher has yet produced a theory presenting authoritative criteria for fixing a means of defining the relation of language to mind especially in the role of predicting the content of intention *via* linguistic expression.[20] So it is not obvious how a form critic can achieve such knowledge, despite the confident moves which are customary. I do not here raise issues for a major treatment of form criticism (which is clearly outside the scope of the present study), but, rather, introduce the relevance of the foregoing for one issue at a linguistic level in form criticism.

(*b*) Koch stated of the "Yahwistic" Genesis 12:1–3 and 7, that 'The writer intends to show how this blessing is transformed from a promise into a fact. This does not happen quickly and straightforwardly, but in a thoroughly complicated fashion.'[21] Unfortunately Koch only spares fifteen lines of general comment to explain why he can know of the writer's intention. However he adds the concession that even if Eissfeldt's opinion, of the narrative's being from a distinct older lay source L,[22] is true, his interpretation holds. Yet this is contrary. If Koch's argument specifically proves the existence of a Yahwist intention, then it cannot exist in conjunction with another different intention (marked as an older L source). This is not to oppose the truth that the same data may consistently be employed to produce different conclusions, nor that the same intentions can be in different minds. It is, rather, to maintain that where Koch has supposed that the conjunction of a Yahwist text and his interpretation implies

[19] See G. M. Tucker, *Form Criticism of the Old Testament*, p. 74.

[20] H. P. Grice reflects a standard admission of this fact, in *Intention and Uncertainty* (British Academy Lecture, London, 1971); also, W. V. O. Quine, *Word and Object* (Harvard, 1960), pp. 80–156; C. F. J. Williams, *What is Truth?* (Cambridge, 1976), pp. 74–96; and G. E. M. Anscombe, *Intention* (2nd edn., Oxford, 1963). See also J. Barr, *The Semantics of Biblical Language*, pp. 257–62.

[21] K. Koch, *The Growth of the Biblical Tradition*, p. 130. It is worth noting that here Koch cannot be construed to be employing 'intends' as 'purpose' (which strictly even then would be postulating knowledge of a mental state in the author). Koch ascribes to the author a psychological state which describes a teleological stance in the author's intention to be implemented at a linguistic level. So 'intends' is not a metaphor for what is written, in Koch's usage.

[22] O. Eissfeldt, *Hexateuch-Synopse* (Leipzig, 1922).

Koch's Yahwist intention, such a conjunction cannot itself be placed together with another hypothesis which holds to a distinct L intention, since this downgrades the specificity of the evidence in the text to support different intentions, and so opposes Koch's usage of it as indicator of his thesis. Of course, beyond this objection is the problem of achieving knowledge of an author's intention at all. Nor may Koch object that it is his interpretation which enables him to achieve knowledge of a Yahwist intention, because no objective criteria have been offered for discriminating between those properties of the semantic values of the text which reflect one or another antecedent intention; further, since the number of alleged sources vary, Koch's type of claim is not only a suggestion about the content of an established referent with intention, his claim has to prove that there is such a referent. And it is here that the downgrading of specificity, by conceding the truth of Eissfeldt's L, produces identity difficulties.[23]

3   Intention and Hypostatization

(a)   From the foregoing it is clear that the identity of an intention is not self-evident in respect of many expressions of it, although this is not to dispute that for a carefully selected class of expressions[24] the description under which a person characterizes himself as acting in fulfilment of an intention can properly advertise intention. However, Anscombe and Jones[25] show that some categories of usage do not fall into this classification. I suggest that the former group can be indicated as intentionalistically transparent, while the latter uses can be marked as intentionalistically opaque. In addition to these two classes, there is at least one other set of uses in literature, which, depending on resolution of problems in analytical treatment, could fall into transparent or opaque categories. Owing to a traditional discussion of them these might hitherto have been ascribed speculatively as having specific

[23] In another context, Koch volunteers similar problems, yet does not apprehend that they oppose his own activity here (cf. his *The Growth of the Biblical Tradition*, p. 119). The problems of identity, identification through reference and description contain a nest of difficulties of which Koch seems unaware, but where philosophers fear to tread for sensitivity over making the mistakes displayed by Koch (e.g. L. Linsky, *Referring* (London, 1967), pp. 67–80).

[24] See G. E. M. Anscombe, *Intention*, pp. 7ff. cf. L. Wittgenstein, *Philosophical Remarks*, sec. 20–24.

[25] See Anscombe, *Intention*, and P. Jones, *Philosophy and the Novel* (Oxford, 1975), pp. 198–9. cf. L. Wittgenstein, *Philosophical Investigations*, sec. 641; cf. 548–91.

intentions associated with them which are, often unwittingly, presented as descriptions of the semantic values which allegedly represent them. I term this hypostatized intention of linguistic phenomena which are themselves hypostatized by scholastic analysis.

Barr's study on hypostatization[26] observed that the standard type of example of this phenomenon (instanced by Bloomfield) 'There is always a *but*' is distinct from another sort of hypostatization popular in theologico-linguistic treatment which 'applies to a word something of the treatment which belongs to realities or really existing relations'. Despite this study, hypostatization still appears regularly in the research literature,[27] even though within that study Barr identified an arena within which confusion could arise. He stated:

> There is a well-known phenomenon of religious hypostatization, which occurs when something like 'the Wisdom of God' or 'the Word of God' comes to be regarded as rather more than a characteristic or an activity of God, as something indeed which may 'come' or 'act' or 'create', for example. Many may wish to regard certain biblical cases of 'the Word' as cases of hypostatization of this kind. This is not hypostatization of a linguistic phenomenon, but hypostatization in the sense of attribution of some kind of independent being to that which might otherwise have been thought of as only the characteristic or the action of another being, and in particular of God.[28]

Barr properly stresses that this second *attributive* hypostatization (as I shall term it, utilizing Barr's description) of 'the Word' is distinct from, albeit related to, the Bloomfield type of example. Unfortunately, some scholars place linguistic phenomena into a category of hypostatization for which there is no warrant. L. Dürr[29] and J. T. Sanders[30] are examples of this approach. Sanders stated:

[26] J. Barr, 'Hypostatization of Linguistic Phenomena in Modern Theological Interpretation', *Journal of Semitic Studies*, VII (1962), 1, pp. 85–6.

[27] See examples in the present section 2.0–2.3 and chapter 4.

[28] J. Barr, 'Hypostatization of Linguistic Phenomena in Modern Theological Interpretation', p. 93.

[29] L. Dürr, *Die Wertung des göttlichen Wortes im Alten Testament und im Antiken Orient* (Mitteilungen der vorderasiatisch-aegyptischen Gesellschaft XLII, I, Leipzig, 1938). For criticisms see A. C. Thiselton, 'The Supposed Power of Words', *Journal of Theological Studies*, 25 (1974), pp. 283–99.

[30] J. T. Sanders, *The New Testament Christological Hymns* (Cambridge, 1971).

Coincident with this hypostatizing process, there comes in
the idea of the word as saviour, as in Ps. 107:20:
He sent forth his word, and healed them,
and delivered them from destruction[31]

Here Sanders assumes some form of hypostatization, but offers
no evidence to support this contention.[32] Perhaps it is obvious
that there is none (partly) because it is the subject 'He' – and
not 'the word' – who 'sent', 'healed' and 'delivered'. This citation
appears to display neither attributive nor any other type of
hypostatization. If one follows a consequence of Lyons's[33]
introduction of personification as relevant to an instrumental
use,[34] that it is an 'actor' and not a 'thing', someone might want to
defend Sanders's hypostatization, in the sense of Barr's religious
hypostatization, as a type of personification, although Sanders
does not refer to such a possibility. However, first, Lyons cites
this as a possibility which he does not appear to favour; furthermore, in Lyons's example above, where there is no 'actor'
referred to overtly as subject or agent, 'He' is the subject. Second,
according to Barr's view that hypostatization of 'the Word' is
not linguistic, but attributive hypostatization of a feature of an
ontological referent, the introduction of the literary device of
personification is contrary to or distinct from the category of
hypostatization. Third, even if Sanders's notion could be reified
to represent a personificatory[35] property of the language, this
opposes his argument as it stands (because of the foregoing) and
lays bare his failure to distinguish between sense and reference in
relation to hypostatization of linguistic phenomena. Such a distinction, although not terminologically expressed in Barr's
account quoted above, is nevertheless compatible with it, and

[31] J. T. Sanders, *The New Testament Christological Hymns*, p. 46.

[32] Notice also that Sanders, characteristically for some treatments, produces
his conclusions from the English, not original languages, and the signs of im-
precise prescriptive language appear, where exact explicit differentiation is
required to reach his conclusion (i.e. 'Coincident with', 'there comes in the idea',
in the latter with a hint of (perhaps unintended) psychologization of data).

[33] J. Lyons, *Introduction to Theoretical Linguistics*, pp. 297f.

[34] Lyons is only laying out certain options to which he does not finally commit
himself; he is concerned with recategorization in, typically, English sentences;
I do not here presuppose a universal category, but abstract Lyons's presentation
as a hypothetical for illustrative purposes.

[35] This usage of 'personificatory' is parallel with the use of the term in J. A. T.
Robinson's *The Human Face of God*, although not the thesis with which he pre-
sents it. An earlier systematic use of personification is in J. Thomas, *Phanerosis*
(Birmingham, 1869).

implicit in respect of hypostatization of sense and hypostatization of referent. Sanders entirely neglects to consider the distinction of sense and reference, or an equivalent designation of the distinction. Other works too fail to relate it to hypostatization, éven though it is central to the status and nature of hypostatization struck with the alleged referents assumed in hypostatization. Sanders constantly moves indiscriminately through levels of usage, albeit while admitting some form of developing process, and seems not to have been properly aware of hypostatizations of differing grades at linguistic and ontological levels. He does, of course, recognize that some subjects apply to gods directly while others refer to properties of referents elsewhere specified.

(b) Irrespective of the quality of Sanders's analysis, and leaving aside the foregoing quotation from his work, the relation of personification to hypostatization is an important aspect for analysis in the arena addressed by Dürr, Sanders and Bultmann,[36] which I here introduce by way of concluding remarks on intention and within that perspective only. At an analytical level, the surface grammar of a sentence can be construed as homonymous in respect of some personification and certain categories of hypostatization, and occasionally indeed of narrative direct speech.[37] I am not supposing that it has this symmetry in every respect in the empirical state when specified in the texts, but that some scholastic description of the texts utilizes features which are homonymous, while asymmetrical properties may reside unexposed in the same texts. Given this, or given a literary analysis which employs prescriptive representation of a sentence, sometimes such texts could contain personification and not hypostatization. On some of these occasions, where this restricted type of scholastic description of the text is adopted, what is deemed hypostatization (of referents)[38] could actually be a literary device involving personification. This does not yield an author's intending to indicate his epistemological assent to an hypostatized referent, but merely a style of writing displaying usage of an expression with a personificatory sense, not reference.

[36] cf. R. Bultmann, *The Gospel of John*, on John 1:1.

[37] If it is possible to interpret *'ny* ('I') in the appropriate way, the following is a case of this category: *'ny ḥkmh šknty 'rmh* ('I wisdom dwell with prudence'), Prov. 8:12. Of course it would be rash to suppose that the author here intended to indicate the personified reference as specifying an hypostatized referent.

[38] 'Of referents' here indicates Barr's above rendering of this type of hypostatization which the scholar confuses.

Where scholars such as Sanders have neglected to take account of Barr's differentiation of linguistic and attributive hypostatization and have collapsed the latter as though it were the former, this conflation can act as a generating point for confusing personification with hypostatization and falsely introducing a referent for personification. This comes about because what is actually a linguistic (literary) device has been taken to be equivalent to attributive hypostatization, as a scholar in confusion sees it; the latter, which is actually a different phenomenon involving onto-logical commitment, is unwittingly (in the scholar's hypothesis) taken to imply a referent for personificatory expressions. Hidden within such a mistake is an unspecified epistemic move: a belief about the relation of the intention producing the text to the text itself is required, although the scholar might be unaware that he has employed this requirement,[39] which the foregoing shows to be a contrary presupposition. In a narrow sense, the conversion of (actually) personificatory expressions into hypostatized items presupposes[40] psychological knowledge of the author, if a scholar has utilized a prescriptive characterization of the text which is, in some sense, homonymous or equivalent in a literary description for both personification and hypostatization.

I do not here develop this issue in relation to John 1:1 since it would involve detailed analysis outside the parameters of the present work. It should, however, be noted that Bultmann[41] assumes that from hypostatization and other points *ho logos* is an 'eternal being', yet the above perspective on personification and its relation to the type of usage in John 1:1[42] raises the need for investigation of criteria for determining differentiation between the two categories, as well as criteria for identifying recategorization in grades of hypostatization which might unpack into personifica-tory expressions. The relation of this problem to the study of criteria for the identification of referents, or of intentional verbs with no referents, is obvious, yet important.

---

[39] For introduction of this type of epistemic move see 2.2, *1* above.

[40] For analysis of presupposition see 5.2, *3* (*d*).

[41] R. Bultmann, *The Gospel of John*, on 1:1, and also J. T. Sanders, *The New Testament Christological Hymns*, pp. 23–4.

[42] I restrict the above comment to 1:1, and do not wish to assume that this concern has to range over 1:14.

1   *Definition of Function*

An aspect of the Fregean specification of semantic value has been refined by Dummett.[1] This can be construed simply as: the semantic value of an (atomic, i.e. simple) sentence is its truth-value – its being true or not true (which is not to be confused with the conditions for its being true or false). One class of expressions which displays semantic value(s) is that of function. (For those who accept a two-valued semantics (that all relevant sentences are true or false), this notion of being true, or being false, is the fundamental criterion in a theory of meaning. Nevertheless, those who advocate a many-valued logic[2] still have to conform to being true in, for example, a possible world. However, as Dummett points out, this is at the expense of having to eject truth as the more fundamental notion.)

Function is a stencil to categorize a certain type[3] of use: the semantic value it takes is a value of the function. The function is itself incomplete, being completed by being attached in use to a subject term (e.g. a proper name, pronoun, etc.), thus being a property (concept) ascribed to the referent of the subject term.

There are a number of formal analyses which determine the necessity of function's being a separable category of usage, albeit incomplete as a unit and dependent on its context for analysis. These I do not rehearse here, but refer to in the above and following footnotes. Beyond this, it is clearly more suitable to show its emergence from usage.

I adopt and adapt the term function by analogy with formal logic's deployment of the item, but make my own use and presentation of it. This produces a comparison and a contrast of function in logic respecting my own application of it, thus furnishing a frame of reference for my suggestions rather than proceeding from a basis of tradition and subjective imagination. (A project of comparison and contrast will not be pursued here because that

---

[1] M. Dummett, *Truth and Other Enigmas*, pp. xxiii, xliv, 19, 74–86; cf. also his *Frege: Philosophy of Language*, pp. 34–53, 204–63.

[2] i.e. arbitrary values other than, or between, true and false. See S. Haack, *Philosophy of Logics* (Cambridge, 1978), pp. 204–20.

[3] The term 'stencil' is from Dummett's formulation.

task is an ingredient of logistic programmes, while my concern here is strictly oriented to applied language studies.)

As Dummett[4] exemplifies it, 'function' is to be unpacked as 'function *of*', since the term 'function' marks a feature of an item (here a linguistic item) in its relation to the other constituent(s) with which it combines to form an expression or a component of an expression. For example, in the expression:

> *bywm hhw' krt yhwh 't-'brm bryt*
> 'In the same day Yahweh made a covenant with Abram'
>   (Gen. 15:18)

the component *bywm hhw' krt . . . 't-'brm bryt* is a propositional function[5] of *yhwh*. In a certain respect, as Prior noticed,[6] this type of example of a function is 'the old-fashioned *predicate*, with the copula treated as an indistinguishable part of it'. The clause (in its use as a term to replace 'sentence') in Hebrew is a suitable type of expression to which one might attach this comparison of propositional function with predicate, because an old-fashioned

---

[4] M. Dummett, *Frege : Philosophy of Language*, pp. 249ff. Such an employment of function is sharply to be differentiated from the theologico-linguistic type of use (in translation) in T. Vriezen, *An Outline of Old Testament Theology* (Oxford, 1958), p. 327. For those who might suspect that I am smuggling in a thesis about hypostatization under the guise of a term different from those criticized above, see W. V. O. Quine's careful discrimination of this function from a nominalist programme by showing that the former falls into a realist category as a marker of an empirical function in language (e.g. *Word and Object*, pp. 233–8). However, this realism is different from and opposed to, for example, D. Hill's (*Greek Words and Hebrew Meanings*, p. 84) because Quine's view is a preservation of an objective entity by representing its context's laws. Generally, where I speak of the value of a function, that value does not include a judgement about tone nor its absence from the associative field of the value.

[5] 'Propositional function' is from Russell (*Principia Mathematica, I*, p. 14, etc.); Quine generally prefers 'statement matrix' instead (for the reason for this, see M. Black, *A Companion to Wittgenstein's 'Tractatus'* (Cambridge, 1964) p. 129). Strictly, one should insert the symbol *n* in place of *yhwh* to produce the appropriate form. I return to functions and subject terms in chapter 3. The notion of propositional function, as Prior has indicated (A. N. Prior, *The Doctrine of Propositions and Terms* (London, 1976), pp. 97–8), is not the same as the ordinary function in mathematics, as for example where 2^2 is a function of 2 and the value of this function for the argument 2 is 4 (although the critical alignment of the two types of function for analytical purposes is a helpful device; cf. P. T. Geach, *Logic Matters*, p. 84).

[6] A. N. Prior, 'Categoricals and Hypotheticals in George Boole and his successors', *The Australasian Journal of Philosophy*, 27 (1949), pp. 171–96, see pp. 191–2.

predicate might, when applied to Hebrew, contain more than one propositional function, whereas one such function of the above sort does not contain more than one predicate.[7]

The above citation from Gen. 15:18 displays a semantic value composed from the propositional function linked with the proper name *yhwh*.[8] Propositional and other functions are incomplete expressions:[9] their usage is in combination with other linguistic entities. Here their values are their uses, and consequent contracted relations.[10] But what of idioms?

An expression such as the citation from Gen. 15:18 can be analysed to yield different types of functions, the propositional function being a larger example from uses where smaller sized features can be distinguished. Selecting just one, *krt* ('made'), in the quotation from Gen. 15:18, would we cite *bryt* ('covenant') as a 'name' to fill the argument-place (or function) X? Namely:

bywm hhw' F yhwh 't-'brm X[11]
'In the same day F Yahweh with Abraham X'.

---

[7] This comparison of function with predicate is of course not employed to suggest that the above function is Russell's 'predicative function' which is a distinct specialized use of a propositional function where there is no quantification over functions (cf. *Principia Mathematica*, I, p. 58). See C. Kirwan, *Logic and Argument* (London, 1978), pp. 84–198. (Here Gen. 15:18 can further be broken into atomic propositions.)

[8] For this usage of 'value', see L. Wittgenstein, *Tractatus*, 3.312–3.318, and P. T. Geach, *Logic Matters*, pp. 108–15, etc.; also, the informative treatment by W. Haas has points of similarity, in 'Linguistic Relevance', pp. 126–7. For my position of exploiting this value as an analogy with truth-values see M. Dummett (*Frege: Philosophy of Language*, pp. 248–9) who sees substantial parallels. However, if I were approaching the application of logic to language from a formalist standpoint, I would hope to explore how functions and their manifolds and maps in mathematical topics furnish some insights for guidance. Relevant to this project is D. J. Shoesmith's and T. J. Smiley's *Multiple-Conclusion Logic* (corrected ed. Cambridge, 1980), and insight would come, I suggest, from scrutiny of function in topological logic employed as an analogy for mapping; cf. S. W. Hawking and G. F. R. Ellis, *The Large Scale Structure of Space-Time* (Cambridge, 1973), pp. 13–15, etc. Also see I. Hacking's 'What is Logic?', *Journal of Philosophy*, 76 (1979), pp. 285–319.

[9] As proved by M. Dummett (*Frege: Philosophy of Language*, pp. 245–63); see also A. N. Prior, *The Doctrine of Propositions and Terms*, p. 99.

[10] cf. L. Wittgenstein, *Philosophical Investigations*, and for the same type of theme in the *Tractatus*, 3.326, 6.211 (statement in parenthesis). For a formalization of use in relation to meaning, see M. J. Cresswell, *Logics and Languages* (London, 1973), pp. 228–40.

[11] F stands for *krt*, and X indicates *bryt*. (This is not, of course, a full formalization; cf. 4.0, *1*.)

A force of this analysis is to expose the issue: is an (alleged) idiom (*krt bryt*) a matter for logic? I return to this in 2.3, *3*; and see 3.0, *3*. (By the way, in assigning the term 'function' to a subject term (and part of a sentence), I am agreeing with Wittgenstein's episodic practice.)[12] A sentence can consistently be described from a number of functional vantage-points to facilitate accurate assignment of descriptions to its use.[13] But logical subject and logically predicative functions are always entirely distinct.

2   Meaning and Usage

(*a*)   The application of the concept of a function to uses in a text necessarily implies that an ingredient of meaning (from which function derives) is usage. One reason for this is because a function depends upon another semantic item for its employment; so the existence of a function in a text (of a relevant sort) entails its use and the use of another expression which completes the function.[14]

While this is an obvious point to make (albeit presented distinctively) recent work on etymology, by E. Kutsch,[15] purporting to extract $\sqrt{brh}$ as the root for *bryt*, is just one example where the point is obscured by hypostatized etymology. Barr[16] has shown that Kutsch neglects operational analysis about how use impinges on meaning in a text, which is being analysed to expose a semantic value (even though in other respects Kutsch is informative).

P. R. Ackroyd[17] has admitted that 'To establish the root meaning

[12] L. Wittgenstein, *The Blue and Brown Books*, p. 21; for care in handling this, note *Tractatus*, 5.02, and also P. T. Geach, *Logic Matters*, pp. 108ff., together with W. Haas's similar use (although set in another conception) which is helpful, in 'Linguistic Relevance', p. 127.

[13] As W. Haas observes, in different terms ('Linguistic Relevance', p. 127).

[14] See the relevant strand in T. J. Smiley's argument on functions: 'Propositional Functions', *The Aristotelian Society*, Supplementary Volume 34 (1960), pp. 33–46. (G. H. Hardy considered that this functional dependence (as he termed it) of a function on a subject term (or variable) for completion is 'the most important in the whole range of higher mathematics' (*A Course of Pure Mathematics* (10th edn., Cambridge, 1958), p. 40.)

[15] E. Kutsch, *Verheissung und Gesetz* (Berlin, 1973), p. 6. (I thank Professor Barr for pointing out this reference to me.) Of course this criticism does not invalidate J. F. A. Sawyer's (*Semantics in Biblical Research*, pp. 89–90) note and J. Barr's positive work of reconstruction to do with sound etymology (see J. Barr's 'Etymology and the Old Testament', *Oudtestamentische Studien*, 19 (1974), pp. 1–28), although Sawyer's root conception is badly confused (see 5.1, *1* below).

[16] J. Barr, 'Some Semantic Notes on the Covenant' in *Beiträge zur alttestamentlichen Theologie*, Zimmerli *Festschrift* (Göttingen, 1977), pp. 23–38.

[17] P. R. Ackroyd, 'Meaning and Exegesis', in P. R. Ackroyd and B. Lindars

of a word does not establish its meaning in a given passage'. Immediately before this remark Ackroyd has a comment about Barr's *Semantics*: 'The warning has been properly given that words cannot be used as counters'.[18] While Ackroyd evidently proposes this judgement unqualified, he afterwards examines a number of examples, the last of which approaches a qualification of this judgement. The qualification is oddly characterized and placed in uneasy apposition with his admission about counters and aspects of meaning. Ackroyd suggests that 'the use of the word *htysbw* ("set yourselves") in 2 Chron. 20:17 may appear to be neutral';[19] and adds 'But it is not unreasonable to hear an overtone here from Ex. 14:13'. From this cogent possibility Ackroyd draws the conclusion that 'Our understanding of 2 Chron. 20:17 is therefore determined not simply by a discussion of the words used and their meanings, but also by this allusion which we may suppose to be present, by which *htysbw* virtually becomes a "counter", inviting reminiscence of a particularly instructive kind.'[20] Ackroyd's use of 'neutral' and 'used' is introduced without definition, but seems to be employed to oppose a (possibly Barr type of assessment of) usage of words, which he thinks cannot allow for a connection with Exod. 14:13. Notice that Ackroyd's employment of 'appear' is perceptual, yet thrust into his argument as an empirical probability about the identity of the semantic item, and he adds it is 'not unreasonable to hear an overtone'. He does not offer grounds for this, apart from the importance of the 'religious experience of the Exodus' (I do not dispute the possibility of an 'overtone', but oppose this presentation). The employment of 'hear' is another perceptual item operating as evidence of an empirical (postulated) feature of the text. Of course, perception is an important consideration, but not one to be conflated with empiricism. What is objectionable is that Ackroyd uses a value judgement identified as a sense datum[21] as evidence, as opposed to information and relations with a text.

So far, he has not offered anything which could polarize 'words used and their meanings' against an 'overtone', except to psychologize data; but later he unwittingly removes the polarity by stating

---

(eds.), *Words and Meanings*, (essays presented to D. W. Thomas, Cambridge, 1968), p. 2.

[18] P. R. Ackroyd, 'Meaning and Exegesis', p. 2, and p. 1 for connection.

[19] *ibid.*, p. 4.

[20] *ibid.*, pp. 4–5.

[21] P. T. Geach's (*Mental Acts*, pp. 45ff., 124–31) analysis of language and judgement in relation to sense data would illustrate this contention.

'May it [$d^c t$ '*lhym* ("knowledge of God"") not also carry the overtone of "religion" in the sense in which this term has often been
understood',[22] where in respect of another expression he concedes
that an overtone is 'carried' by a term (and on the page where
htyṣbw occurs, he writes of 'overtones . . . discernible by the sensitive reader').[23] So even in Ackroyd's usage of 'overtone' there is
a formation which commits him to an agreement that an overtone
is an entity 'carried' in an expression or signified by it. If this is
the case, then it is an artificial organization of data to juxtapose
'words used and their meanings' and an overtone, since the latter
is an item in the former. It may be noteworthy that the hypostatized
use of 'meanings' here – as though *meaning* were something to be
conjoined with *words used*, where the latter is different from the
former – could indicate confusion over the relation of use and
meaning. Of course, one might envisage that Ackroyd's demarcation of 'meanings' here is to advertise a simplistic listing of etymologies, as opposed to a balanced treatment to identify overtones;
but since Barr's viewpoint is the one with which Ackroyd grapples
it is hardly credible that he is ascribing such a view of meaning to
that position.

It is Ackroyd's linking of this polarization with *htyṣbw* – becoming ('virtually') a 'counter' – which is dismantled by the foregoing
remarks. An overtone really is a feature of 'the use of the word
htyṣbw'. Ackroyd's remarks here criticized are only one group of
small elements in his article, yet they systematically affect his
treatment of linguistic phenomena: partial hypostatization of
meanings and uses, resulting in exclusion of a feature like overtone
from the conception and range of use, is a small but pervasive
set of distortions. They are partially generated by a neglect
of the interlocking of terms in expressions, which is portrayed by
the application of function to expressions. A function depends
upon another semantic item for its employment; in this situation,
words cannot be extracted with extra-textual meanings as counters.
Their 'meanings' consist in their textual contract in use, in dependence upon another item, which creates a semantic relation, and
this supports and displays an associative field.[24]

[22] P. R. Ackroyd, 'Meaning and Exegesis', p. 14. For a discussion of overtone
from one standpoint regarding one feature see the following section 4.1, *1*.

[23] P. R. Ackroyd, 'Meaning and Exegesis', p. 4.

[24] cf. J. F. A. Sawyer's comments in *Semantics in Biblical Research*, pp. 30ff.,
and his treatment of a group of terms in their associative field which display a
complex relation: 'Hebrew Words for the Resurrection of the Dead', *Vetus
Testamentum*, 23 (1973), pp. 218–34.

Further, if Ackroyd could show that *htyṣbw* has some feature
which is reproduced from Exod. 14:13, since the term itself
occurs in that text and in 2 Chr. 20:17, it could follow that a
linguistic referent of the term is Exod. 14:13 (this use of 'referent'
arises from the examination in 2.0, 3).[25] Such a result would also
illustrate that the 'overtone' is a feature of the use of the word.
If the earlier, more extreme, cases of the psychologization of
semantic items (by, for example, M. Dahood) are compared with
the foregoing case, while the degree of hypostatization and psychologization is quite distinct, some similarities do obtain at the level
of neglecting the role of use in measuring semantic values.

It is of interest that in reporting Frege's conception in the
Grundlagen Dummett[26] states

> the resort to mental images in an account of the meaning of
> a word springs . . . precisely from the mistake of asking
> after the meaning of the word in isolation, rather than in
> the context of the sentences in which it occurs.

The case of defining 'meaning' has an analogous parallel with
defining a function: a function is incomplete, it is a function of
(something); 'meaning' is a functionally incomplete note of an
expression, correctly expanded it is to be represented as the meaning of an expression p, or a possible expression q. Philosophers[27]
and linguists[28] have sometimes made related points, although not
presented quite like this. They have been concerned to resist the
warps generated by treating meaning (unwittingly or assertively)
as an hypostatization or reification which obscures the operational
importance of use.

Attention to usage of semantic items is not in itself sufficient to

[25] I am not of course agreeing with Ackroyd's proposal as he presents it, and
I am unhappy with his informal deployment of 'overtone'. If it were in fact a
reference to the item in Exod. 14:13, then the referent could be designated an
entity, which would not be a member of the category of tone, which does not
have referential identity.

[26] M. Dummett, *Frege: Philosophy of Language*, p. 642.

[27] See M. Dummett, *Frege: Philosophy of Language*, p. 92. It is instructive to
apprehend a comparison between this hypostatization of meaning and its dis-
sociation from use, and the analysis of truth (in the formulation of truth proposed,
for example, by C. J. F. Williams in *What is Truth?* (Cambridge, 1976)). The
truth of a sentence which is true just is what truth is, since truth is to be unpacked
as shorthand for true assertions made in the use of language.

[28] e.g. J. Barr, 'Hypostatization of Linguistic Phenomena in Modern Theological Interpretation', pp. 85–94.

neutralize a tendency to hypostatize, nor enough to permit usage to dictate the limitation of semantic generalization about use of an expression in one context to other contexts. (I introduce generalization, of course, since an hypostatized notion of meaning is presumed to be a context-independent, albeit context-governing, phenomenon deployed as a type of universal prescription – a theme to which I return in analysis of generality.)

(b) One type of influence distorting attention to use of semantic items, which can produce hypostatization, is when a (fictional) referent (or a wrongly construed referent) is assumed to 'control' the semantic domain of the definite description which is assumed to refer to it. If one accepts R. N. Whybray's examination of the claim that ḥkmy ('wise') refers to a professional class, which he disputes, then we have an illustration of this type of distorting influence. Whybray does not observe what he has performed in relation to hypostatization; but if his conclusions are right, then he has de-hypostatized a semantic value hitherto trapped in a central traditional interpretation of Wisdom terminology, by showing that forms akin to ḥkmy have various descriptive functions, and not the almost titular class of 'the wise men' in Israel,[29] as a semantic value. Attention to a seeming referent had provoked some scholars to organize the identification of ḥkmy as a referential question, whereas, properly, the functional relations of the semantic item in the text ought to have generated the attempt to reach a referent.

(c) An apparently rich source for resolving the values of functions which are actually or allegedly problematic is in comparing, say, an MT text with LXX translation of it where, it is supposed, the corresponding functions can obviate difficulties with the original text. However, this technique is often utilized where interpretation of the item is controversial, and/or the components of the semantic field undetermined. Barr's observation is a point which has not always been rightly positioned to restrict or discipline speculation:

[29] R. N. Whybray, *The Intellectual Tradition in the Old Testament* (Berlin, 1974), pp. 13 and 54. Of course, even if Whybray is wrong, then it still may obtain that some scholars have reached a legitimate conclusion by empirical conjecture about a referent, rather than sound linguistics. (Whybray does rather approach his conclusion as a matter of word-study rather than a refined semantic analysis (cf. W. McKane's review in *Journal of Semitic Studies*, 22 (1975), 2, pp. 243–48).)

In the research operations of comparative philology the scholar uses a list of basic correspondences which have been built up wherever possible with plentiful examples and with the use of words (or grammatical elements) . . . which do not present semantic uncertainties. Only because this list is fairly stable can the more adventurous research into the highly doubtful words be undertaken with confidence.[30]

Even where scholars conform to this type of guideline, their handling of correspondences involves their handling their interpretations of correspondences – as Barr is well aware.[31] Such interpretations are usually concerned with elements that do not present great problems. Conversely, where the criteria of semantic identification are unstable, so are interpretation and research produced under their stipulation. In such cases, special care must be taken, and hypostatized universals must not be unconsciously taken up as a suppressed premiss – required to support the 'identification' of the value of a function.

Of course all employment of universals is not in itself incoherent, although it is a practice of metaphysics. Nevertheless, when the alleged universal is hypostatized (wrenched from its semantic context and texture) it is evidence that consistent routes have not been followed (and perhaps cannot be followed) to achieve the licit adoption of the premiss. For such a device to be used as a warrant for concluding that a function exhibits a given value, in conjunction with the employment of unstable criteria, is a completely uncontrolled situation, masked only by a writer's exclusion of relevant data. Such a position might be slipped into by otherwise careful scholars because the existence of suppressed premisses is, perhaps, assumed to ward off a charge of inconsistency or incoherence. It could be that such a suppressed premiss is itself coherent, yet irrelevant to the value's employment; or it might be that the premiss is inconsistent. Since, mostly, these suppressed premisses are not specified or even mentioned by scholars adopting them, their explicit exposure in the form with which the scholar who uses them might agree is a difficult task. Yet sometimes if the scholar introduces a feature into his argument which is a consequence of a suppressed premiss displaying a universal of

---

[30] J. Barr, *Comparative Philology and the Text of the Old Testament*, pp. 87–8. cf. also J. F. A. Sawyer, *Semantics of Biblical Research*, pp. 31ff.

[31] J. Barr, *Comparative Philology and the Text of the Old Testament*, pp. 44ff., etc.

the relevant type, then the scholar is committed to admitting the existence of the premiss and its incoherence.

For example, P. Walters's study on the LXX text[32] is a monumental synthesis of data, but Barr has shown that there are a number of discrepant treatments owing to confused general conceptions.[33] A case pertinent to the previous observation is where Walters suggested that *thalassa* ('sea') was derived from the Hebrew *t'lh* [3]('trench') which, in 1 Kgs. 18:32 and elsewhere, is rendered by LXX with that term. One aspect of Walters's argument obliquely advertises his suppressed premisses:

> Here we do well to remember the fact that in certain strata of the LXX Aramaic forms were used and Graecized to render the corresponding Hebrew word. Therefore long ago I ventured to reconstruct an Aramaic word which has not been preserved elsewhere. Its sound would be something like *ταελ^eβā* or *ταελ^aβā*. . . . Professor Rahlfs . . . agreed and modified my suggestion by pointing to the Arabic forms *tal˒a* or *tar˒a*, with a transposition of the second and third radical. In conformity with this, the Aramaic form was bound to have been *tl˒t˒*, and from this the Greek homonym *thalassa* was fashioned.
>
> This rendering of *β* by *-ss-* is an example of repeated emergence of certain innate proclivities of Greek. All such examples are valuable for Greek phonetics. In earlier Greek, there is noticeable, in different periods and places and in ways that are not entirely identical in detail, a tendency to use *-ss-* or *-tt-* to express sounds, particularly foreign ones, which were neither $s(s)$ nor $t(t)$ . . . We are unable to define the phonetic value of these sounds. The only thing that we can say with certainty, is that it was neither $s(s)$ nor $t(t)$ . . . The dual spelling which in various ways attempts to express this peculiar consonant is found in many genuinely Greek formations . . . In Asia Minor there is even a special letter for this sound . . . in Carian names . . .[34]

Walters has invoked (rather than constructed) a hypothetical intricate web of relations and premisses, which are for the most

---

[32] P. Walters (formerly Katz), *The Text of the Septuagint: its Corruptions and their Emendations* (Cambridge, 1973).

[33] J. Barr's review of P. Walters, *The Text of the Septuagint*, *Vetus Testamentum*, 25 (1975), pp. 247–54.

[34] P. Walters, *The Text of the Septuagint*, pp. 190–1.

part not specified. He admits that the Aramaic form is hypothetical, yet simply assumes that 'Aramaic forms', used and Graecized to render corresponding Hebrew words, can be attached as a veridical thesis behind the hypothetical Aramaic word. It is interesting that he should follow the opening sentence of the quotation with 'therefore', as though it were a proof to draw a justification for his decision to 'reconstruct' the Aramaic word, while the functional role of 'therefore' is positioned to support an asserted conclusion from that opening sentence.

However, an hypothesis cannot be corroborated with respect to a unique alleged instance of it, if that instance is not observed in the data which comprise the report of examples of the application of the hypothesis.[35] The LXX strata from which Walters extracts his credentials do not display a case of it or its type. Walters switched languages at this juncture to facilitate an alignment with an appropriate Aramaic form, yet he goes to a third language for this ingredient. Barr indicates that[36] the Arabic form (with the inversion of the order of ʿ and *l*) is a precarious basis for such a conjecture. Here Walters[37] requires a group of linguistic universals (which not only quantify over some Semitic languages, but over Greek also), including a cognate-relation universal which permits a transposition of radicals in the relevant situation, for which there is no support. Within this sequence of assumed hypothetical (not empirical) possibilities, theoretical conjectures are promoted to the seeming status of actualities within the later stages of the quotation.[38]

One instance of this smuggling in, concerning an unwarranted promotion from possibility to actuality, is where Walters has, immediately before, introduced the Arabic forms to 'enable' the reconstruction of the required Aramaic form theoretically to be evolved. Walters's account (in the foregoing quotation) continues: 'In conformity with this, the Aramaic form was bound to have been *tlʿt*', and from this the Greek homonym *thalassa* was fashioned.' Here Walters employs an expression 'was bound to have been' which imports necessity for which there is no cogent empirical linguistic nor theoretical proof – not least because of the earlier hypotheticals on which the assumptions themselves rest. Using this necessity 'operator', Walters changes levels from

---

[35] cf. K. R. Popper, *Unended Quest* (London, 1976), pp. 103ff.

[36] J. Barr's review of P. Walters, *The Text of the Septuagint*, p. 251.

[37] For the reason for the detailed comment on Walters, see 6.0, 6 following.

[38] J. Barr defines this modal shift: *Comparative Philology and the Text of the Old Testament*, pp. 285–7, 292ff.

imaginative to empirical constructions, and, by the stage the verb is reached in 'was fashioned', it is made to perform the role of an historical record. Yet the expression 'was bound to have been' is part of a modal fallacy[39] because the modality does not possibly arise from the singular statement which it is supposed to embrace (noted as far back as Boethius[40] as characteristic of this type of fallacy).

In addition to all these features, Walters has conflated the distinction of homophone and homograph in the process of employing homonym (defined inexactly earlier in his treatise, as Barr mentioned)[41] and in the presence of an admission that 'We are unable to define the phonetic value of these sounds'. Further, Walters needs a transitivity between morphological and semantic universals to carry his thesis, and this transitivity is neither evident nor proved. At the graphic level Walters has to move far into other linguistic families, turning to Carian to gain some semblance of evidence for his claim, although he has not furnished any criteria of the relevance of this item for his project.

The above case might be regarded as extreme and untypical, though it does echo some elements of confusion in Walters's general conception of appropriate features of language. Nevertheless, Walters articulates or requires a group of hypotheses hardly any of which are specified explicitly, and none is marshalled into operation with an attached explanation of its grounds of confirmation or qualifications. Of course, it may be responded that, in the case of a treatise like Walters's *Text of the Septuagint*, this is an unreasonable set of strictures. This objection misses the focal point of the criticism: the structural fatigue and speculation, which induce collapse of proposals owing to an organization of priorities, which permits imaginative (theoretical) assumptions to perform empirical roles. Such a situation is largely improved by replacement of expressions such as 'bound to' with 'could possibly' (rather than treatment demanding massive increase in length of analysis). Requisite qualification would indicate the need for exclusion of falsely construed interpretations.[42]

---

[39] cf. P. T. Geach, *Logic Matters*, p. 155; C. L. Hamblin, *Fallacies*, pp. 105–7, 211–12.

[40] A. M. T. S. Boethius, *Introductio ad Syllogismos Categoricus* (Paris, 1860).

[41] J. Barr's review of P. Walters, *The Text of the Septuagint*, p. 249.

[42] I appreciate that Walters's work suffers from being published some decades after it was actually written; and a few of my observations might have been inapplicable had it been published in an earlier state of knowledge of the linguistics of the Bible. Nevertheless, with the book's rapidly becoming a

Walters's explanation amounts to eight premisses (one of which is admitted, two of which are exploded by the concession of ignorance of a relevant phonetic value) needed to sustain his viewpoint. None of them is sound in its connection with or relation to the conclusion; conjoined they generate inconsistency. These premisses are suppressed, except for the hypothesis of the Aramaic form, and even that hypothetical status is disguised (I am not claiming intentionally) by an expression of necessity being attached to it, through illicit use of the Greek term. Some of these suppressed premisses are required to be (by virtue of Walters's use) universals, so that at an hypothetical level they can perform some function. Other problems would also arise when the premisses are made explicit, as for example the lack of synchronicity and mixing of diachronic and synchronic scales (in that order) in the use of data.

An interpretation is no stronger than the premisses by which it is formed. Walters's approach to identifying the relations of the relevant terms advertises that he offers an interpretation in a semantic field which not only has unstable variables, but the stable functions of which have not infrequently been destabilized by his introduction of a regress of premisses of which he appears hardly aware. Nevertheless, he is exploiting the deployment of them to assess the functional relations of *thalassa* and *t'lh*.

The case of Walters on *thalassa* is here presented, partly to illustrate that, apart from the foregoing individual weaknesses, a linguist's appeal to use is often an appeal to his interpretation of that use in its relation to his linguistic world view. Indeed, a scholar will perhaps always bring both his techniques and his value judgements to such a use; I, rather, intend a scholar's injection of an informal 'philosophy' of language, an epistemology of interactions of cultural relations, metaphysical constructs about semantic and other linguistic universals. It is not that I am maintaining it is wrong to hold world views or metaphysical values; but, in the above-mentioned example and previous illustrations, one frequently observes that the implementation of a universal or 'philosophy' of language is in conflict with, and obtrudes onto, the exact linguistic usage in a text. When this unhealthy merger is unwitting, as it often is, or if it runs out of control, unnoticed by its actor, the product is, it might be termed, metaphysical linguistics parading as empirical investigations. Such

---

standard reference work there is a danger of its being misused if these types of points are not made; it is also typical of its genre, historically.

a blend interferes with the text, whether it has its own meta-physic, or is neutral of that feature, or if it happens that there are no universals functioning at the structural linguistic level, or if there are but they differ from those supposed. Often, of course, the result, as in Walters's case, is an hybrid, the edges of which are difficult to detect and so influence irrelevant or distorting items at the descriptive level. Further, in this type of situation a scholar can become entrapped in his own style of discourse, as Walters did (e.g. with 'was bound to have been'). A consequence of such a style is the imposition of a linguistic world view arbitrarily gener-ated from viewpoints held by the linguistic actor and features in the surface structure of his analytical language. It has been shown that this world view, while terminating in a particular thesis about a semantic value, presupposes certain (often incoherent) notions of other linguistic levels which are controversially presumed to underpin a semantic solution.

3   Idiom and Function

Even where a list of words reflects a previous diachronic history with stability of semantic values, this stability is not invariably a resource for predicting the semantic value of a function in con-junction with other items. Cases of idiom are just such instances of deviance from the stability prior to their formation in respect of their components.

(a)   Comparatively little has been done at a formal level on idioma-ticity in the Bible. Barr adapts and adopts a formulation by U. Weinreich:[43] 'an idiom being a complex expression $A + B$, the meaning of which is not expressible as the meaning of A plus the meaning of B'. In an idiom the usual meaning of its constituents with their non-idiomatic values in normal usage cannot be em-ployed, either in principle or in the current state of linguistic

---

[43] In J. Barr, *Biblical Words for Time*, p. 119 n. 5, from U. Weinreich's 'On the semantic structure of language', in J. H. Greenberg (ed.), *Universals of Language* (Cambridge, Mass., 1963), pp. 181ff. In this context J. Barr was dealing with the expression *ka'et hayya* as an idiomatic item wrongly translated by J. Muilen-berg (cf. *Harvard Theological Review*, 54 (1961), p. 236) as 'when the season lives or revives'. If this expression is idiomatic, it follows that, with Barr's analysis, Muilenberg has imposed a non-idiomatic characterization on an idiom; and so missed the asymmetry of words in and out of idiom. (Of course, by current standards, as well as Weinreich's later work and aspects of the article of his cited which Barr does not mention, this formulation of idiom is crude.)

understanding of them, to predict the meaning of the idiom. W. Haas[44] has added the point that it is also the conjunction of the words which has meaning. Such conjunctions are idiosyncratic semantically and syntactically, in that they are not derivable from a standard grammar. However, as W. Haas has mentioned, the constituents of an idiom may, nevertheless, be homophonous with a genuine non-idiomatic construction.[45] Given that an idiom is a completely ossified item, it cannot receive alterations of quantification or have semantic expansions introduced into it. (Those postulated cases of idiom which appear to violate such stipulations, could, on one analysis by A. Makkai,[46] satisfy different criteria of idiomaticity and be placed in a Second Idiomaticity Area. Yet in this class Makkai puts certain types of proverbs.[47] A similar type of Hebrew[48] proverb found in the Book of Proverbs[49] has not been classified as an idiom; these proverbs employ terms which typically have a recurrent contrastive value in and outside such proverbs and component phrases in them receive quantificational modification and have expansions introduced into them. All of this indicates that they are not idioms, if a characteristic specification is to be followed.)

To the element of conjunction in idiom, I would add the feature of a fixed (ossified) order of words. Within this point, though, there is a problem for the notion of conjunction as an element of idiom. I do not wish to oppose the incorporation of conjunction into a formulation of idiom, but want to draw attention to some issues associated with its application to Hebrew and Greek.

(b) In 2.3, *1*, I purposely chose an untypical occurrence of the

---

[44] The above is my own construction of Haas's 'conjunction', and not his. I am grateful for permission to mention it.

[45] Professor Haas furnished the example of 'they were *pulling his leg*, and he fell off the chair'. Clearly, this opens up the possibility of pun language, utilizing such a concurrence. Perhaps it is probable that puzzling expressions in Hebrew could yield such punning duality; for example, in the case of *yš-l'l ydy* ('It is in the power of my hand', etc.) (e.g., Gen. 31:29), where punning polysemy (not ambiguity) occurs.

[46] A. Makkai, *Idiom Structure in English* (The Hague, 1972), especially pp. 124ff. and 117–87 generally.

[47] A. Makkai, *Idiom Structure in English*, p. 124.

[48] W. Haas's and A. Makkai's quite different researches are both largely based on the English language. I am not, in citing them, presupposing that idiomatic cases exhibit universals, or that a definition of idiom is a universal. All research in idiomaticity is, of course, at too early a stage to anticipate the outcome of relevant competing factors. I adopt certain features as hypotheticals.

[49] For data see W. McKane, *Proverbs* (London, 1970), pp. 22ff.

expression *krt bryt* ('make a covenant') where its two components are separated by other semantic ingredients:

> *bywm hhw' krt yhwh 't-'brm bryt*
> 'In the same day Yahweh made a covenant with Abram'

This statement in Gen. 15:18 is the first occurrence of *krt bryt*
in the Bible. Almost all other uses of the expression (if it is to be
deemed the same) have its two components adjacent to one another.
E. A. Speiser,[50] while not treating Gen. 15:18 in great detail,
does not notice the separation of components in the alleged idiom,
although such an item is a relevant consideration when he has
proposed a relation between the idiom and a Mari expression.[51]

Since such a separation of elements could (not must) indicate a
stage in the prehistory of the idiom's components, a synchronic
connection of Gen. 15:18 with, for instance, Davidic covenant
formulae requires proof for linking supposed occurrences of the
idiom in the appropriate texts. Such a connection has been developed by M. Weinfeld[52] and J. Van Seters,[53] as a premiss for a
certain literary relation and dependence concerning the pertinent
texts. Yet none of the treatments by these scholars offers any
observation on or recognition of this phenomenon.

When L. Koehler gave attention to semantic problems involved
with the idiom, he never gave the separation any scrutiny, although
he cited Gen. 15:18.[54] The same is true of Barr's study (cf. n. 57).

Where conjunction and order are properties of an idiom, and
since scholars generally classify *krt bryt* as an idiom, the occurrence
of its two components in an order separating them is in opposition
to what it is to be an idiom.[55]

---

[50] E. A. Speiser, *Genesis: Anchor Bible* (New York, 1964), p. 14; Speiser is
intent on linking *krt* with an allegedly equivalent Mari expression meaning
'to kill [an ass]', and does not appear to notice that the order in the Hebrew items
is distinct from normal distribution of them.

[51] However, see a critical assessment of Speiser's general Mari-Hebrew covenant relations, by M. Held, 'Philological Notes on the Mari Covenant Rituals',
Bulletin of the American Schools of Oriental Research, 200 (December 1970),
pp. 32–40.

[52] M. Weinfeld, *Deuteronomy and the Deuteronomic School* (Oxford, 1972),
pp. 22, 75–80.

[53] J. Van Seters, *Abraham in History and Tradition* (Harvard, 1975).

[54] L. Koehler, 'Problems in the Study of the Languages of the Old Testament', *Journal of Semitic Studies*, 1 (1956), pp. 3–7.

[55] There are two features of order here: a linear 1 to *n* sequence of items, and
the position of those items in the sequence in adjacency or separated by other
external terms.

(c) Nevertheless, the alleged idiom in Gen. 15:18 exhibits certain idiomatic features.[56] Barr's study,[57] of different properties in the idiom in MT, supports such a view and he considers that Gen. 15:18 contains an occurrence of this idiom. In Gen. 15:18 *krt* functions with the value 'to make', if one follows Barr, and not 'to cut'. It is strange that such scholars as J. Bright,[58] while describing *krt bryt* as a 'peculiar idiom', should give it the translation 'to cut a covenant' (and cite Gen. 15:18 as his example to illustrate the idiom), for as Barr states in the above mentioned study:

> ... scholars who offer renderings that capitalize on the literal value, such as 'cut a covenant', misrepresent the normal semantic value in Hebrew: 'to make a covenant' is a much more correct representation. This view is supported by the fact that the idiomatic *krt* could be extended, though sporadically, to govern a term like *dbr* (Hag. 2:5) or indeed could be used without any object at all.

Yet Bright translates the expression in its literal sense, as such a sense is often termed, although the precise designation of 'literal' here is open to question. This is because the translation of an idiom's components (rather than its operational value in use) is a rendering of the terms' prehistory prior to idiomatization. Problems also occur where a morpheme in that prehistory separately (perhaps as an homonym) continues to function synchronically with the idiom.

---

[56] By *idiomatic* I here indicate items which are components in idioms which in Gen. 15:18 have values which are non-normal and thus as such exclusive elsewhere to idiom usage.

[57] J. Barr, 'Some Semantic Notes on the Covenant', in *Beiträge zur alttestamentlichen Theologie*, Zimmerli *Festschrift* (Göttingen, 1977), pp. 23–38.

[58] J. Bright, *A History of Israel* (2nd edn., London, 1972), p. 98. Also, R. Rickards (UBS translation consultant) is typical of some scholars who programme this error into translation work: he stated of Gen. 15:10 (where the verb *krt* does *not* appear) 'The Hebrew term usually translated "make a covenant" in English is literally "cut a covenant" which explains why the carcasses were cut.' ('Gn. 15: an Exercise in Translation Principles', *Bible Translator*, 28 (April 1977), 2, p. 217); immediately after this remark Rickards advocates a rendering of such expressions with the value 'to cut' (but in 15:18 'to make'). Bright and Rickards fail to notice the separation, although quoting texts which present the separated form.

(d)   Of course, pun in a text (e.g. Jer. 34:18) might be confused
with prehistory, as in BDB's[59] account of *krt* (entry 4):

> *cut, or make a covenant* (because of the cutting up and distribu-
> tion of the flesh of the victim for eating in the sacrifices of
> the covenants . . .); *hʿgl ʾšr krtw the calf which they cut*
> Jr. 34:18 (referring to Gn. 15:10)

Here a rare use of pun in connection with *krt* is cited to characterize
the term's normal semantic value by an explanation of cutting:
a pun is used to indicate the word's value outside pun (i.e. the
list of occurrences it introduces) although the mention of 'make'
mitigates this error. Unfortunately, such a mention is not enough
to neutralize the presence of the explanation about cutting.
Also, while the entry is about *krt*, the regress through pun language ends with the reader being referred to a source text Gen.
15:10 where in fact *krt* is not used.

The use of *krt* in Jer. 34:18 illustrates how, for example, pun
can override an idiomatic programme ('to make') and impose an
homonym of the idiom ('to cut') or one of its elements. Where
certain idioms are homographous in unvocalized script, or a text
where vowels are suspect and alternatives have modified semantic
scanning for possible meanings, then a pun may be mistaken for
the normal semantic value.[60]

(e)   Outside untypical contexts of pun, *krt* is idiomatic when
functioning with *bryt*. Barr[61] says the idiomatic abnormality
associated with the former term is not present in the latter word
because *bryt* has, within the idiom, the same meaning that it
bears as the object of other verbs (e.g. *hpr*). This is an important
point, and I take such a contrastive situation as evidence that
bryt is not strictly a member of the idiom. That is to say, *krt* is the
idiom; *bryt* is not, but is merely in constant conjunction with the
idiom. Barr further observes that:

> . . . the idiomaticity of the phrase [*krt bryt*] in actual usage . . .

[59] F. Brown, S. R. Driver, C. A. Briggs, *A Hebrew and English Lexicon of the
Old Testament*, p. 503, col. B. (It is interesting to ask what sense one could make
of the use of *referring* in the above quotation: presumably quotation has a linguistic referent as its source (i.e. the source context).)

[60] Problems of reading which can contribute to this are described by J. Barr,
'Reading a Script without Vowels', in W. Haas (ed.), *Writing without Letters*
(Manchester, 1976), pp. 71–100.

[61] J. Barr, 'Some Semantic Notes on the Covenant'.

attaches to *krt* rather than to *bryt*: it is *krt* that undertakes abnormal functions. But though this is so the idiom still belongs to *bryt*, for it is the meanings attached to it that diffuse themselves through the abnormal uses of *krt*.[62]

The foregoing statement of relation 'the idiom still belongs to *bryt*' requires more explicit characterization for the present topic. 'Belongs to' cannot possess (and Barr evidently did not suppose that it displayed) a relation of full idiomaticity between the two components *krt* and *bryt*, because it is possible for *bryt* to be a substitution instance of *bryt* when in a non-idiomatic context. So there is not the required idiomatic symmetry and status of ossification in *bryt* to perform a semantic role of full idiomatic relation. However, it is quite clear that there is some interference and distinctive association between the two components. Given the above asymmetry between the two components, one is required to place this association in the realm of the associative field of the two items when in conjunction[63] without this fact imputing a relation of idiomaticity between *krt* and *bryt*, since the latter fails the foregoing idiomacy tests.

Such a description of the semantic situation around and within *krt bryt* permits the separation of the two components, as they are found in Gen. 15:18, since the idiom is restricted to *krt* and so does not violate the notions of conjunction and order in being idiom. For *krt bryt* is not the idiom; *krt* is. (The power of the association between *krt* and *bryt* should not be minimized, however, because of the foregoing. The appearance of the expression's equivalent, and with one of its terms reproduced, in for example the Qatna tablets (as [T]AR *be-ri-ti* and TAR *be-ri-t[i]*)[64] is evidence of the expression's pervasive influence.)

The separation of the two items *krt* and *bryt* in Gen. 15:18 will not be further examined here, save to notice that the problem of the separation remains. If the notion of pun be employed to explain the separation, where Gen. 15:10 is the basis for the pun

[62] *ibid.*

[63] For a general account of this associative field see J. F. A. Sawyer, *Semantics in Biblical Research*, pp. 29ff.; also S. Ullmann, *Meaning and Style* (Oxford, 1973), pp. 24f., and cf. 52f. 'Conjunction' in the above may not always entail their being adjacent in position (as in the use of the term in connection with idiom) but also in operational, grammatical conjunction in a sentence.

[64] If one follows W. F. Albright's translation of these expressions (see his 'The Hebrew Expression for "Making a Covenant" in Pre-Israelite Documents', in *Bulletin of the American Schools of Oriental Research*, 121 (February 1951), pp. 21–2).

in terms of the covenant ritual, substantial problems arise, since
Jer. 34:18's punning usage is linguistically distinct from Gen.
15:18 in structure and order. The former text cannot therefore
serve as precedent for the latter. If emphasis be regarded as the
reason for the separation, then no support for this proposal is
forthcoming from Muraoka's[65] study of emphasis in MT Hebrew
formations.

(f)   Often scrutiny of an alleged idiom or idioms is in a context
of other idiomatic uses in the same text, and, as such, an informal
web of associations can be assumed by scholars when assessing
linguistic phenomena. Here there is scope for confusion, if an
unclear, or contrary, use of the identity of idiom is presupposed.

An idiom may be composed of only one word.[66] Weinfeld[67]
supposes that the terms hzq and $'ms$ are idioms:

> The idioms 'be strong and resolute'[68] $hzq\ w'ms$, which occur in
> the book of Deuteronomy only in the context of the *conquest
> of the land* (Dt. 31:7–8, cf. 1:38; 3:28) are employed by the
> Dtr with respect to the general *observance of the Torah*:
> 'Only be strong and resolute to observe and to do according
> to all the law which Moses my servant commanded you'
> (Josh. 1:7). A similar use of these idioms is encountered in
> the Dtr's interpretation of David's testament to Solomon
> (1 Kgs. 2:3–4): though the term hzq in the original testament
> referred to brutal daring in executing dynastic vengeance,
> the Dtr relates it to the observance of the Torah.

The use of 'referred to' in the foregoing reflects a confusion over
referential roles (examined in 2.0, *2* above). The term hzq does
not refer, it describes; nor therefore does it 'refer' to 'brutal

[65] T. Muraoka, *Emphasis in Biblical Hebrew* (Jerusalem, 1969). Muraoka also
informs me that later research in this area has not yielded any other grounds
which can be utilized to establish the presence of emphasis in Gen. 15:18. Pun
might not only arise where a homonym of an idiom component is matched with
the idiom; paronomasia can occur as a by-product of thematic development
(see 3.2, *2* for a case in Exod. 3), and in this sense Gen. 15:10 might give rise to
the separation and hence pun in Gen. 15:18.

[66] See W. Haas, *Writing without Letters*, p. 176.

[67] M. Weinfeld, *Deuteronomy and the Deuteronomic School*, p. 5.

[68] Weinfeld's quotation marks are odd here: presumably 'and' (w) is not part
of either idiom, yet is cited within the marks and reproduced in the Hebrew;
the idioms, thus carelessly isolated, could be later deployed where such distinctions are important to be preserved for identifying distinct functions (as C. Lewy
has shown in *Meaning and Modality*, pp. 1–47, 99–107, and proves that neglect
of quotations produces major distortions in analysis).

daring . . .', although it is employed in that sort of context as a command term.[69] If, on the other hand, Weinfeld construed 'referred to' informally with respect to the term's meaning (and thus avoids the previous criticism, if strict analysis of his language is suspended) and used 'referred to' in the sense of 'has the meaning of', then his explanation contains a mistaken assumption about meaning and idiom. That is to say, if *ḥzq* is taken to be identified as an idiom then one cannot allow two different meanings to be included in its specification (i.e. 'brutal daring', and 'observance . . .'). Against this it might be thought more probable that Weinfeld has used 'referred to' confusedly while only generally associating *ḥzq* with the two sorts of contexts. Yet if this is maintained then one still has warrant to insist on the severity of the referential confusion.

However, Weinfeld has not shown that *ḥzq* is an idiom which, as such, is associated with the appropriate contexts. First, he offers the normal translation of it for when the morpheme is being employed 'literally' and/or metaphorically; he does not even implement his idiom value with a relevant translation. Secondly, 'strong' is a normal translation of *ḥzq* because the non-idiomatic value of this term accurately represents a wide distribution of the metaphoric and 'literal' uses of the morpheme.[70] While the meaning of idiom is not predictable on the basis of its component's or components' prehistory, metaphoric usage can be examined to extract its meaning from its use and constituents; so it is with *ḥzq*. In addition, one cannot introduce syntactic/semantic expansions into idioms, although this can be done with metaphors. Weinfeld's own citations of *ḥzq* advertise a distribution which, together with others,[71] indicate that *ḥzq* conforms to the specification of a metaphor rather than idiom.[72]

The fact that Weinfeld's intricate hypothesis on the Deuteronomic school partly rests upon complex differentiation of linguistic levels, within which semantic shifts of level involving partial

---

[69] cf. M. Weinfeld, *Deuteronomy and the Deuteronomic School*, p. 11. For a discussion of logical issues relating to the analysis and description of commands and imperatives see P. T. Geach, *Logic Matters*, pp. 270–88.

[70] M. Weinfeld, *Deuteronomy and the Deuteronomic School*, as illustrated in pp. 5, 11; and e.g. 2 Kgs. 14:5; Judg. 16:28 (literal); also 2 Sam. 10:12; Deut. 12:23 (metaphors).

[71] Deut. 31:23; Josh. 1:6,9,18; Jer. 23:14, etc.

[72] I think that these objections would generally apply to Weinfeld's other 'idiom' *'mṣ* in view of its usage; e.g. 2 Chr. 11:7; 2 Sam. 22:18; Deut. 2:3,30, etc.

ossification permit or support inferences, renders the foregoing
exposure of confusion a matter for some concern. Where the
establishment of diachronic phases depends on exact identification of synchronic levels, with metaphoric and idiomatic stages of
usage being separated, such a confusion of referential function
and mislaid metaphorization can produce false accounts of linguistic and theological relations and their developments.

(g) C. F. D. Moule's *Idiom-Book of New Testament Greek*[73]
contains a large number of valuable insights, in the form of listing
important deviations from standard grammar and neglected
features of NT semantic phenomena. Moule informed his readers[74]
that the *Idiom-Book* is not a systematic introduction to NT syntax
nor an exhaustive catalogue. Since the *Idiom-Book* is a pioneering
work which serves to describe its field rather than resolve fundamental semantic issues within it, criticism is expedient (although
this will not detract from the practical significance of Moule's
basic compilation of data).

Nowhere does Moule offer any explanation of what it is to be
an idiom or what he would describe or define as idiom. This is a
surprising absence; although, of course, it would be a Socratic
fallacy[75] to move from this to argue that a definition must be
present for there to be knowledge of idiom laid out in Moule's
book. Unfortunately, however, a large group of Moule's cases
do not appear to satisfy a number of specifications of idiom.[76]

Here are some typical instances:
(i) Under the heading of 'Semitisms' Moule[77] deals with some
cases of 'Particular Idioms' one of which is the adjectival genitive,
which he describes as:

> The Semitic idiom whereby *sons of light, of darkness, of life,
> of death, of belial*, etc. means simply *people worthy of*, or

---

[73] C. F. D. Moule, *An Idiom-Book of New Testament Greek* (2nd edn., Cambridge, 1968).

[74] *ibid.*, p. v.

[75] i.e. the fallacy of supposing that to know one is truly predicating of a subject,
entails being able to give a criterion for its being true and being what it is (cf.
P. T. Geach, *Logic Matters*, pp. 33, 164).

[76] This would be the case whether following the above account of idiom, or
Haas's or U. Weinreich's (especially in his later work: *Explorations in Semantic
Theory* (The Hague, Paris, 1972) pp. 89–95) or my use of Barr's distinctions in
the foregoing. cf. also the comments on criteria by A. van Santen (in the review of
A. Makkai's, *Idiom Structure in English*, *Lingua*, 37 (1975), pp. 261–7).

[77] C. F. D. Moule, *An Idiom-Book of New Testament Greek*, p. 174.

associated with light, etc. Thus in the NT we find: Mark ii.19 *hoi huioi tou numphōnos, the bridal party;* Luke xvi.8 *hoi huioi tou aiōnos toutou . . . tous huious tou phōtos;* Matt. xxiii.15 *huion geennēs;* Eph. ii.3 *tekna phusei orgēs* (perhaps = *left to ourselves (phusei) we are destined to suffer the consequences of sin*); Eph. v.8 *tekna phōtos;*

Moule cites cases where two distinct NT words for *sons* are used, although he identifies them as examples of idiom: 'The Semitic idiom'. It is inconsistent to designate these phenomena as a single idiom, and it opposes the notion of an ossified unit of meaning to suppose that substitutions of terms can operate in idiom in this way. Indeed, the fact that two distinct terms can be used in such a type of expression is a test which displays evidence against both being a case of a particular idiom. Further, since the syntax of the examples from Mark and Matthew, for instance, differs in relevant respects, this opposes the syntactic ossification which being an idiom presupposes (if it is a syntactic and semantic idiom, as Moule appears to assume).[78] The singular form of the Matt. 23:15 case is in opposition to the plural states of the other examples where they are regarded as instances of a particular idiom. Such a capacity to pluralize is a property of a metaphor rather than an idiom. Also the semantic value of the postulated idiom's illustrations is predictable from its prehistory by metaphorization, which indicates a metaphor and not an idiom[79] (in a genetic inspection of uses, not referents).

(ii) Dealing with the preposition *pro* Professor Moule categorizes one of its three uses (under the genitive heading) as metaphorical, which is odd in a study of idioms. He cites two examples: 'Jas. 5:12, 1 Pet. 4:8 *pro pantōn, above all*' and adds Col. 1:17 as a possibility.[80]

If *pro* is an idiom, then it cannot be metaphorical.[81] If one admits

---

[78] It cannot, hence, be a syntactic idiom either.

[79] It is true that T. Cohen has argued that metaphors are unpredictable (cf. his 'Figurative Speech and Figurative Acts', *Journal of Philosophy*, 72 (1975), pp. 669–84); but his point is to do with a particular logical sense of mechanical prediction of functions, and not, for example, with the applied linguistic predictability within individual expressions (as in J. Lyons, *Introduction to Theoretical Linguistics*, p. 406, or W. Haas's view that metaphoric value is predictable from its component's prior usage, while idiom is not). cf. Haas's as yet unpublished research on 'Metaphor' (delivered as a John Rylands University of Manchester Lecture, but publication said to be reserved for separate presentation with other research).

[80] C. F. D. Moule, *An Idiom-Book of New Testament Greek*, p. 74.

[81] For example, even though one might guess at the ossified value in 'I'd give

Col. 1:17 as an instance of the category which Moule constructs, then with its feature of priority one might succeed in establishing that *pro* is a metaphor – as a transference from that value to a metaphoric 'above'. Alternatively, but perhaps less probably, the value 'above' might be a paraphrastic rendering of *pro* in the texts Jas. 5:12 and 1 Pet. 4:8, and its actual semantic value is a metaphoric shift from the typical NT usage of *pro* (i.e. 'before', possibly with an LXX type provenance based on the MT *lpny*). Conversely, one might designate *pro* as an idiom formed from the typical NT usage of *pro*, but occurring idiomatically in these two texts. Of course, Moule was obviously aware of this dilemmatic tendency in the data's interpretation, but confusedly combined illicit alternatives.

(iii) Another example of Moule's confusion over idiom and metaphor is evident in his treatment of *loipon*, when, after general introductory observations he stated:[82]

> But sometimes a definite time-significance, *henceforth* (or *thenceforth*), appears to be called for; and once or twice a metaphorical extension of this to mean *it follows that* seems to make good sense.

Moule then furnishes textual examples, one relevant for the above being Heb. 10:13: '*to loipon ekdechomenos* . . ., *thenceforth awaiting* . . .'. It is possible for a metaphor to become an idiom because its or some of its components are unknown to users (as a specialized metaphor). Yet this is not the case here: Moule expressly measures the semantic value of *loipon* in Heb. 10:13 from its other uses (which presumes a predictability relation between the uses); this involves metaphorization not idiomatization, which Moule himself concedes by his classification of it as a metaphorical extension. Yet it appears in a section on idioms.

(iv) The *Idiom-Book* cites the 'general formula "Given certain conditions, certain results follow"'[83] in relation to conditional sentences. Quoting Matt. 6:23, John 11:12 and 1 Cor. 15:16

---

my right arm to be ambidexterous', its pun imparts information from idiom not metaphor.

[82] C. F. D. Moule, *An Idiom-Book of New Testament Greek*, p. 161. Of course, it is clear by now in this brief survey that Moule was unaware of the strict distinction of idiom and metaphoric levels, otherwise no doubt he could have easily implemented the proper classification; but, since his book is widely used and presents linguistic analyses which canonize the confusions, criticism is apt.

[83] C. F. D. Moule, *An Idiom-Book of New Testament Greek*, p. 148.

as characteristic of one category, Moule explained the construction as:

Protasis (if-clause): *ei* with Indic. in appropriate tense.
Apodosis (result-clause): another Indic. (or its equivalent) in appropriate tense.
The negative in the protasis is usually *ou*;

These phenomena cannot constitute conditional clauses as cases of idiom. First, the item (conditional marker) *ei* is the semantic value 'if' as generally elsewhere in Greek,[84] and as such is not idiomatized; neither, therefore, is the conditional status of the protasis which it governs.[85] Second, if Moule is right in describing a phenomenon as an apodosis,[86] then such a view falls under the same type of criticism offered in respect of the protasis. A protasis is a piece of argument of a given logical form, a form which appears elsewhere in the NT together with the foregoing type of protasis examples, and, as such, the apodosis adduced by Moule, in connection with the protasis, is characteristic of non-idiomatic usage in reason. Indeed, it is difficult to envisage what it is to be an idiomatized conditional sentence where *ei* would be a component of it, since logical form is, in the relevant sense, predictable and capable of substitutivity, whereas idiom is not when compared with normal forms.[87] Third, the negative in the protasis

[84] e.g. Matt. 10:25, John 10:35, 1 Cor. 15:13 etc. and in the same general semantic fields or genre as Moule's examples.

[85] Of course, the indicative entities which Moule isolates do not occur with all *ei* uses, but this is irrelevant to the fact that Moule is offering a general formula about a conditional, alleged property of an idiom; and as such the conditional value of *ei* violates the proposal since it is logically and semantically the same in Moule's cases and outside those cases in other NT situations. Perhaps Moule was mistakenly isolating the conditional as the unusual feature, when it is more to do with the clause frame in which the conditional marker appears.

[86] I prefer the terms 'antecedent' and 'consequent', as in standard usage in logic, and employ 'protasis' and 'apodosis' only because Moule introduces them; specifications of the former two terms in standard logic, rather than the traditional explanations of the latter terms, are behind the foregoing comments. (For which see A. Church, *Introduction to Mathematical Logic*, I (Princeton, 1956); and for some of the causal examples used by Moule, cf. J. L. Mackie, *The Cement of the Universe* (Oxford, 1974), pp. 29–58, etc. Also, for some interpretative problems cf. A. N. Prior, *The Doctrine of Propositions and Terms*, pp. 89ff.)

[87] 'Forms' here is not to be confused with strict morphology; 'forms' I reserve for a logical, and morphology for a linguistic, property. It would be a misunderstanding to defend Moule by claiming that he is merely commenting on temporal, morphological, syntactic and semantic peculiarities within conditional sentences (and so avoiding my criticism of his classification of conditional sentences and

(which is normally *ou*) is an operator for negation that has this value in many other (non-idiomatic) NT contexts, hence permitting substitution and so opposing a classification of idiomaticity concerning this case.[88]

The features of ossification, fossilization, non-substitutivity of components and unpredictability of relations of idioms to their components' prehistory or synchronic homonyms are properties of idioms which can be adduced. The foregoing instances of alleged idioms do not conform to descriptions based on these features. On the other hand, the properties which idioms are currently not assumed to have, the *Idiom-Book* regards as idiomatic qualities of words in NT. Consequently, many cases cited by Moule exhibit linguistic phenomena which are not to be associated with idioms. In the perspective of this situation it is not surprising that he erects a complex of classification which has all the appearance of a regular grammar – for that is what the *Idiom-Book* is, to a large extent: and this indicates that it is not an exhaustive treatment of idiom, but an analysis of other phenomena, with a few idioms present, and characterized as idiom, because being idiom opposes the rule-like classification of the *Idiom-Book*.

(*h*) Of course there are some problems of deciding whether a term is an idiom or metaphor, because, among other issues, of the lexical range within which the controverted item appears. For example, in a study on the *nun energicum* and the prefix conjugation in MT Hebrew, T. Muraoka[89] uses the notion of idiom to explain an implication of his research for the view that in early Semitic the jussive and prefix preterite were identical in form. He states:

The use of basically past tense form to express a wish is

---

clauses): because he explicitly addressed a formula and construction of a conditional sentence whose components sometimes (in the case of *ei* invariably) have a parallel logical force in non-idiomatic contexts which comprise the phenomenon (as Moule explains it) of being cases of conditional sentences. And in view of A. R. White's application of philosophical logic to expose some of the canon of indicatives (*Modal Thinking* (Oxford, 1975), pp. 5, 49–103), although problems remain, Moule's indicatives may conform to or violate given forms.

[88] That Professor Moule is giving attention to what he deems logic phenomena is clear from his language: 'logically' (pp. 148, 168); 'implies *obligation, necessity, possibility*' (p. 149); 'formula', 'contingencies' (p. 148); '*implied* protases' (p. 150); 'logically a conditional sentence, one half is not expressed but only implied' (p. 151); 'logically . . . strictly implies a protasis' (p. 151). In this context there is also reference to 'idioms'.

[89] T. Muraoka, 'The Nun Energicum and the Prefix Conjugation in Biblical Hebrew', *Annual of the Japanese Biblical Institute*, I (1975), pp. 63–71.

quite common . . . The English idioms like 'I wish I had more time' or 'It's time you went up to bed' could be similarly interpreted by a man in the street ignorant of the past history of the language. Note also Modern Hebrew *kvar telekh lišon* 'It's time you went to bed' and the like with the striking *kvar*, particle with unmistakable reference to past time. The basic idea lying behind all these usages is that something wished for or urgently demanded is envisaged by the speaker as what has already, or should have long since, materialised.[90]

In a situation where, say, an abstract noun is totally idiomatized, it would be difficult to relate its sense (its idiomatic value) to known homonyms for any guidance about its meaning. Even if it were a metaphor, this would often be a difficult problem, since other homonyms would perhaps have no family likeness in semantics to the metaphor.

However, with temporal lexemes this is rather different: the scope of time-sense is fairly restricted[91] to a specialized group of semantic values whose application in contexts is time-bound. So, even if there is total ossification, would the item's value be completely unpredictable without recourse to external factors? The answer to this is dictated by the position one assumes about the nature of the ossification. That is to say, if the lexeme's non-idiomatic value is that of past tense, would one judge it full idiomatization, if the term came to stand for the future or present? Against this it might be advanced that total ossification has not been achieved because the item is still a temporal word, from which – given that information, one could calculate its value from the context: hence it could be identified as a metaphor, in which case the 'prophetic perfect' would be a metaphorized entity, as would be *kvar*. Now if this is so, Muraoka would be wrong in introducing the term 'idiom'.[92] Indeed, he observed that two examples of idioms (quoted above) 'could be similarly interpreted by a man in the street ignorant of the past history of the language'. This is a condition relating to metaphorization: that one can assess transfer in a synchronic field. Unfortunately, this

[90] *ibid.*, p. 67.

[91] I am not, obviously, assuming any view of time such as that criticized by J. Barr in *Biblical Words for Time*, but merely drawing attention to the functioning narrowness of the temporal field for relevant terms.

[92] Actually Muraoka quotes the full expressions such as 'I wish I had more time' as though they were the idioms; it is more interesting to consider this a slip of the pen or informal characterization, and regard a component of the expression (i.e. 'had') as the idiom.

quoted statement is attached to a judgement of a thing's being idiom, while a feature contingent on idiom is that it cannot be interpreted by a person if he is not initiated into its meaning. It may be that the way to interpret Muraoka's description is to ascribe to the man in the street synchronic cognizance of the idioms, in which case this aspect of the problem is resolved.

In addition to this, Muraoka applies other characteristics to the idioms: the first is something 'wished for', and the second 'urgently demanded'. These are 'envisaged by the speaker as what has already, or should have long since, materialised'. Muraoka writes of the 'basic idea behind all these usages' as a compound of this wish, or imperative, linked with what the speaker envisages. If 'behind' is construed as intention, then it and its related features cannot be semantic values. If this is so, and if the speaker has not synchronic cognizance of idioms cited, then it is wrong to designate the quotations as idioms. Contrariwise, if 'behind' and associated items are specifications of the sense of the quotations, then this would involve a substantial semantic shift quite outside the temporal values of the relevant words, and so these would be idioms because this semantic valuation is not predictable from the temporal lexemes.

In such situations more explicit differentiation between grades of ossification is required and would prevent ambiguity and aid discrimination. Since Muraoka is concerned with the diachronic positions of various related uses of the relevant terms, and because idiom is the final phase of ossification of an expression, often at the end of a lengthy prehistory of progress through other grades of meaning which are an idiom's homonyms, loose criteria of identification for idiom will possibly obscure the relation of an expression to its semantic value at a given level, where the dia-chronic axis is conjectural at certain points. Also, it is clear that separation of mental and empirical levels, relating to associations around idiomaticity, is important because intentionality can dis-tort the empirical status of an expression.

At first inspection, a superficial consideration of idioms and their relations to a logico-linguistic study might (wrongly) con-clude that, because idiom is in extreme states of unpredictability respecting its component historical antecedents, logico-linguistics cannot handle idioms. It has been found that this is not so. Where

---

[93] Nevertheless, this looseness around the term 'idiom' is perhaps recurrent (see T. Muraoka, 'The Status Constructus of Adjectives in Biblical Hebrew', *Vetus Testamentum*, 27 (1977), p. 376). Still, I think this study is extremely fine and valuable, and my point a mere detail.

the actual occurrences of idioms, their functional utility,[94] are the target of investigation, their state of ossification is an aid to realizing the application of some logico-linguistic discussion to pertinent examples and issues. If this is true of idiom it is consistent to conjecture that it applies to less extreme manifestations of linguistic phenomena, at least so as to warrant a full-scale investigation of them.

---

[94] For 'utility' see P. F. Strawson, *Subject and Predicate in Logic and Grammar* (London, 1974), pp. 42ff.

3

PROPER NAMES

3.0 REFERENTIAL FUNCTIONS AND ANCIENT NAMES

1   Reference versus Semantic Value?

(*a*)   It was explained in 2.0, *1* above that reference (the relation, the operation of referring, and the connection of these with their referents) is indicated by proper names and other phenomena.[1] The sense of a proper name (hereafter PN) is its reference; as such it does not display any predicative properties, although the mode of its sense (the way in which it specifies that reference) may vary. The concept of a PN's only having a non-predicative referential function[2] does not obviously comply with many uses of PNs in Near Eastern texts; PNs often can appear to bear the sense of intelligible sentences. For example G. Pettinato, in listing cases of paleo-Canaanite PNs found at Ebla,[3] cites a supposed translation of each PN:

[1] I follow Dummett in his account of proper names (M. Dummett, *Frege: Philosophy of Language*, pp. 54–80, etc.; see also P. T. Geach, 'Names and Identity', pp. 147ff. In a slightly different framework, yet still involving reference of the relevant sort in PNs, ct. J. Bennett, *Linguistic Behaviour* (Cambridge, 1976), secs. 66 and 83).

[2] For this use of function see F. G. Droste, 'On Proper Names', *Leuvense Bijdragen: Tijdschrift voor Germaanse Filologie*, 64 (1975), 1, pp. 1–13. I do not dispute Frege's use of argument whereas *function* is employed above (cf. G. Frege, *Begriffsschrift eine der arithmetischen nachgebildete Formelsprache des reinen Denkens* (Halle, 1879), p. xiii). I replace the term since I wish to avoid its deductive associations, although I presuppose the criteria of identity connected with Frege's term and Dummett's and part of Geach's specification of PNs. Note that the above use of 'only' is strictly related to 'function', not excluding tone, etc.

[3] G. Pettinato, 'The Royal Archives of Tell-Mardikh-Ebla', *Biblical Archaeologist*, 39 (May 1976), p. 50; he lists 20 PNs, of which three typical cases are produced below. The translations were produced by drawing on bilingual data in the vocabulary in text TM.75.G.2000, and other undocumented Ebla texts.

En-na-ni-Il   'Il has mercy on me'
Ip-pi-ḫir   'It has been reunited'
Eb-du-ᵈ Ra-sa-ap 'Servant of Rasap'

Such illustrations may seem to go against a logician's (e.g. C. S. Peirce's)[4] view that 'there is no verb [etc.] wrapped up in a PN'. I wish to maintain that this conflict is not actual, and results only from lack of clarity and discrimination in analysis of linguistic levels (although I do not resist the point that unique nonformal features sometimes surround such PNs).

(*b*)   Before examining aspects of this arena of seeming conflict, a few remarks are pertinent on the treatment of PNs in past scholarship. First, A. R. Millard[5] has shown that some previous scholars made unfounded claims about some PNs. For example, J. A. Montgomery and H. S. Gehman[6] claimed that the Ashur Ostracon presents a more exact transcription of Tiglath-pileser's name than the Hebrew forms in MT. Millard shows that, while the forms adduced by these two scholars supply more extensive phonetic renderings, these renderings are in a later Babylonian form, whereas the Hebrew represents the earlier Assyrian.[7] Consequently Montgomery and Gehman (and also Cowley)[8] ought not to infer that the MT is less accurate or later. Here some of the issues stressed by Barr[9] about semantic presuppositions and

[4] C. S. Peirce, *Collected Papers*, ed. C. Hartshorne, P. Weiss and A. W. Burks (Harvard, 1958), p. 328; cf. P. F. Strawson, *Individuals* (London, 1959), p. 20. (A few logicians who are untypical of most philosophers in the analytic tradition give a certain semantic description of PNs whereby PNs have some sense other than reference (albeit incorporating reference); for the formal work see C. Lejewski, 'On Lesniewski's Ontology', *Ratio*, 1, (1958), pp. 150–76.)

[5] A. R. Millard, 'Assyrian Royal Names in Hebrew', *Journal of Semitic Studies*, 21 (1976), pp. 1–14.

[6] cf. J. A. Montgomery and H. S. Gehman, *Kings: International Critical Commentary* (Edinburgh, 1951).

[7] Tiglath-pileser III: Akkadian *Tukulti-apil-ešarra*; Hebrew e.g. 2 Kgs. 15:29 *tglt pl'sr*; Ashur Ostracon, written in Babylonian, *tkltplsr*. (Millard accounts for differences in other MT texts by regarding transpositions as inner-Hebrew variations, and also the intrusive *n* is treated in this way; cf. A. R. Millard, 'Assyrian Royal Names in Hebrew', pp. 7, 12.)

[8] A. Cowley, *Aramaic Papyri* (Oxford, 1923), pp. 456, 506 (references due to Millard).

[9] J. Barr, 'Reading a Script without Vowels', pp. 82ff. Of course, many of Barr's criticisms of general weakness in semantic analysis of past theologians and linguists also apply to such treatments of PNs, although he did not apply them to this topic (e.g. J. Barr, *Biblical Words for Time* (rev. edn.) pp. 19, 86–100). Barr differently employs 'presupposition' to describe his views, although I take

reading of texts are relevant for assessment and warning, since it is a set of presuppositions linked with a simple item – a PN – which provokes conceptual and linguistic confusions. Description of a PN, even at the graphic level, articulates a set of presuppositions (sometimes unwittingly by both actor and scholar). As Droste expressed it:[10]

> Although they [PNs] dispose of a semantic nucleus, they depend for their functioning in an utterance almost exclusively and essentially on their presuppositional specification.

This specification should be explicit in the case of a scholar characterizing a PN in a text, and it ought to mirror the usage of the PN in such a text; where incomplete understanding prohibits this specification of part of it, scholars need to restrict the domain of their generalization to appropriate parameters – although this is rarely achieved, as illustrated in the foregoing case. Such prohibitions often apply at the juncture where scholars either fail to recognize restrictions or assume warrant to surmount them.

(c)   A second consideration is related to the first: only rarely does a text exhibit a utilization of the alleged non-referential semantic content of a PN, and this is invariably in the context of pun or production of the PN from components in natural language usage. Consequently, there is generally a diachronic and not synchronic relation between the normal use of components of a PN and the normal referential usage of a PN. A synchronic relation between the normal usage of the PN components and the referential use of the PN may exist in strictly separate semantic fields and register with little or no coincidence of the two classes except in pun situations. Contrariwise, etymologization of PNs traditionally has rested largely on an artificial conflation or collapsing of two distinct synchronic axes (separated by a diachronic scale), often also containing dissimilar semantic fields, which are incorrectly

---

it that my use of it represents him accurately. For some explanation of the position on presupposition which I adopt see G. Frege, 'Uber Sinn und Bedeutung', and also S. Haack, *Deviant Logic*, pp. 137–41 (and p. 52 for a criticism of Strawson's interpretation); cf. the helpful remarks, in part, in R. M. Kempson, *Presupposition and the Delimitation of Semantics*, pp. 47–84. cf. also 5.2, 3 below.

[10] F. G. Droste, 'On Proper Names', pp. 1–2; note as well his judgement that 'presupposition coincides with specific reference', in respect of PNs. cf. P. Matthiae, 'Tell Mardikh: the Archives and Palace', *Archaeology*, 30 (July 1977), 4, p. 253, where A.EN.GA.DU^{ki} was wrongly read as A-ga-du EN^{ki} (Akkad) in 1976, but now as unknown A-ru-ga-du^{ki}.

matched or smudged descriptively as one field or symmetrical positions of normality.[11] I return to some such examples after establishing the following distinction.

Two levels of usage are of relevance for differentiating between different uses of PNs. Such levels, although common in logic theory of meaning, are not generally applied in biblical linguistics.[12] They are 'use' and 'mention'. 'Use' is a function or set of functions in the metalanguage: i.e. language as we, or a text, employ language to refer to and describe things.[13] 'Mention' can be that linguistic circumstance (for present purposes) where a referent mentioned is linguistic – a piece of object language – within an expression in a text; in short, where language is used to discuss or mention language. Of course it is not that use and mention are always opposed, mutually exclusive, categories. Mention is a species of use: a mention is an employment of an item in an expression's meaning which perforce involves usage (but where the referent and locus of ascription of semantic values is within the expression). Particularly is it the shift of level, within the hierarchy of usage within the sentence, which is the target of this distinction.[14]

If the foregoing distinction is recognized in operation in Near Eastern and biblical texts, then the function of a PN is solely referential, while mention includes assigning a non-referential semantic value to the PN.

Into the category of mention go PNs which figure as a piece of object language. In some modern languages this shift of level may be indicated by quotation marks,[15] where the name and

---

[11] In 2.1, *4* above, J. J. M. Roberts's treatment of *Rašap* is an appropriate illustration of this. Asymmetry obtains between PNs and their components' prehistory in innovation and intake of PNs (cf. M. L. Samuels, *Linguistic Evolution* (Cambridge, 1972), pp. 61f., and esp. pp. 57–8).

[12] For theory see W. V. O. Quine, *Mathematical Logic*, sec. 4.

[13] Metalanguage and object language distinctions are introduced in 2.0, *3* above.

[14] See P. T. Geach, *Logic Matters*, p. 203.

[15] In logic there are techniques in symbolic language for exposing and preserving this distinction (see P. T. Geach, *Logic Matters*, pp. 50–3, 198–204). Notice that the misuse of quotation marks (which has obscured and confused this shift of levels) occurs amongst some philosophers and users of natural languages, as documented by C. Lewy, *Meaning and Modality*, pp. 23ff.; P. T. Geach, *Logic Matters*, pp. 189–211. Also use and mention are levels which themselves have been conflated and not apprehended on occasions by some philosophers; see examples from Aristotle and Russell in P. T. Geach, *Reference and Generality*, pp. 23f. So it ought not to be surprising if it is discovered that theologians and some linguists have fallen into similar confusions (although such instances may be more obvious and more easily avoided than those to which Geach refers).

sometimes its semantic assignment become linguistic referents. Not infrequently terminology in ancient texts replaces quotation marking. An obvious example of this alternative method of distinguishing use and mention is the introduction of *šm* ('name') and other related terms in etiological formulae.[16] To be sure, such terms were often articulated without an actor's appreciation of the switch in linguistic level. Yet the need to introduce these formulae itself imports evidence of a change of level, in that a PN itself becomes a sort of referent, whereas, prior to the change in level, the morpheme, representing the PN, only referred to an empirical referent. The distinction exposes the structure of an aspect in this changing of levels. From such a truth it is not entailed that the actor had a concept of it – any more than mastery of a piece of grammatical usage by a user entails an ability of that user to specify or recognize the grammatical tendency which the piece displays.

However, it is to be emphasized that such mention of PNs is exceptional and semantically abnormal in ancient Near Eastern texts. Many PNs appear in these texts without ever being employed in mention situations and could only inconsistently or incredibly[17] exist in bizarre theoretical collocations with matching homonyms. *klb* ('bark' of a dog)[18] and *zrš* (Persian: 'mophead')[19] sharply illustrate this. These two names never appear to be used for any purpose other than identification by naming. So in such a usage no paronomasia occurs nor etymological play on the ossified semantic contents of the PNs. Where a person has two different names, he is obviously being referred to by a different mode (or sense) in each name; but this is not ascription of a predicative element in the PN to the bearer. Nevertheless, incomplete understanding of possibility[20] and limitations in our capacity to

I think that the topic of tonal pun and nuance in the context of mention, and its associative relations with the use of a PN, creates a large area for future research. Here the sum of tones in mention is greater than in use.

[16] For which see B. O. Long, *The Problem of Etiological Narrative in the Old Testament* (Berlin, 1968); F. W. Golka, 'The Aetiologies in the Old Testament: I, II', *Vetus Testamentum*, 26 (1976), pp. 410–28; 27 (1977), pp. 36–47.

[17] For the canon of this claim see K. R. Popper, *Objective Knowledge*, pp. 48ff., 119ff.

[18] Num. 13:6. (Perhaps a breakdown yielding 'heart-like' is agreeable?)

[19] Est. 5:10. (I thank Professor Barr for this example.)

[20] A. R. White, *Modal Thinking*, pp. 15–16, 75–89; and in a different context M. Dummett, *Frege: Philosophy of Language*, pp. 126–35; and relating to the premises on which decisions requiring 'rules' rest, see J. Bogen, *Wittgenstein's Philosophy of Language* (London, 1972), pp. 180–220. Of course, these

retrieve the literature which comprised a relevant synchronic field[21] require caution in ruling systematically on certain problematic PNs.

2   Asymmetry of Syntax in PNs

It would be strange if *'bšlwm* were a PN with[22] (ascriptive) semantic value in use (except, conversely, in a situation of pun where a mention of it was a grim satire). This PN typically displays features of internal syntactic abnormality which exists in normal PNs in use in the Bible. For example:

hnh r'yty 't-'bšlm tlwy b'lh
Behold, I saw Absalom hanged in an oak.[23]

In addition to semantic inappropriateness for its context, the PN's syntax has a structure which does not conform to its environment and omits syntax and items relevant for making it a definite description or ascription of semantic value to Absalom.[24] It is certain that, since this PN is typical of the set of the Near Eastern and biblical PNs in use (not mention), the PNs in Near Eastern texts display an apparent internal syntactic structure which does not make a linguistic contribution to its external linguistic environment. Hence, obviously, its external environment does not include functions which contract relations with the PN's supposed internal structure. This is tantamount to the judgement that PNs do not have a semantic value except in their referring value and tonal contracts.

---

uncertainties militate, as well, against those who without proof offer semantic identifications of PNs, since the history of semantics is a series of non-systematic, arbitrary shifts which do not recapitulate logic.

[21] For a review of areas of insight and also ignorance which underlie the employment of possibility here, see N. M. Waldman, 'The Hebrew Tradition', in T. A. Sebeok (ed.), *Current Trends in Linguistics, 13: Historiography of Linguistics* (The Hague, Paris, 1975), pp. 1285–1330. Incoherent yet dogmatically held theses on the 'potentiality' of a word (where hypostatization exists in a scholar's treatment) firmly block access to extant linguistic information which can contribute to the specification of a field; see J. Barr showing this of a particular scholar (regarding a noun) in *Biblical Words for Time*, pp. 6of.

[22] e.g. Absalom in 2 Sam. 13:22.

[23] 2 Sam. 18:10.

[24] Sometimes (e.g. *yhwšw'*) a name seems to ascribe to a person other than its bearer, which presents peculiarly acute difficulties for those who wish to recognize a 'referring' of meaning to a bearer.

The foregoing judgement applies to the various categories of biblical names,[25] such as those listed by Noth[26] and Stamm[27] with features of word names, and word names with constructs;[28] nominal[29] and verbal[30] sentence names;[31] prepositional names;[32] interrogatory names[33] and others.[34] Of course, these PNs' alleged semantic values and actual structure, if characterized as uses, do not concur with their environments, and often contain archaic forms at a linguistic level distinct from, and diachronically separated by, their original use and later occurrence.[35] The widely documented interchange and influence of foreign elements in the formation of PNs reflect a situation where internal syntax and semantics of PNs (although sometimes unsystematically described)[36] do not make a non-referential contribution, in use,

---

[25] I thank Professor Barr for mentioning some of these to me.

[26] M. Noth, *Die Israelitischen Personennamen im Rahmen der Gemeinsemitischen Namengebung* (Stuttgart, 1928).

[27] J. J. Stamm, *Die akkadische Namengebung* (Leipzig, 1939).

[28] e.g. *'by* (2 Kgs. 18:2).

[29] See the ten occurrences in Num. 1:5–15.

[30] e.g. (with noun first) *'lyšm'* (Num. 1:10); (with verb first in perfect) *šptyh* (2 Sam. 3:4; cf. 1 Chr. 12:5).

[31] Some scholars have confused the functional role of epithets/appellations, proper names with one term (e.g. *'Ašerah*) and proper names containing sentences which incorporate such a term, although there is a severe problem of separating the categories of name and epithets in some contexts, which I do not wish to underestimate. However, this hardly gives a permit for a shifting backwards and forwards through the categories without any observations on the change of level, when scholars are attempting to adduce a semantic (predicative) connection between name and sentence; e.g. W. F. Albright in *Yahweh and the Gods of Canaan* (London, 1968), pp. 117–18, 166, etc. Sometimes this shift occurs when a scholar has yet to establish criteria of identification of supposed referents between names and epithets – not infrequently when the naming evidence is drawn from other PNs naming quite distinct items. The god postulated as *'olām* in the form by F. M. Cross (*Canaanite Myth and Hebrew Epic*, pp. 15–18) is such a case; see his identification of it as epithet, then name (and located 'within' the place name of that form in the Shishak List (reference p. 18 note 30)).

[32] e.g. *bṣl'l* (Exod. 31:2).

[33] e.g. *myk'l* (Dan. 12:1).

[34] Hypocoristic formations, and the various forms of abbreviation, with absent (albeit perhaps implied) nouns or verbs, are often taken to be associated with the 'sense' of a PN. Here is a class of PNs which advertises a substantial difference from normal grammar.

[35] Of course someone like F. M. Cross is aware of 'linguistic archaism' (see *Canaanit Myth and Hebrew Epic*, p. 25) and differences in PNs and epithets, but ignores these by making such connections.

[36] e.g. W. F. Albright, 'Northwest-Semitic Names in a list of Egyptian Slaves

to their linguistic environment.[37] This situation does not yet furnish grounds for one to regard the referential function and absence of semantic assignment beyond that role, as universals, but, rather, a law-like tendency. However, at least for the typical PN (and probably all) it is impossible for this not to be the case.[38]

For example, the Amorite 18th-century onomasticon PNs, such as *sumu-la-'il*,[39] show that the item *sumu* ('the name') can be joined on occasions with *'il*. It would not only invoke Russell's Paradox,[40] but also, more importantly, specify a textually non-existent, or competing, reference to assign the seeming internal ingredients of the PN to a functioning level: the bearer is not the subject of the item *sumu*, but it is a component in producing a reference to that bearer; yet this latter point is incompatible functionally with the fact that the alleged internal referent of *sumu* is linguistic (*'il*), which itself does not concur with the PN's referent which is distinct from the alleged referent of *'il*.[41] Certainly, scholars will recognize some difference of priority and role in their description of a PN and its 'meaning' or etymology. This is not disputed; it is, rather, that the actual structure and force of that structure is not appreciated and heeded systematically. Consequently, conclusions are sometimes assumed which would be blocked by accurate description of data.[42]

3   Idiomatization in Proper Names

Quite clearly the foregoing sections, drawing attention to the semantic and syntactic peculiarities of PNs, can serve to indicate the presence of ossification at these linguistic levels: the semantic

from the 18th Century B.C.', *Journal of the American Oriental Society*, 74 (1954), pp. 222–33.

[37] I do *not* exclude the inclusion of semantic tone here.

[38] i.e. where use is admitted to be a criterion of meaning and where reference is held to be a value in a PN.

[39] See H. Huffmon, *Amorite Personal Names in the Mari Texts* (Baltimore, 1965), pp. 165ff., 248ff. For many others cf. another class of PNs in J. K. Stark, *Personal Names in Palmyrene Inscriptions* (Oxford, 1971).

[40] cf. M. Dummett, *Frege : Philosophy of Language*, pp. 530ff.

[41] F. M. Cross (*Canaanite Myth and Hebrew Epic*, p. 11) observes that *su-mu-la-AN* is a name and 'the element *sum-* refers to the hypostatized name of the god'. Cross also uses the internal syntax of such names, all at a level of use, without differentiation of level, to argue certain linguistic relations and influences on Hebrew.

[42] In connection with etymology, J. Barr made a similar point (*The Semantics of Biblical Language*, pp. 158–60).

and syntactic remnants within PNs are frozen elements of pre-history. If one adds to this the resistance of PNs to quantification, there is a firm alignment of main features of PNs with idioms at a particular level of internal redundancy. This internal redundancy operates at the level of use. The causal antecedents of PNs and idioms might be quite distinct, and the residue of their prehistory remaining outside their uses in semantic fields (as homonyms, etc.) will differ, but there will be substantial internal similarities.

These properties of proper names can accordingly be designated idiomatization of PNs. The application of use picks out the idiomatic status here, where a PN is a referring term which does not contribute other semantic (non-tonal) values to its linguistic environment. Mention correlates with a situation involving, for instance, reversal of the status of the PN (i.e. de-idiomatization) by a pun on its ossified component values' alleged, or actual, relation to homonyms, etc., and/or etiology. In this perspective, specification of the PN's role in biblical languages in use (and not mention) concurs with the function of referring,[43] and so this referential feature is capable of analysis as an actual property of a text and not the product of an artificial requirement of a 'logical language'.

(a) *Mention* obtains on the etiology and ascription of non-referential meaning to PNs. In keeping with this (but distinct from it in treatment) J. Fichtner,[44] J. A. Soggin,[45] and B. O. Long[46] have continued the trend of showing that etiological considerations surround apparent ascription of semantic value to PNs. This, of course, relates to the construction, not use, of PNs, although some scholars (e.g. F. Zimmermann)[47] have continued to ascribe predicative properties to PNs, usually where a particular psychological or anthropological thesis is dogmatically presupposed in analysis.

[43] i.e. argument place; such an application is analogous to an equation's specifying what *is* a state to which it refers. Of course since I am dealing with a law-like tendency, I do not dispute that there may be exceptions of an antipathetic sort, but these may result from incomplete understanding; and I have not yet found one.

[44] J. Fichtner, 'Die etymologische Ätiologie in der Namengebung der geschichtlichen Bücher des Alten Testaments', *Vetus Testamentum*, 6 (1956), pp. 372–96.

[45] J. A. Soggin, 'Kultätiologische Sagen und Katechese im Hexateuch', *Vetus Testamentum*, 10 (1960), pp. 341–7.

[46] B. O. Long, *The Problem of Etiological Narrative in the Old Testament*.

[47] F. Zimmermann, 'Folk Etymology of Biblical Names', *Vetus Testamentum Supplements*, 15 (1966), pp. 311–26.

Another level within the category of mention is where a homonym may be overlaid by a PN for narrative pun or irony. Barr[48] has drawn attention to the possibility of the name *nbl*[49] being originally associated with, for example, the (*n-b-l*) epigraphic South Arabian *sent*, with the value 'fool' being ironically matched with the PN for narrative purposes. Here the mention cuts across the prehistory (which is part of the irony) and strikes a contract with a homonym.[50]

Etiological terminology and expressions can on occasions be employed to measure the presence of mention:

wyqr' 't-šmw gršm ky 'mr gr
hyyty b'rṣ nkryh
and he called his name 'Gershom':
for he said, I have been a stranger
in a strange land.[51]

Note that a semantic value is not explicitly injected into the PN, but rather the semantic causality of the reason for the PN is given.[52] There is a sort of causal parallelism alleged, including perhaps *šm-* ('there') in the second element of the PN with the expression *b'rṣ* ('in a . . . land').[53] The general structure of the citation at relevant points is of course:

I: (i) x designates y's name to be PN
      (ii) because x *F*ied.[54]

[48] J. Barr, 'The Symbolism of Names in the Old Testament', in *Bulletin of the John Rylands University Library of Manchester*, 52 (1969–70), pp. 11–30.

[49] 2 Sam. 25:25. It is interesting to note that one of W. Haas's distinctions relating idiomatic forms to the redundant elements in names, and the possibility of striking semantic values for elements in them by pun (although he is treating a quite distinct topic and does not dwell on the connection in the way I do), has a certain helpful parallel with J. Barr's description of 2 Sam. 25:25 (see W. Haas, *Writing without Letters*, pp. 195–6).

[50] The usage of foreign components in PNs in a language, which gives rise to this sort of situation, is widespread in other languages, where no pun on the foreign component is made (cf. K. Charan Bahl, 'Panjabi', in T. A. Sebeok (ed.), *Current Trends in Linguistics*, 5 (1969), pp. 151–200).

[51] Exod. 2:22.

[52] For this type of related, albeit distinct, use of causality and reason, see G. E. M. Anscombe, *Intention*, and cf. her 'The First Person', in S. Guttenplan (ed.), *Mind and Language* (Oxford, 1975), pp. 45–65.

[53] Professor Barr made this suggestion when commenting on a research paper of mine at a seminar.

[54] '*F*' stands for a predicate or part thereof, as is customary in philosophical

The name *gršm* is a piece of object language marked by the term *šmw* ('his name'). Fichtner[55] observed that the items here associated with the name by way of explanation, which (i) and (ii) represent in part, are typical of other uses.

Sometimes, as Soggin and Long point out in the previously cited works, the order of (i) and (ii) is reversed.[56] Also individual terms in either or both may be replaced with similar items; but use of *qr'* ('called') and sometimes also *šm* is characteristic of (i) (though, in one etiology in this class *qr'* is absent).[57] In (ii) *'mr* ('said') is often omitted, yet *ky* ('for') is preserved, or, in some contexts the terms occur in reverse order: *wy'mr ky*.[58] Long proposes[59] that in such naming etymologies there is always a keyword in (ii) which is assonant with the PN in (i).

Fichtner draws attention to another type of name etymology, which can be represented as:

II: Therefore, the name of x is PN.

An example of this type is found in Exod. 15:23:

'l-kn qr'-šmh mrh
therefore the name of it was
called 'Marah'.

In this case, although an assertoric consequent is drawn, it is evident that the operational, functioning role of the PN is not attempting to carry that *mrh* ('bitter') semantic value, which is

---

logic. Note the mentalistic feature in this causality, and relation to Hume, in G. E. M. Anscombe, 'Causality and Determination', in E. Sosa (ed.), *Causation and Conditionals* (Oxford, 1975), p. 65.

[55] J. Fichtner, 'Die etymologische Ätiologie . . . ', pp. 378–80.

[56] Their representation of the types is different from mine, but there is no significant variation of relevance here, although mine reflects a general shift to logic.

[57] Gen. 26:33.

[58] Gen. 26:22.

[59] B. O. Long, *The Problem of Etiological Narrative in the Old Testament*, p. 6. Long, together with Soggin, assumes that there is also mixing of the types producing modifications in MT. The J. S. Mill nominalist confusion deployed by Caird (cf. 1.4, 2 above) foments a linguistics which attracts a failure properly to distinguish predicative and referring roles in the above and other contexts. Caird states (*The Language and Imagery of the Bible*, p. 9) that 'The attachment of a name to a referent is known as predication. Here already we come across a source of ambiguity'. But the ambiguity is in his nominalism, for this 'name' is a predicable (cf. 4. below).

used prior to the operator *'l-kn* ('therefore') in predicative use. There is a pun based on a description, but no more; the term *šm* registers a linguistic gear change which introduces the product of the change, the piece of object language *mrh*. Here the PN's circumstance in an expression is abnormal owing to its becoming a sort of referent for etiological purposes. If the PN's explanation is retrospective, then in II the ossified or suspended semantic values, idiomatized in the PN, are triggered into operation and functioning. It is here that the gear change indicates an ascription to, rather than exposure of, already present semantic values in the PN. This is partly because, if use is incorporated in a criterion of meaning and identification of a unit of meaning, then a use (prior to mention), which does not contract a relation of contrast, which demonstrates the presence of the mention value pun, actually does not 'contain' or retain the value which is produced by II (or indeed I). Such a production in mention of PNs is a generation of an associative value by matching, in narrative, of pertinent causal items. However, once a use of a PN is promoted to a context of sustained mention (although these will be few)[60] it may have to be treated, some may think, as a referring term with a non-referring semantic value attached to it (but only in the situation of mention). This is merely a possibility. A logician might respond by deeming such a mention as a logically definite description.[61]

(*b*) That is to say, a sign which hitherto had been a PN in use, now is a definite description (only in mention) which is homographic with respect to a PN yet is functionally a definite description: i.e. 'The *F*' or 'The *x* that *F*'s'.[62] It might be argued that such a device readily serves to represent Semitic sentential names such as *Ibašši-ilum*[63] – 'The god (the *x*) continually *shows* himself (*F*'s)'. Yet it should, by way of repetition, be emphasized that, if the PN here depicted is in a situation textually of use, then it will *not* furnish contrastive substitutions, which could yield the presence of this definite description's semantic value, but solely a referential value. Hence it is clear that, although it is easy to

---

[60] I consider a candidate for such a category (the name *yhwh*) in 3.2 below.

[61] B. Russell, 'On Denoting', *Mind*, 14 (1905), pp. 479–93; cf. also T. J. Smiley's unpub. notes on his lectures on 'Definite Description', delivered at Cambridge in 1973.

[62] As in A. N. Prior, *Objects of Thought*, ch. 10.

[63] See H. B. Huffmon, 'Yahweh and Mari', in H. Goedicke (ed.), *Near Eastern Studies in Honor of W. F. Albright* (Baltimore, 1971), p. 285.

slide from PN to definite description at narrative and exegetical level, linguistically the two realms are distinct and not to be confused by conflation, if there is a technique for depicting a PN in a context of mention (even then as a possible way of dealing with it) as a definite description.

PNs in logic can be replaced by definite descriptions.[64] However this is not to be confused with assuming that both these items have the same value, since they are only referentially identical. Given this, it is inaccurate to presume that such a definite description merely is an exposure of the semantic value inherent in the use of a PN,[65] although a PN and a description may have the same object.[66] Hence, if a scholar were to insist on applying a definite description to a mention of a PN, he cannot be construed as defining the use of the PN (strictly, the PN's homonymic occurrence in use contexts). Such an application might be interpreted as an indirect, or possibly misleading, attempt to characterize a PN's etiological prehistory or synchronic etiological relations to its contexts. In such a case the foregoing restrictions would apply and the analyst would have gained little headway. I do not see any biblical uses that actually require such a treatment; conversely, if handled with sensitivity (albeit with few germinal results) such a procedure might be considered permissible if confusion is avoided. Nevertheless scholarly confusion is often so apparent (as indicated in some previous illustrations) that usage of the device presents a real danger if deployed with the impropriety with which some other distinctions have been utilized. Caution is warranted here because a representation of a mention of a PN by a definite description cannot consistently be said to be a specification of the meaning in the PN for another reason (which does not oppose a description's value in tone).

A PN's mention is still that PN which elsewhere is in normal use, here switched to being a piece of object language; by the same token, if in use this PN cannot receive a specification of being a definite description, so a mention of it cannot be thus represented. Otherwise, if it happens that a definite description does properly characterize the seeming PN, then there has been a mistaken shift of level prior to making the equation, of PN with definite description, for the PN is a disguised definite description

---

[64] See P. T. Geach, *Reference and Generality*, pp. 123f., 44ff.

[65] For the conceptual confusion in judgements which might lie behind such a muddle, see P. T. Geach, *Mental Acts*, pp. 61–74.

[66] M. Dummett, *Frege: Philosophy of Language*, pp. 196ff.

(e.g. an epithet parading as a PN in analysis). I am not here at all agreeing with Russell's unusual view that PNs are disguised definite descriptions, but quite differently observing that a mention of a PN *m* is a mention of that PN *m* in use, so prohibiting an ascription of descriptive meaning to this PN in either use or mention. A person who has to admit that in normal use a PN is employed solely with a referential value is thereby precluded from consistently being able to introduce the status of a definite description to that PN, since it has not furnished any contrastive value, in its referential role, in use. To suppose that one could etymologize over a PN, as though one were exposing its descriptive meaning, is to ignore and resist this set of distinctions. If it is the case that, for example, somewhere in pre-Sargonic texts *Saṭp(u)-ilim* actually means '(the child) is preserved of the god',[67] then one would here have a case of a definite description (i.e. epithet) aping a PN in surface structure.[68] However, since the expression has the subject component, 'the child', missing, this imports evidence of ossification, which might be taken to imply that *Saṭp(u)-ilim* is a PN, and so cannot be characterized as carrying the meaning of the prehistory of its ossified components.

(*c*) That the opposite of the foregoing position is held in some theologico-linguistic studies, is evident from G. H. Parke-Taylor's remark:[69] 'Since names assigned to human beings are regarded as significant in what they declare about the character and influence of individuals, we are justified in expecting divine names to carry specific meaning.' His expressions 'what they declare' and 'carry specific meaning' are unanalyzed and incoherent designations of the status and function of PNs, given the truth of the foregoing distinctions.

---

[67] cf. J. J. M. Roberts, *The Earliest Semitic Pantheon*, pp. 31–2, 92–3.

[68] For philosophical problems in logic presented by assuming a universalizable substitutivity between PNs and a definite description, see: S. Kripke, 'Identity and Necessity', in M. K. Munitz (ed.), *Identity and Individuation* (New York, 1971), pp. 144ff.; and for a response which reflects my own view, compare D. Wiggins, 'Identity, Necessity and Physicalism', in S. Korner (ed.), *Philosophy of Logic* (Oxford, 1976), pp. 96–132.

[69] G. H. Parke-Taylor, *Yahweh: The Divine Name in the Bible* (Waterloo, 1975), p. 4. Of course, to ascribe actual (non-tonal, non-referential) meaning to a PN is strangely at odds with use (i.e. to 'carry meaning'), especially since such scholars employ the term's prior use in history (or idealized etymology) as though it were a value in the use being examined.

1   *Criterion*

A criterion of a criterion can be explained as, roughly, that which x must be to be y.[1]

Wittgenstein investigated the nature of problems obtaining on meaning and criterion,[2] and noticed their connection with use in language. Geach explains what he understands by a criterion of identity:

> I maintain that it makes no sense to judge whether x and y are 'the same', or whether x remains 'the same', unless we add or understand a general term – 'the same F'. That in accordance with which we thus judge as to the identity, I call a criterion of identity . . .[3]

Dummett[4] has termed the expression 'the same F' as a categorial predicate. Namely, that a predicative expression needs to be introduced to specify the identity of the referent of a PN. An ambiguity in the English 'same' requires clarification: Dummett notices[5] that, for example, where a question involves asking whether a book is the same book as one previously known, there can be a slip from type to token. Is it a question about a specific, particular copy, or merely a question about the same work, any copy of which could fulfil the question's requirement? The sense in the 'same' differs in each case and consequently there are two distinct criteria operating behind the uses. A writer might indeed not be aware that he has committed himself to presupposing a

---

[1] This is my own formulation (in 'An Exhibition of Theological Fallacies: a Critique of Gerhard Ebeling's Analysis of Language', *The Heythrop Journal*, 15 (1974) 4, pp. 423–40) which is an adaptation of G. E. M. Anscombe's (unpub.) definition offered at a Cambridge research seminar, 1973.

[2] L. Wittgenstein, *Philosophical Investigations*, secs. 190, 692.

[3] P. T. Geach, *Reference and Generality*, p. 39; cf. also Geach's related exposition in 'Names and Identity', pp. 139ff., and *Mental Acts*, pp. 69ff. Importantly, see as well M. Dummett's extended development of Frege's criterion in *Frege: Philosophy of Language*, pp. 73–80, 130–46, 179–80, 232–4, 544–83. (My above criterion is a necessity criterion, not a sufficiency criterion.) For the introduction of a part of the above quotation in the context of universals, which pertains to this present point, see above in 1.3, 2 (*b*).

[4] M. Dummett, *Frege: Philosophy of Language*, pp. 76, 546ff.

[5] *ibid.*, p. 74.

particular criterion of identity, but that cannot warrant the pro-
hibition of it because it is his use, not intentions or epistemology,
which is the target of the criterion. In such a circumstance it is
possible for inconsistent criteria to be articulated as though they
were consistent.

F. M. Cross[6] offers an odd mixture of judgements about
ʿAstart's epithet:

> ʿAstart's epithet, sm bʿl, 'Name of Baʿl' found at Ugarit in the
> fourteenth century, and at Sidon in the fifth is semantically
> equivalent to the epithet panē baʿl used of Tannit. These
> epithets belong to a general development of hypostases of
> deity in Canaanite religion . . . Similar tendencies are found
> in Israel's religion. The 'name' and the 'presence' of Yahweh
> act for him . . . The 'Angel of the Presence', or the angel
> 'in whom is Yahweh's Name' is given to Israel to guide them
> in the Exodus-Conquest.

Cross alleges that the epithets sm bʿl and panē baʿl are 'semantically
equivalent'; but this is an impossibility. If they are epithets,
then they have sense and not only referential values. If this is
true, then it is obvious that at least sm and panē are not synonymous,
and so they are not semantically equivalent. One way of attempting
to meet this criticism might be to suppose Cross's view is that
these epithets are hypostatized in such a manner as to convert their
use to being equivalent. Yet this cannot be the case, for Cross
translates the epithets with differing renderings which are not
synonymous. It is also pertinent to observe that the footnote
references to 'Angel of the Presence' and 'angel' 'in whom is
Yahweh's Name' which Cross provides[7] are not normally taken
by commentators, for instance, J. P. Hyatt,[8] to be hypostatized
in the required sense. Further 'in whom is Yahweh's Name' is
only applied to an angel once in MT, so it is illicit to apprehend
'similar tendencies' in Israel's religion (in the relevant sense)
to a 'general[9] development' in Canaanite religion respecting these
semantic values. Nor can Cross be permitted to move to the position of assuming complete hypostatization in the two expressions

[6] F. M. Cross, Canaanite Myth and Hebrew Epic, p. 30.

[7] F. M. Cross, Canaanite Myth and Hebrew Epic, p. 30, n. 102: Exod. 33:14;
23:20,21.

[8] J. P. Hyatt, Commentary on Exodus, New Century Bible (London, 1971),
pp. 250–1, 316. Notice that despite Cross's misleading suggestion, the term
'Angel' does not appear in Exod. 33:14 to which his footnote refers.

[9] My italics.

sm *b'l* and *panē* *ba'l*, where they are semantically equivalent
(allegedly) because of referential synonymy, since he deems them
to be epithets (i.e. with non-referential semantic content), not
only referring terms.

Also, Cross needs the suppressed premiss of the closure of the
wide diachronic gap between the two expressions or universals,
for which he has offered no proof.

Cross is here dealing with some scholars'[10] equation of Tannit
with 'Astarte, in which he supposes that there are acute problems.
He alternatively proposes that at least at Tas Silg the temple was
dedicated to two separate deities, which respectively bore the
epithets. I do not take either side in this debate, but offer the
foregoing and following observations to clarify some features.

Returning to Geach's above formulation of testing with a
criterion of identity, it can be recognized that Cross has not
succeeded in representing 'that same F', nor of correctly differentiating Fs, where 'F' stands for an epithet or a component of one.
Where x is 'Astarte and y is Tannit, is it true that $x = y$,[11] in the
situation where the 'same F' is applied to x and y? This is the
shape of the issue which Cross assumes obtains regarding the
epithets; yet he blocks and obscures a precise characterization
of the issue by conflating two distinct Fs (*sm* *b'l* and *panē* *ba'l*)
in designating them semantically equivalent. Of course, Cross
does not offer any proof of this alleged equivalence. He appears
to have confused two senses of equivalence, analogous to the two
senses of 'the same'; he takes it that on his hypothesis these are
'the same', but it is only by imposing a theological thesis that
he can attempt a theological – not linguistic – equivalence of
type, whereas he is committed to the position of attempting to
claim that this is a linguistic equivalence. However, he himself
quite clearly catalogues differences of value in the internal components *sm* and *panē*. Cross is opposing an equation of the identity
of the referents of these epithets, so it is not in his interests to concede the licitness of what is in fact an illicit conflation of epithets;
but his linguistic procedure is sufficiently muddled to support
such an equation in his opponents' proposed identification.

Cross's employment of 'hypostatization' as a feature of the
object language has not been defined previously by him, and it is
typical of scholars such as Albright[12] that definition is not forth-

---

[10] F. M. Cross, *Canaanite Myth and Hebrew Epic*, p. 29.

[11] See D. Wiggins, 'Identity, Necessity and Physicalism', pp. 97f.

[12] See Albright dealing with the same expression *panē* and claims of hypostatization (*Yahweh and the Gods of Canaan*, p. 117).

coming, but is assumed to be known.[13] Indeed it is clear that Cross's own linguistic approach in part rests upon an absorption of this type of hypostatization, which tends to exist in his accounts as an unanalyzed classificatory response to data (i.e. where data are categorized, but the criteria for identifying and demarcating the categories are not specified).

Nor can Cross assume that hypostatization of this sort is to be salvaged by being aligned with idiomaticity, because the contrastive values for such terms as *sm* and *panē* bear the identical translations (at Cross's hand) both in and without 'hypostatized' epithets.

2 Criterion of Application

Related to the criterion of identity is what has been termed the criterion of application. Using the case of a man, Dummett[14] explains this is that criterion 'under what conditions it is true to say of an object that it is a man'. It is clear that for adjectives attached to items equivalent to *thing* ('*x* is the same divine thing') it is not appropriate to designate them as proper fillers of the categorial predicate. Both they, and on occasions[15] the criterion of identity, require a criterion for application. This is because the specifications yielded by filling the criterion with these types of expressions are not univocal.

However, a number of complex problems surround an analysis of this application in respect of biblical languages. That is to say, (1) the referential status of many PNs and their attached predicates' assignments are disputed as they appear in Near Eastern and biblical literatures: in MT terms purport to refer, whereas form-critical and textual examination applies a demythologization programme whereby PNs and predicates do not perform their apparent role. I do not here address myself to this issue except to note its influence on use of criteria. (2) The criterion of application is required to describe the conditions under which an *F* categorial predicate ascribes. Unfortunately the diachronic history and the

---

[13] This is distinct from metalanguage hypostatization (cf. Barr's helpful description in 'Hypostatization of Linguistic Phenomena in Modern Theological Interpretation', pp. 85ff.).

[14] M. Dummett, *Frege: Philosophy of Language*, p. 547.

[15] For a formal prescription of these occasions see P. T. Geach, *Reference and Generality*, pp. 39ff.; see also M. Dummett, *Frege: Philosophy of Language*, chs. 4 and 16. See M. Durrant, *Theology and Intelligibility* (London, 1973), pp. 56–62, 156–69; one should be aware that Geach argues his work has certain weaknesses.

synchronic relations of some texts are disputed, or unclear, so univocal characterization of the criteria is problematic. (3) A smaller yet significant restriction on one's capacity to specify *F*s is the presence of homonyms as PNs and in predicative position, which not infrequently are classified according to confused criteria which infect clarity, as Barr has shown[16] (albeit in a distinct context). This type of difficulty (e.g. where homonymy precludes differentiation) has indeed troubled philosophers when handling modern languages,[17] so its appearance as a problem in biblical language studies ought not to be unexpected.

(*a*)   The motif of the exposed child linked with Moses (Exod. 2:1–10) can be used to illustrate some of the facets behind (1) to (3). The PN *mšh* ('Moses') in MT Exod. 2:10, in MT is said to be causally related to *mšythw* ('drew him'); this has customarily been taken as a folk etymology in Hebrew,[18] yet is actually based on a probable Egyptian derivation and origin.[19] The semantic causal relations and the postulated textual[20] and scholastic historical provenances here are complex and differ in varying degrees. The detailed intersection of semantics and history is in flux, as well as its relation to the possibility and actuality of there being a referent corresponding to the person Moses. These

---

[16] J. Barr, *Comparative Philology and the Text of the Old Testament*, pp. 145ff.; and 'Etymology and the Old Testament', *Oudtestamentische Studien*, 19 (1974), pp. 1–28. It is sometimes true that linguists do not rightly position the value of possessing a correct theological interpretation as a procedure for identifying which of the homonyms a text employs; but this procedure can easily be circular subjectivity.

[17] e.g. P. T. Geach's comments in 'Names and Identity', p. 155.

[18] cf. J. P. Hyatt, *Commentary on Exodus*, p. 64.

[19] I am not of course following Josephus' *mou/eses* (water/saved), but Sir Alan Gardiner (*Egyptian Grammar* (3rd edn., Oxford, 1957), p. 436) who, among others, associates *ms* (given the Saʿidic form *mōsē*) with the sense 'born'. Clearly, this *ms* was incorporated into many Egyptian PNs; W. F. Albright considers this feature as typical of a general trend and to be linked with other Hebrew-Egyptian PN relations proposed by him (cf. *Yahweh and the Gods of Canaan*, p. 143).

[20] By 'textual' I here intend the provenance proposed in or assumed by the MT text. J. F. A. Sawyer has observed a point related to the foregoing, that contextualization of a text is required for full semantic analysis of expressions (cf. his *Semantics in Biblical Research*, pp. 112–13). This is an important aspect, and should be conjoined with the point he next makes (p. 113) that there are different contextualizations for any one text. I add that the criteria of identity and application are required to fix all of these to their cultural antecedents or provenance, and these are often in dispute, which relativizes assessment, thus sometimes rendering it arbitrary.

problems relate to how one can possess the ingredients for the criterion of application.

This situation has connection with the criterion of identity and intentional objects as discussed in philosophy, where the formulation of the status of the reference is unclear or controverted (as examined in 2.2 above). Nevertheless, it is philosophically peculiar and distinct from that discussion in at least one respect: in most philosophy of language the referents of PNs are those to which predicates are normally applied in usage of language.[21] With a few exceptions, it is usually clear into which category a given narrative falls (e.g. if it falls outside this referential use, and into the category where the referents are mental or referents are fictional). Yet in the case of biblical language it is often a standard point of agreement that the style of language demonstrates that the writers are making referential claims about their subjects (i.e. writing about the referents of PNs),[22] whereas a scholar usually practises some form of referential reductionism in respect of his linguistic treatment. It is no part of present concern to explore this facet of analysis, but rather to emphasize its anatomical relation to a criterion. If a scholar conflates his linguistic semantic description with his theological characterization involving reductionism, then he will have produced a hybrid which in advance enforces reductive suppositions about the status and identity of the semantic values in the text, prior to linguistic identification of the text. (Of course, this type of imposition can be owing to transcendental, rather than reductionist, assumptions.)[23] If attention is paid to requisite qualifications that take into account restrictions of understanding about semantic causality and synchronic positions of a text, a consistent, cautious account of relations will be facilitated. Yet such qualifications may prevent one from reaching a specification of how to build a criterion of application, if there is empirical or linguistic ignorance in pertinent levels; that is to say, where Fs in categorial predicates are not univocal or rest on premises which house speculative theses about diachronic and synchronic relations. Speculation outside such

---

[21] For this see M. Dummett, *Frege : Philosophy of Language*, pp. 196ff.

[22] J. Barr properly strikes this distinction using the terms refer, referent and reference, in *Comparative Philology and the Text of the Old Testament*, pp. 118, 291–3. I do not think that Barr has mentioned that, if his referential characterization is suitable for MT items (as he is right to assume that it is), this shows that the biblical usages are logically consistent respecting empirical reference.

[23] J. Barr's major examination of some conservative theologico-linguists has proved this (e.g. *The Semantics of Biblical Languages*, pp. 107–296).

parameters can easily run out of control without its being noticed, especially if a scholar's linguistic procedure is confused.

(b) The exposed child motif linked with Moses has been variously explained. Redford's[24] study of it and Near Eastern parallels lists thirty-two such motifs in many languages. Hyatt suggests that the closest parallel in the Near East to the MT motif is the Sargon Legend.[25] Hyatt does not mention that the relevant Akkadian texts[26] are dated to the neo-Assyrian[27] and neo-Babylonian[28] periods. The dating of such neo-Assyrian tablets is difficult; there is only one neo-Assyrian copy, and this could be interpreted to display a style of writing the cuneiform wedges, (with altered angles) akin to Assurbanipal's scribes, which would drop the date to a period later than, for example, Tiglath-Pileser I's style which appears earlier than the neo-Assyrian Sargon Legend's wedges. Hyatt[29] observes that the narrative containing the motif in Exodus is assigned to the E source by most scholars, but he (without offering any grounds) judges that this narrative originated with J, while noting that Noth and Rudolph choose the latter source. This reflects a certain type of emphasis in other treatments.[30] I cite it here for illustrative purposes in connection with the criterion of application.

If E is designated as the provenance of the MT motif (circa 8th century B.C.), then the dating is crucial; but acute problems obviously arise in relation to a precise date within that century. The Akkadian material could be dated before or after the MT E source hypothesis; on the one hand, a causal connection with MT and the Sargon Legend might be produced by the analysis; conversely, on the other hand, a causal relation is excluded between 'Akkadian → MT' if the temporal priority is reversed.

[24] D. B. Redford, 'The Literary Motif of the Exposed Child', Numen, 14 (1967), pp. 209–28.

[25] J. P. Hyatt, Commentary on Exodus, pp. 61–3. cf. also B. S. Childs, 'The Birth of Moses', Journal of Biblical Literature, 84 (1965), pp. 109, 114–15.

[26] In translation in J. B. Pritchard (ed.), Ancient Near Eastern Texts Relating to the Old Testament (3rd edn., Princeton, 1969), p. 119 and cf. p. 672.

[27] In Cuneiform Texts from Babylonian Tablets (British Museum), 13 (1901), pl. 42 and 43.

[28] For a reconstructed narrative see L. W. King, Chronicles Concerning Early Babylonian Kings, 2 (1907), pp. 87–96.

[29] J. P. Hyatt, Commentary on Exodus, p. 62.

[30] i.e. in omitting to consider the Legend's date while assuming a possible causal connection (for another example of this see M. Noth, Exodus: a Commentary (London, 1962), p. 26).

The situation is clearer regarding the J source, which is often dated to around 1000 B.C.; here a few hundred years produce a diachronic gap between J and the alleged Akkadian texts, which point precludes the Akkadian material being a causal antecedent of the MT motif, on that hypothesis. While Hyatt is otherwise often cautious and mentions that the Israelites might not have known of the Sargon Legend, he fails to account for his stressing the 'striking' similarities between this legend and MT, as a ground for a possible connection; yet at the same time he chooses the postulated source J, which he, with others, dates long before the Akkadian texts were written.[31] In addition, with perplexing difficulties in the dating of these phenomena, Hyatt ought not to go unchallenged. Further, Hyatt does not take account of Childs's[32] supposition, based on Güterbock's analysis,[33] which ascribes illegitimacy, rather than the MT motif, to the Sargon Legend, and this could alter the relation to be assigned to the two texts. Of course the question would be re-orientated if earlier copies (say, in Old Babylonian) of the Sargon Legend were known; but none has been found. Güterbock presupposes some unattested antecedents for it in his brief remarks on provenance; but he offers no proof or text. (The fact that Sargon II might have lived at the time of writing the neo-Assyrian copy may be of significance.) I do not conclude either way, but merely note a certain lack of disinterested analysis in Hyatt's presentation which reflects some other approaches.[34] (Outside the context of this brief comment using the J and E source hypotheses, I would want to show that the hypotheses are in a state of contrariety and lack empirical coherence, which is partly why they are such a blunt instrument in Hyatt's explanation; but this is not the occasion for debate.)

With respect to Childs's argument, though, there is another feature which makes questionable assumptions. He proposes

---

[31] Of course it is a possibility that one can postulate nonextant earlier copies of this legend in Akkadian, although I have not seen this presented (Hyatt does not mention the possibility) and that would need proof, with criteria.

[32] B. S. Childs, 'The Birth of Moses', pp. 109–10.

[33] H. G. Güterbock, 'Die historische Tradition und ihre literarische Gestaltung bei Babyloniern and Hethitern bis 1200', Zeitschrift für Assyriologie und verwandte Gebiete, 42 (1934), pp. 1–91, see pp. 62–4.

[34] It may be thought that the above sort of conditions are too strict, and censure too severe. Not so; consider how many form-critical theses have rendered Sodom and Gomorrah as non-historical entities, but now we have the Ebla references to these cities, if one follows Pettinato, although E. Sollberger is less convinced.

that the details of foundling, wet nurse plus fixed wage, weaning and adoption found in Exod. 2:5–10 are 'such as to make highly plausible a common Near Eastern tradition which is reflected in Exodus 2'.[35] Childs volunteers the fact that there is no direct evidence for this judgement and admits that nothing is known about the same practices from any Egyptian texts (except that there was adoption). Yet he is not deterred from claiming that the *ana ittišu* bilingual Sumerian-Akkadian legal texts, which contain similar practices, give warrant for his conclusion. There are no grounds for linking the legal texts with Egyptian records, nor for causally associating them with MT, as Childs wants. Such a link requires a set of suppressed premisses about contact and causal connection, for which there is no evidence. Nor is this to oppose the interpretation that these practices were common throughout Egypt and Mesopotamia at the relevant times. Childs seems to be introducing these phenomena as a premiss to show in some sense a causal relation of semantic dependence between Akkadian data and MT.[36] This is an inconsistent connection to allege from the data, because Childs admits that there is no direct evidence to support his view.[37]

Childs has confused two senses of 'the same' which are required to attempt confirmation of statements about 'common' in his remark: 'a common Near Eastern tradition'. Only if 'common' can be consistently associated with evidence of a specific connection between MT and Akkadian sources (to fill the general term in 'the same F') could a criterion of application be formulated. Since there is no evidence of specific contact, let alone proved semantic provenance yielding specification of MT semantic values, then Childs's viewpoint is untenable (although it would be coherent to hold it as an imaginative conjecture). The two senses of 'the same' here are: a type connection illustrating a pattern in linguistic data (not involving semantic causality for identification); or, a type connection in conjunction with causal contiguity of semantic values produced in MT.[38] It is the latter formulation

[35] B. S. Childs, 'The Birth of Moses', p. 112.

[36] e.g. 'These common features [in Akkadian and MT] . . . would tend to confirm the theory that the biblical narrative is working with traditional material' (in B. S. Childs, 'The Birth of Moses', p. 114).

[37] I follow Popper here: where there is no empirical test on the basis of evidence, there is no evidence for the truth (or verisimilitude) of a statement (cf. K. R. Popper, *Objective Knowledge*, pp. 12ff., 52–60).

[38] According to J. T. E. Richardson (*The Grammar of Justification: An Interpretation of Wittgenstein's Philosophy of Language* (London, 1976), p. 114, and

which is required for a criterion of application in the situation where a proposal is being made, not solely about 'the same F' as a member of a pattern of distribution, but where a causal relation producing semantic identification is being adduced. Since there is no extant evidence for synchronic contact (nor causal ancestral connection through intermediate expressions), the data employed to fill a categorial predicate are not univocal. If they are not univocal, then they cannot be applied to the motif as a semantic measure. I am not here offering assessment about the situation in principle, but as construed by the above-mentioned scholars.

The above analysis advertises that relevant features of description in treatment of the motif are unstable in their specifications and so cannot properly be used to predict synchronic and diachronic relations involving other comparative relations. So, whereas the present discussion commenced with an issue about criteria of identity for the bearer of the PN *mšh*, investigation of some approaches to the characterization of the surrounding language for categorial predicates has come up against barriers to furnishing such a specification if the motif is deemed central to the use of *mšh*.

(c) *If mšh* is taken as a non-referring term (as a mythological item), then the foregoing procedure need not be deemed inapplicable (i.e. if the criteria are taken not to apply to a bearer, but to the intentional textual identity of *mšh*). J. Woods has shown[39] that criteria of identity can apply in this circumstance, applying what he terms the 'olim modality'.[40] However, he stresses that the chronological factor in fixing causal relations is firmly tied to applying the identity criteria; and the previous comments display acute problems within hypotheses about the motif concerning diachronic and synchronic relations.[41]

Of course, if the MT is taken to be narrative description and analysed on a monolingual basis,[42] then application of the criteria

---

pp. 104–30), if a proposition *p* is criterial for *q*, it is a necessary truth that *p* is evidence for *q*.

[39] J. Woods, *The Logic of Fiction* (The Hague, Paris, 1974).

[40] *ibid.*, p. 131. The olim modality is, in part, a semantics for formally specifying the above type of usage.

[41] *ibid.*, pp. 42–7. The olim modality, which assesses PNs which do not have extra-linguistic referents, is even more tightly restricted to textual content since it is there that a literary 'personal identity' for the referent resides. So demythologization is not here a brief for imagination.

[42] It is odd that, for instance, J. P. Hyatt's examination of the motif badly

presents no particular problems.[43] Nor does this presuppose that the narrative is true (for it only commits one to the fact that claims are being made about referents – truly or falsely). There is a mapping problem here, of matching structural features which import an ancient writer's intention that a text is narrative. Such a text is now very often designated as mythology, as required by scholarly categorizations of mythology.

In the ancient case, reference is prescribed (where a scholar might identify mythological factors); in a modern work of fiction or mythology no reference is intended. It is as well not to collapse the two genres; nor ought one to suppose that an identity relation holds between mythology and legend,[44] because the latter may strike a true reference (e.g. Sargon) while components in a set of predicates in the legend might not truly ascribe features to the PN's bearer. J. Woods[45] interestingly notices that 'mythology tends to be theology and science fallen into disrepute.' Nevertheless, since an exhaustive formal analysis of narrative references in biblical texts, in conjunction with a systematic formal linguistic and philosophical treatment, has not yet been produced, the question of the status of various references has yet to be adequately investigated.

---

merges and confuses analysis of Hebrew with Akkadian allusion prior to explaining MT semantic values, and so puts aside the important monolingual principle of linguistic analysis (cf. J. F. A. Sawyer, *Semantics in Biblical Research*, p. 116).

[43] See M. Dummett's convenient employment of the PN 'Moses' when dealing with reference, where he lays out some formal work which could be applied to the task (*Frege: Philosophy of Language*, pp. 101–2, 111–12, 135–6). Also see L. Wittgenstein (*Philosophical Investigations*, secs. 79–87) where he uses the PN and biblical predicates to shape some important questions about reference.

[44] J. P. Hyatt employs both terms to explain one another as common properties (in *Commentary on Exodus*, pp. 61–3).

[45] J. Woods, *The Logic of Fiction*, p. 30.

1   Definition

(*a*)   The literature reviewing problems associated with the PN *yhwh* is so extensive, and frequently so repetitious, as to render another survey inadvisable. The following is a brief study of one small set of details related to the foregoing scrutiny of PNs.

There is some evidence of a mystical infection present in some scholars' approaches to this name. For example, G. H. Parke-Taylor claims[1] '... the element of the numinous and the mysterious is present. *yhwh* is not subject to precise and limiting definition. There is a hiddenness, an inscrutability, in the deity who addresses Moses.' Parke-Taylor wrongly assumes that there are definition-resistant elements in this name. This is partly generated by his wielding a referential fallacy: of transferring (presumed) properties belonging to the theistic referent into the semantic value which he presumes represents this item. He collapses ontology into semantics. By the mere fact of its existence, a value in use can be measured for what its use is. Clearly, Parke-Taylor is not advancing this definition resistance because of current ignorance over the item, but saying rather that in the nature of its being the name *yhwh* there is such an (alleged) entailment. It appears that Parke-Taylor has made a similar mistake to that of (incorrectly) assuming that vague predicates cannot for that reason be accurately described.[2] A use can be prescribed for what it is: a use with linguistic proportions and dimensions, a function which, by so being, has a particular specification. In the case of the PN *yhwh*, its value is a referring term whose referential identity is fixed by observing predicates attached to it in MT. Nowhere does the expression *'hyh 'šr 'hyh* ('I will be who I will be') get attached to

[1] G. H. Parke-Taylor, *Yahweh: The Divine Name in the Bible*, pp. 55–6; cf. p. 52. For a coherent use and definition of 'definition' see P. T. Geach, *Reference and Generality*, pp. 120–2, and *Mental Acts*, p. 44. Parke-Taylor is confusing the significance of the referent with the value held by the referring function: the domain of the referent is greater (infinite), but referring is a fixed value.

[2] For proof of this see P. T. Geach, *Logic Matters*, pp. 85–7; L. Wittgenstein, *Philosophical Investigations*, secs. 98–100; cf. W. V. O. Quine, *From a Logical Point of View*, pp. 27–32. For criticisms of a facet of ascribing mystical power to words see A. C. Thiselton, 'The Supposed Power of Words', *Journal of Theological Studies*, 25 (1974), pp. 283–99.

yhwh as a predicate, so there are no problems in that specific connection to oppose the foregoing application of a criterion of identity for defining the PN.[3] In any case other predicates are employed in conjunction with it in relevant MT narratives, where exact items occur to fill a categorial predicate for purposes of identification.[4] Nor does MT usage require that *'hyh 'šr 'hyh* be employed as the only criterion of identity for the bearer of *yhwh*.[5]

Parke-Taylor's allegation of intrinsic 'numinous' elements which are definition resistant is quite distinct from postulated ambiguity (at an empirical textual and not only perceptual level) in an item's specification. For example, Huffmon's suggestion[6] that there are no formal grounds or criteria for distinguishing between the possibilities of causative and a non-causative feature in the form of *yhwh* (and also in the Amorite *ya-wi*)[7] imports nothing about a necessary property of the PN or its author's intentions concerning definition resistance, but relates to the alleged graphic limitations in its writing.

Despite Parke-Taylor's statement on definition resistance, he is committed to the position of having defined the PN when he states ''*lhym* is the generic term for God . . . and as such is often used appellatively as a synonym for *yhwh*'.[8] Matching of two terms as synonyms requires that a description of each item is to hand for there to be knowledge of synonymy in the relevant respect.[9] And this differs from Parke-Taylor's foregoing quoted comments on the name *yhwh*. Perhaps it is clear that he had picked on two

[3] I mention this because Parke-Taylor switches backwards and forwards from PN to this expression as though the latter were a sort of predicate contained in (*sic*) the former.

[4] For an argument opposing an attributive use of PNs where reference of a particular sort is admitted, see A. P. Martinich, 'The Attributive Use of Proper Names', *Analysis*, 37 (June 1977), 4, pp. 159–63.

[5] In which case, of course, Parke-Taylor cannot be allowed to assume what he does: that purported definition resistance in *'hyh 'šr 'hyh* infects specification of the PN *yhwh*.

[6] H. B. Huffmon, *Amorite Personal Names in the Mari Texts*, p. 73.

[7] *ibid.*, pp. 71–2. Huffmon opposes Albright's arguments for a causative in *yhwh*, pointing out that Albright wrongly presumes that there is a symmetry of behaviour between PNs' internal structure and normal usage (see *ibid.*, p. 73, n. 60) in Amorite and related languages which Albright cited. Here, Albright appears to have conflated the components of a PN with their prehistory.

[8] G. H. Parke-Taylor, *Yahweh: The Divine Name in the Bible*, p. 5; and for another occurrence see p. 39; cf. p. 10, n. 50.

[9] For the sense of 'relevant' here, see generally W. Haas, 'Linguistic Relevance', pp. 126ff.

items which are only referentially synonymous,[10] but he failed to isolate and make the feature explicit.[11] However, if Parke-Taylor's phrasing is taken as it stands, then he is in further difficulties, because, to be a synonym of *'lhym*, the term *yhwh* must only be a referring term, since the etymological values ascribed to the terms by Parke-Taylor[12] are not synonymous. If this is true, then the proper name *yhwh* has only[13] a referential value in use. To be sure, one might respond that Parke-Taylor is dealing with folk-etymological connections with the PN in Exod. 3, and solely referential use outside this situation in other comments, where he associates synonymy with *yhwh* and *'lhym*; but nowhere does he present or assume this distinction, nor is a differentiation, equivalent to use and mention, presupposed. The absence of requisite distinctions is a regular feature of Parke-Taylor's treatment, and results in lack of clarity. Parke-Taylor offers nothing new in his analysis of this PN, which none the less is presented as an attempt to clarify the topic further; in this role, indeed, one reviewer stated that Parke-Taylor's book 'deserves attention from all'.[14]

[10] Or, referential identity; J. F. A. Sawyer generally exposes this type of confusion in some examples in *Semantics in Biblical Research*, pp. 75–6.

[11] This reflects a more basic confusion over definition; for example, Parke-Taylor states in a context of explaining meaning and name: 'A change in name means a change of character.' (*Yahweh: The Divine Name in the Bible*, pp. 2–3.) Here a non-formal use of 'means' is indiscriminately merged with a linguistic definitional use, with dire consequences for the external world.

[12] cf. G. H. Parke-Taylor, *Yahweh: The Divine Name in the Bible*, pp. 5, 64, n. 6, 32–45 (for *'lhym*), and pp. 46–78 (for *yhwh*).

[13] But for an hypothesis about a folk-etymological pun in use involving a causal element in the PN, cf. F. Zimmermann, 'Folk Etymology of Biblical Names', *Vetus Testamentum Supplements*, 15 (1966), pp. 311–26, on the analogy of *ḥwh*.

[14] Review by A. G. Auld of G. H. Parke-Taylor, *Yahweh: The Divine Name in the Bible, Scottish Journal of Theology*, 30 (1977), 4, pp. 386–7. Auld himself states that Parke-Taylor has nothing new to present. The lack of adequate definition and specification, resulting in confusion, is part of a facet of biblical studies generally at various levels in Hebrew and Greek analyses; cf. D. W. Gooding, 'An Appeal for a Stricter Terminology in the Textual Criticism of the Old Testament', *Journal of Semitic Studies*, 21 (1976), pp. 15–25, esp. 15–17; E. J. Epp, 'Towards the Clarification of the Term "Textual Variant"', in J. K. Elliott, *Studies in New Testament Language and Text* (Leiden, 1976), pp. 153–73. Apart from the general relation of these two articles to the issue of definition, they also obliquely show that criteria of identity and application of PNs (which are subject terms for a set or manuscripts) are unclear, and so consequently are the domains over which such PNs range. It is interesting that, although H. B. Huffmon's *Amorite Personal Names in the Mari Texts* and W. F. Albright's 'Northwest-Semitic Names in a List of Egyptian Slaves from the 18th Century B.C.', for example, are valuable studies, they do not offer any explanation of what a PN is, nor what it is to be a PN.

Yet such confusions severely limit the value of Parke-Taylor's judgements,[15] since he presents prescription as description.

(b) The question of the reproduction of the name *yhwh* in another language is technically a straightforward affair. PNs are to be transliterated into language B from language A, although the exact status of PNs in their host languages is questionable.[16] It is an obvious test between a PN and a noun that the former is transliterated while the latter is translated.[17] Further, the Geachian criterion of identity cited above in 3.1, *1* applies to test the synonymity of PNs, such that, with respect to sense and reference in language A, a PN *m* shares all properties *F* with its transliterated form in language B.[18] This much seems clear; however, the presentation of PN linguistic material in biblical grammars does not always mirror this. R. W. Funk's[19] translation and revision of Blass and Debrunner has a brief entry:

> *The article with nouns designating persons*
> like *theos, kurios, nekroi, ethnē.*
> (1) *theos* and *kurios* (= Yahweh
> but also Christ) designate beings of which
> there is only one kind.

A PN's translation is only properly understood if it is characterized as transliteration from language A to language B.[20] Therefore, the question of a noun term such as *theos* or *kurios* does not arise as a linguistic candidate in translation where this latter is the matching of an expression's sense and reference (together with

---

[15] Parke-Taylor not infrequently merely lists data without drawing any conclusions (cf. *Yahweh: The Divine Name in the Bible*, pp. 71–3).

[16] P. T. Geach, 'Names and Identity', pp. 139–58.

[17] P. T. Geach, *Reference and Generality*, pp. 26f.; and J. Lyons, *Semantics 1*, p. 226.

[18] See P. T. Geach, *Reference and Generality*, p. 26.

[19] F. Blass and A. Debrunner (trans. of the 9th–10th German edn. by R. W. Funk) *A Greek Grammar of the New Testament* (Cambridge, 1961), p. 133, sec. 254, col. A.

[20] cf. M. Durrant's proof that the item 'God' (which also applies to 'Lord' terminology) cannot be a PN, in *The Logical Status of 'God'* (London, 1973), pp. 1–28. Although, with Geach, I agree that there are some weaknesses in this study (not least the mistaken use of Exod. 15:3 on p. 18) the salient points relevant for the above are sound. Of course, I do not dispute that 'God' in some English theology purports to function as a PN, although in agreement with Durrant I do not think it succeeds; but such cases would be homonyms of the noun (cf. P. T. Geach, 'Names and Identity', pp. 155ff.).

tonal properties if possible) in language A with, ideally, a substitution instance of those properties in language B. Of course, there are problems in achieving this; but the rendering of PNs into another language is not one of them.[21] A treatise on NT grammar should not therefore offer, as a feature of a linguistic rule, a seeming equation which violates this: '*theos* and *kurios* (= *yhwh* but also Christ)'. The equation is quite understandable since NT citations of MT replace (but not substitute) *yhwh* by one or other of these terms. Nevertheless, this is what may be termed exegetical replacement within translations, and not a translation itself. In any case, since the term *yhwh* does not appear in NT, as such, this inclusion of an equation about *yhwh with* an identity sign is not strictly an observation about NT linguistic behaviour. It is, rather, a value judgement on Greek-Hebrew relations with a suppressed premiss (reflected in the unqualified sign ' = ') articulating (on this point) a confused translation hypothesis if the identity sign stands unqualified – as it does. Perhaps this confusion or obscurity can be excluded, if one adopts the value of a hint present in the above grammar, by noticing that the term 'Christ' is linked with *yhwh* as an item which can receive the nouns *theos* and *kurios*. This would be true only if they are connected by the identity sign at the level of reference, not sense, since the Greek for 'Christ' is not a sense synonym of either noun, but they all, on occasions, referentially coincide in the same subject. Utilizing this approach, it is clear that one could claim consistently that the reference of *theos*, *kurios* and *yhwh* all referentially coincide on some counts. However, it is odd that a NT grammar, which is principally to do with the sense of language, should, without any explicit notice, present a referent relation as a piece of grammar in a treatment of the sense and form of words, not least because it seems indiscriminately to have conflated distinct levels of function. It is easy, especially in an informal context where the authors are unaware of the need to distinguish such levels, for the functions of distinct levels to be collapsed and confused;[22] the resulting hybrid is then employed to promote theological theses where levels of functions are exchanged.[23] Yet the Blass-Debrunner

[21] To be sure, where paronomasia produced de-ossification of idiomatized PN components, translation might be in order. But this could hardly be a translation of the PN's value in use.

[22] M. Dummett (*Frege : Philosophy of Language*, pp. 54–203), has shown that this confusion exists in some philosophers.

[23] cf. M. Durrant, *Theology and Intelligibility* (London, 1973), pp. 75–86. See sec. 6.0, 5, note 32, below for Geach's review of Durrant.

grammar appears more than incidentally confused beyond matters of presentation, for it continues by designating *theos patēr* ('God the father') as 'an actual name for God' on many occasions.[24]

It is important that the distinction between exegetical replacement and substitutional translation, especially where the two types are mixed in one reproduction, should be given attention, since it appears to have been neglected. Consequently, understanding of related matters has suffered.

(*c*) J. F. A. Sawyer,[25] in his introduction to Hebrew, a partial improvement on earlier textbooks,[26] appears to perpetrate a feature of this confusion. In his case it is only a misplaced detail, whereas the foregoing type of example is often set in a disordered system of classification. Sawyer states in an introductory study on verbless sentences, considering the definite: 'The Lord is one (Dt 6:4): *yhwh 'ḥd*' that 'This is a *verbless sentence.* The *subject* is *yhwh* "the Lord" ... /*yhwh* "the Lord" is a proper name, and therefore definite.'[27] In other examples in the section PNs are transliterated; and the subject terms in the examples with articled nouns are also translated as nouns with articles. The custom of many OT translations to render the PN *yhwh* by 'the Lord' is an exegetical replacement device which ought not to allow linguistic functions in MT Hebrew to be obscured, especially in the presence of an admission that a given term is a PN, for it will add to confusion where this rendering is posited, in a context of a subset of verbless sentences marked definite. Of course, this is a mere detail; but an important one in the situation of continual conflation of PNs with nouns in linguistic and theological treatments, and where the functional asymmetry between a PN and 'the Lord' is fundamental.[28]

One of Dummett's tests[29] for an item's being a PN is that a

---

[24] F. Blass and A. Debrunner, *A Greek Grammar of the New Testament*, p. 133, sec. 254, col. B.

[25] J. F. A. Sawyer, *A Modern Introduction to Biblical Hebrew* (Stocksfield, 1976).

[26] But see points and corrections in T. Muraoka's review and list together with Sawyer's response, in *Journal for the Study of the Old Testament*, 1 (1976), pp. 56–63, 78–92, 72–5.

[27] J. F. A. Sawyer, *A Modern Introduction to Biblical Hebrew*, p. 17.

[28] I do not think that the separate introductory note which only draws attention to the custom of rendering the PN is sufficient or relevant as a justification for not transliterating the PN, although my point is to draw attention to the merger of two distinct functions, and not to make a protest about this custom (cf. J. F. A. Sawyer, *A Modern Introduction to Biblical Hebrew*, p. 12).

[29] M. Dummett, *Frege: Philosophy of Language*, pp. 59ff.

necessary condition for an *n* to be a PN is that one can infer from a sentence employing the PN, the result of replacing the PN by *x* (or e.g. *hw'* ('he')), and prefixing the appropriate sentence with 'There is something such that . . .' (which bars 'nothing' as a PN and preserves inferential relations). 'Lord' epithets do not pass this and other tests; the upshot of this is that such items cannot be PNs. So this change of gear in exegetical paraphrase needs to be identified and isolated in grammars, not conflated.

2 An Aspect of 'hyh 'šr 'hyh

(a) Sometimes attempted definition produces problems[30] when a PN's sense is said solely to consist in its being a referring term which uniquely satisfies a set of criteria when referring to its referent; the problem here commented upon is where some apparent paronomastic property is present in a PN's context. An applied example of this can be culled from B. Albrektson's fine study on the syntax of *'hyh 'šr 'hyh*,[31] at the juncture where he has made an observation on this expression's connection with the PN *yhwh*:

> It is sometimes thought that the imperfect form of the verb, *'hyh*, is not quite appropriate in this connexion. But it must not be forgotten that the whole phrase is a kind of word-play on the divine name *yhwh* – rather reminiscent of many folk-etymologies of names in the Old Testament – and this of course considerably restricted the author's choice of forms . . . To my mind Vriezen is entirely right in stressing the paronomastic character of the sentence . . .[32]

If one accepts Albrektson's characterization of this paronomastic connection, as a pun contracted between the expression and the PN, there is no threat to the referential value of the sense of this PN. Frege did add the elements of *Beleuchtung* and *Färbung*

---

[30] Some of these types of problems are discussed by P. Ziff in 'About Proper Names', *Mind*, 86 (July 1977), 343, pp. 319–32.

[31] B. Albrektson, 'On the Syntax of *'hyh 'šr 'hyh*' in P. R. Ackroyd and B. Lindars (eds.), *Words and Meanings* (Cambridge, 1968), pp. 15–28.

[32] *ibid.*, p. 27. The citation Albrektson gives for Vriezen is Th. C. Vriezen "Ehje 'aser 'ehje', in *Festschrift Alfred Bertholet* (Tübingen, 1950), pp. 498ff cf. also the brief remark on *šlḥny* ('sent') by J. Barr in 'The Problem of Israelite Monotheism', *Transactions of the Glasgow University Oriental Society*, 17 (1957–8), p. 61.

(which I, following Dummett, represent by the one term 'tone')[33] to the sense of an item, although he did not give the entity tone adequate distinctive attention, as Dummett remarks.[34] I shall adopt and slightly adapt Frege's tone explanation to cover such phenomena as paronomastic properties and contracts of linguistic items, although, with Dummett,[35] I shall ignore Frege's brief talk of mental images in association with tone, since tone is a linguistic and not subjective feature, as Dummett[36] proves. For Dummett's presentation of Frege's view of tone, which I here employ (although applying it to categories which are not illustrated by him),[37] any feature of the meaning of a sentence or expression which is not relevant to determining its truth or falsity (i.e. sense and reference) is part of the sentence's tone. I do not wish to insist that this tone notion rules every linguistic property of an expression outside sense and reference, although this seems a credible conjecture, but that it holds true for a large class of uses, since it requires empirical investigation in the perspective of an exhaustive formal description of all biblical linguistic data. Albrektson's paronomastic thesis is compatible with the notion of tone because the sense and reference of *yhwh* are in primary roles distinct from these pun values.[38] (I employ the latter term 'value', and accordingly introduce tone as having linguistic value, but not the PN's primary truth functional value, although that is not tantamount to supposing that there is no associative connection with, or relation to, truth functional values and tone values.) The reference of a PN is fixed by its being used in conjunction with some predicate(s) for purposes of identification. There is no objection in this to there being some paronomastic play on morphologically or semantically similar values in the

---

[33] M. Dummett, *Frege : Philosophy of Language*, p. 2.

[34] *ibid.*, p. 88; tone did not relate to Frege's central formal interests, which indicates why he gave it little attention; it seems to have been badly neglected by later philosophers generally, as well, for similar reasons.

[35] *ibid.*, p. 85.

[36] *ibid.*, pp. 83–9. 'Tone' covers disparate phenomena in use.

[37] Frege illustrated his tone very briefly, and used an equivalent of 'but'. Dummett employed the following to illustrate tone: 'She was poor, but she was honest' (see *Frege : Philosophy of Language*, p. 86), where the truth functional value of 'but' would be the same as 'and', whereas the tones of 'but' and 'and' are different. The nature of force has likewise been neglected (e.g. assertion, attitude, etc.) cf. *Frege : Philosophy of Language*, pp. 299–63, particularly pp. 319ff. and 331f.

[38] This is not to presume that all phenomena which an applied linguist classifies as 'overtone' or paronomasia *are* tones, i.e. without truth conditions. These could have sense and reference when parsed logically.

predicate's components and the PN's graphic structure, since, if paronomasia is to do with tone, it does not entail ascribing non-referring semantic value to the sense of the PN. Thus the PN can be in a context of use while there is also paronomasia. Conversely, if there is paronomasia where a mention of a PN is employed, the target and component-source of some tone could be the prehistory of the morphemes comprising the PN, albeit explained in conformity with the foregoing, where there is synchronic homonymy or causal etiology.

(*b*) B. O. Long,[39] surprisingly, does not deal with the case of *yhwh* in Exod. 3 as a *possible* candidate for being an (unusual) type of etiology, although, as shown above, Albrektson (basing his view on Vriezen's work) adopts the proposal that it is related to other MT folk etymologies.

All the terminology which marks the Fichtner-Soggin-Long[40] accounts of etiologies appears in Exod. 3, albeit in a more extensive distribution than other MT occurrences. There is also a recital element, with parallel uses of *šlḥ*, which further entrenches the narrative in a naming sequence.[41] I will not discuss the etymologies offered, but, with the foregoing, take it that the data as construed by scholars indicate some form of connection between *yhwh* and *'hyh 'šr 'hyh* in a paronomastic relation.[42]

3   The First Person and yhwh

In a paronomastic perspective, together with the question and answer sequence of Exod. 3:11–15, some alignment between the verb *'hyh* and the PN *yhwh* can be admitted at the level of tone. It is easy to over-state the nature of this interrelation and regard it as a sort of synonymy, where non-referring sense might be

---

[39] B. O. Long, *The Problem of Etiological Narrative in the Old Testament.*

[40] See 3.0, *3* (*a*) above. For *'wt* ('sign') in 3:12 cf. *Jerusalem Bible* note.

[41] i.e.: Exod. 3:10: *w'šlḥk* ('And I will *send* thee'); Exod. 3:12: *wy'mr ky-'hyh 'mk wzh-lk h'wt ky 'nky šlḥtyk* ('And he said, Certainly *I will be* with thee; . . .I have *sent* thee'); Exod. 3:13: *'lhy 'bwtykm šlḥny 'lykm w'mrw-ly mh-šmw* ('God of your fathers hath *sent* me unto you' 'and they shall say . . . What is his name?'); Exod. 3:14: *t'mr lbny yśr'l 'hyh šlḥny 'lykm* ('say . . . *I will be* hath *sent* me unto you'); Exod. 3:15: *t'mr 'l-bny yśr'l yhwh . . . šlḥny 'lykm zh-šmy* ('say . . . *Yahweh* . . . hath *sent* me unto you: this is my name.'). It will be noticed that the above reflects use of the etiology type I terminology (see 3.0, *3* (*a*) in foregoing) built into a sequence around *šlḥ*.

[42] The notion of paronomasia I follow is Barr's, generally illustrated by J. Barr, in *Comparative Philology and the Text of the Old Testament*, pp. 48, 154.

ascribed to a use of the PN; but this would be a mistake, since the relevant feature is paronomasia on tonal properties. A desire to resist this mistake might, nevertheless, provoke a polarity in the other direction which fails to appreciate the influence of the paronomasia. The sequence, first, uses the verb *'hyh* in 3:12 in a context of a revelatory fellowship with a redemptive teleology: *ky-'hyh 'mk* ('Certainly I will be with thee'). From here on to 3:15 the recital motif, marked by *šlḥ*, produces a replacement of *'hyh* by *yhwh*.[43]

I employ the term 'replacement', rather than 'substitution', with the notion that replacement does not require a strictly synonymous value being put in place of that which is displaced, while substitution is concerned with a change of items which are synonymous. Of course, a substitutional[44] relation,[45] where strict synonymy[46] holds, does not exist between *'hyh* and *yhwh* because the former is in the first person. Substitution is to do with a tautologous reification of an expression, whereas replacement is, for example, concerned with the development of a theme.

'hyh is replaced by *yhwh* in the explication of the theme of covenant-naming in a paronomastic and/or etiological context; but it would be a confusion to apprehend synonymy on all counts between the relevant verb and PN. I say 'all counts' without opposing or conceding that there is some level-specific synonymy between these two. For instance, one might be able to measure an unusual type of synonymy within the paronomasia, activating the etiological prehistory of the ossified component within the PN. This would place the pun in a circumstance of mention, or tonal paronomasia, and not normal use.

Scholars such as F. M. Cross have tended to obscure the operational importance of these types of distinctions. Cross[47] notes

---

[43] The definition of 'replacement' in W. V. O. Quine, *Set Theory and its Logic*, p. 88, etc., is different from the above.

[44] This does not exclude the possibility of substitutional relations at the level of tone and force between items. However, *'hyh* and *yhwh* may share identity of reference.

[45] cf. P. T. Geach, *Logic Matters*, pp. 178ff. for a relevant explanation of substitution.

[46] See C. Lewy, *Meaning and Modality*, pp. 64ff. The use of strict synonymy above has some relation to R. Harris's analytic synonymy (*Synonymy and Linguistic Analysis* (Oxford, 1973), pp. 90–1).

[47] F. M. Cross, *Canaanite Myth and Hebrew Epic*, pp. 68–9. Here Cross smudges the borders of first and third person PN forms and, consequently, with other similar moves, ascribes predicative semantic value to the PN's use (p. 67, etc.).

that divine epithets are derived from first and third person formulae in ancient Semitic texts, and moves from this to propose that the original formula (behind 3:14) was *yahwi ḏū yahwi* – using an Ugaritic formula type as precedent for identification of *yhwh*. He does not offer justification for the introduction of hypothetical Hebrew forms or Ugaritic as evidence for this conclusion; nor does he offer proof for employing epithet formulae as evidence for allegedly parallel shifts of syntax in the PN's ossified frozen syntax. However, in a separate context and without seeming to appreciate its import for his later argument he does admit the existence of 'frozen' syntax in other divine names.[48] In this situation Cross obscured the semantic relations in texts by conjectures about the external prehistory, which he imports into being a description of the text; this confusion enables him to discuss 'the meaning' of PNs, as though they functionally display predicative values.[49] Albright[50] was similarly muddled when he wrote of 'causative meaning' without discriminating levels of value in verbs and PNs, using the basically same type of historical background as Cross did.

Nevertheless, there may be some truth in an aspect of Albright's argument, albeit if construed outside the parameters of Albright's thesis about the PN: namely, that *yhwh* is a sort of abbreviation of a longer formula (from Exod. 3:14). It is a possible legitimate way of describing the paronomastic replacement of the verb by the PN in the 3:12–15 sequence, if abbreviation represents this type of feature, and not a PN with a semantic value from Ugaritic (which marks it as being an epithet) in which is rehearsed a highly speculative (postulated) diachronic history. Indeed, this notion of thematic abbreviation of 3:12–14, as an associative feature involved in the paronomasia, would relate the redemptive fellowship strand in 3:12 to the PN (the PN is being interpreted as a form of paronomastic abbreviation of *ky-'hyh 'mk*); but this would be an associative element arising from semantic pun.

The deictic categories have been somewhat conflated in the type of exegesis of linguistics exhibited by Cross. It is only fair to notice that logicians have also dealt with one category of deictic interrelations uncomprehensively; this is the relation between a PN and the first person pronoun. In logic, the generalization is

---

[48] F. M. Cross, *Canaanite Myth and Hebrew Epic*, p. 67.

[49] *ibid.*, pp. 6off.

[50] W. F. Albright, *Yahweh and the Gods of Canaan*, p. 147, etc. I am not objecting to all discussion of apparent semantic values in PNs' ossified contents, but their indiscriminate muddling with textual use and pretextual prehistory.

often assumed that a first person pronoun can substitute a PN, and *vice versa*. A reason for this is because, for the sake of logical considerations, the first person can usually be treated as an empty[51] referring term in a parallel manner to handling of PNs. However, only in certain restricted domains can this substitution operate: it cannot succeed if the bearer of the PN is not writing or speaking, except in quoted speech. Consequently the substitution cannot work if a person is being described in the third person. These evident distinctions need to be allowed for in semantic analysis. Cross's type of speculative permit for an interchange whenever his diachronic thesis requires it might be precluded from being applied owing to such considerations. Unfortunately, these scholars have not yet been able to offer the synchronic deictic[52] co-ordinates on which the alleged changes happened and this is inconsistent with their having proposed them as part of an authoritative historical account, rather than as an imaginative conjecture.

One possible asymmetry between a PN and a first person pronoun is pertinent to current scrutiny. Kant[53] was wary of ascribing referential value to the first person, as Strawson has remarked, although Strawson's own viewpoint opposes this position.[54] J. Lyons is characteristic of many scholars in stating that 'the "first" person is used by the speaker to refer to himself'.[55] G. E. M. Anscombe[56] has maintained that this type of analysis of the first person is entirely wrong. She concludes that the first person is not a referring term at all, although she has not comprehensively specified what it is. This is an intricate area which is only beginning to be explored; discussion here is necessarily preliminary but is warranted because of the import of such an analysis.

Anscombe is not treating of secondary, derivative uses of the first person,[57] nor of its use in types of soliloquy.[58] Anscombe appears to succeed in showing that the first person is neither PN

---

[51] Empty, i.e. non-referring sense values are not present.

[52] For this term see G. Leech, *Semantics* (Harmondsworth, 1974), pp. 77, 168.

[53] I. Kant (trans. N. K. Smith), *Critique of Pure Reason* (London, 1929).

[54] P. F. Strawson, *Individuals*, pp. 82–3; cf. pp. 102–3.

[55] J. Lyons, *Introduction to Theoretical Linguistics*, p. 276.

[56] G. E. M. Anscombe, 'The First Person'. cf. also the important studies of Anscombe's analysis in C. Diamond and J. Teichman (eds.), *Intention and Intentionality: Essays in Honour of G. E. M. Anscombe* (Cornell, 1979), pp. 3–70.

[57] e.g. 'I have hurt my leg' where 'I' is dummy for the subject term to be 'attached' to a leg. cf. I. Ramsey, *Christian Empiricism* (London, 1974), p. 28, for confusion over this.

[58] See P. T. Geach's criticism of misuse of the first person in philosophical analysis regarding soliloquy (*Mental Acts*, pp. 117–21).

nor definite description, nor is it equivalent to the demonstrative pronoun, nor like other pronouns or common nouns, because tests for the applications of members of these categories all fail to apply generally to the first person.[59]

If *'hyh* is in fact a non-referring term, then this is one further property which produces an asymmetry between it and the PN *yhwh*. This provokes no difficulties for descriptions of MT phenomena. For example, in T. Muraoka's valuable research on emphasis,[60] all his examples to do with the first person fit exactly into the conception argued by Anscombe, with Muraoka's exposure of, for instance, the strong link between mental states and attitudes in MT use of *'ny* ('I') which requires nothing in the form of reference.[61] (However, in his preliminary sketch of his working hypothesis (as he terms his introduction) he does write of 'the object referred to by the pronoun'.[62] Yet this expression could be altered so as to exclude reference, and it would not generate a distortion in his following narrative.) One should discriminate between the explicit pronoun *'ny* and the verbal form implied in *'hyh*, a distinction which J. Pedersen[63] has marked in connection with nominal clauses. Albrektson[64] was relying on the same distinction in his analysis of Lindblom's[65] and especially Schild's[66] faulty descriptions of the syntax in Exod. 3:14. Nevertheless, this distinction is a syntactic one which does not dispose of the first person function in verbal forms at the semantic level if one follows normal translation and Lyons's[67] description of this phenomenon. However, Muraoka's account does seem to give weight to the tone of emphasis being placed over the use of the explicit, as opposed to implicit, pronoun,[68] which would explain some occurrences of the phenomenon.

[59] G. E. M. Anscombe, 'The First Person', pp. 49, 53, 61.

[60] T. Muraoka, *Emphasis in Biblical Hebrew*, pp. 32–43.

[61] Muraoka's use of 'self-consciousness' is proper, but according to Anscombe such usage ought to be expanded carefully so as to avoid being linked with a Cartesian Ego theory (cf. Muraoka, *Emphasis in Biblical Hebrew*, p. 38; also G. E. M. Anscombe, 'The First Person', pp. 50–1).

[62] T. Muraoka, *op. cit.*, p. 33. For the philosophical logic of this see H.-N. Castañeda, 'On the Logic of Self-Knowledge', *Noûs*, I (1967), pp. 12–21.

[63] J. Pedersen, *Hebraeisk Grammatik* (2nd edn., Copenhagen, 1933), p. 275.

[64] B. Albrektson, 'On the Syntax of *'hyh 'šr 'hyh*', p. 25.

[65] J. Lindblom, 'Noch einmal die Deutung des Jahwe-Namens in Ex. 3:14', *Annual of the Swedish Theological Institute in Jerusalem*, 3 (1964), pp. 4–10, etc.

[66] E. Schild, 'On Exodus 3:14 – 'I am that I am'', *Vetus Testamentum*, 4 (1954), pp. 296ff.

[67] J. Lyons, *Introduction to Theoretical Linguistics*, pp. 280–1.

[68] T. Muraoka, *Emphasis in Biblical Hebrew*, pp. 32–43. Muraoka believes

Contrariwise, if one considers *'hyh* to have a reference, this relation could also, on one interpretation, display an asymmetry between *yhwh* and *'hyh*. It is the interpretation whereby the first person could be a dangling pronoun[69] which refers back to its antecedent subject term (which in Exod. 3:12–14 is *h'lhym*). In the case of *yhwh* it has a reference of its own. On the foregoing interpretation *'hyh* only has a mediated reference, by its referring back to its antecedent (which is not *yhwh*, but *h'lhym*) and where this antecedent itself makes the referential contribution. So on this interpretation the referential functions[70] of *'hyh* and *yhwh* are asymmetrical and distinct (although the derived reference of the former and the reference of the latter are to the same referent on MT usage). This is a further group of reasons for discriminating functionally between the verb and PN, whatever the tonal paronomastic or etiological or grammatical[71] derivations and thematic associations in MT.[72]

---

that many proposed pleonastic uses, as in Ecclesiastes, are not redundant but emphatic nuances.

[69] For this term, see P. T. Geach, *Logic Matters*, p. 100. cf. generally D. S. Clarke, Jr., 'The addressing Function of "I"', *Analysis*, 38 (1978), 2, pp. 91–3.

[70] For this usage of function in exposition of PNs see F. G. Droste, 'On Proper Names', pp. 1–13; and see 3.0, *1*, n. 2 above. My own view is to follow Anscombe's thesis on the first person, and to see reference *via* substantives.

[71] I have not offered opinions on the status of the grammar apparently articulated in the 'folk etymology' of *yhwh*. The conception of the relations between alleged grammar in these etymologies rests for its criticism on the rule specifications in standard grammars, which notoriously are often insensitive rough-work formalized approximations constructed to reflect the typical formations in extant linguistic phenomena. They are thus inept as a tool to assess an unusual problematic formation which exists in a disputed diachronic position, and where monolingual and multilingual synchronic origins have been variously proposed. A summary of some etymologies can be found in A. Murtonen, *A Philological and Literary Treatise on the Old Testament Divine Names* (Helsinki, 1952), pp. 61–7. W. F. Albright's later views on the PN are to be found in *Yahweh and the Gods of Canaan*, pp. 146–9; cf. also W. von Soden, 'Jahwe 'Eer ist, Er erweist sich"', *Die Welt des Orients*, 3 (1965), pp. 177–87. A fresh viewpoint on the relation of *'hyh 'šr 'hyh* to *yhwh* is reflected in B. Albrektson's study 'On the Syntax of *'hyh 'šr 'hyh* in Exodus 3:14'.

[72] Nevertheless, it is perhaps clear from the above that logic can be used sensi-:ively to construct an account of intricate linguistic thematic features (which :end to be neglected in, for example, criticism of exegetical work by scholars).

4

REFERENCE AND
PREDICATION

4.0 PREDICATE

1 Interpretation

(*a*) A logical predicate is not identical to a grammatical predicate, although there is some analogy.[1] To form an atomic sentence (sometimes a clause, in the Semiticist's use of this term) a subject term *x* is joined to a one-place predicate: '*x hlk*' ('walking'). The variable *x*, when filled with a referring term, refers to the subject, while the predicate ascribes a property to the subject. Subject and predicate share the same sentence, yet their functions are asymmetrical: referring and ascription. A logical predicate does not refer, but applies to a referent, is true of a referent.[2] Logically proper names cannot be[3] tensed; predicates can. This latter feature is obviously true in natural languages at any functional level, while the asymmetry of subject and logical predicate as a property in natural languages, consistently used, is a matter apprehended by a correct description of deep grammar.

(*b*) In the standard interpretation of the predicate calculus one cannot infer '*x hlk*' from '*x hlk ʿrwm*' ('walked naked') since adverbial modification is not represented in the standard constructions within the calculus.[4] D. Davidson,[5] dealing with action

---

[1] cf. P. T. Geach, *Reference and Generality*, pp. 22–46, 108–143.

[2] For the reason for this distinction in the present context, see P. T. Geach, *Logic Matters*, pp. 51–2.

[3] It will be appreciated that paronomasia on the ossified stems in proper names, where these house frozen tense features, does not result in tensed proper names (for which see secs. 3.0 and 3.2 above).

[4] On the significance of this, see W. V. O. Quine, *Philosophy of Logic*, pp. 30–2. Hebrew: Isa. 20:2 (cf. *GK*, 113, *g*, 2).

[5] D. Davidson, 'The Logical Form of Action Sentences', in N. Rescher (ed.), *The Logic of Decision and Action* (Pittsburgh, 1967), pp. 81–120; and D. Davidson, 'On Events and Event-Descriptions', in J. Margolis (ed.), *Facts and Existence* (Oxford, 1969), pp. 74–84.

sentences, attempts to obviate this difficulty and to avoid the need to introduce non-standard logics, by furnishing a device whereby this inference can be made by representing events as subjects. In this approach, the above expression is (roughly) construed as '$(\exists y)$ (y is an *hlk* of x, and, y is ʿ*rwm*)'. The y's value is the appropriate event.[6] This technique facilitates the admission of adverbial expressions to the calculus, and exhibits how, with respect to the relevant class of sentences, the concept of reference can be presented as an entity associated with a type of predicate in natural languages. Davidson's device is not an admission that in the deep grammar of a sentence the deep grammar predicate refers (not least because he is working within the constraint of standard Fregean logic); so it cannot, of course, be employed to support treatment of linguistic predicates as a sort of name, as Boman tends to do,[7] and as GK[8] is rightly criticized by Barr[9] for doing. Davidson's view reflects the presence of hidden subject terms (event-variables) and of simple predicates attached to them in the deep grammar of, what is superficially, a predicate without subject terms in the surface grammar. Davidson's thesis certainly appears an awkward, and perhaps counter-intuitive, logical translation of adverbs, although it is formally correct. It is too soon in the development of his programme to accept or dismiss the theory of meaning (truth) in which he articulates it, although acute criticisms[10] and partial defences of his conception have been produced.[11] However, it is clear that Davidson's application of

[6] The presence of this account of Davidson's device is not because I endorse his overall conception of logic and meaning. My view is very much that of M. Dummett in 'What is a Theory of Meaning?', especially the 'Appendix' (where Frege is compared with Davidson) in S. Guttenplan (ed.), *Mind and Language*, pp. 97–138. The above value of '$(\exists y)$' is (roughly) 'There is a y'.

[7] T. Boman, *Hebrew Thought Compared with Greek* (London, 1960).

[8] cf. *GK*, secs. 141, a; 141, b(d); 126, i and k.

[9] J. Barr, *The Semantics of Biblical Language*, pp. 63–5. It should be noticed that, while Professor Barr is right to criticize Boman's use of *hwʾ hʿyr hgdlh* (in which Boman, effectively, treats subject and predicate as two names), he does not mention that the Fregean type of logic can be applied to preserve, and not obscure, the asymmetry of subject and predicate and that in such logic it would be linguistic usage by imposition of formal logic which would identify the grammatical parts.

[10] For a general introduction and criticism of this aspect of Davidson, see I. Hacking, *Why does Language Matter to Philosophy?* (Cambridge, 1975), pp. 129–56.

[11] See G. Evans and J. McDowell (eds.), *Truth and Meaning* (Oxford, 1976). W. V. O. Quine (*Philosophy of Logic*, p. 31) makes use of the device without adopting Davidson's truth theory.

logic to natural languages is implemented within the parameters of a theory of meaning that is basically a theory of truth (and so perforce has a prominent place for reference). Thus biblical scholars can no longer afford to neglect the relevance of the debate generated by Davidson's contributions, even though his various proposals are not certain to be right.[12]

(c) Presenting right analysis of a sentence's proposition[13] does not entail that there is only one right analysis of it. Adapting the argument by Geach[14] on subject-predicate analysis, and taking as example *wyk š'wl 't-'mlq*[15] ('And Saul smote the Amalekites'), the two proper names can be treated, alternatively, as logical subject: [*w*]*yk* . . . *'t- 'mlq* about *š'wl*; and [*w*]*yk š'wl 't-* a predication concerning *'mlq*. Of course, this is not to employ logic to dictate what is grammar,[16] but a move which excludes traditional grammar as sole canon for indicating semantic relations in use. It is the employment of logic to expose features of linguistic usage, which some traditional logic distorts. It should be noted that the claims of certain modern logicians[17] could give rise to dogmatic implementation of the view that here a dyadic relational proposition[18] occurs, and not a subject-predicate characterization, and thus obscure Geach's insight. However, such an admission, that it is a relational proposition, is not equivalent to designating one of the proper names as a name which itself is ascriptive, although we can apprehend the truth conditions for such a sentence by dealing with it as a type of relational expression.

---

[12] For an alternative approach to adverbial modification, see J. Heintz, *Subjects and Predicables* (The Hague, Paris, 1973), pp. 90–3; cf. A. N. Prior, *Objects of Thought*, pp. 20, 98–9.

[13] 'Proposition' is here used in the philosophical sense used by Geach in *Reference and Generality*, and not in the theologically charged use (see J. Barr, *The Bible in the Modern World*, pp. 123–6).

[14] P. T. Geach, *Reference and Generality*, pp. 28–34.

[15] 1 Sam. 15:7; of course, syntactic alterations are required.

[16] Geach notices (*Reference and Generality*, pp. 28–9) that Aristotle observed (*Analytica priora*, I. 36) a logical subject need not be in the nominative case; cf. also J. Barr, *The Semantics of Biblical Language*, pp. 65–7, who comments on the distorting effect on traditional grammar of the misuse of predicate categories and ill-formed traditional logic.

[17] As Geach points out (*Reference and Generality*, p. 29); E. J. Lemmon, *Beginning Logic* (London, 1965) formalizes an analogous proposition as relational.

[18] For explanation of this terminology, see E. J. Lemmon, *Beginning Logic*, p. 179; this work is also an helpful presentation of ways of formalizing classes of predication not here examined.

(*d*) The Hebrew sentence cited above is comparable to Geach's logic for a related example[19]: '[I]n a two term predicative proposition, only one of the two terms has a predicative role, only one can be regarded as combining with negation to form a term of the same kind and with the effect of negating the whole proposition.' Of course, the point about negation here does not directly apply to the actual MT sentence as it there occurs; but what one can possibly do with it by negation is a criterion for what its use is in MT. It is important at this juncture not to designate '*nkh*' ('smote') the (simple) predicate; for, as Geach shows,[20] the predicate is only correctly exposed by representing its use as 'A *nkh* B' which identifies, in the form of a sentence pattern, a two-place predicate 'identifying a function yielding' the foregoing Hebrew sentence as one of its values. Some find this ejection of proper names and substitution of them by variables to form an incomplete expression reprehensible. It is interesting that biblical usage itself verges on a style reminiscent of some of this segmentation in its employment of 'incomplete sentences', where a subject or predicate needs to be supplied from the context; in the former category, even pronouns are absent (e.g. 2 Chr. 28:21; cf. *GK* sec. 147 *a*, *b*). Such phenomena pertain to a narrow span of MT cases, and they are only indirectly related to this formal device; but they have some value to show that this type of move is not, in all senses, exclusive to artificial languages.

(*e*) A logical predicate can be distinguished from a proper name in virtue of the susceptibility of the former, but the resistance of the latter, to negation.[21] In this perspective, the traditional usage of 'term',[22] which can be indiscriminately employed to indicate an item that is moved from subject to predicate position without a change of sense, must be wrong and so confused. To be sure, some nouns will be equiform with names (e.g. '*dm*: man/red/ Adam), but it is mistaken on that account to conflate them. In

[19] P. T. Geach, 'Names and Identity', p. 146.

[20] *ibid.*, pp. 147–9. Here I am following Geach who I consider is right, as against Dummett, in taking up Frege's view on this detail (and Geach has an analysis of Dummett in the above passage, although clearly they agree over general policy in this area).

[21] This doctrine is developed by P. T. Geach in *Reference and Generality*, pp. 31ff.; Geach takes note of an objection to a facet of his view and offers further analysis in 'Names and Identity', cf. pp. 143–58; see also, *Logic Matters*, pp. 70–4, 78–80. M. Dummett has developed this approach and related topics in his fourth test for being a proper name, in *Frege : Philosophy of Language*, pp. 62–80.

[22] See Geach, *Logic Matters*, p. 71, from where I have taken this point.

short, we can never negate a name; and even where, in the surface grammar, a negation operator is affixed to a proper name, this unpacks into a sign which forms, together with the attached predicate, the contradictory of the proposition of which the proper name is subject. At least this reveals that predicates cannot refer, if the reference is regarded as of the same type as that of proper names,[23] as it is in some following cases.

2 Generality

Some recent employment of theoretical and general linguistic theory to handle the linguistics of biblical language has, at one level, revived a shade of confusion generated in the Middle Ages: namely, the two-class theory of categoricals, mentioned here with respect to its use of reference and class. It is (roughly, for present purposes) where the subject and predicate are assumed or required to denote (or refer to) the classes which they are assumed to indicate, and refer to a relevant part of the class.[24] When this confusion is set, as it is in the following cases, in a theoretically complex presentation, the basic fallacies which it houses are easily ignored, although this is fatal for clarity.

The two-name theory stands behind the two-class theory; that is to say, subject and predicate are classified as names, in seeming to perform as names of classes. William of Ockham principally developed this theory; with the exception of one Polish school[25] whose credibility on this topic is not held in esteem, almost all modern logic opposes the two-name and two-class theories.[26] It is often linked with nominalism, and it is in this sense that the term is here used with its medieval, rather than modern, connections.

[23] I am not at all conceding different sorts of reference, nor reference in predicates; but maintaining, rather, that, if either view is taken, the foregoing criticism explodes the relevant claim.

[24] The terminology 'two-class' and 'two-name' I borrow from P. T. Geach (*Logic Matters*, pp. 49–59); the reader is referred to Geach's works for an authoritative demolition of these theories (see *Logic Matters*, pp. 49–59 and 10.1; and *Reference and Generality*, ch. 2).

[25] e.g. D. P. Henry, *Medieval Logic and Metaphysics* (London, 1972).

[26] cf. P. T. Geach, 'Form and Existence', in A. Kenny (ed.), *Aquinas* (London, 1970), p. 31. Aristotle, countering his earlier subject/predicate distinction initiated a type of two-name theory, although he did not reject his former position.

(a)   F. I. Andersen[27] appears to adopt a position which is reminiscent of a fragment[28] of nominalism when he states:

> When S [subject] is definite and P [predicate] is indefinite . . .
> the predicate has partial semantic overlap with the subject;
> that is, it refers to the general class of which the subject is a
> member. The predicate states the class of the subject.[29]

Andersen does not even attempt to show that predicates refer;
nor does he make any move, consequently, to demonstrate that
such an alleged reference in his study of nominal clauses refers to
a class. These two points echo the foregoing criticism in a different
context (2.1, 2 (d)) where errors were found in his treatment of
MT sentences. I shall assume that these foregoing studies and
my scrutiny of reference support the observation that here 'refers'
and 'class' are false designations whereby a predicate's functional
structure is distorted, not least because an extra-linguistic (seeming) entity, which is paradoxically not the object to which the
linguistic function ascribes a property, is the referent (i.e. 'class')
of Andersen's predicate.[30] His comments above are in a context
of classification, which, as Hoftijzer[31] points out, is crucially
important for Andersen's main thesis. Hence the errors in conception augur badly for its status.

(b)   On other counts Andersen is a case of a revival of philosophical
confusions which long ago entered theologico-linguistics:

> The apparent equivocation in the behaviour of Ns [nouns]
> as P [predicate] with definite S [subject] may be explained
> in terms of the intermediate definiteness of a suffixed noun.
> An indefinite noun like bēn, '[a] son', refers to any member
> of a general class.[32]

[27] F. I. Andersen, *The Hebrew Verbless Clause in the Pentateuch, Journal of Biblical Literature*, Monographs, 14 (New York, 1970).

[28] e.g. as documented by A. N. Prior (*The Doctrine of Propositions and Terms*, p. 100) when he was criticizing some history of philosophy.

[29] F. I. Andersen, *The Hebrew Verbless Clause in the Pentateuch*, p. 32.

[30] Of course, this is an incoherent form of nominalistic presentation; there are much stronger presentations which cannot be dismissed without serious consideration (cf. A. N. Prior, *Papers in Logic and Ethics*, p. 31 on N. Goodman).

[31] J. Hoftijzer, 'Review: the Nominal Clause Reconsidered', *Vetus Testamentum*, 23 (1973), p. 450.

[32] F. I. Andersen, *The Hebrew Verbless Clause in the Pentateuch*, p. 33 and cf.
pp. 46–7.

There are large groups of uses for which a noun plus applicative 'a' plus 'son' does not produce a reference for 'son'. To suppose that 'a son' does of itself refer is to hold, what Geach has called, realist metaphysics and to commit the cancelling-out fallacy,[33] in conjunction with a use of 'any' in a specification. Expressions such as 'a son', 'some son', 'any son', 'any member', do not of themselves refer, and it is a deep-rooted confusion to suppose that they do.[34] This can be brought out relevantly by asking of 'Every woman loves a son' to which son is the noun phrase referring? It is nonsense to assume that there is a reference here; nor can it be retorted that the class of all sons is the referent, since, clearly, every (each) woman is not being said to love all that class.[35] Andersen falls into an extremely dangerous medieval morass, approved only in areas rejected by post-Fregean[36] logic and opposed by J. Lyons,[37] among others. This confusion is well known to legitimize disastrous semantic and conceptual inferences.

(c)   Significantly, Geach notes that 'the doctrine of distribution[38] gets all its plausibility from assimilating nouns and noun-phrases generally to PNs as regards their manner of signification'[39] and he proves this is a fallacious plausibility. Andersen states: 'In some languages even proper nouns can, on occasion, function as count nouns'.[40] This is a typical correspondence of Andersen's

---

[33] P. T. Geach, *Reference and Generality*, p. 61, etc.; i.e. to produce an inference (invalid) from the use of 'a' or 'any', etc., linked to nouns in apposition to PNs.

[34] Geach's major work on this area (*Reference and Generality*, pp. 3–107, 144–91) is the basis for the above and should be taken as its proof. Even with a 'definite noun' ('the man has a son') it is not guaranteed that, by Andersen's specification, a reference is created (*pace*, *The Hebrew Verbless Clause in the Pentateuch*, p. 46), although clearly a PN as S will contribute to a criterion of identity for P. Andersen falls into the error of claiming '*binka* alone would refer to any member of that class' (*op cit.*, p. 46); *binka* alone does nothing of the sort; it lacks criteria (cf. 3.1, *1*, *2*); it is not a PN with reference. The medieval doctrine of distribution (i.e. reference of a term over *all* its quantified domain) here confuses 'being true of' and 'naming' (cf. P. T. Geach, *Reference and Generality*, p. 6).

[35] Notice how Andersen (*The Hebrew Verbless Clause in the Pentateuch*, p. 33) uses Gen. 18:19: *bytw 'ḥryw* ('his household after him') when, without a certain theological view of future contingents (cf. P. T. Geach, *Providence and Evil*, pp. 61–122) to support his analysis, there is no reference for *bytw*.

[36] cf. G. E. M. Anscombe and P. T. Geach, *Three Philosophers*, pp. 132–62.

[37] J. Lyons, *Semantics 1*, pp. 187–8. Elsewhere (e.g. pp. 305ff.) Lyons may not be so clear minded about distribution.

[38] For explanation of this designation see n. 34 above.

[39] P. T. Geach, *Reference and Generality*, p. 6.

[40] F. I. Andersen, *The Hebrew Verbless Clause in the Pentateuch*, p. 40. Observe

positions with the worst of some history of philosophy, which at some stages programmed theology. Andersen, in the following sentence, even acknowledges the truth that 'Biblical Hebrew does not present examples of modification of a proper noun by quantifiers',[41] without appearing to realize that this is a standard point which in principle is taken to exclude PNs from being nouns,[42] and which thus also excludes PN-noun conflation from the domain of his study. Again, this confusion is typical of the cancelling-out fallacy.

(*d*)   If one takes this terminology strictly

> When both S [subject] and P [predicate] are definite, the predicate has total semantic overlap with the subject; that is, each has exactly the same referent.[43]

It is then strange that solely referential identity should be consigned to 'total semantic overlap' (since 'semantic' is centrally used of sense in Andersen), for 'total semantic overlap' imports synonymy. Perhaps Andersen is falling into an incoherent ascription of referring semantic value to a referent, if not just badly specifying reference.

(*e*)   In Exod. 6:2 *'ny yhwh* ('I am Yahweh'), on a certain[44] interpretation of *'ny*, will have a reference in predicate position, but functionally and logically this is a distinct type from Andersen's predicate referents. Hoftijzer has employed the foregoing MT expression to show that Andersen's criteria are formally, semantically illicit, and he states: 'the fact that in Andersen's study no good definition of the semantic and logical/functional criteria used for the identification of subject and predicate is given is a very weak point'.[45] Of course, Andersen's criteria are not even logical, for, if they were, the foregoing example would

---

the unquantified use of the identity sign on this page (lines 2–3) which is exactly the type of device to foment PN-noun confusion.

[41] F. I. Andersen, *The Hebrew Verbless Clause in the Pentateuch*, p. 40. He does not introduce Fregean distinctions.

[42] See M. Dummett, *Frege: Philosophy of Language*, pp. 60ff.

[43] F. I. Andersen, *The Hebrew Verbless Clause in the Pentateuch*, p. 32. cf. his psychologization by 'intention' here.

[44] See 3.2, *3* above for a possible non-referential use of *'ny* where the reference of *'ny* is internal to the subject, which subject is the referring term for the extra-linguistic referent.

[45] J. Hoftijzer, 'The Nominal Clause Reconsidered', p. 470.

not be constructible as a logical predicate in the way a typical ascriptive predicate is; but, rather, as $x = m$,[46] the references of which coincide in the same referent and not as a 'predicate' x (i.e. *'ny*), in which an ascription is made to the referent of m. In such equations, one can admit that there may be a reference from the expression which is attached to the subject term, but this cannot work as a credential for treating all predicates as analogous to identity predicates.[47] Nor can one deal with the combination of a PN followed by a definite description (perhaps illustrated by *yhwh h'lhym* ('Yahweh *be the* God')[48] as though it were a warrant for other types of predicates to be represented in the same way, because only definite descriptions can receive this characterization.[49]

(f) It might be judged that Frege's apparent support for reference to concepts, in respect of other sorts of standard predicates, is a significant counter-example to what has been stated above and even supports a two-name and Andersen type of reference from predicates. I do not think Frege's position is of help in such a deployment. First, Frege gave up this view in his later development.[50] Second, Frege expressly proposed that references, even

---

[46] i.e. where the referents are identical (x is *'ny*, and m *yhwh*). I take note of G. E. M. Anscombe (in 'The First Person', pp. 53–63), but consider this literary use as referentially identificatory, while there is some sense asymmetry. See next note.

[47] There are acute problems in explaining the final form of a decisive account of the first person in relation to PNs; but things are clear enough to go beyond Andersen, in a contrary direction. Whereas the truth of a proposition with a PN as its subject depends on what is said, at least an extra constraint on a proposition with the first person in subject position is who says it (I take this from A. N. Prior and K. Fine, *Worlds, Times and Selves* (London, 1977), p. 30; pp. 28–59 supply requisite explanation). Further, as Geach shows (*Logic Matters*, pp. 238–49), identity can be relative; one can interpret this as, in the same way that 'same' is ambiguous, so with 'identical'; 'x is y' is an incomplete expression, which is (in the relevant context above) presupposing other predicates which display a fulfilment of a criterion of identity. For a different view of identity (but which would still fault Andersen) see W. V. O. Quine, *Philosophy of Logic*, pp. 61–4.

[48] Although this is only one probable interpretation of this expression from 1 Kgs. 18:21.

[49] I am not convinced about which option to choose among Wittgenstein's (cf. A. Kenny, *Wittgenstein* (Harmondsworth, 1973), pp. 78ff.) and Geach's view of Russell's idea (cf. Geach, *Reference and Generality*, pp. 51–143). Geach says that a definite description occurring after the verb 'to be' is to be interpreted as predicative as 'x is an F, and, for every y not identical with x, y is not an F', but this seems rather a prescriptive reification.

[50] cf. M. Dummett, *Frege: Philosophy of Language*, pp. 662ff.

if construed as arising from predicates, could only be guaranteed in a formal logical language, and that it could not *in toto* range over usage in natural languages. Third, the German word he employs, *Begriff*, although it can be translated as 'concept', is uneasily rendered into English by this term, if Frege's view as interpreted by Dummett[51] is followed. He suggests that 'property' would be a more natural word for an English writer to employ for the same type of usage, although neither this nor 'concept' is completely adequate for Frege's *Begriff*. Naturally, the term 'property' moves away from references to conceptions. Importantly, Frege employed *Sinn* (sense) so that 'concept' did not apply to the predicate's sense. 'Concept' Frege applied to the entity itself to which the predicate applied. So there is no room for an abstract concept as a predicate's referent. Dummett's lengthy analysis is, I think, decisive;[52] in it he faults Frege's notion of reference from predicates as incompatible with other features of Frege's conception of language. Dummett shows that, although Frege had drawn reference into a predicate by analogy with a PN's reference, the analogy does not follow through on crucial points.[53] Also, Frege certainly never on any count supposed that a *Begriff* could possibly be a psychological entity,[54] for he was always sharply opposed to psychologization of language. It is precisely this juncture at which some theologico-linguists have posited concepts as mental phenomena, not only in OT but also in NT studies.

(g)   There is a contrary strand in Bultmann's handling of language which introduces predicates as though they refer:[55] 'the *opisō mou* ("after me") refers . . . to the chronological order of the appearance of the Revealer; but the *emprosthen mou gegonen* [("preferred before me"), Jn 1:15] . . . refers to his status.' It is not entirely clear from this whether we are being informed that the seeming referent of 'refers' is a conception of the Redeemer's priority, or

[51] *ibid.*, pp. 173ff.

[52] *ibid.*, pp. 204–44.

[53] *ibid.*, e.g. pp. 240–44.

[54] cf. P. T. Geach, *God and the Soul*, pp. 44–64; C. J. F. Williams, *What is Truth?*, pp. 74ff.

[55] It will be recalled that in 2.0, *3* (*e*) above, related errors by Bultmann were considered from R. Bultmann, *The Gospel of John*, pp. 73–4 (an example similar to the above is also found on p. 235); the above example is from p. 75. From these types of examples it will be seen that what J. Barr ('Hypostatization of Linguistic Phenomena', p. 87) states of mistaken hypostatization of lexical stock ('Some theologians thus think . . . as having "behind" it, a "logic"') is also true for predicates, and the logic is two-class theory.

some alleged empirical referent as a property of the actual, postulated life of the Redeemer. It would be in keeping with Bultmann's
demythologization programme to assume that the former is the
correct way of reading the foregoing quotation, that is, where the
referent is a conception. Of course I am not supposing, even, that
Bultmann was consciously, or explicitly, offering a conception as
a referent of his predicates (though that is a possibility), but that
he is at least committed to that by his descriptive technique. Yet
contrariwise, Bultmann often speaks of concepts as though they
are bits of language in predicates. For example in his treatment of
items in the Prologue of John he lists 'The concepts *zoē* ["life"]
and *phōs* ["light"], *doxa* ["glory"] and *aletheia* ["truth"]'.[56] If
it be asked whether this is not merely a detail of a slip, then
previous examples from Bultmann, together with his hypostatization of referents and terms, show that, far from being a detail,
it is a constituent of a systematic distortion which produces semantic and theological misunderstanding of a text. In the previous
quotation there is the use of a word as though it were a concept,
which reflects the type of error characterized by J. Barr respecting
such scholars as H. Schlier.[5]

[56] R. Bultmann, *The Gospel of John*, p. 13.
[57] J. Barr, *The Semantics of Biblical Language*, pp. 226ff.

5

REFERENCE TO ROOTS

5.0 THE ROOT OF REFERENCE

1 Root Fallacy

Barr[1] dismantled arguments for the view that there is a 'root meaning' which is identical in some sense for all derivations from a given stem. He termed this view the root fallacy. As Barr has pointed out[2] the relation of a word to its root is usually generative, not historical. He draws the distinction of root morpheme (e.g. '-*m-n*) and a word's pattern (e.g. -*ā-ē*) where the former root never appears in an extant text but as a formation (modified by syntax of which it is the hypothetical simple stem) attached to different patterns. Where discussion attempts to reach an assignment of a root (e.g. common to three words) in a synchronic domain within a semantic field, there is a danger of supposing that recurrence of a root morpheme in words indicates the presence of an identical semantic ingredient in the words. There could be, but this would need proof – not merely the assumption that the appearance of the root morpheme has semantic significance. Of course, morphemes have relations to meanings; but root morphemes are bare syntactic skeletons, not semantically significant elements 'contained' in words, unless other evidence yields otherwise.

[1] J. Barr, *The Semantics of Biblical Language*, pp. 100–6.
[2] J. Barr, 'Etymology and the Old Testament', *Oudtestamentische Studien*, 19: *Language and Meaning* (Leiden, 1974), pp. 13–15.

1 An Example

(a) Isa. 7:9, notoriously, contains the statement: 'm l' t'mynw ky l' t'mnw ('If ye will not believe, surely ye shall not be established'). N. W. Porteous,[1] conceding the basic soundness of Barr's criticism of attempts to determine the root meaning and plays on 'mn,[2] suggested that in Isa. 7:9 'the prophet himself plays – and plays in deadly seriousness – on the root meaning common to the two verbal forms. At least it seems reasonable to suppose that more than a mere verbal jingle is involved in this instance.'[3] Barr[4] has responded to this by agreeing that Isa. 7:9 does not exhibit a 'mere verbal jingle', but argues that this is not equivalent to admitting the presence of root pun. Barr states:[5]

(A) A far more probable account of the passage is that the device was collocational in character. It worked through the collocation of the two usage senses, the sense of the *hiph'il* and the sense of the *niph'al*. Both of these are well-known senses, involving no appeal to etymology. The use of two verbs from the same 'root', i.e. having an easily recognizable common consonant sequence, calls attention to the collocation. Putting it negatively, if the prophet had used in one case a verb from a different root, he could not have made his point with the same striking brevity. It is thus indeed possible to say that in a case like this the root sequence furnishes an additional element of meaning which otherwise would not be there. This, however, is not the 'root meaning', whether we understand this as an abstract statement generalizing the

[1] N. W. Porteous, 'Second Thoughts II. The Present State of Old Testament Theology', pp. 70–1.

[2] J. Barr, *The Semantics of Biblical Language*, pp. 168ff.

[3] N. W. Porteous, 'Second Thoughts II. The Present State of Old Testament Theology', p. 71. The two articles misprint Isa. 7:9 (as 7:8).

[4] J. Barr, 'Did Isaiah Know about Hebrew "Root Meanings"?', *Expository Times*, 75 (April 1964), 7, p. 242.

[5] Porteous's and Barr's treatments of the question are brief, owing to the nature of the journal in which they wrote. I do not suppose that either of their viewpoints is adequately laid out for their full structure to be exposed.

meanings in usage or as a historical statement referring to origins. The additional element is the significance of the collocation. What is indicated is not the root meaning but the meaning of the fact that the two words are used together.[6]

J. F. A. Sawyer[7] has taken up the issues raised by Porteous and Barr. Sawyer observes that 'the root of a Hebrew word is peculiarly obtrusive, a fact which may be due to three factors: its predominantly triliteral character, the relatively small number of basic word-patterns superimposed upon it, and the truly remarkable stability of the radicals in the face of more than 4,000 years' phonetic development.'[8] Sawyer asks 'is there any evidence that the "root" in the second sense, that is a recurring group of consonants common to several words, carries with it some common semantic element?'[9]

Sawyer clarifies one aspect by differentiating with translation examples between a 'verbal jingle', i.e. 'sure'/'endure'; and verbal jingle plus etymology, i.e. 'trust'/'trusted'.[10] He maintains[11] that 'certain recurring sequences of sounds, consonantal or vocalic or both, perform as independent sense-bearing elements . . . The important point is that the root of a word can be considered as just such a recurring sequence of sounds, with these same properties.' In inquiring how we can know this, *in vacuo*, of the biblically unattested root '-*m-n*, Sawyer insists that the root-meaning (proposed by many commentators), if it is right, 'must be based on . . . presumably the comparison of all words containing the sound-sequence '-*m-n*.'[12] Admitting that the exhaustive treatment of relevant phenomena is not practicable in current states of classification of MT fields, Dr. Sawyer nevertheless offers two fields[13] in which there is an overlap where *'emūnā* and *ne'eman* are common to both, in addition to other collocations. Sawyer concludes this feature by stating:[14]

---

[6] J. Barr, 'Did Isaiah Know about Hebrew "Root Meanings"?', p. 242.

[7] J. F. A. Sawyer, 'Root-Meanings in Hebrew', *Journal of Semitic Studies*, 12 (1967), pp. 37–50.

[8] *ibid.*, pp. 39–40.

[9] *ibid.*, p. 41.

[10] *ibid.*, p. 43.

[11] *ibid.*, p. 42.

[12] *ibid.*, p. 43.

[13] *ibid.*, p. 45. Sawyer mentions the collocations of *kēn* and *nākōn*.

[14] *ibid.*, pp. 45–6. cf. related comments in J. F. A. Sawyer, *Semantics in Biblical Research*, pp. 49–50.

(B) When it appears from the above survey that the roots of three common words for *true* also appear in three common words for *pillar*, in several Semitic languages, it seems possible that, whether or not the Semitic speaker was aware of the history of the words and their etymological connexions, the words for true in these languages had for him certain common elements relating them with words meaning *established, firm*. If this pattern appeared only in one case, there would be little to go on; but when it appears three times, we are not justified in dismissing the idea that the etymological group of words has some common semantic element in it too: that the root '-*m-n*, in other words, is a sense-bearing element in the two words collocated by Isaiah in his famous pun, communicating in both *ta'ᵃmīnū* (believe) and *tē'āmēnū* (established) some idea of firmness after all.

(*b*)   The term and notions traditionally associated with 'root' no longer appear in many linguistic dissertations. For instance, it is absent from Lyons's *Semantics 1*,[15] but in a major study Hoenigswald[16] has a use for the term. Sawyer is careful in the foregoing quotation to note that his conclusion is to be graded as 'possible'. Within this parameter certain restrictions exist owing to other possibilities which can be adduced. First, the recurrence of the same three radicals in separate words in one semantic field does not entail that a *sense*-bearing element appears as a property of the recurrence. For example, in Ps. 89:30 and 45 *ks'w* ('throne') occurs (a slightly different form of the stem also appears in verses 5 and 15 with the same meaning); but in Ps. 89:37 exactly the same form is used yet with the sense of 'moon'. Certainly there are some strong differences between this case and Isa. 7:9, not least that here in Ps. 89 the sample is to do with nouns, not verbs as in Isa. 7:9.[17] (However, see J. Barr's[18] own example hinted at in his previously mentioned piece on Isa. 7:9, where he placed it in a common category with Ps. 137:5 in which *'škḥk* ('I forget thee')

[15] J. Lyons's earlier work (*Introduction to Theoretical Linguistics*, pp. 20, 195–6) does mention 'root' briefly, but merely to point out its use in diachronic (Sanskrit) linguistics, and its influence historically.

[16] H. M. Hoenigswald, *Studies in Formal Historical Linguistics* (Dordrecht, 1973). On pp. 25ff. Hoenigswald writes of rooted trees and their roots; but this is, of course, quite a distinct notion from the foregoing root use by Sawyer.

[17] A more extreme example would be *zrw'* ('arm') in Ps. 89:14, 22, but the radicals also appear in *zr'* 'seed' v. 5.

[18] J. Barr, 'Did Isaiah Know about Hebrew "Root Meanings"?'.

and *tškh* ('wither' *NEB*) are placed together, where no common sense-bearing element exists in both, but a nuance is generated by the collocation.) The status of both the Isa. 7:9 and Ps. 89 cases is distinct in a number of ways, although it is possible to see an extended sort of contrast in Ps..89 between 'throne' and 'moon' whereas matching in Isa. 7:9 is of adjacent items (but Barr's Ps. 137 instance is such an adjacent matching, and does not fall into the excluded class of Sawyer's comments on MT folk etymology).[19] I take it that Ps. 89 and Ps. 137 are typical of other MT phenomena; in this role, they are counter-examples to the viewpoint that, in principle, the occurrence of the same radicals entails the presence of an identical sense-bearing element in these radicals. Further, Ps. 137:5 and Ps. 89:30, 45/37 illustrate that an identity relation between some radicals in a collocation has to do with contextual tone which produces an associative field (where not even pseudo-hyponymy[20] is implied) importing nuance or pun. When such a collocation generates intense associations and relations between terms, confusion arises by designating such features as common sense-bearing properties of the root morpheme in each term, if the different sorts of semantic phenomena have not been successfully separated. I shall show this to be the case with Sawyer's assessment of Isa. 7:9. Also, if other evidence Sawyer offers (on the significance of similarities in distinct vocabulary) is inconsistent, which will be argued in the following, he is left with a bare claim of root-morpheme identification at the semantic level, which rests solely on a morphological parallel: that is, the morphological root fallacy of using form as an implicit criterion of meaning, thinly disguised by misuse of synchronic/diachronic relations.[21]

(c) An alternative possibility of preserving some root allusion is to investigate pun on root by a user's play on a diachronically earlier semantic value associated with the morpheme in question,

---

[19] J. F. A. Sawyer, 'Root-Meanings in Hebrew', p. 41.

[20] This term and its related theory is adopted from D. A. Cruse's 'Hyponymy and Lexical Hierarchies', p. 30, and is connected with his differentiation of the second major subtype 'any X must be capable of being regarded, or used, as a Y' (e.g. *knife* and *weapon*). cf. also J. Lyons (*Semantics 1*, pp. 292ff.), although Lyons does not take account of Cruse's earlier criticisms of his work.

[21] To be sure, Sawyer does grade his thesis at one stage as a possibility ('Root Meanings in Hebrew', p. 46); but the article and his later references to it (*Semantics in Biblical Research*, p. 50, etc.; *A Modern Introduction to Biblical Hebrew*, p. 167) accept it as true and to be generalized.

analogous to de-ossification of frozen[22] items in idiom in pun.
Sawyer wrote of the 'small number of basic word-patterns superimposed upon' a root and 'the truly remarkable stability of the
radicals in the face of more than 4,000 years' phonetic development'.[23] It is, however, proper to add that, with such restrictions
at a morphological level, there must have been a proportionately
abnormal incidence of homonyms which therefore undermines
the viability of an appeal to recurrence of stems as evidence for
semantic equivalence. But within this perspective there is scope
for pun between identical forms, some of which (like *škḥ* in Ps.
137:5) are apparently diachronically unrelatable; but others could
be diachronically linked in early stages, yet in MT fields be synchronically semantically unconnected.[24] This state of affairs
(diachronically causally connected, but synchronically semantically unrelated at a later stage) is a fertile circumstance for pun,
analogous to de-ossification of an idiom.[25] Such puns do not entail
any common sense-bearing element between two words, but a
play on their prehistory (the idiom *krt* ('cut')/'make') outside pun
situations could not be said, when idiomatically used (as 'to
make'), to possess a common sense-bearing 'cut' ingredient as a
part of its function). I think that this could obtain with regard
to Isa. 7:9 and the items Sawyer cites, for the most part, although
it is not the case that all candidates for root meaning are disposed
of by positing puns. The type of possibility here envisaged would
not at all require reference to 'root meaning', nor concede its existence, because neither term in such a contracted relation possesses
the property induced through pun; that is why a pun has to be contracted, for its value is not already in functioning use.[26] I think
that the Isa. 7:9 type of usage is just such a collocational relation,
where the relation is what carries the value as an associative property of the semantic field.[27] It seems that the ascription of semantic pun value to a stem (as a constant sense-bearing value) is

[22] See 2.3 above.

[23] J. F. A. Sawyer, 'Root-Meanings in Hebrew', pp. 39–40.

[24] e.g., possibly, Lachish ostracon 4: *hdlt* may mean 'door', or indicate a
column of writing on a papyrus roll (cf. respectively Deut. 6:9, and Jer. 36:23);
see D. Diringer and S. P. Brock, 'Early Hebrew Inscriptions', in P. R. Ackroyd
and B. Lindars (eds.), *Words and Meanings* (Cambridge, 1968), pp. 42–3.

[25] See 2.3, *3* above.

[26] I believe it is a weakness to argue of an intrinsic sense-bearing stem that it
does not allow for semantic reversal, the activating of ossified elements.

[27] As in truth-functional definition in logic, so here: to define a value (e.g.
a conjunction) in terms of other values must not be confused with being those
values.

a confusion arising from the inversion of this relation's effect as cause (where cause here is (falsely) construed as the constant sense-carrying item(s) in the terms which allegedly display the root(s)). Adjacency (e.g. in idiom) can be a semantic value.

(d)   Sawyer notices that the same stem recurs in three terms with two other stems paralleling this interesting feature:[28]

Root	Truth/true	Established	Pillar(s)
ʾ-m-n	ʾᵉmet	neʾᵉman	ʾōmᵉnōt
y/n-ṣ-b	yaṣṣib	niṣṣab	nᵉṣîb, maṣṣēbā
k-w-n	nākōn	mūkān	kēn

This correlation which Dr. Sawyer exposes is certainly of special interest. Yet I do not judge that it requires the interpretation attached to it in (B) above, for this displays a style of self-evident entailment ('When it appears . . .') without detailed analysis of exactly how this consequence arises from the correlation (though it is later sometimes qualified as a possibility).[29] Of course, this opposes the view that the fact of there being this correlation implies a common sense-bearing element associated with the 'root' ʾ-m-n. The grounds for such opposition are twofold: first, without other evidence it is a piece of morphology not semantics; second, the root ʾ-m-n itself is not empirically attested in MT and so is unsupported by empirical proof. Of course, Sawyer's care in specifying that it is (only) a possibility itself advertises that it requires further evidence. Such evidence would need to go beyond that which leads to its being a possibility, in order to reach with empirical force a conclusion that the sense-bearing element exists. Given this, ʾ-m-n is a metaphysical construct.[30]

(e)   These general considerations can be related to the theory of empirical root descent in the following ways (which are only a selection of options). (1) It is probable (even given Sawyer's[3] observation that the radicals of the Hebrew word are subject to

---

[28] J. F. A. Sawyer, 'Root-Meanings in Hebrew', p. 45.

[29] cf. J. F. A. Sawyer, 'Root-Meanings in Hebrew', p. 46.

[30] This usage of 'metaphysical' is not derogatory but descriptive (cf. L. Wittgenstein, *Tractatus*, sec. 6.53). Although depending on the outcome of the item, it indicates (if it is non-veridical, then) it is critical cf. L. Wittgenstein, *The Blue and Brown Books*, pp. 18–66).

[31] J. F. A. Sawyer, 'Root-Meanings in Hebrew', p. 40.

'remarkable stability [over] ... 4,000 years') that some lexical shift of meaning occurred at a primary stem level.[32] Taking this together with evidence of distinct primary values appearing as differentiated items in the above list (i.e. truth/true, established, pillar(s)), then there is a probability to account for, in respect of a propensity for change, which could obliterate the root-stem sense in some cases, at a time after differentiation of the stem into the above terms. (2) Related to this are Hoenigswald's[33] six groups of (in all twenty-two) trees, with different patterns of development involving change, which have some general applicability to assessing the nature of change in a glottochronological situation involving three linguistic entities,[34] and their possibly 'bleeding' (losing) semantic content, or acting as a target for 'feeding' (reception) of semantic modifying influence; both movements of which could entail root change in function.

The metaphysical construct, here the postulated root '-m-n, stands at the vertices marked by X[35] as the hypothetical common point of origin.[36] In Figure 1, A represents 'mt; B stands for n'mn; and C indicates 'mnwt; all of these with the sense of carrying the stem '-m-n with a propensity for change at this root level (where the root is proposed as a sense-bearing element).[37] The direction of the lines from X represents the flow of time, although it stands for a direction and not in length a determined, but only a possible relative, time.[38] The nodes can indicate the points at which the stem ceases to widen or narrow its original scope[39] and reaches the final stage of bleeding or being a feed-point for semantic influence. Here semantic change[40] leads to a sequence whereby

---

[32] cf. J. Barr, *Comparative Philology and the Text of the Old Testament*, pp. 184–7; I am not assuming that the glottochronological approach is valid in making the above point, but presuming that, where roots are postulated as sense-bearing phenomena, it is legitimate to expect a hypothesis of this sort to be tested by available techniques which might indicate its status; the preliminary and disputed state of roots and glottochronology is a limitation on the proposal of roots as much as an admission of weakness in that arena of criticism.

[33] H. M. Hoenigswald, *Studies in Formal Historical Linguistics*, p. 30.

[34] *ibid.*, pp. 46ff.

[35] And of course for y/n-ṣ-b and k-w-n if required.

[36] *ibid.*, pp. 26ff. X is subsumed in the first temporal item (or vertex) where it is not cited.

[37] H. M. Hoenigswald, *Studies in Formal Historical Linguistics*, p. 46.

[38] *ibid.*

[39] See H. M. Hoenigswald, *Language Change and Linguistic Reconstruction* (Chicago, 1960), pp. 34ff., 45.

[40] H. M. Hoenigswald, *Studies in Formal Historical Linguistics*, p. 11.

the root-semantic value snaps[41] from the continuance of its morphological and/or phonological values; these then carry a new semantic value.[42] The congruence of direction of the lines (or edges) is proportionate to their agreement with or deviation from the lexical value of X, or the line which joins it as ancestor

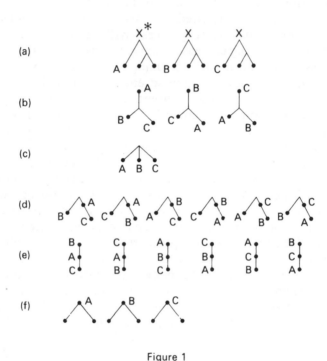

(a)

(b)

(c)

(d)

(e)

(f)

Figure 1

* Only the first three vertices have X positioned for illustrative purposes; it should be taken that X is at each vertex.

[41] For this usage see J. F. A. Sawyer, *A Modern Introduction to Biblical Hebrew* p. 169.

[42] H. M. Hoenigswald, *Language Change and Linguistic Reconstruction*, pp. 29ff. If it be a matter of concern that one relies on a rule-like stipulation to reach this empirical possibility, it should also be recalled that the rule-like framework, whereby one partly reaches decisions about the provenance of an X root sense-bearing item, is itself liable to collapse at points and can exhibit a conflict of laws (for which see M. Y. Chen, albeit in a non-Semitic arena, in 'Relative Chronology: Three Methods of Reconstruction', *Journal of Linguistics*, 12 (1976), pp. 211–14, etc.).

to its descendants.[43] Group (b)'s three ancestors, not arising from any root, are deviant, with non-rooted trees.[44] Sawyer's view does not allow for such a possibility. Group (e) follows a line which is shared by A, B and C; this could be illustrating the lexico-statistical loss through times t_1 and t_2·(these are relative and not chronologically fixed periods).[45] If one takes Hoenigswald's hypothetical percentage,[46] which is of the same order as that which Barr[47] cited, by the end of the second phase (from A to C), the retention of lexical stock is 64 per cent, and in practice may be much less. (This application is capable of implementation in other trees.)[48] Such an illustration indicates that some loss is to be expected; unfortunately it is the case, as J. Greenberg[49] stated that 'it is often difficult to know what is retention and what is innovation, for a semantic change in one direction can just as easily occur in reverse fashion'. Hoenigswald[50] quotes this in support of his own view. Without the reversal problem, difficulties still remain; and these act to weaken arguments for, and against, sense-bearing elements in roots. This is true even where, as Sawyer observed,[51] 'the root of a Hebrew word is peculiarly ob-trusive, a fact which may be due to . . . [e.g.] the truly remarkable stability of the radicals in the face of more than 4,000 years' phone-tic development', because, as Hoenigswald showed, 'a great deal of semantic change takes place within remarkably stable morpheme systems.'[52] In view of this and the above observations, Sawyer's use of 'root' here cannot be seen to infer a sense transfer or source;

---

[43] H. M. Hoenigswald, *Studies in Formal Historical Linguistics*, pp. 26ff. cf. an applied oblique corollary of this in J. Barr, *Comparative Philology and the Text of the Old Testament*, pp. 198–9.

[44] H. M. Hoenigswald, *Studies in Formal Historical Linguistics*, pp. 32–3, 40–1, but cf. p. 39. Of course, one of these descendants can bear X, or in certain unusual states simultaneously merge without X being retained.

[45] cf. H. M. Hoenigswald, *Studies in Formal Historical Linguistics*, p. 47.

[46] *ibid.*, pp. 47–54.

[47] J. Barr, *Comparative Philology and the Text of the Old Testament*, p. 185.

[48] H. M. Hoenigswald, *Studies in Formal Historical Linguistics*, pp. 27, 48f.

[49] J. Greenberg, *Essays in Linguistics* (Chicago, 1957), p. 53.

[50] H. M. Hoenigswald, *Studies in Formal Historical Linguistics*, p. 42.

[51] J. F. A. Sawyer, 'Root-Meanings in Hebrew', pp. 39–40. If one follows the Lees and Gudschinsky proposal reported in *Comparative Philology and the Text of the Old Testament*, the range of results is 86·4 to 74·4 per cent of words retained per 1,000 years, though it appears that the diachronic range of time in which the postulated stem '-*m-n* occurs is unknown because only a few terms in the field are being assessed, and with ignorance about other features of the history behind it (cf. S. C. Gudschinsky, *Word*, 12 (1956), p. 203, etc.); but cf. p. 185 and n. 1.

[52] H. M. Hoenigswald, *Language Change and Linguistic Reconstruction*, p. 45.

it is a piece of morphology. As such, the three terms may fit the (c) type tree.

(*f*)   It is important to notice that Sawyer is standing on a specifically diachronic suppressed premiss in the above use of '4,000 years', although his is an allegedly synchronic analysis. Sawyer cannot utilize the standard average 80·5 per cent retention per 1000 years either, because there the required prediction involving a package deal of the three terms plus sense bearing root involves distribution which reduces this figure. And there is no large enough empirical field trial of core terms in which to set the small sample in this package deal to give it confirmation.

(*g*)   The foregoing reduction of probability is even greater if Sawyer intended or is committed to propose the common semantic pattern in '-*m-m*, *y*/*n-ṣ-b*, and *k-w-n* as empirical evidence for the sense-bearing element 'true/firm' owing to the low probability which results from distributing the figure through the series. Also Sawyer[53] draws on allegedly similar relationships in Syriac, Akkadian and Arabic. But if these are causally connected in roots, how does Barr's[54] judgement, that the diversity of the Semitic group could go back 20,000 years, structure Sawyer's opinion? With a twenty per reduction every thousand years on lexical stock, the location of a root consonant parallel in distinct languages serves up no semantic probability worthy of mention.

(*h*)   Sections (*a*) to (*g*) above generate a *reductio ad absurdum* against Sawyer's contentions. He appeals to the fact of 'true'/ 'firm' in the semantic field within a group of terms, reflecting three separate stems, to show that '-*m-n* $\sqrt{}$ 'true' or 'firm' occurs within one subset in the group; but this is precisely the conclusion which has to be proved, and is not. Prescription articulating the desired conclusion masks description of the data. Sawyer has not presented a synchronic analysis which exposes 'true' or a common stability component in the words. In offering some diachronic considerations blocking his conclusion I have not supposed his to be a diachronic investigation, but that the diachronic assumption's probabilities, which produce the appropriate semantic fields, massively militate against any credibility being placed on the positioning of a common root as an assumption operating in

[53] J. F. A. Sawyer, 'Root-Meanings in Hebrew', pp. 45–6.
[54] J. Barr, *Comparative Philology and the Text of the Old Testament*, pp. 184–5.

Sawyer's study. And, certainly, the foregoing shows that he used suppressed diachronic premisses.

(*i*) Sawyer[55] ends his article with a short sketch on problems about 'overtones', which he concludes with:

> ... the question of the part played by a root in the meaning of Semitic words is still an open one, particularly when, as in Isa. 7:9, there are such striking similarities in the root, the form, the context, and associations of two words – or two parts of the same word.

It is worth emphasizing the alternation in 'the associations of two words' and 'two parts of the same word'. What is 'the same' here? 'Word' is analytically redundant owing to the question of identity between the two words (with the stem '-*m*-*n* in Isa. 7:9). Therefore it does not perform a logical role of acting as a determinative description separating the words, either as tokens of one type or as tokens of two distinct types (from the standpoint of the inclusion of an identical sense-bearing root).

How is root related to overtone? 3.1, *1* above explained that a criterion of identity[56] is required in uses of the 'same'. This criterion also applies to lexemes in predicate position, in which, as Dummett[57] shows, it is easy to misplace items because of the greater complexity of issues involved with predicables. So it is an analytical fact that the practical difficulties adduced above are reflected by the theoretical framework of specifying a root-portion of a term. Still, the disjunction of 'the associations' and 'two parts of the same word' in the previous equation should be strictly preserved against the tendency to conflate the two. It is nevertheless clear that, on some occasions, features in an associative contract between two words result in the absorption by either or both words of that relation, as a semantic value of the words' uses, but at this juncture the use changes gear, because the functional values of the terms alter. One ought not to confuse this situation as evidence that the relations are, or have been, or become, the lexemes prior to its happening; nor indeed should it be supposed that because it happens, the resultant value always was an intrinsic value of the relations of the word thus specified.

[55] J. F. A. Sawyer, 'Root-Meanings in Hebrew', p. 50.

[56] A criterion of application will also be required; this might not be supplied till '-*m*-*n* is shown to be an empirical, and not only unattested theoretical, construct, which might thus block conclusions being drawn about root meaning.

[57] M. Dummett, *Frege: Philosophy of Language*, pp. 233ff.

(*j*) In disposing of the term 'overtone', it can be replaced by 'type tone' to indicate the postulated sense-bearing element in a root such as '-*m-n* and its contracted relations. 'Tone' can be employed to represent suggested properties which can include some relations between some expressions in a text. It is often inexplicitly assumed that all type tones are tones (i.e. all root meanings are overtones). But if, as is frequently stressed, a root is a diachronic phenomenon which is so ancient[58] that its root form is unattested, and in any case is purported to exist prior to its later appearance within a lexeme in some texts, then the equation of type tone with tone is at least an unstable identification and at most generally misleading. Moreover, it is equally often emphasized that[59] an 'overtone' is an item which is produced by a context and has to be explicated as a feature of a known context. Sawyer observes that 'a word constantly used in a popular idiom[60] *acquires* overtones which it carries into other contexts'[61] (my italics). This is true, and it would be odd to agree with such a point and yet expect that, prior to the acquisition, the linguistic item which is the 'overtone' was a sense-bearing element holding that 'over-tone' property.[62] This is also true of Sawyer's example of the word 'missionary', which 'has accumulated unsuitable overtones',[63] and 'sex'.[64] Perhaps it is appropriate to notice that, since the lexical stock employed in biblical and other texts exists prior to the production of those texts, the distribution of tones in contracts with lexemes will reflect the context of situation[65] in which the texts were produced, with respect to some items. But the fact that these tones are acquired, for the most part, as functional by-products of association in the situation of use, after creation of the stem, enables it to be inferred that the stems do not act as semantic fixed containers or markers for the accumulation of tone at later stages. There is, however, no reason why there should not be exceptions to this: the foregoing is concerned with general ten-

---

[58] cf. J. Barr, *Comparative Philology and the Text of the Old Testament*, p. 185.

[59] J. F. A. Sawyer, 'Root-Meanings in Hebrew', p. 47.

[60] For *idiom* cf. 2.3, *3*.

[61] J. F. A. Sawyer, 'Root-Meanings in Hebrew', p. 46.

[62] I am not supposing that Dr. Sawyer disputes this point.

[63] J. F. A. Sawyer, 'Root-Meanings in Hebrew', p. 47.

[64] *ibid.*, p. 48.

[65] J. F. A. Sawyer ('Root-Meanings in Hebrew', p. 47) gives a balanced stress to this facet of analysis; for a view from the vantage point of a psychological relation of memory and choice to lexemic usage, see G. A. Miller, 'Lexical Memory', *Proceedings of the American Philosophical Society*, 116 (1972) 2, pp. 140–44.

dencies. This asymmetry between type tones and tone is often blurred or neglected, and employed as an unwitting interchange for hypotheses about roots which collapse under the weight of critical evidence, and are converted into an overtone group of hypotheses while still seeming to perform as root theses.[66] To neglect this asymmetry and draw converse consequences, together with the implementation of resulting confusions, would be a sort of nominalism where *in vacuo* stems (roots) were held to be names for semantic values.[67]

(*k*)   Hence to presume that 'overtones' indicate the presence of root meanings, or are produced by such synchronic roots, is a muddle about lexical identity and relations of both diachronic and synchronic functions. This judgement, as Barr observed,[68] also applies to those who defend etymology by emphasizing nuance. Sawyer[69] appears to be guilty of an aspect of this muddle in his later utilization of his article in his book, when he cites the conclusions he draws about root meanings to generalize about associative field and semantic interference in principle, implicit in his article on root meanings. Given the foregoing analysis, it follows that Sawyer's examination of roots commits the root fallacy, and this situation is obscured by his prescriptive employment of fragments of general linguistic theory. Once this is cut away from his proposal, it is revealed as an attempt to preserve an approach which has been discredited by an aspect of developments in semantics[70] and the current analysis.

[66] I can appreciate that some tones could be so entrenched in usage with a particular term that they are in constant conjunction with it; but this would be distinct from the tone's being identical with a particular unattested stem which allegedly appeared in the lexeme. 2.3 above dealt with *analogous* phenomena regarding idiom words which are in constant conjunction with certain terms when they are in idiomatic status, while the terms are not.

[67] Or perhaps unwittingly used markers for 'overtones' which are contracted in synchronic contexts and not diachronically remote texts allegedly displaying the root.

[68] J. Barr, 'Etymology and the Old Testament', p. 22.

[69] J. F. A. Sawyer, *A Modern Introduction to Biblical Hebrew*, pp. 166–7; but cf. his *Semantics in Biblical Research*, p. 50, where a diachronic factor is envisaged as relevant to the values.

[70] i.e. J. Barr, *The Semantics of Biblical Language*, pp. 76–205.

1   Damaged Terms

The misuse of etymology can damage terms which are subjected
to this violation[1] respecting the characterization such terms receive. Not infrequently the ascription of a root meaning to a term
is taken as an entry permit for introducing a conception into a
narrative text – mischievously implementing a theological abstract
object as the (seeming) function of the term with the root meaning
as its 'name'.

2   Root and Concept

(a)   Sometimes the conception of a root is assumed to be con-
vertible into the equation of a root's being a conception, which
by no means follows. J. Lyons[2] has observed:

> A particular manifestation of the failure to respect the dis-
> tinction of the diachronic and the synchronic in semantics
> (coupled with a failure to keep distinct the descriptive and
> prescriptive point of view in the discussion of language) is
> what might be called the etymological fallacy: the common
> belief that the meaning of words can be determined by investi-
> gating their origins. The etymology of a lexeme is, in prin-
> ciple, synchronically irrelevant.

Not infrequently, perhaps in a witting or unwitting attempt to
evade or exclude the sort of indictment Barr has rightly produced
concerning root meanings,[3] scholars disguise the structural
procedure of their appeals to roots as conceptions by directly
linking their allegation of semantic value with the social contexts
in which the purported root appears, often in different languages.
This may on occasions be mere confident confusion resulting
from inattention to analytical distinctions.

F. M. Cross[4] exemplifies this tendency with his discussion of

---

[1] 'Damaged terms' is by analogy with 'damaged propositions'; see A. N. Prior
and K. Fine, *Worlds, Times and Selves* (London, 1977), pp. 40–2.

[2] J. Lyons, *Semantics 1*, p. 244.

[3] J. Barr, *The Semantics of Biblical Language*, pp. 76–291.

[4] F. M. Cross, *Canaanite Myth and Hebrew Epic*, pp. 267–8.

bryt. The only etymological comment he has on the term, which is used to articulate and seemingly support a centrally positioned thesis about the MT *bryt* conception, is:

> The most troublesome etymology is that of *bryt*. Two plausible derivations have been suggested. One relates the term to Akkadian *birītu/birtu*, 'bond', and the Egyptian loanword (from West Semitic) *bi-ri-ta*, 'treaty', found in twelfth-century texts. The other derivation takes Hebrew *bryt* as a loanword from the Akkadian preposition *birīt*, 'between'. The former view is more likely.[5]

Immediately after this quotation Cross moves to implement his conclusion by explaining the MT uses of *bryt* by usage of 'secular covenants' and suzerainty treaties, often respecting vassal kings, in Hittite. His linguistic data on the other hand come from Akkadian and Egyptian, and his appended Assyrian example (Šamši-Adad I) is synchronically irrelevant (as are most of his other examples), coming from about 1748 B.C. Of course, it is analytically incoherent to introduce the widespread treaty custom as a relevant quasi-universal which can be instantiated, at whim's dictate, anywhere in discussion, merely because the phenomenon was in regular use, albeit in a distinct sociolinguistic level to that of *bryt*. In the perspective of Cross's usage of his root observations, he has employed the occurrence of *bryt* as though it were equivalent to the Akkadian/Egyptian uses of the relevant postulated cognate (contrarily illustrated mostly by Canaanite parallels, not in Hebrew) with the residue of these uses and their conceptual associations (as conceived, as being in the language, by Professor Cross's hypothesis). In short, this type of process of diachronic linkage involves not only the etymological fallacy, but presents the connection of *bryt* with its purported etymology, as an entry permit for a conception (strictly) in which the cognate terms occur in ancient usage; but since the synchronic links and the conjunctions of the MT item with other Near Eastern items cannot – at this strong level – be equated with the summation of the contexts in which the comparative phenomena appear, then Cross is committed to articulating a root as a marker for this (fictive) conception. This is not only because his proof fails, but also owing to his not having attempted to link data and interpretation in the relevant way, since he lifts out the root as a self-evident focus of

[5] *ibid.*, p. 267.

(not just *for*) the conceptual content he is programming into his book.

It may be objected that Cross only asserts that 'The former view [of *bryt* being linked with *birītu/birtu/bi-ri-ta*] is more likely',[6] not that it is self-evident. However, Cross[7] implements his thesis here by following it with such expressions as it 'is apparent' in relations of etymology and of empirical properties in the required historical contexts. It is characteristic of Cross's (and some other American)[8] presentation that a list of data is cited and an alleged consequence is merely added, as though it were an evident truth, and not speculative conjecture, to the end of a string of information, although selection and prescriptive representation has, of course, played a part. Once a grading of probability is introduced (e.g. 'more likely') it is sometimes quickly excluded as a qualification, or sloppily ignored, and replaced by an assertion of stronger value.

A feature of the prescriptive presentation is reflected in the bald suggestion, and presumption, that the Akkadian-Egyptian noun option is more likely than the prepositional derivation. There are strengths in the latter possibility which are entirely neglected by Cross, and which could reverse the probabilistic priority,[9] although this is not to be taken as an admission that the etymological 'value' of *bryt* has anything to do with its functional value in MT.

This type of example from Cross's work is roughly analogous to some medieval treatises.[10] Often in these, the distinction of predicates and names is confounded.[11] By comparison, a general term such as *bryt* is taken as a name of a property. The relation of proper names to referents is functionally simple (i.e. that criteria of identification require only that any aspect of the same referent be the subject for the reference to be successful, even where different predicates are applied on distinct occasions of usage of the name), while the relations of predicates to referents is mediated

---

[6] *ibid.*, p. 267.

[7] *ibid.*, p. 268. Even on this probabilistic reading of his hypothesis, he is still faulted by the foregoing since he offers no proof for that grading nor criteria of grading.

[8] e.g. W. F. Albright, *Yahweh and the Gods of Canaan*, p. 92.

[9] For a discussion of 'more likely', see A. R. White, *Modal Thinking*, pp. 59–74. See J. Barr, 'Some Semantic Notes on the Covenant' for linguistic proof assumed above.

[10] cf. N. Wolterstorff, *On Universals* (Chicago, 1970), pp. 180–93.

[11] P. T. Geach, *Reference and Generality*, p. 35.

and complex[12] (i.e. the subject term is the referring item, and usage of a predicate ascribed to a referent on one occasion cannot in principle guarantee its applicability in other uses with the identical referring term). It follows that the confusion of the functional status in analysis and textual usage of 'predicates as names' is fatal when one is assuming or applying some discovery procedure for the identification of a term. Of course, Cross has not directly identified $\sqrt{b\text{-}r\text{-}t}$ as a predicate; he treats it as a predicate item,[13] and as a subject term where it has that use. In analysis he supposes that the mere occurrence of it as a subject term in an ancient text gives one carte blanche to cull items from the predicates attached to it, and when it is in predicate position he employs the subjects in those non-MT texts as information to explain the MT. Also, this feeding of semantic ingredients, from subject-to-predicate-to-root, is additionally multiplied by there being domains of discourse in different languages which are utilized as resources, without evidence of synchronic connections. There are, of course, substantial dissimilarities between what I might term root nominalism and two-name nominalism. First, in the latter the whole predicate is a name, whereas in the former a component is treated as such, usually. Second, in the former there is an analytically provoked alleged reference to roots as a genetic, and not functional, referential property; this is often conflated, by a sort of genetic fallacy,[14] with its being the semantic value of the textual use, or construed as a type of psychological analogue (or, a Platonic Form),[15] whereas in the latter the reference is said to be part of the 'predicate-name's' value. It is, rather, the naming of an ascriptional property, as though the referent of this act were a conception, which is the point of parallel I wish to draw.

(b) R. Bultmann has a variation on this type of mistake where the concept itself (which has been referred to by being an MT or NT textual word) also has the apparent property of referring to an empirical[16] referent. The following case illustrates this:

[12] cf. M. Dummett, *Frege : Philosophy of Language*, pp. 204–63.

[13] Cross and many others nowhere strike the distinction of a predicate and predicable; Cross's use is usually that of the latter – as an abstracted item, highly stylized.

[14] cf. C. L. Hamblin, *Fallacies*, p. 45 and see also the reference to the fallacy of pseudo-simplicity on that page.

[15] See J. Barr's analysis of Boman's use of Plato (*The Semantics of Biblical Language*, pp. 105–6).

[16] If one takes at all seriously Bultmann's use of the term 'referring', he seems committed to some such referent (see the following quotation from his work).

. . . such concepts as *pneuma* ['spirit'] and *rwḥ* ['spirit']
refer in their proper sense to a mode of human existence,
inasmuch as the latter is aware that it is at the mercy of the
mysterious, of a superior power. Thus both *pneuma* and
rwḥ refer to the divine power, whereby the latter is conceived
not as in itself, but as it impinges on human existence.
This means to say that there are two constitutive elements
in the concept of spirit: 1) the element of the *miraculous* . . .
Here the precise object to which the concept pneuma or
'pneumatic' refers varies . . . This does not however cause
any variation in the *concept* of pneuma itself. 2) An active
element;[17] here pneuma is spoken of . . . as an event worked in
man.

Quite simply, Bultmann has converted the referring function
associated[18] with *pneuma* and *rwḥ* into seeming to be the referring
function of the concept which these two words are said to be.
Of course, it may be retorted that this is just a manner of writing;
but since we are considering, and Bultmann is handling, precisely
those properties which inhere in being word *or* concept it is evidence of confusion so to deal with them (*not* merely *as if*) in
terms of their being in one-to-one relations.

(*c*)   This slip is not a mere stylism on Bultmann's part, but evidently a programmatic norm (as is Cross's, although in a distinct
theologico-linguistic stream of consciousness). What Bultmann is
required to do, as a first descriptive correction, to legitimatize his
'concepts as *pneuma* and *rwḥ* . . . refer to the divine power', is to
admit that a quantificational variable is absent when it is needed
in his analysis. If he opposes this need for correction, then he is
committed to displaying the type of incoherent word-concept
thesis which Barr[19] has so forcefully exposed in other writers.
Conversely, if he admits the need for correction, the alternatives
lead to an exposure of deeper inconsistency. First, if Bultmann's
account of John 3:5, quoted above, is taken as the textual base for
quantification, since his language needs reification[20] concerning

---

Still, it is clear that the distinctions of intentional identity and reference involved
in verbs of worship and believing and their subject terms (cf. P. T. Geach,
Logic Matters, pp. 146–65) are not known to Bultmann, although it is crucial for
consistency in such topics.

[17] R. Bultmann, *The Gospel of John*, p. 139.
[18] For how this might be thus associated see 2.0–2.2 and cf. J. Lyons, *Semantics I*, pp. 174–97.
[19] J. Barr, *The Semantics of Biblical Language*, pp. 207–43.
[20] On reification see 2.0–2.1 above.

'*concept* of *pneuma*' in 3:5, then this is of no assistance because the NT does not there offer a concept of *pneuma*. As P. T. Geach wrote of 'Socrates is wise',[21] this quotation is not 'about' the concept 'wise', although there is, in such cases, information in the quotation which is constructible with other ingredients into an explanation of a concept. Again, to follow Geach:[22]

> . . . the number of times a concept is realized cannot be a mark (*Merkmal*) of the concept itself. The marks of a concept are properties of the objects that fall under it; but unity and plurality cannot be significantly ascribed to any object; it does not make sense to ask concerning an object whether it occurs once or more often, whether there is one or many of it. Unity and plurality can be ascribed only to concepts under which objects fall, i.e. to properties of objects, expressible by predicates.

Moreover, there is a deep muddle over singularity and plurality in Bultmann's language; he writes of the concepts '*pneuma* and *rwḥ*'. Since the latter does not appear in NT texts, and Bultmann's immediately prior use is quite generally to 'the Hebrew *rwḥ*' without reference to any MT or other texts, he is to be interpreted as generalizing over some common meaning of the term in texts. In sum, his use is a sort of concept name for the set of uses which are alleged to be exemplified as this concept, but which is the word itself; in fact Bultmann himself admits, in the passage following the quotation, that there are different uses of the terms.[23] Yet taken in this way the employment of 'concept of spirit' is merely the type of word concept, examined by Barr, as mentioned above, and hypostatization[24] of the relevant terms. Why? First, if there are different uses of *pneuma* and *rwḥ*, which Bultmann agrees, then one one-word designation cannot possibly represent, yet alone specify, different uses.

C. Lewy[25] has formally proved that a concept is not a recognitional capacity (that is, a person might have the concept of a parent, but he does not distinguish between all parents and non-parents because of that, in virtue of that). So, even given Bultmann

[21] P. T. Geach, *Logic Matters*, p. 29.

[22] *ibid.*, p. 215.

[23] R. Bultmann, *The Gospel of John*, p. 139, n. 1.

[24] J. Barr, 'Hypostatization of Linguistic Phenomena in Modern Theological Interpretation', pp. 85ff.

[25] C. Lewy, *Meaning and Modality*, p. 85.

has a concept, it does not at all show that it is articulated in harmony with the properties which comprise the phenomena, the (alleged) instances of the conception. Lewy has demonstrated a consequence of this which has relevance for the current issue: one must distinguish between different concepts of the same concept.[26] Bultmann does not isolate what it is to be his concepts which are the words *pneuma* and *rwḥ*; and yet he insists that there is no 'variation in the *concept* of pneuma'. Since these words are in distinct languages and each term has different uses, and owing to the phenomenon of there being concepts of concepts, it is false to draw this conclusion after having volunteered a semantically significant distinction (1 and 2 in Bultmann's assessment quoted above).

Consequently, a second point emerges from this situation. Taking Bultmann strictly, he cannot be allowed to concede 'the precise object to which the concept pneuma or "pneumatic" refers varies'[27] for the following reason. The 'concept of *pneuma* or *rwḥ*' would involve the instantiation[28] of that concept, because the reference of the expression is a function of the reference of *pneuma* or *rwḥ*; thus the sense of the expression must be a function of the sense of the word *pneuma* or *rwḥ*.[29] Given this, the sense of the concept determines the reference, if the concept is consistent. Only if it is inconsistently formulated will it purport to be a concept which is composed of terms (*pneuma* and *rwḥ*) which 'refer in their proper sense to a *mode* of human existence' (my italics), yet in which there is also the claim that 'the precise object to which the concept refers varies', since these are viciously contrary specifications; for if the mode really is the referent of the concept, then 'the precise object to which the concept pneuma or "pneumatic" refers varies' cannot possibly be true. That is to say, if the reference of a concept is specified, then either *but not both* above uses of 'refers' can be a candidate. If it is the mode, then it is not an object which varies, and if it is an object which varies then it cannot be the mode.[30] I conclude that, since the foregoing are typical

---

[26] *ibid.*, pp. 82ff.

[27] R. Bultmann, *The Gospel of John*, p. 139, n. 1.

[28] This term is used in a roughly similar sense to J. Lyons's *Semantics 1*, p. 13, where tokens instantiate their type. I vigorously oppose Lyons's explanation of a concept as defined in terms of an idea, thought or mental construct (p. 110).

[29] C. Lewy, *Meaning and Modality*, pp. 88–95 where Lewy offers an outstanding proof of this type of implication, on which the above is based.

[30] Of course, there is an obvious route to attempt to redress this by claiming that Bultmann is being sloppy, and, in respect of the latter varying reference,

examples from Bultmann, chronic weaknesses exist in his linguistic procedures, especially when treating sensitive intricate
material which requires precisely the delicate description which he
obscures.

3   Idealization of Values

One aspect of idealization is to be considered here: misuse of
synonymy as a category of relation. There is a tendency for some
scholars to employ the term 'synonymy' in conjunction with two
terms not so related, as a bridge to join two features of theses
which are judged by the analyst, to be linked. It might – in terms
of the generative syndrome – be assessed as a parallel route to
using word concepts to synthesize an hypothesis. It is not infrequently the case that such hypotheses (owing to their conjectural infirmity) have not been supported by anything other than
such a procedure; and consequently they will collapse when the
structural fatigue in making relations is exposed. It is not my task
to pursue this feature, but rather to exemplify the logico-linguistic
aspects of the use of language in this state of affairs. This idealization of a semantic value to force a (seeming) synonymy I designate
as 'theological synonymy' parading as linguistic synonymy.

(*a*)   Synonymy is a sign for a relation which can obtain at a particular level or levels between expressions, in virtue of the corresponding values of each expression. The relation is misleadingly
marked by being stated as '*x* is a synonym of *y*', because the nature
of the 'is' masks,[31] yet requires an exposure of, the nature of that
relation. J. F. A. Sawyer has generally noticed this problem in
respect of some traditional terminology applied to Hebrew poetry

---

merely loosely speaking of the swopping of objects which display this characteristic mode. However, Bultmann is being quite explicit and offering a definition of
a concept, and the two contrary strands are a systematic property of his exposition
of language. A rather weaker case of this concept-word treatment is to be found
in R. Bultmann, with contributions by G. von Rad and G. Bertram, *Life and
Death*, Bible Key Words from Gerhard Kittell's TWNT (London, 1965),
pp. 14ff. Incidentally, the fact that Bultmann reserves the original type of Hebrew
and Greek script for most expressions involving concept words stresses further
the word-concept error thereby emphasized unwittingly.

[31] P. T. Geach's criterion of identity (*Reference and Generality*, pp. 39ff.),
which is developed in sec. 3.1, *1* above, stands behind the formal assumptions
here. This masking which wrongly 'produces' an illicit theological synonymy
is not a new phenomenon, and has a rich illustration in C. von Orelli (cf. J. Barr,
Biblical Words for Time, pp. 89ff.).

which 'while indicating that a meaning-relation exists between two or more terms, does not provide a built-in definition of what relation it is'.[32] 'Is' in 'is a synonym' masks (and sometimes bewitches perception of)[33] the functional relation of '*a* has the property F which is shared with *b*'.[34] This is never appreciated or even intuitively articulated in the relevant way in such works as that containing the following example, from Albright:

> There are two old words for covenant in Hebrew: *běrît*, which has now been found in extra-biblical sources from pre-Mosaic times; and *'edût*, a term rendered 'testimony' but which is undoubtedly a synonym of *běrît*.[35]

Albright has already idealized the terms here cited, since he is employing them to generalize in principle over the occurrences of the words, not just in MT but in other texts (e.g. Qatna tablets), as though his mention of the words were a name for the totality of uses.

Many uses of each term *bryt* or *'dwt* require distinct translations and appear in differing semantic fields;[36] the former is unpluralizable, while the latter is pluralizable; the former is opaque,[37] but the latter is transparent;[38] these features combine to deny any room to sustain a claim of synonymity, yet alone in the unqualified form Albright maintains. He also relates the alleged etymology of *bryt* to the Akkadian *birītu*[39] and that of *'dwt* to the Assyrian *ādê* (although this latter term may only appear around the eighth century B.C., but Albright postulates earlier occurrences in non-extant texts). These two hypotheses are employed to produce a semantic connection between the two Hebrew terms, via their proposed etymological origins in respect of the usage of the etymons in Akkadian and other ancient texts; this connection Albright then assumes as relevant support for the semantics of biblical

---

[32] J. F. A. Sawyer, *Semantics in Biblical Research*, p. 75.

[33] 'Bewitch' here is a term of art from L. Wittgenstein, *Philosophical Investigations*, sec. 110ff. cf. my previous uses on pp. 64 and 84.

[34] For the formal work behind this sort of formulation see P. T. Geach, *Logic Matters*, pp. 84–5, and *Reference and Generality*, pp. 39ff.

[35] W. F. Albright, *Yahweh and the Gods of Canaan*, p. 92.

[36] e.g. respectively all uses in Genesis, and Ps. 81:6, Exod. 30:36, etc.

[37] My use of this term is that of J. F. A. Sawyer (*Semantics in Biblical Research*, pp. 49f.) and not J. Lyons (*Semantics 1*, p. 192).

[38] See J. Barr, 'Some Semantic Notes on the Covenant'.

[39] W. F. Albright, *Yahweh and the Gods of Canaan*, p. 92 nn. 135 and 136; F. M. Cross has the same view (cf. 5.2., 2 (*b*)).

religious history and covenant.[40] Here etymology and root fallacy are (in a perspective of the generative syndrome) associated with synonymy, which is actually pseudo-synonymy – thus blocking the interpretation Albright wished to generate through its relation. That *bryt* and *'dwt* appear to have some regular – but not universal – collocations with each other as complementary values, can be used to infer that they only share class membership, and not semantic identity; so, if this is true, Albright has made a category mistake, and committed etymological fallacies in inducing (falsely) an unqualified synonym.[41]

(*b*) B. Lindars[42] furnishes a collective example of this type of error in his attempt to reach a theological conclusion about *twrh* ['law']. Lindars states[43] that in Deuteronomy 'the concept of law is expressed much more frequently by a variety of synonyms, generally used in combination and in the plural form, *mšptym* ['judgements'], *ḥqym* ['statutes'], *mṣwt* ['commandments'], and *'dwt*.' Again, here there is no quantification of the nature of the synonymy; so, taken as it stands, it involves unqualified synonymy. Since it is crucial to Lindars's theological thesis that synonymy holds between these items, and it is a subtle affair to avoid misplacing the level at which synonymy may hold, it is not sufficient for Lindars to assume a relation not specified, for it has been shown above (in this section and in 3.1, *1* and *2*) that this is fatal to semantic clarity. Even by the latter part of his analysis, Lindars has not made any grading[44] in synonymity, but merely asserts: 'The most remarkable feature of the book's usage is the occurrence of all these words as synonyms, usually in combinations of two or three of them.'[45] Concerning *ḥqym* and *mšptym* in combination with *mṣwt* sometimes, he alleges: 'It is impossible to assign any distinction of meaning to them.'[46] This extremely strong claim Lindars does not prove, but only supposes to be true. His employ-

[40] W. F. Albright, *Yahweh and the Gods of Canaan*, p. 93.

[41] It is significant that (according to J. Barr's analysis, *Biblical Words for Time*, pp. 89ff.) C. von Orelli in *Die hebräischen Synonyma der Zeit und Ewigkeit genetisch und sprachvergleichend dargestellt* (Leipzig, 1871) commits the same mistakes (although my formulation is different from J. Barr's analysis) concerning synonym, etymology and theological conception.

[42] B. Lindars, 'Torah in Deuteronomy', in P. R. Ackroyd and B. Lindars, *Words and Meanings* (Cambridge, 1968), pp. 117–36.

[43] *ibid.*, p. 117.

[44] But *ibid.*, p. 126.

[45] *ibid.*, p. 128.

[46] *ibid.*, pp. 128–9.

ment of the word 'impossible' requires that if a possibility of distinction of meaning is produced, then his view is wrong.[47] I do
not here examine the semantic field, since my quarry concerns
another matter; however, one possibility can easily be cited, by
comparison of the collocations of *ḥqym* with *mšpṭym* in their
semantic fields in Deuteronomy (and restricted to that context).
Concerning *dbry* ('words'), it appears in conjunction with *ḥqym*,[48]
while with *mšpṭym* it never does. This indicates that there is not
a maximally equivalent semantic contract between the two terms.
Further, the item *dbry* is a value connected with words which is
linked with the domain of *ḥqym*, but not *mšpṭym*. This leads to the
possibility of constructing a semantic difference between these two
MT words whereby *dbry* contracts a relation with *ḥqym* because
the latter is also to be interpreted at the level of *statutes* [of words]
whereas (hypothetically) *mšpṭym* is a value related to the conceptual level. From this consideration it seems that Lindars's assessment that it is impossible to assign any distinction of meaning is
false. It could be that these two terms are to be regarded as hyponyms, in which case Lindars has wrongly quantified a level-
specific relation as a universal permitting identification at all
levels. Indeed, this even may turn out to be pseudo-hyponymy[49]
since Lindars admits that outside Deuteronomy the relevant
words have different meanings to that within the book, and he is
not in the position of being able to argue that this group of terms
within the book are only homonyms of those outside it in MT.
Another possibility is that these terms can be what might be
expressed as referential hyponymy, where they share the same
reference and a common-sense semantic feature, but not others.

However, these distinctions are quite outside the type of analysis offered by Lindars. He articulates possibilities as certainties,
and sometimes relates sensitive semantic questions to crude etymological conclusions. For example, he asserts: 'The root [*ḥqh*]
means "to cut in", which implies that the original usage was in

[47] It appears that with using 'impossible' Lindars requires a mathematical
absolute identity, which is difficult to discover semantically even in formal logic
(cf. P. T. Geach, *Logic Matters*, pp. 238ff.).
[48] See Deut. 17:19 *lšmr 't-kl-dbry . . . hḥqym* ('to keep all the words of . . .
statutes').
[49] cf. D. A. Cruse, 'Hyponymy and Lexical Hierarchies', p. 30 (Cruse cites the
example of 'poisonous creatures and other snakes'). In employing 'level' above
I am not assuming that hyponymy is to be interpreted in terms of a lexical
hierarchy as in J. Lyons, *Semantics 1*, pp. 291ff., although that approach might
be utilized to exemplify how Lindars has confused levels of function as though
one level governed others.

connection with carving enactments on stone slabs for the sake of permanence. This explains why *ḥq* often carries with it the idea of an unchangeable decree, being frequently combined with *'wlm*.'[50] The only way in which the root could be so used is for it to be construed either as a name for the consequent (i.e. the statement affixed to 'implies'), such that the consequent can be drawn from it, or at least as a marker for all the information contained in the consequent. However, this would involve almost all the fallacies and confusions adduced in foregoing examples. First, the etymological fallacy has been committed;[51] second, a referential fallacy is generated by the first mistake because there is no information in the specification of a root value[52] that there ever was a corresponding historical/empirical situation presumed in the consequent. This also reflects a modal fallacy at two levels: of confusing[53] imaginative possibility with empirical possibility, and of promoting this empirical possibility to being history. Of course, fourth, since these are fallacies, in asserting that the root 'implies' the consequent, an implication fallacy has been committed. Used in this way by Lindars, the root is made to perform the role of a conception of the history in the theology he is offering; and this point is perhaps an indication of why such connections have come to be made.

(c) The foregoing type of misuses of synonymity is evident in quite distinct theologico-linguistic approaches. For example, R. Bultmann,[54] when dealing with the expression *eiselthein eis tēn basileian tou theon* ('enter into the kingdom of God') John 3:5, stated that '*eiselthein* ("enter") is synonymous with *idein* ("see") in v. 3' (presumably because the latter appears in the expression *idein tēn basileian tou theou* ('see the kingdom of God'). As is customary with Bultmann, he offers no explanation of this equation in a linguistic perspective, nor does he offer an explanation of

---

[50] B. Lindars, 'Torah in Deuteronomy', p. 127.

[51] This is partly because an allegedly later text (Deut.) has an occurrence of a form related to the root in one synchronic level, while this level is identified semantically with a hypothetical, prior synchronic level contemporaneous with the proposed usage of the root, and the intervening diachronic gap is collapsed or absorbed into either. (cf. J. Lyons, *Semantics 1*, pp. 243–5.)

[52] This is not least because the root is a verb form without any specified reference which is required to make any link with a historical circumstance of cutting stone slabs.

[53] J. Barr classifies a related confusion (*Comparative Philology and the Text of the Old Testament*, pp. 291ff.); see 2.0–2.1 above.

[54] R. Bultmann, *The Gospel of John*, p. 138, n. 2.

his conception of synonymy elsewhere. However, it appears that his equation is straightforward. He has a conception of the sameness between perception of and entry into the kingdom of God; unfortunately he thrusts this onto the Greek as though it exposed a semantic equation which is semantically isomorphic. (Nor can this be excused on the grounds that he is doing theology, for the above quotation is not in the main text, but in footnotes handling the Greek text and linguistic matters.)

The Greek appears to be a didactic parallelism of language, rather than usage of synonymy, and in any case it is evident from such cases as John 3:4 (where *eiselthein* is related to entry into *ten koilian* ('womb')) that *idein* could not be taken or used as a substitution instance for *eiselthein*. This is theological 'synonymy', not any form of linguistic synonymy; and I would agree that in the use of 'synonymy' in 'theological synonymy' the term is used metaphorically. Of course, the mistake is so obvious and trivial that in itself it has little interest, except that it is typical of a class of mistakes which Bultmann makes. If some of his linguistic NT connections have so slim a basis in the functions of NT language, then this clearly raises questions about the status of his interpretation of the text. What is more cause for criticism is that Bultmann should permit such a usage of synonymity, obviously faulty, and unqualified in its scope; for it leads to scant attention to the linguistic in NT analysis and imposes the inconsistent theological motif into the text as a criterion for what is applicable to language relations. Such a procedure is the mythologization of linguistic relations; perhaps therefore 'mythological synonymy' would be apt as a term to designate the use of expressions which are semantically distinct and in different value classes, yet which are deemed synonymous because of being components of a common sentence fragment in two uses.

(*d*)   The foregoing case reflects the adoption of presuppositions in a suppressed premiss held by a scholar which on occasions can seem to dispose of the requirement that linguistics be descriptive. This often happens when one scholar is discussing another. A. C. M. Blommerde[55] cites Job 12:23 together with his translation:

[55] A. C. M. Blommerde, *Northwest Semetic Grammar and Job*, Biblica et Orientalia, 22 (Rome, 1969), p. 64. The use of 'presupposition' in the foregoing is roughly that of S. Haack (*Deviant Logic*, pp. 137–41) following the general type of approach used by Frege and developed by Haack and Smiley, which for present purposes can be construed to indicate that a scholar's own language is used as the

mśgy' lgwym wy'bdm
šṭḥ lgwym wynḥm
Some nations he raises, then makes them perish
(in Sheol),
Other nations he disperses, then leads them
(into Paradise).

Immediately following this he states:

> Most commentators and translators consider the stichs of
> this verse as synonymous, cf., e.g., Pope's rendering:
> 'Makes nations great, then destroys them
> Expands nations and leads them away.'
> 'Makes great' is a synonym of 'expands'; 'destroys' is syno-
> nymous with 'leads away'.[56]

One might be forgiven for concluding from Blommerde's language
that Pope's judgement has been mentioned by Blommerde,
because Pope has offered that opinion together with his translation. One looks in vain for this opinion in Pope's study on Job;[57]
Pope has no comment at all on that aspect of the verse, but Blommerde imposes synonymity on Pope's translation, and in a manner
which requires Pope's expressed judgement in that context.
Here is an example of a presupposition expressed as a property of
the scholar's view which is being criticized, when it is Blommerde's
presupposition (if only[58] for the purpose of criticism) which he
ascribes to Pope as an assertion of Pope's.[59] I term this faulty move
on Blommerde's part 'presupposition-failure'.[60] It is especially
characteristic of scholars who see others from an institutionalized
linguistic point of view.[61]

---

criterion for the identification of true, false and neither true nor false features in
textual items.

[56] A. C. M. Blommerde, *Northwest Semitic Grammar and Job*, p. 64.

[57] M. H. Pope, *The Anchor Bible: Job* (New York, 1965); cf. also 3rd edn.
(1973) p. 88.

[58] The distinction I assume here between asserted and (as an exception under
'if only') unasserted expressions in use (which is a neglected feature in biblical
studies) is what Geach (*Logic Matters*, p. 255) calls 'Frege's Point'.

[59] I am punning on the use of presupposition/assertion distinctions here, for
which see D. Wilson, *Presuppositions and Non-Truth-Conditional Semantics*
(London, 1975), pp. 72ff., although I suspend judgement about her thesis.

[60] Adopted from D. Wilson, *op. cit.*, p. 68.

[61] A. C. M. Blommerde, *Northwest Semitic Grammar and Job*, pp. 64–5.
cf. H.-N. Castañeda, *Thinking and Doing: the Philosophical Foundations of
Institutions* (Dordrecht, 1975), pp. 157ff.

Blommerde adequately shows that the Hebrew parallelism is not synonymous,[62] though he offers an alternative which takes the MT to be Ugaritic. However, Blommerde appears genuinely confused about what it is to be a synonym, for he still has offered the opinion that, for example, 'destroys' is synonymous with 'leads away', as he interprets the items. There is no contrastive equivalence in use for these, only complementary parallelism of collocations. Of course one might charitably construe his presentation such that he is actually alluding to the Hebrew behind these expressions, which is not properly an acceptable concession since he does not cite the Hebrew in this connection at all, but specifically shifts attention to the English. In that case one might then be able to construct an argument for some form of hyponymy, but not synonymy.[63] It is an important consideration that if such confusions exist in the procedure of a scholar who is advancing the tide of links to be conjectured between Ugaritic and MT Hebrew (and certainly in some form there are strong links between them in the fourteenth to twelfth centuries B.C.), then his criteria of comparative identification will be accordingly muddled owing to contrary presuppositions. That is to say, where a scholar has a crassly vexed notion of what a synonym is (having perhaps totally ignored the related question of what it is to be a synonym) in one language (i.e. Hebrew), and equates hyponymic or even semantically disparate (paralleled) terms as semantically identical in two languages, there will be a proportionately multiple probability of producing mistakes. Further, since such approaches will argue from presuppositions which mask data, there will often be a self-confirming circularity which evades external questions.[64]

(e) It is crucial to the consistent articulation of a presupposition (whether or not it be empirically true or deemed false) that the distinction of sense and reference[65] be properly recognized and allowed for. Many biblical theologico-linguists such as D. Hill[66]

[62] cf. also the occurence of *śgh* in Job 8:11, and *šth* in Ezek. 26:5, 14 where there is contrastive change.

[63] I do not think that 'destroys' and 'leads away' are even cognitive synonyms (e.g. begin/commence) or dictionary synonyms (e.g. murder/kill) although each imply the same type of terminus (but implications are distinct from what implies them).

[64] For a not unrelated group of neglected aspects, see J. Barr, 'Hebrew Lexicography', in, P. Fronzaroli (ed.), *Studies on Semitic Lexicography* (Florence, 1973), pp. 103–26.

[65] For reasons, see S. Haack, *Deviant Logic*, pp. 137ff.

[66] D. Hill, *Greek Words and Hebrew Meanings*, pp. 286–7.

write as though the distinction did not exist, and they never raise it as a pertinent topic nor coherently presuppose it or an equivalent way of producing the distinction. Hill[67] does employ the term 'refer', but apparently as something which gives rise to the (supposed) synonymity of sense, which is an impossibility. He observes:

> Twice in the Gospel [of John] (11:33 and 13:21) the word [pneuma] is used in the psychological sense. That the phrases refer to disturbance of the human spirit of Jesus . . . is clear from the former passage where 'in the spirit' is synonymous with 'in himself'.

Even given that the references of 'spirit' and 'himself' are identical (with referential identity),[68] it does not follow that the senses of both phrases are identical, that is, synonymous. However, I can see that Dr. Hill has not explicitly drawn his synonymy from reference, although he relates the two in a common cause. There is no evidence of idiomaticity in the structure or meaning of *pneuma*, so it is appropriate that its semantic value as 'spirit' be taken into account when measuring it with the reflexive pronoun. In this permutation it is impossible to produce synonymy between the pronoun and noun.[69] This is not least because Dr. Hill locates the focal points as 'the seat of the emotion',[70] and 'the human spirit *of* Jesus', *not 'being* Jesus' (my italics). If it is responded that with the uses of the preposition 'in', both relate to something in Jesus and that this something is the same, I answer that to utilize this entails a referential fallacy. First, if two items have the same reference it does not imply that they have the same sense. Second, even given that they both refer to the same referent (i.e. referential feature within a person), the pronoun merely measures up to, but does not include, what that referent *is* (since a pronoun is essentially a hollow term referring (by assumption of the antecedent PN, in this case *Iēsous*, to a person, and here within him),

---

[67] *ibid.*, p. 286.

[68] cf. J. F. A. Sawyer, *Semantics in Biblical Research*, p. 76.

[69] Even if one were to extend the discussion beyond linguistics into philosophy of mind, it is highly questionable that an analogical form of synonymy between the referents of 'himself' and 'spirit' could hold, for in the case of 'himself' it is a referring term through the subject (which is either a PN or (if the indirect reflexive (in classical Greek marked by *he, hou, hoi*)) the first person) – and it is a PN in 11:33 and 13:21, not *pneuma*.

[70] D. Hill, *Greek Words and Hebrew Meanings*, p. 286.

while the term *pneuma* measures – by an additional sense component which the pronoun does not possess – a property of that state of that referent). And here, to produce (a seeming) synonymy would involve falsely shifting some empirical property associated with the referent of the pronoun, but not specified by the pronoun, to produce an apparent synonymous match with the sense of the noun *pneuma*.[71]

In this example there is a dominance of unspecified psychological presupposition,[72] where a conception of terms and their projected connection with personal identity control semantic equations to provoke synonymy. However Hill never makes this type of presupposition explicit, often appearing unaware of just what it is and how it regulates and is required in his analyses. In this way, it will be appreciated that a presupposition amounting to theological and theologico-linguistic theses stands behind the use of the term 'synonymous'; and this type of term contrarily instantiates such theses in linguistic phenomena as descriptive (but actually prescriptive) assessment.

I term this presuppositional characterization of linguistic relations. It is comparable with a scholar's regarding the referent of a word as a concept, in that, now, a relation between two words has been produced illicitly by appeal to, or assumption of, a conception – not of relations, but of semantic values. These in turn faultily explain some, often theological, feature of language. For example, synonymy is an unwitting signpost[73] for a conception which is applied to the expressions alleged to bear synonymity. If one inverts this, it is clear that these expressions do not display the conception in their functions, which is one reason why the fiction of synonymity is a resort of the theologico-linguist: it is a concise method of achieving the (seeming) implementation of imagination as a value of a textual expression.[74]

---

[71] This empirical mistake is documented in a distinct context by J. Barr, *Comparative Philology and the Text of the Old Testament*, pp. 291ff.

[72] For 'psychological presupposition' cf. D. Wilson, *Presuppositions and Non-Truth-Conditional Semantics*, p. 65.

[73] For this usage of 'signpost' see L. Wittgenstein, *Philosophical Investigations*, secs. 85–7, 198. The foregoing comparison of being a signpost with referring is only an analogy, and not that 'synonymous' refers.

[74] The fact that Dr. Hill assumes much from *TWNT* is relevant for the above presupposition. For other aspects, see J. Barr's review of Hill's book in *Biblica*, 49 (1968), pp. 377–87, entitled 'Common Sense and Biblical Language'.

6

GENERALITY: CONCLUSION

6.0 THEORY OF MEANING

1 Generality

The employment of 'generality' here depicts an orientation respecting the possible scope of generality for expressions constructed by scholars to explain the nature of biblical linguistic phenomena, and not the discussion of quantifiers[1] in MT and NT. Wittgenstein's use of the term is analogous to my concern:

> We predicate of the thing [e.g. biblical language] what lies in the method of representing it. Impressed by the possibility of a comparison, we think we are perceiving a state of affairs of the highest generality.[2]

> The more narrowly we examine actual language, the sharper becomes the conflict between it and our requirement. (For the crystaline purity of logic was, of course, *not a result of investigation*: it was a requirement.)[3]

This is a warning to those who, by imagination or misuse of reason, would regiment biblical language into permissible forms by imposing a belief or attitude as criterion of meaning, although there may be a possibility of constructing an adequate system at a certain level;[4] but candidates scanned in the preceding sections generate law-like collision of presupposition with data and con-

---

[1] e.g. *kl* ('all').

[2] L. Wittgenstein, *Philosophical Investigations*, sec. 104.

[3] *ibid.*, sec. 107.

[4] I do not ignore the problem of equating *Philosophical Investigations*, sec. 107 with *Tractatus* 5.5563 and sec. 108 (the portion not cited above), but refer the issue to G. E. M. Anscombe (*An Introduction to Wittgenstein's Tractatus*, pp. 90–7) where it is resolved (cf. also *Philosophical Investigations*, sec. 102).

sistency. Nor ought one to acquiesce in subjective response to individual linguistic cases, for the above analysis shows Wittgenstein's[5] judgement to have peculiar force in characterizing many biblical theologico-linguistic treatments.

> The question 'What is a word really?' is analogous to 'What is a piece in chess?'[6]

> These [problems] . . . are solved, rather, by looking into the workings of our language . . . *in despite* of an urge to misunderstand them. The problems are solved, not by giving new information, but by arranging what we have always known . . . a battle against the bewitchment of our intelligence by means of language.

> 'Language . . . is something unique' – this proves to be a superstition (*not* a mistake!), itself produced by grammatical illusions.
> And now the impressiveness retreats to these illusions, to the problems.[7]

> The problems arising through a misinterpretation of our forms of language have the character of *depth*. They are deep disquietudes; their roots are as deep in us as the forms of our language and their significance is as great as the importance of our language.[8]

These remarks apply both to the apprehension of biblical languages and to scholastic use of modern languages to characterize analyses; it is an additional factor for concern that some linguistic phenomena from the former class have become part of scholastic modern language which infects and distorts recognition of semantic differentia. Since the Latin grammar is not the universal language, the applicability to Old Babylonian grammatical paradigms[9] of

[5] L. Wittgenstein, *Philosophical Investigations*, secs. 108–10.

[6] i.e. an item is to be explained in terms of its complex uses. See an alternative formulation of this point in L. Wittgenstein, *Philosophical Remarks*, sec. 18.

[7] This important use of 'impressiveness' is relevant here partly for its allusion to the previous employment by Wittgenstein earlier in his argument, quoted on the previous page above (from *Philosophical Investigations*, sec. 104).

[8] L. Wittgenstein, *Philosophical Investigations*, sec. 111.

[9] See the fine analysis by T. Jacobsen, 'Very Ancient Linguistics: Babylonian Grammatical Texts', in D. Hymes (ed.), *Studies in the History of Linguistics* (Bloomington, 1974), pp. 41–62.

substantial aspects of a Latin paradigm method (the latter appearing to subsume some scholars' linguistic stances) might, ironically enough, hint obliquely at the depth of these forms of language which mirror disquietude in assumptions of linguists. The problem is exacerbated because, as Jacobsen observes,[10] the Akkadian interpretation blurred the Sumerian grammatical scheme at points. The foregoing criticism of examples displays the grip of these forms exerted on some scholars at a specifically semantic level.

F. I. Andersen[11] entirely misses one category of bewitchment. He states:

Explanations of the exceptions to the supposed rule S-P are often given in terms of *emphasis* or *importance*, which have no empirical status.

. . . The facts are the same, no matter what theoretical model is used to interpret them.[12]

'Facts' – empirical bits of stuff – can only be perceived and so designated via theory-laden senses, which are impressions of linguistic referents, not neutral markers of the empirical world; so there is no guarantee of sense synonymy in respect of 'facts' and the term's alleged linguistic textual referents. Also, records of sense data are always non-universalizable in their empirical scope since they are omnisciently vacuous, because of abstraction and selectivity contingent on perception. Of course, Andersen distinguishes between 'facts' and their uses in a theoretical model; my point is that pre-formal observations also implement an implicit linguistic world-view which requires that 'the facts are' not 'the same' (except in a way inaccessible to current description), but differ in proportion to different scholars' sense data of the empirical MT material. Indeed, this comes out obliquely in Andersen's peculiar assumption that emphasis, for example, does not have empirical status. Position possibly can be a semantic marker for force,[13] and to oppose this in principle entails a conjectural exclusion via interpretation. This conclusion is indirectly reflected by reviving (from 3.1 above) the consideration that uses of 'the same' need expansion into the property F, in respect of

[10] *ibid.*, p. 55; of course, the analytical skill of the authors of the texts is not here being minimized.

[11] F. I. Andersen, *The Hebrew Verbless Clause in the Pentateuch*.

[12] *ibid.*, p. 18.

[13] cf. T. Muraoka, *Emphasis in Biblical Hebrew*, p. 5, etc.

which one fact shares (allegedly or actually) some feature with another fact. Yet Andersen's 'facts' are not the identical 'facts' many other scholars assume, for he criticizes them even outside their theoretical contexts – so there is no synonymy here; in this case Andersen's use is wrong. Andersen's error is advertised also by noting that 'same' does not carry a universally quantified domain of shared properties for 'facts' because one needs to discover in what respect, and to what extent, properties are shared between groups of 'facts'.

Despite Andersen's concern with fairness to data, his model is extremely holistic, and thus requires a teleological investment regarding its exact relation to the 'facts'. As he states: 'The descriptive model used in this study is holistic rather than analytical'.[14] If the investment is not consistent with the actual language over which it extrapolates, then description becomes prescription. Hoftijzer's study[15] and comments quoted in chapters 1 and 4 above give warrant to this tension.

Dummett has properly raised discussion over this type of tension and the wisdom of adopting a holistic conception of language.[16] His classification of types of theories of meaning is helpful to adopt and adapt here:[17]

(A)   A theory of meaning will contain axioms governing individual words, and other axioms governing the formation of sentences: together these will yield theorems relating to particular sentences. If a theory correlates a specific practical capacity with the knowledge of each axiom governing an individual word, that is, if it represents the possession of that capacity as constituting a knowledge of the meaning of that word, I shall call it *atomistic*; if it correlates such a capacity only with the theorems which relate to whole sentences, I shall call it *molecular* . . . since, with unimportant exceptions, the unit of discourse . . . is the sentence, there can be no general requirement, of a theory of meaning, that it be atomistic. What a speaker knows, in knowing the language, is how to use

[14] F. I. Andersen, *The Hebrew Verbless Clause in the Pentateuch*, p. 25.
[15] J. Hoftijzer, 'Review: the Nominal Clause Reconsidered'.
[16] M. Dummett, 'What is a Theory of Meaning? (II)', in G. Evans and J. McDowell (eds.), *Truth and Meaning* (Oxford, 1976), pp. 67–137, cf. p. 79. (Of course, my articulation of 'use' is holistic, as is Wittgenstein's; but this is of an entirely different order from Andersen's presentation of an exhaustive complex holistic grammar.)
[17] M. Dummett, 'What is a Theory of Meaning? (II)', p. 72.

the language to say things, i.e. to effect linguistic acts of various kinds. We may therefore require that the implicit knowledge which he has of the theorems of the theory of meaning which relate to whole sentences be explained in terms of his ability to employ those sentences in particular ways, that is, that the theory be molecular. But his employment of words consists only in his employment of various sentences containing those words, and hence there need not be any direct correlation of that knowledge which is taken as constituting his understanding of any one word with any specific linguistic ability. The ascription to him of a grasp of the axioms governing the words is a means of representing his derivation of the meaning of each sentence from the meanings of its component words, but his knowledge of the axioms need not be manifested in anything but the employment of the sentences.

I do not here rehearse the formal argument Dummett offers to support this theory of constraints on the theory of meaning. However it is significant that it concurs with, for instance, J. Barr's dismissal of atomistic, as opposed to molecular, semantics.[18]

If Dummett's explanation is right, it shows that the type of atomistic approach assumed by such scholars as R. Bultmann, G. R. Driver, M. Dahood and D. Hill (who, interestingly, nevertheless display widely different theologico-linguistic and theological motivations) is doomed to be incapable of yielding a theory of meaning for biblical languages which could adequately characterize sentences and their relations to words; yet this word/sentence pivot is precisely the important correlation for a theory of meaning. The unwitting atomistic axiom-type stance, where a constraint on discovery procedures for semantics is destructive of generalization over actual functions, is well illustrated in Bultmann. Bultmann's inclination to adopt an axiom of word concepts is a particularly apt example of this. Of course, this failure to operate at the sentential level of analysis is not a mere absence of progress in such scholars, for the above analyses demonstrate that to produce a sustained defence of this atomism (as I shall call it), the functional relations and levels in texts are smashed by the constraints of the atomistic axiom assumed. Sometimes

---

[18] Of course, Barr does not formulate the contrast in this way; however I believe it represents a developed reformulation consistent with his relevant theses in his *The Semantics of Biblical Language*.

this is disguised by positing or assuming that the resulting seeming uniformity provoked (by the smoothing of disparate levels whose distinctions have been obscured) is a property of the text itself, as in the case of Hill's use of synonymy, where asymmetrical items are supposed to share identity. Often conjoined with this is the move which I designate theological axiomatization of semantic values (as Hill's position shows); this is the association of a theology to warrant a linguistic attitude (word concepts through hypostatization on the part of Bultmann, or a conservative theological programme, as appealed to by Hill).

Dummett's proposal, about the molecular (or sentential) orientation of linguistic analysis for a theory of meaning, concurs with the choice of a molecular formulation (as I wish to term it) of linguistic problems by such as Barr, where a sentence is the prime semantic unit, although not the only one. This approach is implemented in the work of J. A. Fitzmyer, J. T. Milik and T. Muraoka, as well as others. In addition, it is clear from previous studies in the foregoing investigation that logico-linguistic aspects of biblical languages firmly present interdependences and functions which support the molecular theory of meaning as applicable to dead languages; and, conversely, repeatedly logico-linguistic delineation of atomistic scholastic treatments has revealed incoherent prescription of linguistic phenomena based on a misunderstanding of the functional identity of sentential components. Therefore the sentence-orientated linguistics and theory of meaning (or what I indicate by molecularity) reflects empirical findings in biblical linguistics. Accordingly (a carefully quantified) molecularity is not a requirement[19] but a finding: not a hypothetical universal canon, but a formal characterization which mirrors an empirical discovery. Hence it can operate as a constraint on the attempts to produce a theory of meaning in respect of biblical languages (but to be discarded if empirical discoveries later falsify this constraint).

The previous discussion in 1.0 to 5.0 examined some scholars who, often inexplicitly, adopt a roughly molecular approach at a pragmatic level (W. F. Albright, F. M. Cross, J. Gray, and J. A. T. Robinson, with J. T. Sanders) who nevertheless focus justification of their approach, on occasions, on an atomistic treatment of

[19] I here allude to L. Wittgenstein's terminology cited above (*Philosophical Investigations*, sec. 107). For a possible strict analogical parallel between this physical nomenclature ('molecular', etc.) and symbolism in scientific language and natural language, see P. T. Geach, *Reference and Generality*, pp. 57, 138, and, for its limitations, p. 102.

phenomena. Namely, molecularity is presupposed and adopted at non-crucial[20] junctures; but collides with atomicity in analysis. Cross's sequence (3.1, *1*) utilizing a confused synonymity for *sm b'l* illustrates this. It appears that these molecular pragmatic attitudes, which devolve on an atomistic proof, are examples of accidental molecularity (as I describe it), where there is no sustained consistent exposure or construction of sentential usage. Perhaps this hybrid occurs because a theologico-linguistic premiss is suppressed and motivates selection and assessment of phenomena. Cross exhibits such a tendency since his book[21] offers a theology of history which construes linguistics as (what I consider to be) theological linguistics, where an axiom declaring or assuming molecularity is sharply regulated and restricted by a theological or cultural axiom which conceals a particular teleology of linguistic and theological history.

Sometimes the molecularity is admitted as an explicit structural feature of an explanation of biblical language (although not in the form here adopted), but atomistic concerns thwart the realization of attention to the functional qualities of sentential components. For instance, E. A. Nida and C. R. Tabor (see 2.0, *3 (g)*) offer a structural account of sentences and components, but, for example, locate the reference of an expression in the wrong (actually non-referring) term and consequently distort encoding of language. Theorization which dictates such matching clearly has not determined atomic axioms, yet alone molecular ones.

Some features of F. I. Andersen's treatises were examined above and shown to display comparable structural confusions. They also exhibit the additional characteristic of introducing structurally misleading definitions, inclining to the two-name theory, which itself viciously destroys functional description at a sentential level by inaccurate symmetrization of components, whereby references are invented for ascriptive terms (see 2.1, *2 (d)–(e)*) (G. B. Caird's confusion over reference and denotation has a family relation to this category of error; see 1.4, *2 (c)*). This weakness is exacerbated by Andersen's holism and eschewing of an 'analytical' approach, the latter being precisely the weakness that provokes error in his interpretations, and which, as Barr[22] has observed, is typical of some other studies. There is a certain theoretical opposition between molecular axiomatization and holistic analysis of language which, given the weaknesses attested

---

[20] i.e. 'non-crucial' from the standpoint of the protagonist's thesis.

[21] F. M. Cross, *Canaanite Myth and Hebrew Epic*, pp. 29ff., etc.

[22] J. Barr, *Biblical Words for Time*, e.g. pp. 198–9; cf. 1.2, *1*.

in Andersen's research, becomes a major matter for concern. It is well put by Dummett:

> (B) The difference between a molecular and a holistic view of language is not that, on a molecular view each sentence could, in principle, be understood in isolation, but that, on a holistic view, it is impossible fully to understand any sentence without knowing the entire language, whereas, on a molecular view there is, for each sentence, a determinate fragment of the language a knowledge of which will suffice for a complete understanding of that sentence . . . On a holistic view . . . the relation of dependence is not asymmetric, and in fact obtains between any one expression and any other: there can be nothing between not knowing the language at all and knowing it completely.[23]

The latter criticism is akin to objections which can be raised against some transformational linguistics. It is clear from Andersen's work, as criticized by Hoftijzer and the comments in Chapters 2 and 4 above, that the former's holism is not successful, for reasons comparable to Dummett's points. Andersen's metaphysical linguistics (as I suggest they are) fail because he has not fully described the data in holistic form, and perhaps cannot, and not least because he prescribes molecularity by holism.

Dummett's axiom could be taken strictly, or as an analogous way of representing features here. It need not itself be holistic: in (A) Dummett proposes that ascription to a linguistic actor of axioms 'need not be manifested in anything but the employment of the sentences'.[24] Correspondingly, one might concentrate on applied analysis of particular sentences to expose this manifestation, with appropriate characterization of increasing generality as more sentences are thus represented.

2   Use

Of course, introduction of the notion of use into constraints on a theory of meaning is not merely the trivial feature that an item is

---

[23] M. Dummett, 'What is a Theory of Meaning? (II)', p. 79. I also wish to allow for the interconnectedness of groups of sentences both at a textual level and where the meaning of a sentence A can be explained by matching with a sentence (or translation) B.

[24] ibid., p. 72.

employed; it is, rather, that a necessary condition for being an operation in (textual) language – being a use – entails contact and contracts with a context whose texture is a means to assessing what it is to be that use. To be sure, 'necessary condition' and 'entails' have a holistic ring here, if positioned as a requirement and not a discovery. But it is on the basis of foregoing analysis (and other scholars' work) that use emerges as an empirical property, not metaphysical holism.[25] I am not here presuming that holism of all sorts be disbanded, but solely measuring use against misuse of holism as observed above.

It is a property of the generative syndrome (see 1.3, 2 (c) that, in the case of G. R. Driver, for example, empirical data from languages and contexts irrelevant to, and distinct from, the object language being analysed are employed as a rule for biblical usage; or, as is the practice of J. A. T. Robinson and others (cf. 1.4–2.1), conceptual entities are assumed to be the referents of non-referring terms whose usages are being judged. Both these treatments are atomistic in technique and aimed at the atomic level in the object language, while yet purporting to produce estimations obtaining at the molecular level or multi-molecular (i.e. sets of sentences, linked at a literary) level. Such treatments are superficial re-mappings of texts, which cohere in falsifying the functional topography of textual features, which instantiate an actually inapplicable frame of reference. This frame of reference, because it is a consistent projection of false premises, has a certain attractiveness and coherence by which its champions deflect and discard criticism. This they often do by feeding into its parameters newly discovered empirical data interpreted in the perspective of their norms and reinforced by a 'logic of discovery' which obscures the disconfirming aspects of the data (see 2.1, 4 and 2.3). Consequently, the generative syndrome has a systematic status and influence in preserving and defending theologico-linguistic world views; and, as such, it is exceedingly difficult to dislodge from a position of implicit arbiter in many scholars' assessment of criticism of it, as Barr found in some reactions to his work[26] and as with the foregoing cases of revival and re-

---

[25] Of course, no one has cited an employment of a word which is not a use of it; and it is difficult to posit a situation where this could be otherwise! So use appears to be necessary to there being linguistic discourse, not merely trivially necessary as a hypothetical. So here the status of use cannot be aligned with, for instance, Andersen's holism.

[26] i.e. in J. Barr, *The Semantics of Biblical Language*. I also believe that the generative syndrome occurs in Barr's own theological writing, e.g. *Fundamenta-*

presentation of the fallacies he detected which appear in more recent research literature.

3 Function

The realization of the applicability of functions to describe uses in the biblical languages (2.3, 2 etc.), and the resultant anatomy thereby displayed, clearly imports, at every examined point of use, that there is a dependence (not always symmetrical) within the atomic layer of usage of one word (or set of words) upon another for completion of the word's (or words') function. This feature yields a support for defining a word in terms of its functional dependence upon and relation to its context. This in turn provokes a proof that the molecular level is the grade at which the focal point of analysis ought to be; hence, atomistic and psychologistic priorities will distort linguistic analysis. It is worth noting that a theory of understanding, and its relation to a theory of meaning, is an urgent requisite for sociolinguistic and philosophical semantics,[27] and, although the word is not the prime linguistic unit, it requires special consideration in semantic analysis.[28]

Wrong description of functional relations is inconsistency; hence the inconsistency examined in the foregoing investigation is a matter of practical linguistics as much as a feature of philosophical significance. Contradictions exposed above in scholastic analysis cannot properly be resisted or pushed aside on the ground that the indictment arises from application of logical canon, since this misses the fact that such a procedure discovers textual features and measures inconsistent treatment of them. This is also true where a scholar's handling of an individual value results in the introduction of his presupposition to mask a term in a text; for example, by hypostatization (in 2.2, 3) or imposition of an abstract object such as a root meaning onto a term (as with 5.1).

If someone were to object that this is acceptable for those whose concern is with linguistic theory, but not applicable to those who,

---

lism (London, 1977), which proceeds at points, rightly or wrongly, by assuming the truth of consensus views.

[27] See M. Dummett, 'What is a Theory of Meaning? (II)', pp. 69ff.; but cf. also W. V. O. Quine, 'Mind and Verbal Dispositions', p. 87, etc., and see J. Barr, *Biblical Words for Time*, pp. 195–9.

[28] See J. Krámský, *The Word as a Linguistic Unit* (The Hague, Paris, 1969); also, J. Lyons, *Semantics 1*, pp. 18–25 for details of classifying words. An expected defence of the word as the primary linguistic unit (perhaps illustrated by A. J. J. de Witte) would have to explain away the essential dependence of a word component in an idiom upon its idiom members to make its (*sic*) semantic value.

like theologians, are employing biblical languages for their own ends, that would merely be an uninterestingly inventive way of misunderstanding the previous observation. Lindars's mistaken treatment might be cited as just such a case of a scholar whose priorities are more theological than linguistic (see 5.2, *3 (b)*); but this completely evades the point that his theological thesis stands or falls on his usage of synonymy. It would be rather like attempting to justify a grammatical error, which involved identifying the wrong subject, because the user was not a grammarian.

4   Sense and Reference

Traditional logic in the hands of a scholar such as T. Boman or W. F. Albright is a philosophical distortion foisted onto a text with damaging results for the representation of semantic values in that text. Frege's formal logic has exposed sense and reference as ingredients of semantic functions in natural languages. The occurrence of sense and reference in biblical texts is important for a theory of meaning, although, equally, one should not conflate Fregean presupposition with biblical phenomena. Allowing for this, nevertheless, there is a quite awful confusion at the referential level in theologico-linguistic treatments of biblical phenomena. This also has the effect of distorting or destroying accurate characterization of referential entities and attached functions, as 2.0–2.2, 3.0–3.2, for example, showed; in some refined theoretical formulations of MT linguistics (see 4.0, *2*) parallel misunderstandings exist. Frequently, this referential mythologization (as I prefer to term it) induces a scholar such as Bultmann (see 2.0, *3 (d)–(e)*) to warp the measurement of relevant and related sense (predicated and predicable) items to support (or, actually, to cover up the confused internal structure of) the interpretation he attaches to the referential argument.

Of course, it is important not to fall into the error of defining meaning wholly as sense and reference, since, given the foregoing evidence of usage, they are components of, or constraints for, such a definition. 'Meaning' here should be carefully expanded into (roughly) a set of necessary and/or sufficient conditions which represent the axioms manifested in the totality of a set of textual uses at a molecular level. Indeed it is not yet clear what is the scope of language(s) which comprise the object language for this definition. Among other things, it is contingent on what registers of usages and molecular domains are coterminous[29] in respect of

---

[29] See J. Barr's discussion 'The Language of Religion'.

'natural languages' and 'religious language(s)', together with the unanswered question of the relation of semantic universals to the level at which such possible universals operate at the point of authorship, either as creative or residual elements. However, it is evident that massive prescription of semantic phenomena which mishandles reference, and consequently produces a caricature of sense as well, is doomed to prevent a consistent empirical answer to these issues, not to speak of Bultmann's (see 5.2, 3 (c) universalized mystical theologization of language in NT,[30] or the different but questionable theologization of MT language by M. Weinfeld (see 2.3, 3 (f)). The evidently close connection of reference to fundamental questions about meaning, and particularly theological language, renders the lapses documented above (with some of them displaying systematic obscuration of data) an alarming facet of biblical language studies.

5　Theological Referents

Dummet remarks that

> . . . in the case of proper names, the crudest picture of a speaker's grasp of the sense of a name would be as consisting in an ability to determine effectively, for any given subject, whether or not it is the bearer of the name. On any credible theory of meaning, this account must be generalized . . . we should have to say that a grasp of the sense of a name consisted in a capacity to recognise whatever is to be taken as conclusively establishing, of a given object, that it is the bearer of the name.[31]

There are certain basic problems associated with attempting to refer to theological referents, together with well-formed logical solutions[32] of which biblical studies has not yet taken account,

---

[30] The high regard in which Bultmann's *John* study is held by many only serves to emphasize the problems raised.

[31] M. Dummett, 'What is a Theory of Meaning? (II)', p. 135.

[32] Notice how this confusion of reference and purported identification of theological referents is often bound up with the two-name theory (cf. P. T. Geach, *Logic Matters*, pp. 289–301). M. Durrant, *Theology and Intelligibility*, pp. 45–144, and *The Logical Status of 'God'*, pp. 1–80, has attempted to tackle some of these problems. Durrant is largely articulating work produced by scholars such as Anscombe and Geach; since they are much clearer than Durrant, it is better to read them for proof. Geach has a review of Durrant's two books which is extremely critical of them (*Second Order*, 6, No. 2, pp. 111–14).

although the foregoing case-histories of mistaken usage of reference expose a number of the issues and routes to solutions. Yet allowing for these difficulties, 2.0–2.2 above, together with 3.0–3.2, portray examples of scholastic confusion which can and ought to have been avoided, as, for example, where hypostatizations of extra-linguistic properties at an empirical level were transported (by J. J. M. Roberts) into seeming qualities of a referent said to be specified by MT Hebrew. In these examples no attention was given by the scholars concerned to the distinction between intentional identities and actual identities, or between intentional identities and identities declared by an author to be actual, when references were assumed by the scholars for scrutiny, although the pertinent distinctions are crucial. Nor, related to this, has any attention been given by these scholars to the connection of intentional verbs with this issue in securing an account of the demythologization of some referents. In many treatments of data the whole arena is filled with disparate unsystematic conjectures grown into metaphysical theological programmes, be it in a conservative theological context or a perspective of comparative religions. Theological referents constitute a central group of subject terms in biblical languages. Concerning these, if Dummett is right, a theory of meaning must supply an account of in what a grasp of the sense of a PN consists, in order to establish conclusively, of a given object, that it is or is not the bearer of the PN. It is quite obvious that this aspect of biblical linguistics is in a theoretically primitive state regarding the formation of a theory of meaning, for not only does one need to secure such an explanation, but one is required to generalize it if it is to yield explanatory power. Criteria of identity and remarks on criteria of application have been introduced in the foregoing analysis in the context of criticism as a move both for detecting inconsistent attempts at classification of referring terms and referents, and to outline criteria within which applied analysis can produce consistent explanation.

6 Universals

It has been found, in some of the above cases, that where the analytical and/or empirical texture of a scholar's treatment and proposal is weak or faulty, then this is supplemented by universals, which have an actually hypothetical status but which are required as factual entities. The example of Walters's analysis of *thalassa* was offered in some detail, although it itself was only a small facet of Walters's approach. Yet it is typical of a group of phenomena which he treated, since it demonstrates that even in a highly technical and scholarly work one can discover assumption, adoption or invocation, of a web of universalized notions to cover analytically improper proposals and prescriptive shifts in discussion. This often happens when a scholar's general conception of language is weak, where, in fact, he appears not to have given the relevant conception of a conception of language any attention. In such instances, as with Walters's examinations, there is often an impressive degree of technical competence, but this is, often unwittingly, used as a mask to conceal the illicit articulation of universals. Further, this adsorption of empirically unsupported universals necessitates excessively strong linking terms, such as 'therefore' (see 2.3, 2) as assertion signs to seem to carry the universalized loading of the data. As was shown in criticism of Walters's suggestions (where also a modality of 'must' was introduced), the analytical defects in this type of mixture of universal and improperly employed data collapse under their own weight when measured against a requirement of consistency.

Against this trend, however, it is interesting to observe the general mention of the notion of semantic universals by J. F. A. Sawyer;[33] but he committed the root fallacy. Work by such scholars as F. M. Cross (see 3.1, 1) produces the same type of error as that found in Walters. For example, he supposes that a synonymy universal obtains, which actually only serves as an attempt to exclude a diachronic gap between two expressions; this gap if investigated is found to contain data which disconfirm synonymy. Unfortunately this is an overwhelmingly dominant trend in quantitative respects. J. J. M. Roberts (noticed in 2.1, 4) hypostatizes diachronic sequences as though they can apply at any synchronic axis, although phenomena come into hypostatized operation from not only distinct synchronic levels but in different languages (in this regard, Roberts parallels Bultmann and J. A. T. Robinson in NT semantics). Such a move consists in being the Babel fallacy and also exhibits the segmentation fallacy (see 1.3, 1 and 2).

In a certain respect, PNs are universals[34] (to be distinguished, of course, from the view that universals are names). If identifica-

[33] J. F. A. Sawyer, *Semantics in Biblical Research*, pp. 28–9. However, surely biblical linguistics is at too early a stage to prove that universals obtain in a way symmetrical or asymmetrical respecting other languages (cf. p. 115).

[34] See P. T. Geach, 'Names and Identity', p. 152; and cf. J. Lyons, *Semantics 1*, pp. 111–12.

tion of a PN is made with its referent, it is a powerful device for generating interpretations. The pressure of a desire for generality has provoked some scholars to employ this device where a PN is only equiform to, and not referentially coincident with, the function of, another morpheme or component of it, as in the example of J. J. M. Roberts (2.1, 4), despite the fact that his study is an investigation of PNs. There is an inclination to conflate a PN with a common noun, which was found where the noun's semantic field was improperly used, either to enrich or to produce a conception illicitly linked with the PN.

It has not been part of the current research to relate logico-linguistic confusions to the theologies which they induce (or *vice versa*), but many examples were selected for analysis because in addition to their logico-linguistic weaknesses (or one might say because of them) they have been employed to construct a theology or exegesis of the relevant texts. In this perspective it is significant to note that F. M. Cross,[35] for instance, attempts to programme the MT text with theologico-linguistic presuppositions employed as universals; once these are implemented they hold the status of a sort of suppressed premiss acting as the criterion for whether a textual reading is original (*sic*: acceptable), so that a theology can be received by the text. For example, concerning *h'l* ('the God') in Gen. 46:3 (which has no variant readings in BHS, and for which Brockington[36] has no conjectural or semantic emendations) Cross,[37] in a mere brief footnote, assures the reader that this occurrence of the article, which is a counter-example to his theologico-linguistic theological equation concerning PNs and common nouns in West Semitic and MT at one juncture, was not in the original text but is a later addition. This textual and semantic surgery which requires exact criteria of identity and application has, in other contexts, been rightly criticized by Barr,[38] but still regularly appears in current literature.

A distinction between theological and linguistic assessment has often been merged into a deployment of synonymy hypotheses, with dire consequence for semantic description. Perhaps a most extreme case of this is in B. Lindars's study of Deuteronomic law (5.2, 3) where four fallacies characterize fundamental confusion

[35] See sections 3.0, 2; 3.1, 1; 3.2, 3 above.
[36] L. H. Brockington, *The Hebrew Text of the Old Testament* (Oxford, 1973), p. 7.
[37] F. M. Cross, *Canaanite Myth and Hebrew Epic*, p. 12 n.
[38] J. Barr, *Comparative Philology and the Text of the Old Testament*, pp. 288–304, etc. cf. also his *The Semantics of Biblical Language*, pp. 288–96.

over relation, modality, word/concept and etymology, and reflect the type of mistakes present in the works of W. F. Albright[39] and R. Bultmann (also documented in 5.2, *2*).

Synonymy universals are seminal assumptions for semantics, which if misused encode such features as roots and conceptions as though they were the semantic values of the equated terms – as Lindars's case advertised. Not infrequently, in the few cases where a scholar gives any attention to his metalanguage (e.g. 'synonymy') he lays bare his confusion over what it is to be that item, as illustrated in A. C. M. Blommerde's treatment of Job and Northwest Semitic texts (5.2, *3*). A concomitant of this is that representation of not only ancient texts is inadequate, but that it reflects a tendency generally to misunderstand and/or wrongly depict scholarly treatments (cf. Blommerde's reproduction of Pope, and Hill's discussion of Barr, 5.2, *3*).

Simplifying considerations, in the spirit of Ockham's razor,[40] are structural features of semantic explanation which can be prescriptive or descriptive. Only the latter have value, but the former prescriptive simplicity often holds ground against description. Description is more complex and perplexing to those who prefer, in advance of empirical description, an exhaustive classification of semantics simply contrived, although complexity is not a categorial measure of the presence of descriptive work (as F. I. Andersen's systems show, being highly prescriptive). This simplicity is actually incorrect hypostatization of linguistic phenomena which can only destroy the basis for generalization. A clear example of this is the still fashionable appeal to roots, which the structures of influential lexicons play no small part in preserving. Moreover, some scholars like J. F. A. Sawyer (5.1, *1*), B. Lindars (5.2, *3*) and G. R. Driver (1.3, *2*) provide regular examples of metaphysical speculation; although J. F. A. Sawyer's analysis of some roots is an advance over previous studies, but I have shown it to be unsuccessful as a proof for their existence.

Influential research in the comparative Semitic arena in

---

[39] In addition to 5.2, see Albright errors reflecting these confusions when commenting on logic and language (dealt with in the Appendix below).

[40] E. Sober (*Simplicity* (Oxford, 1975) p. 41, n. 2) gives notice that the Ockham maxim 'entities must not be multiplied without necessity' does not actually appear in Ockham in that form. A. N. Prior (*Papers in Logic and Ethics*, p. 31) confessed a lack of zeal for the maxim. I think it can be misunderstood; for where there is no complete linguistic knowledge of dead languages, there is no basis for universalization to reduce entities at a systematic level, except in proportion to description of entities.

Ugaritic-Hebrew connections has not provided an analytical basis from which universals can be adduced, since subjectivism (as in the case of M. Dahood – see 2.1, 4) has generated psychologization of data and recurrent fallacies (e.g. fallacies of modality). Simultaneously, hypostatization of items and referents (although not in object language as hypostatization) regularly invent an illusion of generality (cf. 2.3, 2 and 2.1) to which the scholars concerned retreat to synthesize policies rather than engage in exploratory analytical descriptive procedures.

No single class of descriptions of a semantic class in biblical language has yet been formulated at all empirically or theoretically specified in a way which receives a universal classification. This situation, together with the foregoing documentation of systematic confusion and fallacy, shows that finalized discussion of or objection in principle to universalized semantics is premature.

7   Logico-Linguistics

Even among scholars who have explicitly accepted Barr's critique of semantics,[41] there has been a sizeable minority who have in practice opposed it (e.g. P. R. Ackroyd – see 2.3, 2). Ackroyd's case illustrates that grasp of a concept[42] is not the possession of a criterion of, or recognition of, how to apply it; in practice he psychologized use and distorted its functional texture. So it is not entirely unexpected that some errors exposed by Barr still pervade the literature, and others, more extreme, such as Bultmann's were not unveiled.

The almost complete inattention to refined analytical procedures by those scholars criticized above has its trajectory measured by the discovery, via the application of logico-linguistics, of substantial misunderstanding, confusion, contrariety and inconsistent generalization. Wherever convenient, this logico-linguistic representation was matched by applied linguistic considerations to show that the logico-linguistic characterization was functional, and not artificial novelty. That it succeeds as a device, exhibits the applicability of logical analysis to applied linguistics, which, while a main objective of this study is to denounce error, is in itself a positive contribution to the production of sophisticated analytical procedures. Further, the logico-linguistic description of linguistic phenomena can map some textual operations and functions with

[41] J. Barr, *The Semantics of Biblical Language.*
[42] Bultmann's case illustrates this. Cf. 5.2, 2, where I offer an analysis of concept which relates to the above point.

sensitivity, if the previous study is in principle typical of what is possible generally. Logico-linguistics has been able, in this perspective of functional priority, to offer some conditions for analytical consistency which are urgently needed, and until now often ignored and systematically countermanded in some linguistics, theologico-linguistics and biblical studies.

Such an analytical empiricism is also important for producing an arena within which semantic conceptual questions can be formed so as to construct a route to a theory of meaning. One of these questions concerns the core ingredients at a functioning level for this theory respecting sense and reference (as Dummett formulates the issue).

The foregoing treatments of linguistic phenomena, together with the documentation of systematic confusion and error, forces the need for a reassessment of the theological conclusions which have been drawn on the basis of such a state of affairs. It would be a mistake to assume that this requires only minor alteration of synthesis and conclusion, for it has been shown above that even primary elements in language (e.g. reference) have been often grotesquely described and misused. This is a matter of structural and fundamental defect. Since major theological developments have been enjoyed with this inconsistent situation as warrant for them, reassessment in the perspective of the foregoing study needs to extend to some of the most basic assumptions in theology. Will this be the foundation for programmes of future research?

7

APPENDIX

7.0 W. F. ALBRIGHT'S USE OF 'LOGIC'

1 Scope

Only in one extremely narrow sense is the following note to do with 'logic'; it concerns how Professor Albright employed the term (and its various formations) in contexts where he gave reason a position of structural significance in, and for, his treatment of biblical and Near Eastern data.[1] Despite the supporting role 'logic' has in Albright's conceptual foundations, scholars have tended, as it were, by omitting to deal with his 'logic' as a structural feature, to construe charitably rather than imitate his remarks. In view of the confusion which Albright displays, this is commendable; but since the presence of confusion in a position of structural support has consequences for what it is alleged to hold up, it is proper to expose a cause of potential collapse. Compared with Albright, other scholars[2] exhibit only occasional employment of the word (and its forms).

2 Pseudologic

(a) W. F. Albright[3] adopted (and after 1940 adapted) a distinction of three types of logic from Lévy-Bruhl, which the latter later retracted. They are, with relevant quotations from Albright:

[1] e.g. W. F. Albright, *Archaeology and the Religion of Israel* (5th edn., New York, 1969), pp. xiv–xvi, etc.

[2] Sometimes such uses are careless, rhetorically present to give warrant where no reasoning is used (e.g. J. T. Sanders, *The New Testament Christological Hymns*, pp. 40–1); at other times (e.g.) 'logical structure', 'form and logic of the Hebrew sentence' are warranted (examples from J. Barr, 'b'rṣ-molis . . .', in *Journal of Semitic Studies*, 20 (1975), 2, pp. 150 and 164) but entirely unexplained, though such identification is of crucial value in use of the terms.

[3] W. F. Albright, 'Neglected Factors in the Greek Intellectual Revolution', in *Proceedings of the American Philosophical Society*, 116 (1972), pp. 225–42.

(i) *Proto-logical*[4]
'It is distinguished by an inability to control by ordinary human experience, dream life, religious phenomena . . . etc.'[5]

(ii) *Empirico-logical*[6] (or *Empirical Logic*)
'The Hebrew Bible is probably the most remarkable example of a work characterized almost throughout by empirical logic'[7]

(iii) *Formal Logic*[8]
'The shift in ways of thinking . . . among the Hellenes . . . consisted essentially in an introduction of generalized modes of thought as well as of reasoning with the tools of formal logic'[9]

Logicians have never used (i) and hardly ever (ii),[10] and while (iii) is used by logicians, it tends usually to refer to post-18th-century A.D. logics, and Albright's subsequent explanations of it are distinct from standard accounts.[11]

(*b*) Albright observes[12] 'none of the characteristics of Greek philosophy is found in the Hebrew Bible. There is no logical reasoning.' While agreeing with the former statement, one might wonder what the last expression exactly negates, especially since in another place Albright stated:[13] 'the Hebrew Bible is the greatest existing monument of empirical logic . . . and this logic is more exact than formal logic in some important respects.' Presumably the comparison relating to exactness is composed by like-kinds. How is it possible for one logic to be more exact than another without 'logical reasoning' being involved in each?

(*c*) This ambiguity (or worse, if it is interpreted strictly) reflects

[4] *ibid.*, p. 225.
[5] W. F. Albright, *New Horizons in Biblical Research* (London, 1966), p. 24.
[6] *ibid.*, p. 25.
[7] W. F. Albright, 'Neglected Factors in the Greek Intellectual Revolution', p. 225.
[8] W. F. Albright, *History, Archaeology and Christian Humanism* (New York, 1964), pp. 54f.
[9] W. F. Albright, 'Neglected Factors in the Greek Intellectual Revolution', p. 225.
[10] 'Empirical logic' has occasionally been used, but not as a standard term and in any case not with the above sense.
[11] For which see W. and M. Kneale, *The Development of Logic*, pp. 1ff.
[12] W. F. Albright, *History, Archaeology and Christian Humanism*, p. 91.
[13] W. F. Albright, *Yahweh and the Gods of Canaan*, p. 154.

systematic confusion in Albright. He maintains:[14] 'It is impossible to derive Greek logic and philosophy from Egypt, Babylonia, or Phoenicia', yet elsewhere, while agreeing that 'there is no indication whatever that the principle of the syllogism as such was recognised anywhere', adds: 'On the other hand, ancient law . . . does show the practical use of the syllogism.'[15] The Mesopotamian law Albright is concerned with has a syllogism in it, if it shows the practical use of the syllogism, if Albright has employed the designation 'syllogism'[16] properly. Albright has produced a disguised contradictory, assuming he escapes its consequence by introducing 'practical'.[17] In addition, if it is 'impossible to derive Greek logic . . . from . . . Babylonia' (in which he needs to have the sense 'any logic', if his proposition is true), how could this be evidently compatible with the existence of 'use of the syllogism'? Professor Albright makes matters worse by asserting in another place,[18] concerning Eshnunna case law 'that the seeds of formal syllogistic reasoning are already there.' It is not straining at a metaphor to assume, if this is so, which it is not, that some 'Greek logic' can be 'derived' from Babylonia.[19]

(d)   Albright was nevertheless concerned to stress that 'primitive customary law'[20] cannot be transformed into or reduced to terms

[14] W. F. Albright, 'Neglected Factors in the Greek Intellectual Revolution', p. 227. Of course, it is possible that Albright lost track of contrary statements within his various analyses.

[15] W. F. Albright, 'Neglected Factors in the Greek Intellectual Revolution', p. 225.

[16] cf. J. D. G. Evans, *Aristotle's Concept of Dialectic* (Cambridge, 1977), p. 22 n. 53 and p. 74.

[17] Albright's basic mistake is in judging a thing to be empirical because its subject matter is empirical (or a different non-syllogistic syllogism because it is a syllogism which has practical material); M. Przelecki (*The Logic of Empirical Theories* (London, 1969), pp. 6ff.) gives formal warrant for showing Albright is wrong, although surely it is obvious enough anyway. I am not here referring to practical reasoning, for which see P. T. Geach, *Logic Matters*, pp. 285–8.

[18] W. F. Albright, *History, Archaeology and Christian Humanism*, pp. 97–8.

[19] It is interesting to note that in the Akkadian Laws of Alalah *šumma* normally has its verb in the present/future, not preterite (cf. G. Giacumakis, *The Akkadian of Alalah*, Paris, 1970, p. 52) thus giving (only) a vestige of support to the notion of a partly formalized system rather than case law. Aristotle's taking the consequence relation as primitive (undefined) – 'follows of necessity' – renders incorrect Albright's alignment of an aspect of it with the Eshnunna use of consequence. For this whole area, which Albright neglects, see J. Lear, *Aristotle and Logical Theory* (Cambridge, 1980), pp. 4ff.

[20] See W. F. Albright, *History, Archaeology and Christian Humanism*, p. 98. He criticizes such an attempt by E. A. Hoebel, *The Law of Primitive Man* (Cambridge, Mass., 1954), pp. 67ff., 100ff., 127ff., 211ff.

of formal logic; nor can it be claimed that this product would be what was understood by early Babylonians who used the laws. Contrariwise, he chooses to demonstrate (allegedly) that the 'seeds of formal syllogistic reasoning'[21] appear in Babylonian case-law by employing the following example from Eshnunna,[22] together with its proposed transformation produced by Albright:

(A) If a man cuts off a man's finger he shall pay two-thirds of a silver mina.

(B) A man who cuts off another man's finger shall pay two-thirds of a silver mina;
This man has cut off another man's finger;
Therefore he shall pay two-thirds of a mina of silver.

A relevant question is whether or not Albright is right to suppose that there is any actual connection *in* logic between the Eshnunna case-law (A) and the syllogism (B), in the appropriate sense he requires to designate 'seeds' in (A). It is not sufficient to deem the act of transformation as evidence of a transfer of the relevant item from (A) to (B), for a number of reasons. First, as Albright[23] insists elsewhere, there is no generalized ancient system, or any system, of reasoning reflected in, or which produces, (A); nor is (B) employed as a deductive item in Eshnunna case-law, even though (as Prior[24] rightly says of 'if') *šumma* is of itself an abstract semantic value. Second, since (as Anscombe reports Wittgenstein[25] to state) 'in logic every proposition is the form of a proof', form is essential to the question of possible and actual connections between propositions; in this perspective (A) and (B) have no identical formal features which are common to both.[26] (The con-

[21] W. F. Albright, *History, Archaeology and Christian Humanism*, p. 97.

[22] Law § *43*; W. F. Albright, *History, Archaeology and Christian Humanism*, pp. 97–8.

[23] W. F. Albright, 'Neglected Factors in the Greek Intellectual Revolution', p. 230.

[24] A. N. Prior, *Objects of Thought*, p. 32, cf. pp. 29–30, where he also mentions 'implies' in the same category.

[25] G. E. M. Anscombe, *An Introduction to Wittgenstein's Tractatus*, p. 114; cf. L. Wittgenstein, *Tractatus*, 6.1264.

[26] On the question of the relations of 'If . . . then . . .' and 'therefore' see M. Dummett, *Frege : Philosophy of Language*, pp. 305–63, where the two are shown to be not similar in the relevant sense.

tent is no evidence[27] because the relevant concern of logic is form.)[28] Third, since Albright employs 'seeds' in the plural and relates it to the topic of 'formal syllogistic reasoning'[29] (not just one aspect of either or both), notice that Eshnunna law cannot generate the 256 standard instances[30] of the pattern of the syllogism.[31] Fourth, even for the alleged immediate Greek[32] influence on the origin of the syllogism there is uncertainty and dispute, and with no evidence of a synchronic link or diachronic ancestral chain of connection between Eshnunna law and Aristotle, it is rash speculation to suppose that Albright's connection can be held as an unargued evident explanation. Fifth, it is a chronic confusion to suppose that the operation of transforming (A) into (B) proves that the author or user of the former employed any elements of reason in (A) which are logically genetically related to (B), since a logically possible transformation does not entail a genetic connection.[33] Sixth, many scholars[34] might be interpreted to oppose Albright's alignment of logic with legal laws.[35]

(e)   Albright made various assertions about MT law in equating it with his 'empirical logic',[36] but on the basis of a (seeming)

[27] Of course there is formal semantics; but syllogism is to do with form, not semantics.

[28] In 'Neglected Factors in the Greek Intellectual Revolution', p. 232, Albright stated that Eshnunna law has an 'almost complete lack of systematic classification'.

[29] W. F. Albright, History, Archaeology and Christian Humanism, p. 97

[30] J. Łukasiewicz, Aristotle's Syllogistic (Oxford, 1957).

[31] Main features such as quantification do not appear in Albright's example, nor of course the syllogistic form itself (although a conditional 'If/then . . .' does appear within some syllogisms).

[32] cf. M. A. Stewart and R. K. Sprague, 'Plato's Sophistry', The Aristotelian Society, Supplementary Volume, 51 (1977), pp. 21–8, 45–61. It might be said that Albright may incur the fallacy of misplaced credit (cf. Sprague, p. 46) in ascribing to Eshnunna seeds of syllogism.

[33] To oppose this would be to agree to the genetic fallacy which Albright commits (cf. C. L. Hamblin, Fallacies, p. 45) 'of confusing temporal or historical origin with logical nature' (although in this case Albright has the origin wrong as well).

[34] B. A. Wortley's occasional use of Aristotle does not utilize any aspect which has an alleged equivalence with Eshnunna law types in Albright's hypothesis (cf. Wortley, Jurisprudence (Manchester, 1967), pp. 293–302). J. Rawls (A Theory of Justice (Oxford, 1972), pp. 424ff.) is characteristic in using Aristotle's mean without any of his logic to expound law; W. Haas suggests from a linguistic standpoint that law is to be construed as a tendency ('Meaning and Rules', pp. 152–5), which I think goes against Albright's formal presupposition.

[35] See W. F. Albright, New Horizons in Biblical Research, pp. 23–4.

[36] W. F. Albright, New Horizons in Biblical Research, pp. 28ff.

identification and description of relations between Mesopotamian Akkadian law and Greek logic. Since these attempts have been summarily shown above to be very confused and mistaken in respect of the two latter features, it follows that Albright's (usually unargued) assertions about MT 'empirical logic' and law will reflect the same type of distortions; consequently it is not worth while giving them detailed attention, except in regard to one additional phenomenon. The examples Albright cited to illustrate the category 'empirical logic' often belong to distinct classes, in such cases as can properly be related to any logics. The 'famous Pythagorean theorem'[37] is cited as an example of the 'tremendous progress in empirical logic'.[38] Diophantine algebra, surgery, mensuration, the poetry[39] and law[40] of the Hebrew Bible are all

[37] W. F. Albright, *History, Archaeology and Christian Humanism*, p. 71. A theorem is a piece of deductive, a priori reasoning (e.g. P. F. Strawson, *The Bounds of Sense* (London, 1966), p. 286; B. Russell, *Our Knowledge of the External World* (Chicago, 1916), pp. 5, 112ff.); surgery is not, so Albright has conflated distinct classes by characterizing both falsely. Also, a priori reasoning exists long before Albright assumes: cf. the text dated by T. Baqir at 2000 B.C., where a theorem is applied ('An Important Mathematical Problem Text', *Sumer*, VI (1950), 1, pp. 39–54). This is a counter-example to Albright's identification of non-generalization in Akkadian mathematics since, although to do with a specific problem, it employs generalized forms.

[38] W. F. Albright, *History, Archaeology and Christian Humanism*, p. 71.

[39] W. F. Albright, *New Horizons in Biblical Research*, pp. 29–30.

[40] Albright mentions 'Thou shalt not kill' (*History, Archaeology and Christian Humanism*, p. 97) as an example of empirical logic, law and extreme generalization. However, it is not generalized (with quantifiers) but is a singular imperative (although I agree it serves to govern the domain of people, with 'thou' being a dummy term; but my point is about the absence of specified generalization). More important is the feature of its being an imperative; no well-formed logic of imperatives yet exists (cf. P. T. Geach, *Logic Matters*, pp. 278–85) and its link with, and status respecting, commands are disputed (cf. M. P. Golding, *Philosophy of Law* (Englewood Cliffs, 1975), pp. 24–51; cf. also p. 120 on the procedural nature of MT law, as opposed to Albright's suggestion). So Albright's assumption of the self-evidence of MT law being any form of logic in terms of his logic specifications is highly questionable. Indeed, it might be possible to construe the imperatives as analogous to theorem-hood premisses. A. Phillips (*Ancient Israel's Criminal Law* (Oxford, 1970)), albeit in a sort of analysis distinct from the present one, proposes that the ten commandments can be interpreted as a type of group of premisses placed behind the criminal law (Exod. 21:1–23:5); but on Albright's interpretation (*New Horizons in Biblical Research*, p. 29) the criminal law is to be separated from the empirical logic of the ten commandments and related to the Akkadian laws. However, a neglected feature of Exod. 21:1–23:5 is its internal systematic interrelations; e.g. the conditional markers *ky* (21:2, 7, 14, 18, 20, 22, 26, 28, 33, 35–7; 22:4–6, 9, 10, 14, 16, 27) and *'m* (21:3–5, 8–11, 19, 23, 27, 29, 30, 32; 22:1–3, 6–7, 10–12, 14, 16, 22, 24–5) (excepting oath formulae) appear on occasions to be functionally substitution instances of

given as examples of 'empirical logic'. However, geometry and algebra are a priori reasoning, surgery is no reasoning but inductive practice (or ritual practice); and poetry shares no logical properties with surgery. If Albright is unwittingly using 'empirical logic' as a metaphor (regarding the last term especially) this falsifies his thesis on its own terms of being a claim about logic; but even in such a revised form it incoherently attempts to classify disparate groups under one category. Albright, as previously noted, committed the genetic fallacy[41] of confusing temporal and historical origin with logical nature. That is to say, he classifies geometry and some algebra as empirical because, he observes,[42] they are used in connection with specific problems about empirical issues of size, land, building, etc.; but, if the mathematical status of those calculations in the relevant texts,[43] is generalized algebraic quadratic equations, as Neugebauer[44] has shown them to be, then they are a priori phenomena, and their subject matter is (in the appropriate respect) irrelevant to the logical nature of the reasoning. Hence Albright cannot be permitted to conflate the two empirical and a priori categories. Consequently, his attempt to foist a classification on to MT texts which gives them the seeming 'logical' status of Babylonian mathematical texts is viciously confused. This is so not least because MT texts are not algebraic and are concerned with empirical issues in a manner distinct from the geometrical texts in Akkadian.

---

one another where consequences are drawn from antecedents. This reflects a degree of organization and systematic integration of values, a product absent from paralleled Akkadian law codes.

[41] cf. C. L. Hamblin, *Fallacies*, p. 45 (Albright committed this fallacy in other related contexts (see the foregoing) thus generating the generative syndrome (cf. Ch. 1 above) and fallacious family resemblances (cf. 1.3, 2 above).

[42] W. F. Albright, 'Neglected Factors in the Greek Intellectual Revolution', pp. 225–42.

[43] O. Neugebauer and A. Sachs, *Mathematical Cuneiform Texts* (Newhaven, 1945), and C. J. Gadd, *Brown University Studies*, 18 (1954). Of course, the significance of these analytical texts should not be overstated; alongside the mathematical description of near space was a more extensive contrary adoption of a mythological universe: cf. T. Jacobsen, 'Religious Drama in Ancient Mesopotamia', in H. Goedicke and J. J. M. Roberts (eds.), *Unity and Diversity* (Baltimore, 1975), pp. 65–97.

[44] O. Neugebauer, *The Exact Sciences in Antiquity* (Copenhagen, 1951), pp. 42ff.

INDEX OF BIBLICAL
PASSAGES

INDEX OF NAMES AND
SUBJECTS

References which can be discovered by use of the Contents list are not reproduced here; the citation form for foreign words is that of their appearance in the book; the Semitic consonants ' and ' are indexed before 'a' and 'p' respectively.